Nevada Gunsmoke

Nevada Gunsmoke

*Frontier Fighters
of the Boom Years, 1850–1890*

ELMER D. MCINNES
with LAURETTA RITCHIE-MCINNES

McFarland & Company, Inc., Publishers
Jefferson, North Carolina

LIBRARY OF CONGRESS CATALOGUING-IN-PUBLICATION DATA

Names: McInnes, Elmer D., 1958– author. | Ritchie-McInnes, Lauretta, 1967– author.
Title: Nevada gunsmoke : frontier fighters of the boom years, 1850–1890 / Elmer D. McInnes, with Lauretta Ritchie-McInnes.
Description: Jefferson, North Carolina : McFarland & Company, Inc., Publishers, 2022
Includes bibliographical references and index.
Identifiers: LCCN 2021059322 | ISBN 9781476686318 (paperback : acid free paper) ∞
ISBN 9781476644080 (ebook)
Subjects: LCSH: Pioneers—Nevada—Biography. | Gunfighters—Nevada—Biography. | Mining camps—Nevada—Biography. | Frontier and pioneer life—Nevada. | BISAC: HISTORY / United States / State & Local / West (AK, CA, CO, HI, ID, MT, NV, UT, WY) | HISTORY / United States / 19th Century
Classification: LCC F840 .M45 2022 | DDC 979.3/01—dc23/eng/20211209
LC record available at https://lccn.loc.gov/2021059322

BRITISH LIBRARY CATALOGUING DATA ARE AVAILABLE

**ISBN (print) 978-1-4766-8631-8
ISBN (ebook) 978-1-4766-4408-0**

© 2022 Elmer D. McInnes and Lauretta Ritchie-McInnes. All rights reserved

*No part of this book may be reproduced or transmitted in any form
or by any means, electronic or mechanical, including photocopying
or recording, or by any information storage and retrieval system,
without permission in writing from the publisher.*

Front cover images © 2022 Shutterstock

Printed in the United States of America

*McFarland & Company, Inc., Publishers
Box 611, Jefferson, North Carolina 28640
www.mcfarlandpub.com*

Acknowledgments

by Elmer D. McInnes

As is usually the case with a project such as this, it cannot be accomplished alone. Numerous individuals and institutions have contributed to the compilation of the book now before you. I would like to acknowledge those contributions and thank all involved for their input in the assembling of this volume.

Nevada: Dianne Pickett and all other staff members—Getchell Library, University of Nevada, Reno; Nevada Historical Society, Reno; Chris Driggs—Nevada State Library and Archives, Carson City; Gayl Siemer—White Pine County Library, Ely; Corinne Hogan, Lisa C. Lloyd—Lincoln County Clerk's Office, Pioche; Mary Jo Castaneda—Eureka County Clerk's Office, Eureka; C. Bloomsburg—First Judicial District Court, Carson City; Lander County Clerk's Office, Battle Mountain; Lied Library, University of Nevada—Las Vegas.

Other locations: California—Alfred W. Janske, Oakland; California State Archives, Sacramento; Truckee Library, Truckee; Charles Dyer and Isabel MacLean Drown—Carlo M. De Ferrari Archives, Sonora; Robert Chandler—Wells Fargo Bank History Museum, San Francisco; Colorado—Mark R. Jones, Centennial. Utah Julie Kroff—Third District Court, Tooele; Fifth District Court, St. George; Fifth District Court, Cedar City; Susan Christopher—Gerald R. Sherratt Library, Southern Utah University, Cedar City; David Yardley, Iron County Clerk, Parowan; Deborah M. Jukes—Fifth District Court, Beaver. Illinois—Cheryl Barnhart—Circuit Court Clerk's Office, Princeton. Texas—Chuck Parsons, Luling.

We also thank the many staff over the years at the Yorkton Public Library in Yorkton, Saskatchewan, Canada, for all their assistance in our research.

Last, but not least, I thank my wife Lauretta Ritchie-McInnes for all her love and support over the years. As not only wife but research assistant, manuscript reader, editor, typist, publisher liaison and idea consultant, Lauretta goes above and beyond the call of duty every day.

To anyone we inadvertently may have missed, please accept our humblest apologies but know your efforts toward this volume are greatly appreciated.

Table of Contents

Acknowledgments by Elmer D. McInnes   v

Introduction by Elmer D. McInnes   1

1. A "Cool and Courageous" Man: Thomas Coleman   5
2. "The Best Fighter in Nevada": Dick Prentice   19
3. The Hard Luck Gunman: Dick Paddock   31
4. A Savage Life and a Dishonorable Death: William Bethards   43
5. Boss Fighter to Political Chief: Leslie Blackburn   58
6. A Dedicated Law Man: William McKee   70
7. The Fighting Irish: Irish Tom Carberry   83
8. Two Dangerous Men: Jack White and Bob Mellon   93
9. "Something of a Noted Rogue": John Burke   105
10. "One of the Worst Men in the Country": James Harrington   120
11. A Full-Fledged Fighter: George Kirk   136
12. A Venomous Desperado: Rattlesnake Dick Darling   148
13. Eureka's Paul Revere: Billy Martin   162
14. The Ghost of Ely: Hank Parrish   170

Epilogue by Elmer D. McInnes   187
Chapter Notes   189
Bibliography and Source List   217
Index   221

Introduction

by Elmer D. McInnes

The mining rush to Nevada, ca. 1859–1878, though on a somewhat smaller scale than the mammoth California gold rush of ten years before, nonetheless witnessed a prodigious influx of ebullient humanity into the formerly barren, sunbaked landscape. The discovery of valuable silver deposits in the rock of the region proved to be the impetus for the human development of the nation's 36th state. In imitation of California, however, who set the North American precedent, the Nevada rush also saw that unique development called the "mining camp gunman" or "Chief of the camp." That violent, domineering individual, armed with a brace of huge so-called "horse pistols" and a wicked looking, long bladed "Bowie knife," strode the plank sidewalks and dirt streets of many of the region's bustling communities. They would be a fixture for most of Nevada's boom years and would add their own brand of excitement to the days of auriferous wealth accumulation.

The first known white man to set foot in what would later become the State of Nevada proved to be a group of fur trappers led by the legendary mountain man Jedediah S. Smith out of St. Louis, Missouri, in 1825. Although only passing through on their way to California, Smith and his party were the first to describe various features of the landscape of the area. Smith was subsequently followed by various other exploring parties, including those of Peter S. Ogden, Milton Sublette and the great "Pathfinder," John C. Frémont. These expeditions, plus the parties of gold seekers who crossed the Great Basin in the late 1840s on their way to California, helped to familiarize the rest of the country with the seemingly uninhabitable region.

With the establishment of Utah territory on September 9, 1850, the area now encompassing the present-day State of Nevada became part of the Territory of Utah. That same year a party of Salt Lake pioneers set out for California. Reaching the base of the Sierra Nevada Mountains in the Carson Valley, the group tarried long enough to discover slight traces of gold in the feeder streams of the Carson River. Although this created some interest it was not deemed of great importance and the area continued to be ignored as a place for settlement.

Though prospecting had been sporadic and largely unpromising, by 1851 the Carson Valley of the West portion of the territory began to attract settlement, principally at the camp of Mormon Station, later renamed Genoa. Slowly, more and more settlers and gold seekers began to arrive and other camps began to spring up throughout the Valley. Eventually, the officials of Utah Territory at Salt Lake City split the region of present-day Nevada into various counties, including the organization of Carson County in 1855. By this time the discovery which would cause this sparsely settled wilderness to explode in a paroxysm of greed, violence and heady adventure had already come to pass.

Despite the fact of the search for gold having been, to a great extent, disappointing, the quest for silver still had some promise. In 1853 the Grosh brothers of Pennsylvania, E. Allen and Hosea, discovered important silver deposits in the Carson Valley near the future site of the town of Silver City. At length the discoveries began to be announced at a steady pace, including possibly the biggest of all, the so-called Comstock Lode, on June 12, 1859. This would be the genesis of perhaps Nevada's greatest boomtown, Virginia City, as well as numerous others in the area. With the first influx of humanity from the California gold fields, the Nevada rush began in earnest.

The mining discoveries quickly had a pronounced political effect on the future of Nevada. There had always been a strong autonomous movement within Nevada lobbying for self-government. With the apparent prosperity of the region assured by the riches being dug out of the hard earth, those seeking independence finally triumphed on March 2, 1861. On that date the U.S. Congress approved the bill establishing Nevada Territory. With the continued prosperity of the Nevada mines, a little over three years later, on October 31, 1864, a presidential proclamation ushered Nevada into the Union as a full-fledged state.

Within the development of the State of Nevada lay an underlying crust of conflict and turmoil. The white intruders' relations with the various Piute and Shoshone Indian tribes had rarely been cordial. This led to a worrying succession of raids, battles, ambushings and death, culminating in the brutal battle at Pyramid Lake in May 1860. Although this proved a disastrous encounter for the whites, resulting in almost total annihilation and a resounding Indian victory, soon, as happened almost everywhere in the West, the native population became mere bystanders and relics in the whites' rush for wealth and industry.

As highways and railroads began to crisscross the state, the mining discoveries continued through the '60s and '70s. Like periodic explosions, first here, then there, people ran in the directions of these "booms" as if attracted by the noise, looking to see what they could acquire from the resultant debris. As the Virginia City mines continued to pump out millions of dollars of ore annually, other discoveries such as the Esmeralda rush, centered at Aurora in 1860; the Reese River discoveries around Austin in 1862; the Eureka boom of 1869; the White Pine rush at Hamilton in 1869; Ely District run to Pioche of 1870; and countless others of a lesser degree throughout the state in the 1859 to mid to late 1870s time period kept Nevada in a constant state of frenetic activity.

As had manifested itself in the California gold rush, and would again in mining rushes of the future, the Nevada mining boom attracted thousands of adventurous souls to every developing and established mining camp. Also, in common with every other mining area, some of these arrivals proved to be men of the gun and knife, men who brooked no insult and would fight at the drop of a hat. This was not a unique phenomenon in the American west of the 19th century. Be it a mining camp, end of the track railway town, cattle town, or lumber camp, all such vibrant, frontier communities attracted these types of individuals. Why this is so is, perhaps, a matter of speculation. Naturally, men of an adventurous, independent spirit, wishing to make money off the other individuals in attendance via gambling, liquor, women and any other vice imaginable, were men used to protecting themselves and their interest by means of violence if necessary. Men of the criminal mind were likewise attracted to such communities, not only for possible monetary gain, but simply looking for a place to hide away from the more established areas of civilization. A largely male population gathering in dance halls, gambling dives and saloons, mostly all armed and believing in the credo "protect yourself, as all men must," proved a recipe for violent conflict and often sudden death.

In the book *History of Nevada*, published by Thompson & West, Oakland, California, 1881, editor and early Nevada historian Myron Angel gives an exhaustive listing of all the known homicides occurring in Nevada between 1859 and 1880 in a section headed "Homicide, And Some of Its Causes," pages 343–356. To preface the listing Angel states, in part:

> In the list of homicides we give below it will be seen that the total is 402. Those for which trivial causes, or none at all, is assigned are more than one half. The majority of these can safely be set down as having begun in frivolous bravado, and never would have occurred had men not gone unnecessarily armed and congregated in places where their cooler thoughts were usurped by those begotten by the insidious wiles of strong drink. There are thirty cases in which the causes are stated to be gambling and drunken quarrels, which properly should be classed as of "no cause." In newly-settled countries, where all are squatters alike, it would seem as though disputes about land titles ought to be a more prolific source of quarrels than all else; and yet such is not the fact, for there are only twenty-eight homicides reported as having been caused by quarrels about title of land, money and other property. Quarrels about women are fifteen. The unsettled state of a new mining community, where the preponderating number are males, and a great many of the females not of the best class, makes their presence no inconsiderable factor in the cause of death by violence. There are thirteen cases given where death resulted in resisting arrest. Most of these can be attributed to intemperance; for no offender against the law, unless incorrigible or inebriated, will risk his life in a contest with officers, but, when cornered, gracefully accept the situation, and peaceably yield—trusting to juries and the law's delay for future liberty. Those whom officers kill for resistance of arrest can be set down as brave, foolish, reckless characters. In all the long list which follows below there are only twelve of those who were murdered for money. By this the inference can readily be drawn that, as a class, the settlers in a new mining region are not the sordid, cold-blooded sort, who kill for lucre alone—though there are a few who do so. The justification of self-defense is given in eleven cases.

All the men dealt with in the chapters of this book, save for Hank Parrish, whose career of mayhem did not begin until after the *History of Nevada* was published, are mentioned in these listings. Perhaps Angel's introductory goes some way to helping us understand the motivations and circumstances of the individuals herein chronicled. Then again, possibly the only avenue toward some form of understanding is to do as I have done, present their respective lives as they lived them and let a clear reading guide our judgment.

1

A "Cool and Courageous" Man
Thomas Coleman

Like many other fighting men who traveled throughout the Nevada mining camps of the 1860s and '70s, Thomas Coleman was a native of Ireland.[1] Born about 1831[2] the youth early decided to emigrate to America, likely during his teenage years. According to one source he first landed in New York City where he quickly connected himself to one of the gangs of political thugs who worked in support of their chosen political cause.[3] Eventually, by at least the early 1850s, young Coleman followed various other gamblers and shoulder strikers, such as the well-known Billy Mulligan, James "Yankee" Sullivan and Jim Hughes, to the West Coast.[4] Here, in gold laden San Francisco, Coleman again ensconced himself into the gambling and back room political scene. In San Francisco he may have made an attempt at starting a family, as he was known to have at least one son living there in 1873.[5] Who they were and what became of them, however, has been lost to time.

Following at least ten years of roaming between the various California mining camps engaging in the gambling and sporting lifestyle and hiring out his gun to assorted political and business causes Tom Coleman was a seasoned, hardened tough. By 1861 the 30-year-old Coleman had gravitated to the thriving city of Sacramento, California. It would be in Sacramento that he would participate in his first recorded act of violent confrontation.

Established at the confluence of the American and Sacramento rivers, by the early 1860s the city of Sacramento boomed along with California's gold rush economy. This proved most evident along the wharf district, the Embarcadero, first established by California pioneer John Sutter in the late 1840s. By 1860 many steamship companies realized that freighting goods and passengers into and out of Sacramento could be a most lucrative operation. Quickly competition between the numerous shipping concerns began to develop. This in turn engendered the hiring of so-called "wharf runners," men whose job it was to steer prospective passengers and freight owners in the direction of their employers' respective steamships as they sat docked at the wharf. As could be expected, this state of intense competition soon led to much friction and confrontation between runner gangs.

By the time of Coleman's arrival in 1861 or 1862 the steamship companies had taken to hiring toughs to guard their respective runners and intimidate rival crews.

The Steam Navigation Company hired Tom Coleman for just such a purpose. Gunfire and a chain reaction of death would soon follow.

By early 1862, Coleman found himself at odds with the leaders of a rival runner crew, Edward "Ned," George and Thomas Lloyd. The Lloyd brothers, operators of the Mountaineer Saloon in Sacramento, were also hard characters.[6] In fact, shortly before arriving in Sacramento Ed Lloyd had killed a teamster named Thornton in a confrontation in Oroville, California.[7] Coleman and George Lloyd were known to have had at least one verbal shouting match.[8]

The afternoon of Saturday, March 22, 1862, found Coleman, accompanied by Fred N. Smith and Joe McGee, a special policeman on the Sacramento city police force, walking the crowded wharf on Front Street, just opposite the foot of K Street. While Smith and McGee faded into the crowds working to load the waiting steamboats shortly before their departure, Coleman happened to pass Ed Lloyd almost in front of the What Cheer House Saloon. Nearby stood his brother George and their brother-in-law Patsey Callaghan.

Thinking he heard Ed Lloyd make a disparaging comment to two ladies passing by, Coleman strode up to the man and upbraided him.

"You are a scrub," Lloyd shouted at Coleman.

Coleman wagged his finger in Lloyd's face. "If so, I'm the best scrub in this crowd," he barked back.

Suddenly Lloyd reached out with his left hand and slapped Coleman's face. With that both men quickly took a number of steps back and reached for their pistols. Coleman came up first and jerked the trigger but heard only a click as his gun misfired. Lloyd's pistol exploded a fraction of a second later, the ball flying wide of its mark. Both men then fired two or three more shots, none taking effect.

As Coleman and Lloyd fired at each other, Fred Smith appeared out of the crowd in front of the What Cheer House with a revolver in his hand. With Lloyd's back to him, Smith swiftly ran up, placed the muzzle of his revolver against Ed Lloyd's side and fired; the slug passed through Lloyd's body, perforating his liver.

"I've got you now," Smith yelled.

Lloyd could only gasp "Yes" as he grabbed his side, doubled over and staggered down the street to fall a short distance away.

Seeing his brother receive the shot from Smith, George Lloyd, being unarmed, ran over to Callaghan, to whom he had lent his knife a short time previous.

"Give me that knife, they've killed Ed," he exclaimed to his brother-in-law.

Just as Callaghan handed George Lloyd the knife, he spotted Joe McKee standing at the corner of the What Cheer House, his revolver resting over his arm pointed at them.

"Look out," Callaghan shouted. At the same instant McGee began shooting.

Hit in the right shoulder, Lloyd dropped the knife. "I'm shot, Callaghan. Look out for yourself," he groaned as one of McGee's bullets grazed Callaghan's hip.

While the action between George Lloyd, Callaghan and McGee had transpired, Coleman motioned Smith to him and exchanged his revolver for Smith's. He now strode toward George Lloyd, his revolver presented in front of him. Seeing Coleman approach, Lloyd moaned out, "Coleman, don't shoot me, I'm shot bad."

"Are you?" Coleman said. Reconsidering the shooting of an already wounded man, Coleman stopped and turned off.

At this juncture, Sacramento police officer Macintosh ran onto the scene and an already diffusing situation was contained.[9]

Bystanders hastily carried Ed Lloyd to a room in the nearby National House Hotel. Dr. Clapp was summoned; however, the gravely wounded man was beyond help. Lloyd died 15 minutes after Clapp's arrival.[10]

Coleman, Smith and McGee quickly saw the inside of the Sacramento lockup as a result of Ed Lloyd's killing. Authorities convened an inquest over Lloyd's body that same evening. Following the testimony of various witnesses to the affair the jurors concluded:

> We, the jury summoned to ascertain the cause of death of the deceased, now before us, do find that his name is Edward Lloyd, a native of the County Limerick, Ireland; that his age is 22 years; and that, in our opinion, he came to his death in the city of Sacramento, California, this 22nd day of March, 1862 from the effect of a pistol shot wound from the hands of Frederick Smith.[11]

The afternoon following his death Ed Lloyd received burial in St. Rose's Church Cemetery in Sacramento.[12]

It had first gained report that George Lloyd was in a serious condition.[13] By the second day after the fight, however, his condition was upgraded to "much improved."[14]

Meanwhile, the three considered responsible for Ed Lloyd's death, Coleman, Smith and McGee, contemplated their fate in the Sacramento jail. The court set the hearing for Thursday, March 27.[15] Following a week of adjournments and testimony, including that of George Lloyd, who appeared in the courtroom heavily bandaged with his arm in a sling, Judge Gilmer decided that Fred Smith should be held to answer a charge of first-degree murder in the death of Ed Lloyd. He also decreed that Joe McGee be held on a charge of committing a deadly assault on George Lloyd. Tom Coleman, however, was cleared of all charges and walked out of the courtroom a free man.[16]

All of the principals involved in the March 22, 1862, gun battle would go on to meet violent ends. The first of these would prove to be Fred Smith. While in the Sacramento jail Smith more than once commented that when he eventually gained his release, he would make every member of the Lloyd family "hunt their holes." After languishing for over five months in the local lockup he finally gained his freedom on Tuesday, September 16, 1862, as a result of the grand jury's decision to ignore indictments against him as well as Coleman and McGee, the latter having previously gained his freedom by posting bail bond.[17]

Smith's freedom would prove short-lived. After being on the Sacramento streets for only a matter of some 15 minutes he chanced to meet George Lloyd. Having been informed of Smith's release Lloyd was prepared. Pulling out his pistol he pumped two bullets into the 45-year-old Smith's body killing him instantly.[18] Despite being arrested and facing numerous court actions Lloyd eventually gained his liberty from prosecution.[19]

Patsey Callaghan and Joe McGee went on to experience similar violent fates to

Ed Lloyd and Smith. In about 1863, Callaghan engaged in an encounter with one Thomas Sherman in Sacramento's Bank Exchange Saloon. In the ensuing battle Sherman succeeded in stabbing Callaghan fatally.[20]

McGee would go on to a rather more notorious career in Nevada, engaging in a number of shooting scrapes and killings before being shot to death in the St. Nicholas Saloon in Carson City on December 9, 1863.[21] Nevada and its stories of mineral wealth, prosperous mining towns and easy money would also attract two more of the Sacramento sextet from the 1862 gun battle. Tom Coleman and George Lloyd were destined to meet one last time.

By 1863, Coleman had been attracted to the Nevada mining excitement. He moved west to the lively silver mining town of Aurora, just over the border from Bodie, California. Gaining employment with one of the mining companies as a guard to protect their interests against rival companies, Coleman also embedded himself into the gambling and saloon milieu of Aurora's tenderloin.[22] In this environment he once again met his old enemy George Lloyd.

Lloyd also relocated to Aurora around the same time as Coleman. Even though he had at one time fought a vicious fistfight with him earlier in Sacramento he aligned himself with the associates of John Daly, a notorious gang leader, gun man and gambler working to rule the vice order of Aurora. It was inevitable that Coleman and Lloyd would eventually come together and sparks would fly. The only question seemed to be when it would happen.

The answer came on October 24, 1863. This Saturday evening proved an especially raucous one at the Del Monte Exchange Saloon in Aurora. This proved even more so with the presence of Tom Coleman, George Lloyd and Tom Daly. At length, between drinks at the bar, the three men began arguing amongst themselves. Rival mining company alliances have been speculated as one possible cause despite the fact that both Lloyd and Daly worked as muscle for the Pond Mining Company, aside from Lloyd's alliance with Daly's clique. This most likely had no effect on Lloyd, however, who was the type of individual to challenge any show of authority, legal or extralegal. Knowing the history behind Lloyd and Coleman it is abundantly clear where their mutual animosity took root.

Be that as it may, soon the armed and dangerous trio were exchanging loud oaths. Suddenly, all three grasped revolvers and commenced firing, Coleman and Daly shooting at Lloyd and Lloyd returning the fire. As everyone in the crowded saloon dived for cover or stampeded out the front door, George Lloyd hit the sawdust-covered floor perforated by at least one fatal bullet. Neither Coleman nor Daly was injured.[23]

Most sources list John Daly as the killer of George Lloyd. Some sources, perhaps most tellingly, more contemporary to the time in question, give Tom Coleman the credit for firing the shot that killed Lloyd. A few years after the occurrence the *Stockton* (California) *Independent* would state, "several shots were fired and Lloyd was killed. It was generally believed that the fatal shot was fired by Coleman."[24] Likewise, the *Eureka Sentinel* of Eureka, Nevada, would report, "Coleman afterward killed [George] Lloyd."[25]

Whatever the circumstance, Tom Coleman had a hand in killing his old enemy

Aurora, Nevada, 1865, about one year subsequent to Thomas Coleman's residence there (courtesy Digital Photo Collection, Image # UNRS-P0483-1, Special Collections and University Archives Department, University of Nevada, Reno Libraries).

George Lloyd and would soon be the last of the Sacramento six still standing following the death of Joe McGee in Carson City that December. Shortly he would be looking for greener pastures.

After Lloyd's death, in early February 1864, the citizens of Aurora decided to crack down on Daly and his nefarious activities with the formation of a vigilance committee. In the cleanup Daly and a number of his henchmen ended up hanging at the end of lynch ropes.[26]

Although not connected with John Daly and his gang, apart from their mutual shooting of George Lloyd, Coleman found the atmosphere around Aurora decidedly unhealthy for anyone who circulated in the gambler, gunmen, saloon crowd. By late 1863 he had picked up stakes and moved some 135 miles northeast to the burgeoning mining camp of Austin, Lander County, Nevada.

While searching for strayed horses in Pony Canyon in May 1862, stage station employee William Talcott accidentally discovered a major silver quartz vein. The town of Austin quickly developed on the site. By the time of Tom Coleman's arrival in early 1864, Austin was an incorporated city with stores, banks, schools, churches, public halls, private dwellings and many saloons, gambling dens, bordellos and dance halls. The surrounding hills were dotted with numerous mining operations and stamp mills.[27]

Coleman's exact means of making a living in the area are unknown; however, he quite possibly followed his usual custom of hiring himself out as an enforcer to one of the multitudinous mining companies operating in the so-called "Reese River District." The Nevada mining frontier would be known in history for its epidemic of feuding mine companies. Many men known to be handy with firearms and with a reputation as "fighters" made a living as muscle for the various companies. Tom Coleman was one of these.

In Austin, Coleman once again ran into an old California traveling companion, Billy Mulligan, who arrived in town around the same time as himself. Accompanying Billy was his brother Barney. In December 1863 Barney declared himself as a candidate for the post of Mining Recorder at the nearby camp of Amador. At the election held that month Coleman also attended in some capacity and he and Barney Mulligan fell into a heated quarrel. This caused a distance and animosity to simmer between himself and the Mulligan brothers.[28]

The feud smoked and smoldered until the evening of Austin city election day, Tuesday, April 19, 1864, when Coleman and Billy Mulligan came together in Jim Leffingwell's Austin saloon. Quickly Coleman reached for and palmed his pistol. In a calm voice Mulligan admonished him to put the gun away and not to shoot in the crowded saloon. Instead he proposed a duel for early the next morning to be held on the outskirts of town. Coleman acquiesced and the two immediately went about preparing for the next day's festivities.[29]

Adair Wilson, editor of the local *Reese River Reveille* newspaper, and the man who would later present himself as a fan of duelists like Tom Coleman and Billy Mulligan in particular and the duello in general, witnessed the resultant episode. Springing out of bed early Wednesday morning, Wilson quickly dressed and with great anticipation hastened to the designated duel site on the outskirts of Austin which he would later describe as "the head of the Upper Grade, … near the Junction House, only half a mile from the courthouse" and "this side of the graveyard."[30]

Editor Wilson was about to witness an event which would have a great impact on him and would stay at the forefront of his memories for years to come. According to his eyewitness account printed in the next day's *Reveille*:

> Messrs. James Dunican and P. Haynes, acted as seconds for Mulligan and E.S. Bradshaw and C.H. Patchen, acted as seconds for Coleman. Dr. Morton acted as surgeon for the latter party, and Dr. Davis for the former. Both parties proceeded to the ground about daylight, and found assembled about one hundred men, and two women, to witness the fight.
>
> The preliminaries were now gone through with, Bradshaw for Coleman, winning the choice of place, also the call. The weapons were to be six shooter revolvers, to fire at the word, and continue until the six shots were expended. The distance was measured off, ten yards, the marks were made, and after carefully changing about to avoid all lines of the ground or other objects that would aid one party in his aim, the principles were placed in readiness. While the forms necessary in such cases passing, some remarks were made showing the extraordinary coolness of the parties, Mulligan offering to bet the drinks that he would drop his opponent the first fire. Coleman exhibited equal imperturbableness. All being arranged, the men took their places for the firing. Facing each other, the usual questions were asked, and the word to fire given. Coleman having been instructed by his second to fire low, his shot struck the ground about eight feet short, that of Mulligan's was not traced. The firing continued without casualty until the third shot of Mulligan struck the third finger of Coleman's right hand, while in the act of cocking his pistol. Although slightly wounded he continued firing quite deliberately, but very poorly, as out of his six shots, not one took effect. The shooting done by Mulligan was but little

better, notwithstanding his aim was as painstaking and deliberate as if a post had been his target instead of a fellow being, armed, and seeking his life. The last shot of Billy's inflicted a slight wound in the fleshy part of Coleman's thigh which will probably lay him up for a short time, and make a horizontal position much pleasanter than a sitting one. As the firing was over the surgeons now took charge of their men. Dr. Davis, after examining Mulligan and finding him unhurt, assisted Dr. Morton in his care of the wounds of Coleman, finding them not serious, all returned to town. Coleman's finger is quite badly injured, but Dr. Morton thinks that it may be saved.[31]

Wilson then went on to extol the two duelists in terms both glamorous and supportive of the duel culture:

Neither man needed proof of courage or firmness of nerve, their well-known reputation in many rencountors [sic] had long since established the fact. Since the meeting a complete reconciliation has taken place, and now, those so lately seeking each other's lives are now the dearest of friends; and why shouldn't they be?, [sic] each, at a personal sacrifice, having furnished the other with capital sport. It is so funny to shoot at another, particularly when it is done in so neat a manner, and then to read all about it in the papers, the romantic reconciliation, the chivalrous bearing, the smiles of the fair, the congratulations of the men, the general admiration of all, the attention even of those who hypocritically condemn, are the flowers cast in the path of the duelist. Laws may forget the practice in vain; the greatest and best, as well as the meanest of the land have thought; and while fighting calls forth many qualities and the fair, as well as the sterner sex, honor bravery, the duel will be an institution of the land, for physical courage covers a multitude of faults.[32]

Shortly after his injuries, Coleman was back on the streets of Austin. Billy Mulligan would go on to further gun fighting adventures before being killed in a major battle with San Francisco police a little over one year later, on July 7, 1865.[33]

Tom Coleman's movements for the next two years or so are largely unknown. In July 1864 he still resided in Austin. On July 18 he was one of the men who assisted City Marshal Lew Bodrow when the lawman accidentally shot himself in the foot.[34] After this his trail goes dim until December 1866 at which time, he appeared in Gold Hill, a town near Virginia City, Nevada, working at Mike McCluskey's Theatre Saloon.[35]

The 1867 discovery of extensive silver deposits in the White Pine Mountains of eastern Nevada quickly fostered another of the state's many so-called "mining rushes." By 1868 thousands of boomers from all over Nevada, California and elsewhere in the country flocked to the White Pine area. Mining camps began to sprout on the previously barren hillsides. One of the richest locations proved to be a prominence know as Treasure Hill. To illustrate the richness of the district one small shaft operated by one mining concern, 70' by 40' by 25', would eventually yield $3 million in ore in a very short time.[36]

Almost at once three communities sprang to life on mineral rich Treasure Hill, all within two to three miles of each other. Hamilton, situated on the northern base of the Hill, became the transportation and freighting hub of the area containing a population of some 6000 inhabitants by 1869, many businesses and many of the mills utilized by the mines farther up the Hill. Treasure City developed near the summit of Treasure Hill at 9200 feet altitude. Most of the mines were clustered around Treasure City. On the southwestern base of the Hill, Shermantown came into being. The smallest of the trio, Shermantown owed its existence to its proximity to wood and water used by the various mills and smelting works in the district.[37]

Being the center of the mining district Treasure City quickly developed a reputation as a fast, raucous town. By 1868 the camp boasted a population of about 5000 people. With some 200 mines in the vicinity one newspaperman was prompted to expound, "Treasure is the great mining town, and its streets, if not like those of Paradise, paved with 'pure gold,' come nearer being paved with pure silver than those of any other town in the universe."[38] By early 1869, Treasure City contained some 50 to 60 business buildings, including about one dozen saloons to wet the whistle of the thirsty miners. The fraternal organizations built impressive brick Masonic and Odd Fellows lodges. Treasure City could even boast its own stock exchange.[39]

Two of those to strike out for the new bonanza would be Tom Coleman and his buddy Mike McCluskey from Gold Hill. The pair would have followed the route taken by most of the White Pine rushers which consisted of catching a Central Pacific Railroad train to Elko in northeastern Nevada. At Elko they would have bought a ticket on one of the many newly organized stagecoach lines and traveled the 115 miles due south to Hamilton.[40] They most likely arrived sometime in the fall of 1868 or spring of 1869 to find a town the character of which Coleman was abundantly familiar and in much need of adequate law enforcement.

Another example of the prevailing state of pistol promiscuity took place on Friday, January 29, 1869. On that afternoon, with the main street crowded with ambulating pedestrians, two miners, James Marcuse and Joseph Byron, pulled revolvers and blazed away at each other over the affections of a soiled dove. Though neither man was hit nor, miraculously, no innocent bystanders perforated, an unlucky horse did receive a fatal head shot. The citizens proved unimpressed. As the local *White Pine News* editorialized, "Yesterday a great many advocated hanging the shootist, and another exhibition of the kind will in all probability lead to a worse one—that of one or more men dancing on nothing."[41] Into this milieu stepped Tom Coleman.

While Mike McCluskey busied himself setting up his usual saloon enterprise on Treasure City's main thoroughfare, Coleman probably once again hired himself out to one of the numerous mining companies in the area or simply hung out in McCluskey saloon waiting for opportunities. This presented itself in June 1869 when both Coleman and McCluskey decided to run in the local Treasure City town elections. McCluskey won himself a City Trustee position. Coleman defeated John Leconey 360 votes to 207 to win the office of City Marshal on Monday, June 7.[42]

The following Monday, Treasure City Mayor S.W. Boring announced his new police force: City Marshal Thomas Coleman; Deputy City Marshal Richard Paddock,[43] a well-known gunman and officer from Virginia City; policeman Thomas Hughes, Paddock's partner from Virginia City; and one Michael Dolan, an all-around rough and enforcer lately from Idaho.[44] Within two years Dolan would play a prominent role in Coleman's ultimate fate.

Coleman wasted no time in taking up his duties. On Sunday, June 13, he and Paddock arrested a pair of prize fighters attempting to hold an illegal boxing match on the outskirts of Treasure City.[45] The new City Council also kept him busy enforcing the defective stovepipe regulations.[46]

Tom Coleman's performance of his duties was apparently appreciated by the citizens of Treasure City. A number of his friends got together on the evening of July 6 and presented him with a silver City Marshal's badge. Much more serious troubles lurked just around the corner.

Early Wednesday morning July 14 a serious shooting affray broke out on the streets of Treasure City. The battle involved a group of miners including John Mitchell, John Reilly, Frank Fitzpatrick, Dan Murphy, John Donahue and Pat Lamb. The entire affair ended with Reilly shot in the chest at the hands of Mitchell. Fitzpatrick also received a slight wound. Racing to the scene Coleman arrested all six men and locked them up in the local jail. There were rumors that the fight had something to do with the Miners Union League, the organization having recently infiltrated the area and initiated a strike of members in an attempt to acquire for the miners a higher wage than the standard $4 a day. Most, however, decided it was simply a drunken brawl brought on by too much whiskey.[47] Subsequent events involving the Miners Union and the self-same Dan Murphy may have shown that those advocating a Union connection to the fight may have been closer to the truth.

Only one week later, Wednesday, July 21, another shooting affair shattered whatever peace and tranquility Treasure City had managed to attain. At 10 o'clock that morning, following a protracted drinking bout in the Bureau Saloon, two miners, Barney Flood and John Flarety, fell into a disagreement over who was to pay for the next round. Both men reached for pistols and fired at least three shots before Flood dashed out the front door ending the fracas, no one being injured. Making his usual speedy appearance on the scene, Marshall Coleman placed both men under arrest and carted them off to the city jail. Both were bailed out within a short time.[48]

Flood, a 39-year-old native of Ireland, was well known to Coleman as the two were next door neighbors in Treasure City.[49] Flood was also a well-known rounder who sometimes would hire out his gun to any of the mining concerns requiring extra muscle. What actually occurred during Coleman's apprehension of Flood is unknown. That there may have been some sort of hard feelings engendered, however, seems a possibility when considered in light of future events. Flood, like policeman Dolan, would go on to be a major player in Coleman's ultimate destiny.

The summer of 1869 was not fated to be an easy time for Coleman. This would be in large part due to the activities of the Miners Union League on Treasure Hill. The marshal's heightened sense of awareness peaked on Tuesday, July 27, when he and Assistant Marshall Paddock spotted a large group of men, including Dan Murphy of the July 14 shooting bee, parading down Main Street headed for the South Aurora Mine just outside of town. Soon the sound of shouts and gunshots were echoing down the Hill.

Gathering up the rest of the small police force Coleman and Paddock raced to the scene. It became apparent that the force of men had been a group of Union Leaguers attempting to recruit members in a drive through the mines. Unfortunately, their tactics soon degenerated into force and intimidation, the gunshots having been fired into the sky in an attempt to cow the working miners. Rounding up as many of the peace disturbers as they could, Coleman and Paddock marched the men off to the Treasure City calaboose.[50]

Only six days later the Miners Union staged a repeat performance on the mines of Treasure Hill. A local newspaper felt moved to praise Coleman and his officers on this occasion for being "most efficient in the discharge of their duties."[51] Indeed, this time, with the help of White Pine County Sheriff Irwin and his deputies, Coleman and his men nabbed Miners Union President Peter Leonard, Treasurer Justin McCarthey and a number of other rank and file, including Dan Murphy, and trooped them to the jail to await charges of riot.[52]

At this juncture, Coleman unexpectedly came under fire from various sources for allegedly hiring some of the same individuals who had participated in the riots, on the side of the Union, as special police to patrol the town after the fact. One correspondent complained bitterly:

> I assert that no member of the League who was arrested for firing on the Nevada men ever fired one single shot, but a member of the League did some of the firing, and an American who was no member of the League. Only three men did the firing, and those three are now packing their Henry rifles and shotguns, and receiving $20 per night to guard against the acts being recommitted which they themselves did.... We hope our Marshall can clear his skirts of it.[53]

Marshall Coleman's reaction to this criticism is not known. Shortly, however, all the miners being held in the local jail were released after the paying of a minimal $25 fine.[54] This seemed to clear the air and the mining trouble seemed to subside.

At this point Coleman probably felt he needed a break from Treasure City and his duties as City Marshal. Apparently, he had retained his interest and connections in the San Francisco political scene. Late in August he left on a brief sojourn to the Bay City to "assist in the election of the Irish municipal ticket of that place."[55] He may also have taken the time to pay a visit to his son who appears to have resided with friends there.

Returning to Treasure City shortly after, Coleman once again took up his duties as City Marshal. In October another well-known Nevada shootist and lawman, William Bethards,[56] gained appointment to the police force under Marshall Coleman.[57] Coleman himself gained appointment as a deputy sheriff of White Pine County in conjunction with his Treasure City responsibilities.[58]

In December Coleman would be forced to use his gun in the discharge of his duties, the first and only recorded instance of such an occurrence during his residence at Treasure City.

All throughout the evening of Thursday, December 16, and well into the early morning hours of Friday the 17th a group of men had been on a protracted bender traveling from one Treasure City saloon to the next. While ambling down the street making their way to another drinking establishment, they chanced to meet one of the city's Chinese residents and "beat him over the head in a shameful manner." At length, while the others continued to imbibe in another saloon, one of the men staggered out into the street with a revolver in his hand. Concealing himself behind some dry good boxes in front of Haas & Co.'s store the man hollered at the first person to come along, George Rutherford, editor of the local *White Pine News*, to stop, at the same time aiming and pulling the trigger of his pistol. Fortunately for Rutherford the gun failed to fire. Hearing the click the newspaperman quickly scampered down the street and out of danger.

Unfortunately for the would-be ambusher, the next person to come along proved to be City Marshal Tom Coleman, walking home following the windup of his shift for the night. Following the same procedure, the tipsy man jerked the trigger. Again, the weapon failed to fire. Hearing the snap of the gun's hammer but at first not seeing anyone Coleman quickly moved to the middle of the street, at the same time pulling his revolver.

"Stand, you son of a bitch," the man barked.

With that Coleman spotted his attacker moving toward him. The man again attempted to shoot with no results. Instantly, Coleman fired, at the same time calling for him to surrender. The ball struck the man in the left groin, passed through his body and lodged under the skin of his back.

"I will," he groaned and collapsed to the street.

In examining his victim Coleman was shocked to find it was an individual named John Sheehan, a man he had befriended some days previous and for whom he had found employment upon learning he was in dire straits. Upon examining Sheehan's Remington revolver Coleman found the weapon fully loaded but with only two of the caps in place.[59] Eventually, Sheehan made a full recovery.[60]

Eighteen sixty-nine would prove to be Treasure City's busiest and most prosperous year. By the end of 1870 it would be almost dead. Tom Coleman continued to serve as Treasure City Marshal throughout 1870, but most of his duties proved routine and unexciting. Despite being a rough man inured to violence he could also, at times, show a kind and altruistic side. Such proved to be the case in March 1870 when a miner named Donahue was severely injured in a mining accident. Along with two other individuals Coleman organized a committee and managed to raise $950 for the injured man's benefit.[61] Soon there would be very few miners, or anyone else for that matter, left on Treasure Hill.

The year 1870 saw ore values plummet. Many of the silver veins on the Hill pinched out and many of the mines ceased production. At its peak in 1869 Treasure City's population reached almost 6000 inhabitants. By late 1870, in the space of about one year, the population had dropped to around 500 people.[62]

By late October 1870, Coleman still resided in Treasure City.[63] Soon, however, he, along with most others from Treasure City, would be moving on to other, more prosperous, locations. Apparently, he gained himself a position with one of the mining concerns at still booming Pioche in Lincoln County, Nevada.[64]

According to the local Treasure City newspaper, the *White Pine News*, their 39-year-old former Marshall had a strange premonition of doom before leaving town. He reportedly told friends that "he should not probably be seen here again alive." He went so far as to have "his life insured a day or two before he left for $10,000, as he felt that the chances were against him."[65]

Evidence would seem to suggest that Coleman knew he was stepping into a hornets' nest by going to Pioche due to "some transactions on the Hill, that happened six months or more ago."[66] Something had transpired between Coleman, his neighbor at Treasure City and one time arrestee and purported friend Barney Flood, his former

The booming mining camp of Pioche and the Ely Mountains about the time of Thomas Coleman's residence (courtesy Maureen and Fred Wilson Collection, Image # snv001085, UNLV Libraries Special Collections & Archives, University of Nevada, Las Vegas).

underling on the Treasure City police force and purported friend, policeman Michael Dolan, and a notorious Nevada gunfighter and all around rough named Morgan Courtney. Just what happened would remain a mystery.

Some three or four months after moving to a cabin in Pioche, on the evening of Wednesday, February 22, 1871, Tom Coleman decided to host a get together at his home at which refreshments of the alcoholic variety were readily available. A number of men of the town accepted his invitation including supposed friends Barney Flood, Mike Dolan and Morgan Courtney. The ribald conversation continued with the consumption of liquor well into the early morning hours of the 23rd. By about 2 a.m., Coleman, as well as a few others, were allegedly in a state of intoxication.

According to one story the conversation began to revolve around some previous incident that Coleman, Flood and Dolan had been involved in, presumably in Treasure City. The argument quickly became heated at which point Flood decided to leave, "as he did not wish any quarreling amongst friends." Flood called for his hat at which point Coleman supposedly refused, yelling at Flood, "you shall leave at once!"

With that Coleman physically attacked Flood, throwing him to the floor while at the same time reaching for a large splitting knife leaning against the wood pile by the stove. At the same time, Flood produced a knife and in the tussle that followed stabbed Coleman five times about the body. Pistols were also produced and some shots fired, however, no one was hit. Coleman would be dead within hours of the fight.[67]

Most likely due to his reputation, but also possibly because of some vague conspiracy rumors, lawmen arrested Courtney shortly after the melee. Officials tracked Flood to his rooms later that morning and placed him under arrest.[68] Lawmen also sought Mike Dolan; however, he quickly left town and would not be seen in the area again for another eight months.

As soon as news of the incident began to circulate rumors ran rife. One newspaper surmised:

> Coleman was as cool and courageous a man as we ever knew and was possessed of many noble traits of character. His slayer, when under the influence of liquor, is one of the most treacherous, vindictive and desperate men in the State; one who would treasure up a fancied wrong with a malevolence as misery as if it were a real one, and it is not altogether improbable that Tom Coleman's manly and fearless course as an officer during the riotous times on Treasure Hill in July, 1869, had something to do with his untimely end.[69]

The March Grand Jury of Lincoln County failed to indict anyone for the Coleman killing.[70] The December Grand Jury, however, saw things differently. On December 12 they returned a true bill against Barney Flood, Morgan Courtney and Michael Dolan for the Coleman murder.[71] Authorities arrested Morgan Courtney in March 1872.[72] By this time Flood and Dolan had left the area. Released on $6000 bail that same day, Courtney would gain total freedom on Friday, April 5 when the District Attorney failed to prosecute.[73] Courtney went on to further violent encounters before meeting his own death by gunshot on August 1, 1873, in Pioche.[74]

Eight months after the death of Coleman, Michael Dolan suddenly appeared back in Pioche from his home in Connecticut. Stepping off the stage on Sunday, October 13 he willingly submitted to arrest.[75] Released on a $6000 bail bond the next day, Dolan likewise had little to worry about.[76] In November the District Attorney entered a nolle prosequi in Dolan's case and he was a free man.[77] Dolan, who was called in the newspapers "Mike McCluskey's right-hand man," eventually wandered to Tucson, Arizona, where he died of consumption in September 1880.[78] His connection with Coleman's old pal Mike McCluskey also throws that relationship into question. The mystery would never be solved.

In the summer of 1873 it gained report that the body of Tom Coleman was to be disinterred from Pioche's cemetery and shipped to San Francisco for reinternment, possibly to be nearer his son who was reportedly "attending school at Oakland."[79] This was never carried out, however, as to this day he still remains buried in Pioche's historic Boot Hill Cemetery.[80]

Adair Wilson, still editor of Austin, Nevada's *Reese River Reveille* newspaper, would continue to be enamored with the likes of Tom Coleman for the rest of his days. When a shooting scrape broke out in an Austin saloon on the evening of May 21, 1873, Wilson declared himself unimpressed. After pouring forth his disdain for the two pistoleers of the night before, Wilson commented in his next day's issue:

We have no desire to unduly excite the public mind against the parties to this affray; as we said before they are both strangers in this community, and do not understand the character of our people. We, of Austin, have seen better fighters than these men are.... Besides, after seeing the Mulligans, the Coleman's, the Irish Tom's,[81] the Vances, the Ridgeley's, our people are rather fastidious in the matter of fighters.[82]

Tom Coleman would have been proud.

2

"The Best Fighter in Nevada"
Dick Prentice

Not much can be said concerning W.D. "Dick" Prentice's pedigree or origins.[1] In fact, not much is known about the man at all. He has been described by someone who knew him personally, Comstock newspaper editor Wells Drury, as "a silent, sidling little 'shotgun miner,'" and "a quiet acting, little dried up looking fellow."[2] On the other hand, a contemporary newspaper gives us a totally different impression of the man when it referred to him in 1878 as being "considered the best fighter in Nevada."[3] Both sources may have been accurate in their descriptions. Although Prentice may have been small and unimpressive looking, what little is known of him are his many and varied shooting scrapes and physical encounters. Indeed, he may have been one of early Nevada's most feared roughs and gunmen.

Following a routine which he would stick with for most of his adult life Prentice usually toiled underground as a miner for any concern willing to hire him. His avocation and what he enjoyed most, however, were the occasions on which he could hire out his gun during times of strife between rival mining companies. Any outfits looking for extra muscle knew they could find a willing fighter in Dick Prentice. On these exigencies he could take a break from the backbreaking toils of the underground, pack his pistol, shoulder his favorite weapon, a double-barreled shotgun, and patrol the company grounds waiting for a fight. It soon became clear that Prentice was not loath to use his chosen weaponry in displays of deadly force.

The gun fighting miner first came to the notice of Nevada periodicals on the Comstock, Monday, February 8, 1864, as an employee of the White and Murphy mining concern near Virginia City. On this occasion a man named Peter O'Connell sat in his small cabin, located in a most unfortunate spot directly below an embankment, above which was situated the tailing dump of the White and Murphy mine. All at once the dwelling shook to its foundations as large boulders from the mine dump suddenly rolled over the embankment and landed on O'Connell's roof.

Quickly hastening his way to the mine O'Connell swore an oath at the workmen, one of whom proved to be a young Dick Prentice. After receiving a few choice words in return from Prentice, O'Connell angrily made his way back to his cabin. A few minutes later, while sitting by an open window in his home, O'Connell spied Prentice a few yards away pointing a revolver at him. Before O'Connell could react, Prentice fired. Luckily for the aggrieved householder the ball zipped past his head, lodging

Six Mile Canyon from C Street, Virginia City, 1860. Within four years Dick Prentice would make his first mark by gunfire in this city (courtesy Digital Photo Collection, Image #UNRS-P1997-06-34, Special Collections and University Archives Department, University of Nevada, Reno Libraries).

in the opposite wall. Having made his point, Prentice lowered his pistol and slowly ambled back to the mine.[4]

O'Connell hastened uptown and reported the incident to Virginia City police. Making his way to the White and Murphy claim, police officer Ben Lackey arrested Prentice without incident and lodged him in the city jail on a charge of assault with a deadly weapon.[5] The result of the next day's court hearing is not on record. It could not have been too severe, however, as the shootist would be back working for White and Murphy within a short time.

Three months later White and Murphy Company found themselves embroiled in another dispute seemingly centered around their tailing dump. In early May a group of men led by H.B. Blackwell erected a bulkhead around a portion of the dump, apparently in a partial attempt to hold in loose rock debris. According to White and Murphy Superintendent O'Reiley's way of thinking, however, the barrier fenced out some 50 feet of White and Murphy property. Wednesday morning, May 4, O'Reiley, along with mine foreman John Pierson, Dick Prentice and a number of other employees set to work and commenced pulling down the offending construction.

At about 11 o'clock Blackwell and five or six supporters suddenly rushed O'Reiley's party and a general melee quickly followed. Fortunately for everyone, Prentice must have been unarmed and unable to reach a firearm as none was employed. As a result, the men utilized pickaxes, steel bars and rocks to full effect. After the serious injury of a number of men and one woman (Blackwell's wife who, in attempting to assist her husband, fell down the side of a rock pile), Virginia City police arrived and ended the free-for-all.[6]

The following day Dick Prentice, H.J. O'Reiley, H.B. Blackwell, John Pierson, John Fleming and A. Stoddard appeared before Judge Davenport. Davenport set their cases for the next day.[7] Unfortunately no record exists as to the consequences, if any, of the White and Murphy/Blackwell imbroglio.

In the meantime, Dick Prentice continued to reside and work as a miner and mine guard in the Virginia City area for the next six years. In the fall of 1870, he would again come to the attention of the public due to his involvement in Virginia City's so-called "Water War."

Virginia City faced a serious water shortage by late summer 1870. The one company contracted to supply the necessary fluid, the Virginia and Gold Hill Water Company, suddenly saw a major decrease in their sources which they tunneled and flumed from the nearby mountains. Not only were the mills and other mining related operations suffering. The Virginia City and nearby Gold Hill fire departments were despairing in case of fire. In such arid conditions as the Nevada desert presented the city streets needed regular sprinkling or risk being buried in a mountain of dust. Worst of all, even potable drinking water for residential consumption was in short supply, some people resorting to buying ice and melting it for household use. Anyone who could supply the area with usable water had a major opportunity for making large monetary returns.[8] As the *Virginia City Territorial Enterprise* commented: "a strike of 15 or 20 inches of water ['measured as it flows in a flume without pressure'][9] would be worth a mint of money to the Water Company."[10]

The situation worsened when the V.& G.H. Water Co.'s only reliable source of water, a shaft of the Cole Gold and Silver Mining Co. located in Seven Mile Canyon, about a mile or two east of Virginia City, was suddenly turned off. The Water Company had been leasing the Cole tunnel and using their own pipes to transport the water to the city. When the lease expired at midnight, August 31, the Cole company decided to renegotiate the agreement, greatly increasing the value of the lease. The V.& G.H. refused to pay. With that the Cole officials proposed to provide the area with free water until they could put in their own pipes, provided the V.& G.H. would allow the temporary use of their pipes and sluices. The V.& G.H. refused to comply.[11]

This state of affairs soon engendered the birth of a second water company in competition to the Virginia and Gold Hill Co. Christened Peake and Company the concern was formed by the Cole Gold and Silver Mining Co. to oversee what Cole executives saw as their potentially lucrative water operations. An intense rivalry soon developed between the two companies. At length the adversarial entities began the hiring of "fighters" to protect their respective interests, properties and equipment in the canyon near Virginia City.[12]

By late October, Dick Prentice found himself one of those hired by Virginia and Gold Hill Water Co. The two sides warily spied each other for a time before the fireworks finally exploded on the afternoon of Tuesday, October 25.

In what he would later claim was an attempt to make peace between the two sides, Prentice stuck a pistol into his belt and, followed by another Peake soldier named William Sheik, a 32-year-old tough from Virginia City who would figure in future Virginia City shooting affairs,[13] made his way over to the Peake and Co.'s camp.

In Peake and Co. territory Prentice encountered one of their men, a known shootist named Leslie Blackburn,[14] lounging on a rock pile. Also sitting nearby proved to be another V.& G.H. Company fighter, gunman Dick Paddock. At the time both Blackburn and Paddock were unarmed.

Prentice spoke to Blackburn concerning the troubles between their respective employers. Blackburn apparently took umbrage with the remarks and angrily told Prentice there was no use talking about it. According to Prentice's later testimony, at this point Blackburn picked up a rock and advanced on him. According to Blackburn, he had dismissed Prentice when the latter suddenly flew into a rage and pulled his revolver.

At any rate, the ball now opened as Prentice fired a shot at Blackburn, the slug perforating Blackburn's coat but missing his body.

Running up on the scene Paddock hollered to Blackburn, "Are you hurt?"

In the excitement of the moment, thinking he had been wounded, Blackburn replied, "Yes, I believe I am, but I'll get even."

Before Prentice could fire another shot, Blackburn slammed a rock into the side of his attacker's head, knocking him to the ground. Stunned, Prentice laid prostrate while Blackburn began mashing his face and head with the rock. Looking up, Blackburn saw Sheik running toward him, a pistol in his hand.

Jumping up, Blackburn told Paddock to take over the pummeling of Prentice while yelling for another of the Peake fighters, Robert Lindsay,[15] to bring up their guns. With blood streaming down his face, Prentice grasped Paddock and the two grappled and rolled on the ground before finally rolling over an embankment. Upon hitting the bottom Paddock slammed into a concrete barrow, shattering his shoulder bone.

With Paddock hors de combat, Prentice staggered to his feet just as Lindsay appeared on a rise, aiming a rifle. Lindsay squeezed off a shot which failed to hit either Prentice or Sheik. Backing away, both Prentice and Sheik returned Lindsay's fire with their pistols. One of the shots struck Lindsay in the right leg below the knee. At this juncture both Prentice and Sheik turned and fled the scene, leaving the Peake and Co. men in command of the field.[16]

Gradually, the wounded of the Seven Mile Canyon fight began to straggle into Virginia City. Walking the short distance from the Canyon into the city, Dick Prentice was the first to appear. He presented a horrible sight as he shuffled to the office of Dr. Heath, his head, face and clothes covered in blood, several lacerations in his scalp, a deep and ugly cut between his eyes, his upper lip split open. After the ministrations of Dr. Heath, however, he made a quick recovery.[17]

The others of the fight also eventually recovered from their injuries. Paddock and Lindsay however, were laid up for some time before they were ambulatory once more. Despite the violence of the encounter, any legal action as a result of the fight is not of record. Eventually the water problems were solved and the Virginia and Gold Hill Water Co. continued to operate in the area for years thereafter. Dick Prentice, in fact, continued unhindered. Only a couple of weeks later he appears on the voter's list for the First Ward, Virginia City, in anticipation of the November elections.[18] He would still be in the area two years later when, again, he would make headlines with his gun.

2. "The Best Fighter in Nevada"

The *Gold Hill Evening News* of Wednesday, February 21, 1872, blared the headlines:

>DARK AND BLOODY DEED!
>A MAN SHOT IN THE ENTRY
>OF A HOTEL AND IN-
>STANTLY KILLED!
>HIS BOWELS TORN OPEN BY
>THE SHOT!
>A SICKENING SCENE!

Gold Hill, a mining community about a mile South of Virginia City, was simply an extension of the Comstock mining area. Despite being almost a part of Virginia City, the burg had its own town structure, police force, fire department, hotels, stores and saloons. By 1872, Dick Prentice would seem to have been employed by the Caledonia Mine near Gold Hill.

The evening of Tuesday, February 20 found Prentice drinking in the bar room of the Piute House Hotel in Gold Hill where he had his rooms. At length he fell into a disagreement with a ca. 29-year-old miner and native of Ireland named Patrick O'Rourke.[19] O'Rourke, who perhaps had been imbibing even more than Prentice, was soon extremely intoxicated. He made himself so obnoxious that, at length, Prentice suddenly grabbed a bottle and broke it over the Irishman's head, inflicting a nasty scalp laceration.

Thinking he had ended O'Rourke's hijinks for the night Prentice went upstairs to his room and went to bed. O'Rourke, however, would not be cowed.

A few hours later he decided to confront Prentice. At about three or four in the morning, with a candle in one hand and a revolver in the other, he made his way to Prentice's room. Opening the door, he called to Prentice, "are you ready to fight me?"

Stirring himself, Prentice could see that O'Rourke was almost staggering drunk. "I don't want to fight," Prentice said. "As far as our little difficulty in the bar room, I will leave it to all who were present to say who was right and who was wrong."

Temporarily stymied, O'Rourke left the room and eventually made his way to the hotel porch. Taking his revolver, he fired a shot into the air. He attempted to squeeze off two more shots but the revolver failed to fire. Someone standing near the front of the hotel told him the weapon was no good whereupon O'Rourke stuck it in his back pocket and reentered the hotel.

Having heard the revolver shot, Prentice got out of bed, grabbed his double-barreled shotgun and went out into the hall. Suddenly, he encountered O'Rourke in the hallway.

"Are you ready for a fight now?" Prentice growled.

"All right," O'Rourke slurred.

Without raising the shotgun to his shoulder Prentice fired both barrels from the hip. The charge caught O'Rourke in the abdomen nearly cutting him in two. The mortally wounded man died within seconds of hitting the floor.[20]

When Gold Hill City Marshal Tom Harkin arrived on the scene, he was met with a picture of carnage rarely witnessed. In a large pool of blood some ten feet in width lay the body of O'Rourke, his perforated liver, ribs and intestines exposed.

Blood, flesh, bits of bone, and internal organs coated the wall behind where he had been shot. Dick Prentice was nowhere to be seen. Harkin, along with policeman Morrow and Isaac Hubbel, an acquaintance of O'Rourke's, set out in pursuit. Prentice, however, had simply walked out to the Caledonia Mine where he left his shotgun, then hiked into Virginia City and gave himself up at the County Jail.[21]

A story soon became general around town which had much to say concerning the pragmatism of a local physician who had been summoned to attend O'Rourke on the night of his shooting. According to the *Gold Hill News*:

> Early, day before yesterday morning, shortly after the killing of O'Rourke, by Prentice, a man came rushing to see Dr. Hall, telling him that he was wanted down at the Piute House, right away, as a man was shot through the bowels. "How badly is he hurt?" inquired the doctor. "Hurt, is it? Why the whole belly's blown off him, and he's dead!" "Ah, well, then what does he want of a doctor?" "Yes, that's so," says the messenger, reflectively, and left. The doctor went to bed again. Some people, apparently do not think a man is officially dead until a doctor pronounces him so.[22]

Indeed, the coroner's jury of February 22 just as pragmatically pronounced Patrick O'Rourke dead, "by gunshot wound, said gun being in the hands of W.D. Prentice, and said wound being given in self-defense and preservation of his own life."[23] Justice Putnam was not convinced. Deciding Prentice's actions were not totally blameless he decided to ignore the last part of the Coroner Jury's decree and bind the gunman over to appear before the next Grand Jury on a charge of murder. Putnam did allow Prentice to post a bail bond of $5000.[24] Sitting in early March the Grand Jury apparently agreed with the Coroner's edict and decided to ignore the charge against Prentice.[25] The battling miner had dodged another bullet.

The incident that could be termed Dick Prentice's defining moment took place in October 1874. The genesis of the entire affair started some 175 miles away in the board rooms of San Francisco. By late summer a conflict had developed between members of the Board of Trustees of the Justice Mining Company, located on lower Gold Hill. Evidence seems to suggest that three of the board, J.P. Jackson, John F. Hill and E. Hestres were of the opinion that the other two board members, A.P. Minear and J. Clem Uhler, who owned a minority of the stock, were trying to depress stock values in an attempt to buy back into the company.[26]

By September 1874 rumors were rife concerning a possible takeover bid by certain factions of the Board using as leverage the Superintendency position at the Justice. It also gained report that the two factions, one supporting current superintendent T.F. "Fred" Smith and the other behind possible replacement George F. Kellogg, a native of New York, were developing at the mine. It became common talk amongst locals that there was bound to be a fight sooner or later. All sides, it was reported, were hiring "fighters," one of the recruiting agents being well-known Virginia City gambler and lawman Tom Hughes, although he would later deny the charges in court.[27]

The spark that ignited the Inferno came on the afternoon of Saturday, October 3. That afternoon George Kellogg received a telegram from certain members of the Board of Trustees in San Francisco informing him that he had been hired as the new superintendent at the Justice to replace Fred Smith. A short time later board member John Hill telegraphed Fred Smith to hold the mine at all hazards, at least until Kellogg presented him with the proper injunctions.

Managing to acquire the proper paperwork, Kellogg, with the added support of Gold Hill Constable Tom Harkin, trooped out to the Justice Mine and informed those at the main office that he was the new superintendent. He then set out to attempt to locate Smith and inform him of developments. Unsuccessful in his quest, by early evening Kellogg began making plans to relieve the men at the Waller Defeat shaft and hoisting works of the Justice mine complex which was still being held by Smith supporters. In the meantime, according to his later testimony, Smith, informed of Kellogg having obtained the proper paperwork, wrote out a note to John Dunn, foreman of the Waller Defeat shaft, instructing him to turn the buildings over to Kellogg.[28] Before this note could arrive at the mine works, however, developments would render it a missive of little consequence.

At about 6 o'clock that evening Kellogg ordered his brother, 42-year-old William Kellogg, a New Yorker like himself, to gather up a posse and take possession of the Waller Defeat. Recruiting a number of men including Michael Caine, W.D. Shiftlett, John Brown and Michael Rieley, William Kellogg led the way to the Waller Defeat shaft. While still a number of yards away, the group spotted four or five heavily armed men inside the hoisting building while another, likewise armed, stood by the open door in front. The identities of any of the armed party holding the Waller Defeat would never be determined for a certainty. All that is, save one. It became common knowledge throughout the Comstock after the incident that one of the men, probably wielding his trusty shotgun, was Dick Prentice.

According to one of the closest witnesses to the events to follow, one G.W. Werk,[29] a member of Kellogg's party, when the group were within 30 feet of the building the outside guard shouted at them, "Men, hold on! Don't come any further!"

The men continued to push forward. "Hold on!" Kellogg yelled, attempting to keep his men back. Two of them, 37-year-old Michael Rieley and Michael Caine, 35, both natives of Ireland, pushed past him, pulled revolvers from their belts and dashed for the door.

With that, the guard quickly jumped inside and a regular fusillade erupted from inside the building. Both Rieley and Caine dropped dead in the doorway. Another man farther back in the crowd, a 37-year-old native of Pennsylvania named John Brown, fell to the ground, dead with a bullet in his chest. Immediately the door to the hoisting works slammed shut.

Shocked by the turn of events, Kellogg called out to the men in the building, "For God's sake, stop this! Let me say a few words to you!"

"Talk on," a voice came from inside.

"Shall I come inside?" Kellogg asked.

"If you fetch anybody with you, we will fire on you," the voice came back.

"I will come alone," Kellogg answered and moved with trepidation toward the door.

The door banged open as Kellogg stepped to the threshold. Despite his admonitions, a number of the men pressed in close. One of them, Harry Foster, had an image burned into his memory which may not have left him for a long while. As he would later testify:

> I saw a man inside with a shotgun; he pointed it apparently at me; I dropped on one knee and slid away; McMartin and Humphreys went down with me; the man with the shotgun had black whiskers.[30]

This was probably Dick Prentice. Foster was lucky to have "slid away" for the action was not over yet.

As Kellogg began to speak with the men inside, his followers continued to jostle in the doorway. One of the defenders repeated himself two or three times. "Don't come in," he warned. Still the men pushed. All at once, more shots rang out. Hit in the stomach, Kellogg doubled over and stumbled out the door. As everyone turned and ran for the rise leading away from the Waller Defeat, 47-year-old Virginia native W.D. Shiflett fell, shot in the back. He would die early the next day.

As Kellogg staggered past G.W. Werk he gasped, "I believe they have got me. The Indians couldn't have done worse. I had no idea that they would shoot." He would also die later that night.[31]

Informed of the shooting, Constable Tom Harkin and Storey County Sheriff Thomas Atkinson hastened to the scene. With all the casualties cleared from the battleground the two lawmen employed guards to surround the Waller Defeat shaft and buildings in an attempt to besiege the gunmen inside. It was daylight the next morning before someone finally found the courage to enter the structure. The building was empty of life, the men having flown, possibly in the initial confusion of the end of the fight or sometime during the night. All that was found inside, besides the large pools of dried blood where Caine and Rieley had fallen near the front door, was a box of 100 cigars, two half empty demijohns of whiskey, a Henry rifle, three revolvers, a small caliber pistol, a double-barreled shotgun and various ammunition.[32]

Gold Hill News editor Alfred Doten, 1870. In October 1874, Doten would express his disgust with the Waller Defeat affair (courtesy Digital Photo Collection, Image #UNRS-P1393-1, Special Collections and University Archives Department, University of Nevada, Reno Libraries).

As news of the tragedy became general, many felt revolted by the spectacle of another violent episode connected with their local mines. Alf Doten, editor of the *Gold Hill News*, expressed what many people felt when he editorialized in the October 5 issue:

> Five good men and citizens have been most needlessly slaughtered, and the public eagerly desire to know where the blame lies. Contending trustees and stakeholders in San Francisco are the most guilty parties, according to our idea, directing a sudden, absolute and preemptory change in the Superintendency and management of the mine.... Why could not the parties wait until morning and let the proper officers of the law interfere if necessary?... Five good men and citizens are killed in consequence, and Gold Hill is disgraced forever.

Later, on the morning following the shooting, Sheriff Atkinson and Constable Harkin encountered three men camped near Silver City, three miles or so south of Gold Hill. Realizing the trio were Dick Prentice, Thomas Murphy, and Dan Askew, all suspected in the Waller Defeat battle, the lawmen placed them under arrest and trooped them to the County Jail in Virginia City. The next day another suspect, Patrick Peters, joined the three in jail.[33]

On the same day as the funerals of the five Waller Defeat victims, Storey County Coroner Holmes convened a coroner's inquest on Monday, October 5.[34] After two days of testimony the jury came to the conclusion that the five men died "from gunshot wounds inflicted by the hands of parties to us unknown."[35] Despite this ruling, Prentice and his cellmates remained locked up pending the Grand Jury investigation later that month.[36]

In a somewhat surprising development, on Wednesday the 7th, officers arrested former Justice superintendent Fred Smith. This arrest proved to be the result of a warrant sworn out by George Kellogg charging him with "aiding and abetting in the killing of William F. Kellogg."[37] This charge would eventually be ignored by the Grand Jury. In fact, Smith eventually would have the last laugh.

Work had only been suspended at the Justice Mine for less than a day following the battle of the 3rd. The following day, under new superintendent George Kellogg, production resumed.[38] Back in San Francisco, however, stockholders were not happy. In mid–October a majority demanded the removal of the present Board of Trustees who were largely blamed for the debacle at the mine. E. Hestress would be the only one to survive the purge. On October 20 the new board removed Kellogg as superintendent and replaced him with former superintendent T. Fred Smith.[39]

Dick Prentice also would have reason to be pleased with the outcome of his case. Reporting on Tuesday, October 27, the Grand Jury, led by foreman Lloyd Rawlings, ruled, "It is a lamentable fact that, although the community has been startled with the commission of the greatest outrage ever committed in the State, we have been unable to ascertain the name or names of any persons who were engaged in the killing.... We have been unable to present an indictment against a single person connected with this killing."[40] The jail doors were flung open and Prentice and his companions strode out, free men once more.

Although the official legal tribunals were unable to come to any conclusions, most everyone else in western Nevada who knew anything about the case knew, or at least strongly suspected, that Dick Prentice had been one of the shooters at the Waller Defeat shaft of the Justice Mine that day in early October 1874. It affected his persona to such an extent that from this time onward he came to be known to many on the Comstock as "Waller Defeat" Prentice.[41] This reputation was no amelioration to his personality and according to some, he began to see himself as "chief"[42] fighting man of the area. On at least one occasion, however, according to well-known Comstock newspaper editor Wells Drury, Prentice would have his peacock feathers ruffled, albeit ignorantly, by a man unaware of his identity.

As Drury described years later in his book of reminiscences, *An Editor on the Comstock Lode*, a soon-to-be friend of his named Arthur McEwen had recently arrived on the Comstock to assume the assistant editorship of the *Gold Hill News*. Shortly after the killings at the Waller Defeat shaft of the Justice Mine, McEwen happened to be sitting in Donovan's Saloon in Gold Hill having a drink. As Drury related the story:

> A quiet acting, little dried up looking fellow, in a faded brown suit of clothes, sidled up to him and said:
> "Hello, Mac, old boy. How do ye open up this mornin'?"
> McEwen did not let on to hear him, but the other fellow didn't mind that, but in an off-handed way remarked:
> "Gimme a cocktail, too, barkeep. I guess I'll drink with Mac."
> "I guess you won't," snorted out the bristling editor. "I pick my companions as a general thing and when I want you to drink with me, I'll ask you."
> "See here!" Said McEwen, turning to the barkeeper. "What makes you let a bum like this lie around your place to insult gentlemen when they come in for a drink?"
> "Get out of here," he fairly shrieked, turning to the intruder again. "Get out of here right quick or I'll bust your jaw and throw you out."
> The quiet little fellow turned on his heel, like a man who had been misunderstood, and walked over to the stove, where he stood blinking out of his beady black eyes, in a wicked sort of way. It would be hard to say which was more surprised, the barkeeper or the little fellow who invited himself into McEwen's company.[43]

Little did McEwen know that he had just told off Dick "Waller Defeat" Prentice.

Later, Drury and a group of his friends, realizing that McEwen was ignorant of what he had done, praised the man for his courage. Confused, McEwen asked them to explain. According to Drury he replied to McEwen:

> "This morning, what you did over in Donovan's saloon, you know, when you showed your nerves like that; when you wouldn't let Prentice drink with you, you know and—"

> But he wouldn't let me finish what I was saying.

> "What!" he demanded, "Was that Prentice I was talking to and threatening to smash in the jaw? Is it possible that is the man I have heard so much about? How did he know me I'd like to know?"
> "Yes," says I, "that was him. That was Prentice. He knows everybody, and that was his way of introducing himself. He felt, of course, you'd be proud to meet him."
> "But that's not Waller Defeat Prentice," he says, aghast. "Not the fellow that killed five men when they tried to capture the Waller Defeat Shaft, and him inside loaded up with shotguns and six shooters and Bowie knives?"[44]

When he finally realized who he had insulted, McEwen was determined to rush out, track the man down and apologize profusely to him. His friends, however, convinced him not to do it but to enjoy the reputation he would garner for having called down such a character. As Drury told it, Prentice "kind of dropped the subject. He said he didn't want to have anything to do with a man who didn't know enough to be afraid of the boss of Gold Hill."[45]

Prentice continued to pursue his avocation. Two years later, in January 1878, a dangerous situation developed between the Justice and Alta mines when two of their respective shafts were expected to intersect, both entities claiming the disputed ground.[46] Both sides followed the standard procedure of hiring "fighters" to protect their interests at $10 a day, a princely sum when compared to the standard miners wages of $4 per day. Of course, one had to have the boldness of character and dexterity with firearms to claim the flush prize. One of these was Dick Prentice.

This time Prentice hired himself out to the Alta Mine. One of those hired by the Justice proved to be Robert McDonald, a former Virginia City police officer who had killed Tom Hughes in the famous Virginia City gunfight that also resulted in the death of Dick Paddock in January 1877. It would be while describing these various fighting men that one Nevada newspaper would call Prentice "the best fighter in Nevada,"[47] a testament to whatever dubious distinction the dangerous shootist had garnered for himself.

With the bone of contention being the underground shafts, the two rival companies placed gunfighters underground in anticipation of the fireworks expected when one or the other broke through into the competitor's shaft. This did not sit well with the Miner's Union claiming, rightly so, that this state of affairs placed the regular miners in grave danger. In this case, common sense prevailed for once and the company fighters were barred from the underground. This forced the Justice and Alta to come up with other, nonviolent, means to solve the difficulties. By January 18, Prentice and the other fighters were relieved of their duties.[48]

In subsequent years Prentice continued to make his abode in the Virginia City–Gold Hill region. He also continued to live by the gun. Early on the morning of Sunday, October 31, 1880, Prentice, making the rounds of the various Virginia City saloons, managed to run afoul of former Bodie, California, gunman, law man and exhibition wrestler Eugene Markey.[49] At length the two began to quarrel. When it appeared to Markey that Prentice was reaching his hand to his gun, Markey pinned Prentice's arms to his side and refused to let go until Prentice agreed to calm down and depart in peace.

Later that same morning, at about 5 o'clock, the pair came together again in the Delta Saloon. As two other men seemed to be about to begin fighting, Markey stepped between them and attempted to act as peacemaker. Seeing this, Prentice, for some reason, took umbrage.

Pulling his pistol from under his belt Prentice moved toward Markey. "You big fighter, what do you want to meddle for?" He roared at Markey.

In a move straight out of a later Hollywood B-Western, Markey kicked the gun out of Prentice's hand. Picking it up where it landed on the floor Markey fired a shot at Prentice with his own weapon. The slug caught Prentice in the fleshy part of his left arm near the shoulder. Markey squeezed the trigger a second time; however, the pistol refused to fire. Realizing the weapon was now no better than a bludgeon, Markey swung the revolver at Prentice's head. The gun connected with Prentice's skull, opening a large gash and knocking him to the floor. At this juncture the fight was all out of Dick Prentice and the conflict came to an end.[50]

Assisted to the County Hospital, Prentice had his wounds tended and quickly made a full recovery. Authorities arrested Eugene Markey on an assault to kill charge. Released on a bail bond of $1000, it is very doubtful that any further action was taken against him.[51]

Dick Prentice resumed his residence on the Comstock Lode for the next ten years. During this time, he failed to engage in any newsworthy physical encounters and perhaps he had a chance of living the remainder of his life in peace and dying of the proverbial "natural causes." If anyone was inevitably destined to fulfill that ancient axiom "those who live by the sword shall die by the sword," however, Prentice was that man.

In about the summer of 1890, Prentice entered into some financial dealings with Jerry Mulligan, a rancher in Six Mile Canyon, just east of Virginia City. Subsequent to this, Prentice felt that Mulligan owed him some money which the rancher was overly slow to pay. Prentice commenced uttering threats against the man's life. One day he appeared on the doorstep of Mulligan's ranch house in Six Mile Canyon and made an attempt to collect the supposed debt by force. Knowing Prentice's reputation and fearing for his life, without much ado Mulligan grabbed the nearest weapon, ironically enough a double-barreled shotgun, and emptied both barrels into Prentice's body. Dick Prentice died on the spot.[52]

The resultant Coroner's Jury deemed Mulligan's actions as in defense of his own life and decreed the rancher blameless.[53] As newsman Wells Drury so succinctly put it, W.D. "Dick" "Waller Defeat" Prentice had finally reaped his "persistently sought fate."[54]

3

The Hard Luck Gunman
Dick Paddock

If a fearless reputation and willingness to use a gun in personal combat were the deciding factors in measuring the worth of an Old West gunman, Dick Paddock would rate high on any list. If luck, however, was the determining factor Paddock would fail miserably. His reputation in early day Nevada was such that at one time a local newspaper was prompted to comment that he "would rather look down the barrel of a gun than waste wind."[1] Many feared him as a man best left alone. Perhaps it was this fearlessness combined with recklessness that caused him to receive serious injuries in almost every one of his known encounters. At one time he challenged one of the most noteworthy shootists of the Old West era. The result almost caused his death in his first known gunfight. This proved to set the tone of events to follow until Paddock finally received the most serious injury of all, a mortal one, in his last battle.

A native of Ireland born in about 1838,[2] Richard "Dick" Paddock eventually made his way to America. His movements before the early 1860s are unknown. By 1863 he had located to the mining camps of Nevada, finally gravitating to the capital of Storey County at Virginia City. It would be in Nevada where Dick Paddock made his mark as a man "with sand."

Dwelling in Virginia City during early 1863 proved to be a notorious gambler and shootist named Langford Peel. Known by the cognomen "Farmer" Peel because of his habit of dressing in homespun's and coveralls when he wished to dupe a sucker at a game of three card monte or thimble rig, Peel was a tough customer. Having killed men in various shooting scrapes from Texas to Utah, Peel quickly ascended to the position of dominant sport in Virginia City. To all, that is, except young Dick Paddock who would meet Peel in one of the few face-to-face, walk-down gunfights, to actually occur in the real old west.

Encountering Peel in one of Virginia City's many saloons one night, Paddock instigated an exchange of hot words over something in which he felt slighted. Years later a local newspaper described the incident:

> One day Paddock and Peel had a few words in Robinson and Gentry's gambling saloon on B Street, south of Sutton Avenue, and Paddock asked Peel to step into the street and fight. Peel coolly walked out, and taking the centre of the street drew simultaneously with Paddock, who was on the sidewalk. Peel's first shot pierced Paddock's side. The wounded man, throwing his arm around a post, steadied himself for the return shot, but was too weak from the shock of his wound to take a correct aim, and the ball scattered the dust at Peel's feet. Peel continued to

answer his antagonist's desultory fire by deliberate shots, each ball knocking the splinters from the post behind which Paddock was trying to shelter himself, and passing into Paddock's body. Three or four bullets took effect, and one passed through his stomach. Peel was unhurt. After the fourth shot Paddock threw down his pistol and remarked, "Boys, I'm a dead man," and sank down at the foot of the post. Peel put away his revolver, and walking back into the saloon, resumed his seat as if nothing had happened, while Paddock was taken to the hospital.[3]

Paddock remained in the hospital for several months in critical condition. Physicians felt his many wounds, especially the stomach wound, would eventually prove fatal. The injured man showed himself to be made of stern stuff. In time he made a full recovery.[4] Peel, meanwhile, made a court appearance gaining his release on the grounds of self-defense.[5]

Farmer Peel went on to kill "El Dorado Johnny" Dennis in a similar street fight in Virginia City before moving on to other locales and adventures. Occasionally he would return to Virginia City[6] before finally meeting his death in a Helena, Montana, shoot-out at the hands of John Bull on July 23, 1867.[7]

As 1863 turned to 1864 the fully recovered Dick Paddock was a mainstay in the service, social, political and sporting scenes of Virginia City. His display of bravado in challenging the formidable Farmer Peel had acquired him a respected reputation in the city's dives. Most every night he could be seen in these places, socializing with friends and being treated as a dangerous man.

Often seen carousing and gambling at night, by day Paddock could call himself a valued member of the Virginia City Fire Department, Eagle Engine Company No. 3.[8] In fact, on February 8, 1864, while answering a fire alarm, Paddock received painful injuries when the engine wheel struck a barrel. The tongue he grasped jerked sideways, mashing three fingers and his leg against the outer wall of Kirk and Co.'s drugstore.[9] He quickly recovered and was back on duty within a few days.

Despite his service to the community Paddock was by no means a model citizen, often finding himself in trouble with the law. In early July, Virginia City police officer Clarkson arrested Paddock on a warrant charging him with assault. On July 7, he was found guilty in recorder court and fined $25.[10] Again, on September 7, Virginia City Mayor Arick took it upon himself to arrest Paddock for being drunk and disorderly.[11] Paddock spent the night in the drunk tank where he slept it off and nursed his woozy head.

Another of Dick Paddock's interests proved to be state politics in which he took an active part. A staunch supporter of the Democratic Party he gained appointment as teller at the Storey County Democratic Convention held in Virginia City during the week of October 18, 1864.[12] This would be one of the many positions he eventually held with the county Democrats. He may have been considered a so-called "political rough," using his muscle and reputation at the polls, political rallies, etc.

By early to mid–1865, Paddock held a number of responsible positions concurrently in the growing city. In March city officials appointed him to the office of fire warden with power of arrest in regard to violators of the city's fire ordinances.[13] In May the energetic young man gained an appointment as a police officer on the Virginia City Police Force.[14] Simultaneous to this he received a promotion within the fire department to the rank of Second Assistant Engineer at a salary of $83.33 for the month of May.[15]

Despite these positions of responsibility Paddock had not shelved his fractious nature. November 7, 1865, election day in Virginia City, commenced with the usual hustle and bustle. At nine that morning, Paddock and fellow fireman J.S. Pitzer met at the B Street polling station. For some reason the pair argued before being separated by friends. Later that afternoon the two men came together again at the First Ward polls located in the Music Hall.

Pitzer sat in his buggy on the street while Paddock walked up from behind. Suddenly Pitzer's horses backed up causing the back-buggy wheel to narrowly miss Paddock's foot. Paddock spat an oath. With that Pitzer pulled a revolver and fired a shot, the slug cutting a narrow furrow along Paddock's shoulder. The pistol was so close to Paddock's face when Pitzer pulled the trigger that his face was slightly powder burnt.[16] Paddock quickly drew his own revolver and fired an answering shot. The bullet just missed Pitzer's neck as he jumped from the buggy. At this juncture the two men were separated and the pistol duel came to an end.[17] Paddock made a speedy recovery from the slight flesh wound and soon was back on the streets.

Paddock and Pitzer were not the only fighting firemen in Virginia City. On the evening of March 2, 1866, Paddock's friend and fellow fireman Ben Ballou was shot and killed by Billy Sheppard, an actor performing at the Music Hall, in a fracas at the

Fire engine along with crew on a Virginia City street, 1866. Although none of the men are identified, Dick Paddock may well be in this photograph as he was known to be a Virginia City fireman during the time of the photograph (courtesy Digital Photo Collection, Image #UNRS-P0132-1, Special Collections and University Archives Department, University of Nevada, Reno Libraries).

Capital Saloon on C Street.[18] All the engine companies in the city followed Ballou's body to its temporary resting place in Virginia City. One of the many mourners in the cortege probably included Dick Paddock. Eventually Ballou's remains were shipped to San Francisco, California, where he received interment in the Fireman's plot of Lone Mountain Cemetery.[19]

By early 1866, Paddock had become somewhat domesticated. He had married his 22-year-old-wife Anna. This year also saw the birth of the couple's first child, Benjamin.[20] Ben would be followed two years later by Richard Jr. and then little Mary in July 1870.[21]

He also continued active service in the Fire Department. In January 1866, members of Washoe Company No. 4 nominated him to run against William Pennison for First Assistant Foreman in the upcoming elections.[22] The election, held one day after the funeral of Ben Ballou, March 5, almost ended in gunplay between opposing factions within the fire company due to ballot box stuffing. That Virginia City might bury another fireman or two was feared. Eventually, however, cooler heads prevailed and Paddock lost the First Assistant position to William Pennison by a mere four votes, 203 to 199.[23]

Paddock continued to serve despite the loss at the polls. He is recorded as having made two arrests during the month of March in his capacity as Fire Warden of the city.[24] The entire Fire Department received a severe test of their skills on the morning of Sunday, June 18, when nearly 100 houses burnt to the ground as fire raged through a residential district of Virginia City.[25] Dick Paddock and his fellow fire fighters performed sterling service in battling the blaze and saving many buildings.

Some time in late 1866 or early 1867, Paddock quit the fire company in order to work full time on the Virginia City Police Force. The local *Territorial Enterprise's* "Recorder's Court" column often lists him as the arresting officer in various cases of drunk and disorderly, disturbing the peace, carrying concealed weapons, etc.[26] Paddock seems to have been one of the most aggressive members of the force. According to the City Jailer's records for the month of July 1867, Paddock executed 27 arrests out of a total of 108, the most of any member on the force.[27]

There is evidence to suggest that Paddock may have been a bit overly aggressive. On Tuesday, December 24, 1867, the *Territorial Enterprise* printed the following item:

> Board of Police Commissioners–The Board of Police Commissioners held a special session at the City Hall last Saturday evening to investigate charges preferred against police officer Richard Paddock, for conduct unbecoming an officer. A number of witnesses were examined touching the case, and after a full and critical examination Mr. Paddock was honorably acquitted of the charges preferred against him.

The exact nature of the charges was not reported. Having been cleared of all wrongdoing, Paddock continued to act as a city policeman for at least another six months.

One of the most noteworthy episodes during Paddock's service on the Virginia City force would have to be the Russian Pete incident of July 1868. Peter Hill, or Russian Pete as he was known, was a native of Finland. One observer termed him "a very large, muscular and exceedingly fierce-looking man ... peculiarly animal and ferocious-looking."[28] His specialty was petty larceny and on the evening of July 26 officers spotted him in Virginia City.

Upon being hailed by Storey County Deputy Sheriff Gregory, Pete showed his defiance by turning and dashing down the street. Eventually a party of county and city officers, including Sheriff Mulcahy, Deputy Gregory, Constable Ash and policeman Dick Paddock, trailed the wanted man to an abandoned mine shaft located on the outskirts of the city. In answer to a call for his surrender Russian Pete hollered that he would not be taken alive, that he had a revolver and would kill as many men as he could who attempted to get him out of his refuge.

A few yards back from the mouth of the disused shaft the timbers had caved in causing a hole, which extended to the surface. In order to seal off one avenue of escape, and perhaps cause the desperate man to feel that he was being trapped, the officers began to fill in this hole by caving in the loose earth on the side. By this time a crowd of some 200 individuals had gathered on the scene to watch the excitement and some began to take a hand in the work. One of these, a blacksmith named Walter Williams, moved to the south side of the hole in order to pull down a large mound of loose dirt. Taking no heed of Sheriff Mulcahy's repeated warning that the south side would expose him to fire from the shaft, Williams went to work. Suddenly a shot rang out from inside the shaft. Gasping, "Oh God!" Williams almost fell into the hole before being caught by Paddock and some others who carried him off to the side. Shot in the chest directly through the heart, Williams died almost instantly.[29]

Keeping the men working from a safe angle, Mulcahy also employed the tactic of pumping water into the shaft in an effort to flush the desperado out. At the same time, Mulcahy, Ash, Gregory and other officers concealed themselves behind various breastworks in front of the mouth of the tunnel. Armed with a Henry rifle, Paddock lay down behind a bank of earth some 50 yards in front of the shaft, leveled his rifle over the top and awaited developments.

Concealing himself behind timbers, Russian Pete made his way to the opening of the shaft and fired two shots at his pursuers. With that, Mulcahy, Ash and Paddock opened up, firing a number of shots into the mine. Following this initial volley all was quiet for a few seconds before another report echoed inside the shaft. Eventually one of the men ventured inside. He discovered Pete had stuck the barrel of his pistol into his mouth, pulled the trigger and blown his brains all over the walls of the old mine shaft.[30] He had saved the county the expense of another trial.

By June 1869, Paddock had relocated to the booming mining camp of Treasure City. In the mid–June town elections Paddock won the position of Deputy City Marshal under Marshal Tom Coleman. Paddock's old friend Tom Hughes gained appointment to the Treasure City Police Force at the same time.[31] Dick Paddock only served on the Treasure City force for about one year. The federal census for 1870 shows the 32-year-old Paddock living in Virginia City with his wife Anna, 26, and their three children.[32] He is listed as working as a miner. Their next-door neighbor at this time is Paddock's friend and future business partner Thomas Hughes, also listed as a miner.[33]

Although working in the mining region, Paddock (and possibly Tom Hughes as well) was not toiling in the mines at this time. "Miner" was probably just a convenient title to give to the census taker. Paddock had hired his gun to Parke & Co. in what could be called Virginia City's "Water War."

By the fall of 1870 water was a valuable commodity in Virginia City simply because the city, at one point, was not getting any. Virginia City's water supply was piped in from Seven Mile Canyon a few miles outside the city. Beginning in the summer of 1870 two opposing water companies, the Virginia and Gold Hill Water Co. and Parke & Co., began to wrangle over right of way through Seven Mile Canyon. In a move reminiscent of mining wars and later railroad wars both sides hired known fighting men to act as guards and protect company property and interests. Parke & Co. hired Dick Paddock as one of their hired guns.

The situation had reached such a serious level by October that, for a time, Virginia City was not getting any water at all except that being pumped up from the bottom of the Ophir Mine works. The *Territorial Enterprise* termed this "most unwholesome, if not positively poisonous." Drinking water was not the only worry. In Nevada's arid climate the streets had to be sprinkled on a regular basis to keep down the choking dust. If the streets are not sprinkled soon the *Enterprise* complained, "we shall all be buried in dust as were the inhabitants of ancient Pompeii in ashes."[34]

The affair reached a climax on the afternoon of October 25 on the disputed ground of Seven Mile Canyon. Who precipitated the scrimmage is a matter of contention, both sides laying blame on their opponents. At any rate, it is clear that Dick Prentice,[35] a Virginia and Gold Hill guard, approached Dick Paddock and Leslie F. Blackburn of Parke & Co. as the pair lounged on a dump pile near their camp. Both Paddock and Blackburn were unarmed, having left their guns in camp. Prentice carried a small derringer in his coat pocket. Why Prentice crossed over to confront the enemy camp is unknown; however, it may have been an effort to promote peace between the two factions. If this was his goal it backfired badly.

Quickly an argument developed between Prentice and Blackburn. At length Prentice pulled the derringer out of his pocket and fired at Blackburn. The ball passed through Blackburn's coat.

Startled, Paddock jumped up. "Are you hit?" he yelled to Blackburn.

"I think so," Blackburn snarled, "but I will get even."

Scrambling to his feet Blackburn grabbed up a large rock and, before Prentice could get off another shot, smashed the improvised weapon into Prentice's head. This opened a large gash between Prentice's eyes and knocked him down. With Prentice on the ground Blackburn dealt him another couple of blows to the skull before he spotted William Sheik, another Virginia and Gold Hill man, rushing at him with a pistol in his hand.

With Sheik hollering that he would shoot him the enraged Blackburn left Prentice where he lay and charged the armed man. At the same time, he called to Robert Lindsay[36] at the Parke & Co. camp to come on the run with their guns.

In the meantime, Paddock took over the pummeling of Prentice. In the tussle both men ended up rolling down the side of the dump pile. When they hit the bottom Paddock forcefully struck his left shoulder on the corner of a barrow, breaking the bone near the socket. Prentice, blood streaming down his face, quickly jumped up. Leaving Paddock writhing on the ground in agony he ran to join Sheik.

With Prentice and Sheik retreating, Lindsay arrived on the scene and managed to fire a shot after them. Turning, both men answered Lindsay's fire with shots of their own. Struck in the right leg just above the knee Lindsay dropped to the ground. Continuing their retreat, Prentice and Sheik scampered off the field of battle and the fight came to an end.[37]

Eventually all the combatants straggled into Virginia City for medical treatment.[38] Paddock's broken shoulder proved to be a very serious and painful injury. It would be a number of months before he fully recovered. For all intents and purposes this brought an end to Virginia City's "Water War." Both sides quickly shipped more fighters out to Seven Mile Canyon; however, shortly the dispute was settled. Within a short time, the Virginia and Gold Hill Water Company was piping fresh, clear water into Virginia City once again. Any legal wrangling resulting from the Seven Mile Canyon battle is unknown.

Sometime after finally recovering from his broken shoulder, Dick Paddock pulled up stakes and left Virginia City. He and his family's movements are questionable for the next year or so. By 1872 they were living in Carson City where Paddock served as Sergeant-at-Arms in the State Legislature for that year.[39] In the spring of 1873, Paddock and his family passed through Eureka, the well-known mining community located in east central Nevada some 225 miles east of Virginia City. Apparently little Mary had died in the interim as the family at this time consisted of only Paddock, his wife Anna and their two sons, Ben and Richard Jr.[40] It seems he liked what he saw for, by March 1874, the Paddock family returned to make their home in Eureka.

In March, Paddock purchased the Eureka Saloon located in the Eureka Hotel Building.[41] His ad in the local *Daily Sentinel* proclaimed, "None but the best brands will be found at the bar. Call and test the hospitalities of DICK PADDOCK."[42]

As a Eureka businessman, Paddock prospered. Fortunately, his saloon was spared by the devastating flood, which swept through Eureka on Friday, July 25. Some 15 or 16 lives were lost and over $100,000 in damage to various buildings was sustained before the waters finally subsided.[43] This time Paddock's luck held.

Paddock continued to involve himself in the social and political scene of Eureka as he had done previously in Virginia City. He and his wife could often be seen attending the horse races at the tracks outside of town.[44] In September, Paddock, having suddenly switched his allegiance to the Republican Party, played a prominent and active role at the Eureka Republican County Convention held in Eureka's District Courthouse. Named to a number of committees and as a delegate to the State Central Committee, Paddock made his presence felt at the 1874 convention.[45]

Although through most of 1874 he found the Eureka Saloon profitable, by late in the year the saloon, and Eureka itself, began to sour for Paddock. Twice in a row, in October and December, he suffered burglaries at the saloon in which money and valuables were stolen.[46] On February 23, 1875, he almost came to gunplay with an absconding customer as reported in the *Virginia City Territorial Enterprise*:

> Dick Paddock starts out to Make Collections.
> Eureka, Nevada, February 24th.
>
> Some excitement existed yesterday afternoon in the vicinity of the stage office, occasioned by the appearance of Dick Paddock, armed with an ax halve and vowing vengeance on J. Darnes, a person who was booked for passage on the railroad. The cause of the trouble was the latter

owing the former money for drinks, sundries, etc. and his intention to leave without paying for the same. Darnes was struck several times with the weapon in Paddock's hands, when he retaliated by going for his assailant with a bottle, striking him over the head and inflicting a scalp wound of some extent. Paddock then drew a pistol and wanted to finish the business in the approved style, but Darnes succeeded in getting aboard the stage and left. Sometime after the melee, Constable Kelley started out to collect the bill or bring Darnes back. He succeeded in the latter.[47]

The next day, his head stitched and bandaged due to the severe scalp wound inflicted by Darnes, Paddock appeared in Police Court and received a fine of $20 as a result of the affair.[48]

Apparently, by mid-1875, Paddock decided to sell the Eureka Saloon.[49] He soon fell back on his reputation and gun to make a living. At about this time he gained employment with the K K Consolidated Mine on Ruby Hill outside Eureka as a night watchman.[50] His occasional violent proclivities continued to surface. Sometime in May 1875, Eureka police arrested Paddock for committing an assault upon one J. McDougal. Appearing before Police Court Judge Beatty on May 26, the fractious former saloon man received a hung jury. The final outcome of this particular case is not of record.[51]

Dick Paddock continued to live in Eureka relatively quietly for the next year working at the K K Consolidated Mine. By spring 1876 the urge to return to his old haunts struck him. Packing up the family he tied up his affairs in Eureka and headed back to Virginia City.[52]

Upon returning to Virginia City, Paddock quickly stepped back into the city's mélange. He joined in partnership with his old friend and former neighbor Tom Hughes in a cockpit located on North C Street. Every night hundreds of dollars would change hands as those of a gambling bent wagered on which rooster could best his opponent. He also joined the Montgomery Guard, a local militia company in which Tom Hughes was First Lieutenant.[53] At about this time, although it may have been earlier in Eureka, Anna Paddock gave birth to another child, a baby brother for Ben and Richard Jr.[54]

Perhaps remembering a time nine years earlier when he himself had faced similar charges, Paddock appeared as a witness before the Board of Police Commissioners on September 8. The case on this occasion involved City Jailer R.H. Robey and police officers Daley, Curby, and Iby charged with abusing prisoners.[55] The charges were eventually dropped. Though he did not know it Dick Paddock had only another four months to live.

The early morning hours of Tuesday, January 2, 1877, arrived with a cool crispness in the air. A few still celebrated the New Year in the various saloons of Virginia City. One of these groups, composed of Dick Paddock, Tom Hughes, John Clark, James Sumner and two or three others, had continued their revels in the Delta Saloon well past midnight. The gathering, led by Hughes, began to sing Irish folk songs and rejoice in a decidedly unrestrained fashion. At about 4:30 or 5:00 in the morning a group of miners, led by Richard Anderson and John Richard, entered the Delta. Anderson, Richard and company began singing the same songs Hughes, Paddock and their friends had been singing. Hughes, Paddock and Clark decided that the group carried off the performance in a mocking, insulting style and confronted the miners. At this point a general melee ensued in which a number of punches were thrown. During the brawl Hughes pulled a pistol, which he flourished about the crowd. Dave Shaw and Peter Dunn, bartenders in the Delta, and W.H. Bartlett, a friend of Hughes and Paddock and Special Policeman on the Virginia City Police Force, attempted to stop the fight.

Notified of the trouble at the Delta Saloon policeman Robert McDonald ran to the scene. McDonald had earned the enmity of Tom Hughes by arresting a friend of Hughes' on Christmas Eve. When McDonald entered the Delta the already agitated Hughes flew into a rage.

"What are you doing here!" Hughes yelled at McDonald, again drawing his revolver from his coat pocket.

McDonald stepped up to Hughes and told him to put his gun away or he would have to arrest him.

Bellowing, "You son of a bitch, get out of here or I'll kill you!" Hughes raised his revolver and brought the barrel down in a glancing blow on McDonald's head.

At this juncture McDonald reached out, grabbed Hughes, and told him he was under arrest. Rushing between the two, Paddock, Clark, Sumner and Bartlett pulled Hughes out of McDonald's grasp and hustled him to the center of the saloon.

"Hughes has done nothing," Paddock said to McDonald. "Let him alone and I will take care of him."

Taking no heed of Paddock, McDonald strode over to Hughes and took hold of his arm in another attempt to place him under arrest. Again, Paddock and Clark pulled McDonald off of Hughes. Hughes once again struck the policeman over the head with his pistol, this time knocking McDonald down to one knee. As McDonald rose up, Hughes fired, the slug missing McDonald and passing over his left shoulder. McDonald swiftly drew his pistol and at almost the same instant as Hughes fired a second time, McDonald answered with four shots of his own. Hughes' second shot also missed its intended victim. McDonald connected with each of his four shots, hitting Hughes twice in the left breast near the heart, once in the upper right portion of the chest and once through the right hand. Hughes staggered over to the wall. Placing his hands on the wall he slowly slid down to his knees, then fell over dead.[56]

Although the testimony is confusing and conflicting apparently Dick Paddock stood either between Hughes and McDonald or behind McDonald when the shooting commenced. At any rate, soon after the first shot, Bartlett saw Paddock "down on the floor crawling toward the wall; he acted like a man bewildered or stunned; supposed he was hit by the first shot; he did not get up after that."[57] It was believed that Paddock had been shot accidentally by a stray slug from the gun of his friend Tom Hughes.

As officer McDonald was led to the police station by officer Bartlett, Paddock was laid out on a keno table. Physicians were summoned and it was found that, although unconscious, Paddock still lived. He had been shot once in the forehead over the left eye out of which wound large quantities of blood and brain matter flowed. He had also sustained two large fractures to the top of the head, which no one was able to explain and which remained a mystery.[58]

Shortly after the tragedy, Anna Paddock received word of the affair. Frantically grabbing one of her children she rushed to the scene. Policeman Barney Murray and an officer named Glen were guarding the doors of the Delta Saloon when Mrs. Paddock and her son arrived. A large, agitated crowd milled about in front of the building, many brandishing knives and revolvers. The young Paddock boy pushed through the crowd ahead of his mother and asked officer Glen to let him inside. Not knowing who the lad was, Glen told him "it was no place for boys." Bursting into tears the boy said that his father lay inside and he wanted to see him. By now Anna Paddock had made her way through the crowd to the door. An apologetic Glen quickly let them inside. It was said that the sight of the distressed mother and child did much to diffuse the angry crowd.[59] Eventually, Paddock was delicately carried to his home, his death anticipated at any moment.

Of the dead Tom Hughes the *Territorial Enterprise* eulogized:

> Hughes was a married man and leaves a wife and three children. Four years ago, he was elected Constable of Township No.1 and served his term out worthily. He was a man who never knew fear and was frank, open and generous-hearted. He was also a man of strong passions and when under their influence was reckless of consequences, as the affray of yesterday shows. At the time of his death he was a member of the Knicker-bocker Engine Company No. 5 and First Lieutenant of the Montgomery Guard.

Concerning the gravely wounded Dick Paddock the paper continued:

> He has been somewhat reckless of his life before and will now lose it because he went to the assistance of his friend. He did this through known danger and was endeavoring to interfere when the bullet from his friend's pistol found his brain.[60]

On the Thursday morning following the shooting a coroner's jury found that Thomas Hughes, "a native of Ireland, aged about thirty-five years," came to his death, "in consequence of gunshot wounds inflicted by Robert McDonald, a policeman of the city of Virginia, and that said policeman was acting in the direct line of his duty, and inflicted said wounds in self defense, and was justified in doing so."[61]

One year later, in January 1878, McDonald went on to work as a hired gun for the Justice Mine in the war of right-of-way between the Justice and Alta mines. In another interesting connection with Dick Paddock, the Alta Mine also hired Dick Prentice, the man who had fought against Paddock in the water war of 1870, for the same purpose.[62]

On the afternoon of January 3, Thomas Hughes' funeral took place from the Montgomery Guard Hall.[63] That same day Dick Paddock's condition gained report in the local press:

> At latest accounts last evening Dick Paddock was still alive. In addition to the bullet wound the unfortunate man has his head fractured in two places. Over two ounces of brain have exuded through the hole in his forehead, yet he was conscious yesterday and spoke to his wife, and lifted up his baby and kissed it. It is possible that he may recover. Such cases have been known, but they are extremely rare.[64]

If nothing else Dick Paddock was definitely a tough customer. On the 4th he showed some improvement. When anyone called his name, he would open his right eye, "the

View of Main Street, Virginia City, 1878, a few months after Paddock's death (courtesy Digital Photo Collection, Image #UNRS-P1993-20-02, Special Collections and University Archives Department, University of Nevada, Reno Libraries).

only sound one," as one observer put it, and often spoke with those around him. Another stated that "the quantity of brain matter oozing out yesterday was considerably less than on the day before." A grim pronouncement indeed, yet some were optimistic of his pulling through.[65]

All optimism faded quickly on the evening of Friday, January 5. Paddock fell into a coma at eight o'clock. By about 10:30 he took a few short, shuddering breaths, and then lay still in death.[66]

Two days later, Sunday afternoon, Dick Paddock was laid to rest in Virginia City's Catholic Cemetery. The Montgomery Guard, of which the deceased had been a member, led the funeral procession. Also participating were the Emmet and Sarsfield guards, the Exempt, Monumental and Knicker-Bocker fire companies, as well as Rippingham's band playing the mournful dirges.[67]

Both Paddock and Hughes left wives and children behind. The people of Virginia City showed their support for the grieving women and children by holding a theatrical benefit for them on Monday evening. Interestingly, one of the actors in the entertainment proved to be Robert Lindsay, Paddock's former fellow fighter during the water war of 1870. Many tickets were sold, the proceeds of which were turned over to the Paddock and Hughes families.[68]

January 10 a coroner's inquest concluded:

In the matter of the inquisition upon the body of Richard Paddock:

We, the undersigned jurors summoned to appear before D.F. Hodges, Coroner of the county of Storey, at Virginia City, on the 8th day of January, AD 1877, to inquire into the cause of death of Richard Paddock, having been duly sworn according to law and having made such inquisition, after inspecting the body and hearing the testimony adduced, upon our oaths, each and all of us do say that we find the deceased was named Richard Paddock, was a native of Ireland, aged about thirty-nine years, and that he came to his death on the 5th day of January, AD 1877, in this county, from a pistol-shot wound received on the 2nd day of this month, and in the opinion of the jury it was an accidental shot from the pistol of Tom Hughes. All of which we duly certify by this inquisition in writing by us signed this 10th day of January, AD 1877.

Richard Ross,
William Meadows,
Charles M. Lawrence,
J.C. Hampton,
F. Fredericks,
H. Butenop,
Franklin Ward,
Peter Daley,
J.L. Black,
Jurors.[69]

What became of Dick Paddock's wife and children is a mystery. It is known, however, that at least two years following Paddock's death his family still resided in Virginia City. In early October 1879 newspapers reported that Richard Paddock, Jr., then 11 years old, was seriously injured in Piper's Opera House in Virginia City. Apparently full of mischief, the lad had been sliding down the banister of the establishment when he tumbled off and fell 30 feet to the floor below. At first it was thought that his injuries would be life threatening but he eventually recovered.[70]

It seems that the boy not only inherited his father's daring attitude but the Paddock luck as well.

4

A Savage Life and a Dishonorable Death
William Bethards

Upon occasion of the brutal murder of William Bethards by a fellow prisoner at the Nevada State Prison in 1878 the editor of the *Carson Morning Appeal* eulogized:

> This writer…, knew him as long ago as 1851 in Downieville, and was one of his mining partners there. No kinder hearted boy than he ever packed a blanket or swung a pick. His subsequent misfortunes—misfortunes incident to a deficient training and false education—shall not deprive him of this tribute. He was as brave a man as ever lived, true to his friends and defiant of his enemies. Many a man in Carson remembers him with the kindest of feelings.[1]

The editor of the *Ward Weekly Reflex* located at Ward, Lincoln County, where Bethards had operated in the early 1870s, countered this sentiment:

> The above [the Carson newspaper man's writings on Bethards] makes Bethards out not only a good man but an injured one. It is a little bit strained, to say the least of it. We hardly thought William was such an exemplary Christian. Those who knew him in Pioche will be pleased to learn that he was a man of generous impulses. He would not do anything worse than wantonly kill a man or, jump a mine and betray those who joined him in such an enterprise. A few more such laudatory notices of State Prison birds might have the effect of inducing a number of young men to emulate William H. Bethards' noble example.[2]

The foregoing are two extremes of a man who could apparently generate friendship and hatred, loyalty and mistrust. Who was this man who could produce such divergent opinions in his contemporaries?

A forgotten man of the frontier and one of Nevada's premier gunfighters, William H. Bethards, or Billy as he was often called, was born ca. 1835[3] in Delaware.[4] At the tender age of 14 or 15 he left the familiarities of home and traveled to the California gold fields. Here, in about 1851, he toiled over a sluice box along with others whom he would later know in Nevada.[5] It would be in such camps as Downieville and Goodyears Bar that young Bethards would cultivate his staunchest friendships. It would be these same men who would be his strongest supporters years later in his new base of operations in the state of Nevada.

Somewhere along the way the young miner managed to acquire a wife and start a family of his own.[6] About the year 1865 the Bethards family moved to the Nevada state capital at Carson City. It would be in the capital that Bill Bethards' proficiency with firearms would lead him into a position of law enforcement. Soon after his arrival, he received appointments as both night watchman of Carson City and as a deputy sheriff of Ormsby County under Sheriff Tim Smith. By all accounts, Bethards made an efficient officer of the law in Carson.

An example of the kindheartedness referred to by the *Carson Morning Appeal* editor in writing of Bill Bethards eight years later would be manifest by him in May 1865 and reported by the local press. On the evening of May 18 parties called the night watchman to look after an intoxicated lady wandering around the city with an infant in her arms. Having dealt with the lady and her child to what he thought was everyone's satisfaction, a few hours later Bethards received another call. This time the woman had been found sleeping in a stable on Third Street, the baby lying in the filthy straw beside her. Taking the child to his house the lawman gave it over to his wife who bathed the infant

Tom Bedford seated, William Bethards standing, ca. 1860 (courtesy Mark R. Jones).

and dressed it in clean clothes. Although forced to lock the intoxicated mother in the County Jail for the night Bethards gave her every convenience he could and turned her and her child over to the proper authorities the following day.[7] This act of humanity not withstanding, frequently Bethards' law enforcement position would lead him into acts of frontier violence.

The first known instance of Bethards being forced to use his gun to enforce the law occurred on July 1, 1865. On that day a young man named Edward Griffin, an employee at Frisbie's Saloon in Carson City, looted his employers safe and quickly hotfooted it down the American Flat road toward Visalia, California. Hitching a ride on an outgoing wood wagon Griffin bounced along atop the pile of lumber until being overtaken by Bethards and fellow deputy sheriff Haswell who had set out in pursuit in a one-horse buggy.

At Haswell's command of "I want you!" Griffin jumped off the wagon and dashed for the roadside timber. Unlimbering his pistol Haswell leaped from the buggy and unleashed two wild shots at the fugitive. Undaunted, Griffin continued his flight. Seeing the possibility of the young felons' escape, Bethards whipped the horse into a gallop and rode directly toward the running man, at the same time, with his free hand, firing a shot at Griffin with his pistol. Under this barrage of gunfire Griffin stopped short and threw his hands into the air in surrender. With Frisbie's loot recovered and the robber in tow the two deputy sheriffs rode triumphantly back into Carson City later that night.[8]

Bethards continued to perform sterling duty as both a deputy sheriff and night watchman throughout the summer of 1865. In August he appeared as a witness in Justice's Court against James Barker, a thief he had been investigating.[9] Five days later, on August 8, he and Haswell, along with other officers, spent an entire night in a pounding rainstorm attempting to track down a group of highway robbers who were operating on the roads just out of Carson City. Although this time the pursuit proved unsuccessful, Bill Bethards had displayed his undoubted tenacity in the game of outlaw catching.[10]

Sometimes the duties could be more mundane as reported by the *Carson Daily Appeal* of Sunday, November 12, 1865:

> Arrested.—Officer Bethards arrested a boy named James Holland on Friday night for being drunk and disorderly. This lad is one of a party of young scapegraces who style themselves "the Scallywags" and who seem to think that they are gaining an enviable reputation as "fast" young men by perpetrating the most rude and uncouth practices, by cursing and blackguarding in presence of ladies and gentlemen, and by getting drunk and making rowdies of themselves. We hope that Bethards will take occasion to arrest every lad that he catches running around loose after night fall. A reform school would be a good thing to improve the manners and habits of the "Scallywags."

Time was not always spent as a stern enforcer of law for Billy Bethards, however. He and his wife apparently moved with grace in the social circle of Carson City as well, as is shown by this January 23, 1866, notice in the local newspaper:

> Ball To-Night.—Mr. Bethards called at our office yesterday and desired us to state that the grand ball which he advertised for last evening would be postponed until this evening. Every preparation has been made to render this a very delightful evening's entertainment. All our ball going friends should be in attendance.[11]

The worm would soon turn on the socialite lawman. Within a year he would go from being one of the social elites of Carson City to being a pariah of Carson society. In the meantime, Bethards continued to serve the people of the capitol city. As a member of Carson City's volunteer fire department, he struggled shoulder to shoulder with his fellow firemen when a major blaze broke out in the Head Quarters Saloon on the morning of February 27, 1866. Though the Head Quarters was gutted and extensive damage incurred by the St. Charles Hotel, Muller Hotel and the Pioneer Stage Company stables the fire companies managed to prevent a catastrophic conflagration from engulfing the rest of the city.[12] At the conclusion of the near disaster, Officer Bethards found that he had lost his Dragoon six-shooter, "for the delivery of which at the Sheriff's office he will pay a reward of ten dollars."[13]

Whether or not he recovered his Dragoon revolver, only four days later Bethards would once again be forced to use a firearm in the performance of his duty. Early on the morning of Saturday, March 3, while making his rounds, Bethards came upon an attempted burglary in progress at the Magnolia Saloon. At the appearance of the lawman the two would-be-burglars turned heel and ran in opposite directions. Sprinting after one of the men, Bethards was gaining on the felon when the thief suddenly turned with a pistol in this hand and fired at Bethards and another man who had joined the pursuit. Both Bethards and his sudden assistant pulled their revolvers and returned the burglar's fire. The man enveloped himself in darkness, however, and managed to make his escape.[14]

Billy Bethards continued to serve as Carson City night watchman and Ormsby County deputy sheriff for almost another year. At the end of this stretch he would be confronted by the incident which would change his life. Although an apparent accident it would prove to be an unfortunate tragedy, after the commission of which, Bethards would never again be quite the same. His stature in Carson City would be ruined and life from this point forward would be a downward spiral into murder, prison and death.

Receiving a complaint concerning the activities of a Mexican woman who operated as a prostitute in Carson City's sporting district, Bill Bethards ventured forth on the evening of February 20, 1867, and placed the courtesan under arrest. At about three o'clock on the morning of the 11th, Bethards encountered Henry Sherwood, the brother of Bethards' friend and fellow fireman John Sherwood, in the Sazerac Saloon. For some reason never explained, Henry Sherwood began berating Bethards for his arrest of the prostitute, even going so far as to insult Mrs. Bethards. Infuriated, Bethards drew his revolver and attempted to strike Sherwood on the head with the barrel. Seeing the fracas, John Sherwood jumped between the pair and, in attempting to protect his brother, grasped at Bethards' flailing revolver. While in John Sherwood's hands, Bethards revolver discharged, the bullet slamming into Sherwood's chest. While everyone looked on in shock, bystanders carried John Sherwood to his rooms. Nothing could be done for him, however, and eight hours later the popular fireman died from his wound.[15]

Everyone in Carson City lamented the death of the well-liked John Sherwood. The *Carson Daily Appeal*, under the heading "Fatal Shooting—Death of A Favorite Citizen" perhaps best expressed the feeling of many in the capitol when it commented:

> We are not disposed either to rake this matter over with a relentless hand, nor are we disposed to gloss it over with a few common-place, lachrymose sentences. Henry Sherwood was guilty of conduct the most inexcusable. Bethards had only done his duty by arresting the woman in question. But, abused and even threatened as he was, Bethards, a peace officer, had no right to draw a weapon in the manner in which he did. The provocation was very great, but it was only a taunt, and not an assault justifying extreme violence. The value of the life that is gone attests this. Perhaps Bethards is enough punished by the distress of mind that this great calamity has

occasioned him. We are not disposed to seek for or to counsel his punishment for an accidental homicide which is more the fault of the brother of the dead man than his. But we have no right to make public mention of this matter and not talk plainly of its participants. A most painful, sad, and heart-rending fatal accident has resulted from a brawl which should never have been allowed to proceed to such lengths as it did.[16]

The heavily attended funeral of John Sherwood on February 12 served to make even more pointed the situation of Bethards in Carson City. As Bethards stood on the sidelines and watched his comrades in the various volunteer fire companies lead Sherwood's body to the grave[17] he saw the writing on the wall. He likely realized his position in Carson was now untenable. He quickly resigned his commission as deputy sheriff and night watchman, Sheriff Smith appointing Gus Lewis to the vacant position.[18]

All that now held William Bethards in Carson City proved to be a judicial decision in the courts as a result of the February 11 tragedy. Despite the serious outcome of the affair many in the capitol still held a measure of respect and sympathy for the former lawman due to his actions of the past. Although the popular Sherwood had been killed authorities decided to charge the man responsible for his death with only a rather minor indictment of assault and battery.[19] On Monday, April 1, Bethards appeared in District Court and entered a plea of guilty.[20] Seven days later, the same day as petitions in the matter of the estate of John Sherwood were heard in the same courtroom,[21] Bill Bethards received a judgment of a $100 fine in his assault and battery case.[22] This he paid without delay. With nothing now holding him in Carson City and no reason to remain he quickly packed up his family and shook the dust of Carson from his boots.

The movements of Bethards for the next year are unknown. In May 1868 he turned up in Austin, Nevada, some 155 miles east of Carson City, in Lander County. On May 12 he applied for the position of special city policeman and night watchman under Town Marshal Frank Wheeler.[23] At the City Council meeting of May 26, Bill Bethards defeated the only other candidate for the job, James Gray, by a vote of 5 to 1 to become the new Special Policeman at Austin.[24]

Quickly, Bethards stepped into the new position. Three days later he arrested one James Gilpatrick on a charge of disturbing the peace.[25] The following week Laurence Hunt took a shot at an individual known as "Chileno George" in a dispute over a horse. Luckily, Hunt's bullet missed and Bethards rushed to the scene and placed Hunt under arrest before any further damage could be done.[26]

Bethards was not destined to remain in Austin for long. By summer 1868 the new mining excitement centered about 120 miles further east in White Pine County was drawing speculators from all directions. Austin City Marshal Frank Wheeler was one of those who headed for the new diggings.[27] Shortly after, Bill Bethards would follow his former boss, tendering his resignation to the City Council in late July 1868 and heading east.[28]

Like many attracted to the region Bethards likely hoped to make his fortune as a freelance speculator. When he failed to strike the mother lode he gradually drifted back into his career of choice, that of a lawman. In October 1869 he landed in the mining camp of Treasure City where he gained employment as an officer on the

Treasure City police force.[29] By December he had gained the position of a deputy sheriff of White Pine County under Sheriff J.D. Patterson.

Despite his full-time employment as a peace officer, Bethards continued to keep his hand in at the avocation of a prospector. In late January 1870 the local newspaper listed him as one of a party of mining speculators heading to the recently discovered mines "at the southern end of White Pine Mountain."[30] It would seem that Bethards' various mining ventures never did amount to a great deal despite his continued interest.

William Bethards would never be far from controversy. February 23, 1870, he was called to testify at a notorious murder trial taking place in Hamilton. Almost two months before, on December 26, 1869, Samuel P. Howard, a local auctioneer and saloon owner, shot and killed one James Cartwright in a dispute over unpaid rent.[31] During the trial Bethards testified to a conversation he had with Cartwright at Treasure City about ten days before the killing. According to Bethards, Cartwright told him that Howard owed him "for rent of saloon, and said if he did not pay it he (deceased) would 'make it hot for him,' or put him out of saloon."[32] Although the effect of Bethards's specific testimony is debatable, Howard was eventually found guilty of second degree murder on February 25[33] and sentenced to a term of 12 years in the state penitentiary.[34]

The fate of Howard aside, perhaps the most poignant and ironic aspect of the Howard trial from Bethards' standpoint, in hindsight, proved to be the appearance of another witness in the proceedings. Testifying on the same day as Bethards was another resident of Treasure City who had been an eyewitness to the encounter that had taken Cartwright's life.[35] A native of Ireland,[36] born ca. 1840,[37] Thomas Flynn[38] was a soon to be nefarious sneak thief and burglar who often operated under the alias of Matt Rafferty. Flynn would often cross paths with Bethards in Treasure City. It would be an association both unpleasant and regretful for the mining camp lawman.

In the meantime, Bethards continued his service to the residents of White Pine County. In mid–March he and Deputy Sheriff Irwin took charge of Sam Howard and another prisoner named Charles Jones, transporting the pair to their new home at the state prison in Carson City.[39] One can only imagine the feelings of Bethards as he returned, albeit briefly, to his old hometown at Carson.

Beginning in the summer of 1870 things were starting to heat up some 100 miles south at the most fabulously wealthy mining town in Nevada, Pioche. The cut-throat competition between mining concerns could often be violent and sometimes deadly. William Bethards would be drawn into this maelstrom of savagery. It would end up as an episode in his life that would do him very little credit.

A correspondent signing himself "Cela" gives possibly one of the best descriptions of conditions at Pioche that summer. Writing to the *Elko Independent* newspaper in Elko, Nevada, Cela wrote:

> Pioche City, July 20, 1870.
>
> Editors *Independent*—this is a hot place—decidedly hot, hot men and hot times among the mine owners. You can get your head blown off for three words and get buried for nothing. Parties coming here contemplating a speedy demise need no money for funeral expenses, as either Pioche or Meadow Valley companies have an undertaker and a supply of coffins on hand, and

are looking anxiously for recruits for their new graveyard; this is, judging by the determination they manifest to bring about a collision between the citizens and men in their employ; keeping at all times a patrol of armed men, who make it their business to stop unoffending citizens upon public highways and at all places near the Great Mogul's works. This would be a serious thing in this American country if it were not simply absurd, and how the officers of this company, good Christian members of high-toned churches in San Francisco, can countenance such a proceeding passes our ken, but pray for our souls and send more Henry rifles. There are somber men here, and any of those becoming tired of life can shuffle off this mortal coil by paying a visit to our mines.[40]

With his reputation as a man handy with firearms Bill Bethards made his appearance in Pioche that summer. The 1870 federal census of Pioche, enumerated on August 2, lists him as living in Pioche amidst a number of other men all described as "Silver Miners."[41] Although listed as a silver miner there can be little doubt that Bethards real purpose in Pioche was acting as a guard for one of the feuding mining corporations, he having hired out his gun to the highest bidder as a mining company "fighter." Future events would point to this likely assumption.

It would seem that at this time Bethards traveled frequently between Pioche and his home in White Pine County at Treasure City. Later, in August 1870, in his capacity as a deputy sheriff of White Pine County, he would be involved in the arrest of Thomas Flynn on a multiple robbery charge.[42] This arrest resulted in Flynn being sentenced to the Nevada State Prison for a stretch of years.[43] Here Flynn would prove himself an incorrigible convict, being involved in more than one prison break and other acts of defiance toward prison authorities. It would also be here where Flynn would nurse his grudge toward Bethards for his arrest, little believing he would eventually be able to carry out his revenge.

In October 1870, Bethards, back in White Pine County, received the Republican nomination for constable at Hamilton.[44] He soon returned to Pioche. One of the biggest mining companies in the Pioche district, the Raymond and Ely Company,[45] needed fighters in a hurry. Bethards and his gun answered the call.

The trouble for the Raymond and Ely Company began in the fall of 1870. Charles Gracey, chief engineer for Raymond and Ely, in his later years, set down his reminiscences for the Nevada Historical Society. As Gracey remembered it:

> The first trouble occurred at the Washington and Creole. Tom and Frank Newland had made a location above the Washington and Creole mine, which latter was owned by Raymond and Ely. The Newland boys asked for the privilege of starting a tunnel below the Washington and Creole to run through the same which at this time was not considered of much value. Raymond and Ely gladly granted the privilege, for the Newland boys were newcomers and needed encouragement. The boys ran in their tunnel about thirty feet underground, or from the face, and struck the Washington and Creole ledge as was expected. But, contrary to expectation, the ledge at this point was very rich, averaging about three hundred dollars per ton. It proved to be nine feet thick. Before much was known about the strike, the Newland boys went to Raymond and Ely and secured the privilege of taking out ore on the Washington and Creole for thirty days.[46]

The Newland brothers slaved night and day in their tunnel. At the conclusion of their 30-days lease they had succeeded in removing $100,000 worth of high-grade ore.[47] Raymond and Ely officials were shocked at the opulence of the Newland's discovery. So were the Newlands. As Gracey put it:

Raymond and Ely Mine, the focal point of mining company's fight with the Newland brothers in 1870 (courtesy Lincoln County Museum).

> A mountain of ore worth three hundred dollars a ton will worry anyone when it is in plain sight and everyone is allowed to see it. Before long the Newlands got some of the new men from White Pine to help jump the mine. They built a fort in the night and manned it with men and guns for defense. Then they commenced to take out and ship the ore to Silver Peak, where there was a ten-stamp mill. There was no law in the country, and no one to stop them.[48]

After a week of the Newland brother's defiance Raymond and Ely decided they needed to take decisive action. They put out feelers for willing muscle. William Bethards saw an opportunity to take advantage of the situation. Teeming up with Morgan Courtney, perhaps the most notorious gunman in Nevada history, and two other fighters of note named Michael Casey and Barney Flood, the Bethards group approached Raymond and Ely. In return for a written promise that they would be allowed to work the disputed ground for 30 days, Bethards, Courtney and company proposed to drive the Newlands and their gun hands off the Washington and Creole property. Raymond and Ely agreed.[49]

Wednesday, November 9, Bethards, Courtney, Casey and Flood decided to make their move. Early that afternoon the quartet arranged for a number of bottles of whiskey to be shipped to the Newlands and their guards. Thinking the libations had been sent by some magnanimous supporter, the barricaded men, which included Jack White, another notorious Nevada gun handler, imbibed freely. Meanwhile, Bethards and his partners hid in a dense growth of nut pine trees on a hill overlooking the mine awaiting their chance to strike.[50]

By about mid-afternoon the four gunmen decided the time was right. Unlimbering their revolvers, they suddenly charged down the hill toward the Newland's fort, shouting and firing as they ran. The Newland party fell into confused, whiskey befuddled, disorder before some managed to regain their wits, retrieve their weapons and return a scattered fire. W.G. Snell, a Newland man, caught a bullet and fell dead. Others continued to resist, in some cases fighting hand to hand battles with the four intruders. At one point Casey was seen to swing his rifle like a club and knock a Newland fighter some 70 feet down a mine shaft. Incredibly the man lived, receiving only a few bumps and bruises.[51]

After some 60 shots had been fired, Bethards and company managed to drive the Newland group from the mine and take possession. Snell proved to be the only fatality, while Morgan Courtney and Newland men Jack White, James Finley, Al Doliff, John Morgan and Tom Newland received various painful injuries.[52] Tom and Frank Newland quickly made their departure from Pioche and disappeared to parts unknown.

The day following the "Washington and Creole Battle," Bethards, Courtney, Casey and Flood allowed themselves to be arrested by Lincoln County Sheriff John Kane and his deputies. With the property returned to the ownership of Raymond and Ely the four fighters waved an examination in Pioche court on the morning of November 10. Justice Clapp ordered them held under a bond of $5,000 each to appear at a later date for the death of Snell.[53]

Raymond and Ely fulfilled their agreement with the four men. While out on bail, Bethards and his partners worked the rich mine until their 30-day time limit expired. At the end of the allotted time the gunmen managed to harvest some $60,000 worth of silver laden ore which was purchased by Raymond and Ely,[54] provoking one chronicler to remark:

> Since the Newlands had cleared $100,000.00 in the same period of time, it could be assumed that, in working for a living, there were too many "chiefs"[55] in the mine, and not enough Indians. But, even at that, they were well paid for the work they did.[56]

With his $15,000, a sizable fortune for the time, Bethards traveled back to White Pine County. In late December he returned to Pioche to face his indictment for the Washington and Creole fight and the killing of Snell.[57] His case would be carried over until early April 1871. At that juncture Lincoln County authorities finally decided to ignore the true bill against Bethards.[58] Although no details of this particular case seem to be in existence, apparently, if later comments hold any meaning, Bethards was far from loyal and true to his friends in the Pioche mine battle. Whether he might have turned state's evidence and testified against Courtney, Casey and Flood is not known. However, when a future newspaper editor wrote derisively, "He would not do anything worse than wantonly kill a man or, *jump a mine and betray those who joined him in such an enterprise*"[59] (author's italics), it leaves one wondering if Bethards eventually went back on his pals in order to alleviate his own circumstances.

While violence continued to plague Pioche,[60] Bethards continued to make news in White Pine. By August 1872 the shootist had moved from Treasure City to the new mining camp of Ruby Hill in the Schell Creek Range of mountains. Prospectors discovered rich ore ledges in the area in 1871 and by the time of Bethards arrival the camp boasted some 200 to 300 residents.[61]

Evidence leads to the conclusion that the gunman managed to keep a well-maintained revolver and a contentious nature. In mid–August 1872 it gained report that he entered into some sort of fracas in Ruby Hill with a man named McFarland. Both individuals apparently drew forth weapons and exchanged eight shots. Neither man sustained injury although an unlucky bystander was said to have taken a wild slug in the leg.[62]

It is sure that Bethards was delving into dangerous territory at this time. Using a small portion of the $15,000 reward he had earned in Pioche in late 1870, the former lawman purchased for himself and family a cabin on Ruby Hill's main thoroughfare across the street from Scott's Saloon.[63] What had become of the balance of the money is a matter of conjecture but immediately upon his arrival Bethards was seeking employment. He found it in the usual place, as a hired gun.

Simultaneously with the evolvement of Ruby Hill there developed two opposing factions in the town. One, the so-called "town lot faction," quickly purchased large sections of the town site as a business proposition. One of the leaders of this group was a local entrepreneur and saloon owner named John Wagner. The other coterie, termed the "anti-town lot faction" believed in a freer enterprise type organization. One of its leading lights was a hard-drinking miner named James Brophy. The two factions soon fostered a bitter antipathy.

After his arrival in Ruby Hill, Billy Bethards hired out to John Wagner as a guard for his various town lot properties.[64] This brought him into direct conflict with many in the camp, chief amongst them James Brophy. One bone of contention proved to be a "little log pen" claimed by Brophy which encroached on Bethards own lot. According to Bethards later testimony the situation got so bad between him and Brophy that at one point Brophy shouted at him, "Yes, God damn you, you will catch a rope the first thing you know!"[65]

Brophy pulled no punches in expressing his ill will toward Bethards. Many in Ruby Hill would be witness to these expressions of aversion. One was Ruby Hill constable Ed Brannan. During a local election campaign Brannan encountered Brophy on the street. Brophy angrily warned the constable that if he were re-elected and showed any partiality or appointed Bethards or S.L. Winslow, a friend of Bethards, as a deputy constable he would, as Brannan quoted him later "hit you with a rock."[66] On more than one occasion Brophy reportedly told various witnesses that he would never stand idly by and let Bethards come after him.

Soon Bethards tired of the constant bickering. Around the end of September 1872, he resigned his employment with Wagner, telling Frank Alman, "He was sorry that he had to work for Wagner—as everyone was down on him for it—but that his bread and butter depended upon it for his family."[67] He soon got himself a job in the local mill. Although no longer employed by Wagner the feud between Bethards and Brophy continued to simmer through the fall.

According to the later testimony of saloon man John Scott, one night he caught Bethards peeking in the window of his saloon. On being discovered, Bethards assured Scott it was not him but James Brophy he was spying on. Going inside, Bethards confronted Brophy who sat at a table drinking with some friends. At issue seemed to be the ownership of a certain town lot.

"I'm going to hold my lot," Brophy said to Bethards.

In a sarcastic tone Bethards replied, "Well, you won't Jimmy!"

When Brophy reiterated his determination to hold the lot, Bethards reportedly shouted, "I am chief of all you sons of bitches!"[68]

On this note the two enemies parted company and went their separate ways. Further trouble was on the horizon.

The evening of November 4, 1872, Bethards and some friends spent their time celebrating in the various saloons of Ruby Hill. As the frivolities dragged on into the night, Bethards made his way from John Wagner's saloon toward his home when he noticed loud activity emanating from Scott's Saloon just across the street from his cabin. Entering, he found a crowd of revelers drinking and carrying on at Scott's. A large number of both the pro and anti-town lot companies moved within the throng, drinking and discussing the upcoming primary elections.

"Hurrah for Hanford," Bethards hollered as he passed through the door, expressing his support for one of the political candidates in the forthcoming vote.

"That suits me," answered one James Sheridan in support of Bethards sentiments. "Let's take a drink."

At this point Bethards spotted Winslow and James Brophy engaged in an apparently heated discussion at the bar.

Knowing that his friend Winslow also had a dispute with Brophy over the town lot issue, Bethards made his way over to the pair. "What are you arguing about?" he asked them.

Despite being assured by the men that they were not arguing Bethards again asked, "What are you fighting about?"

Exasperated, Brophy looked him up and down. "We are not fighting and if we were it is none of your damn business," he snarled.

"You are a damn liar if you say it is none of my business," Bethards shot back.

Jumping up from his chair, Brophy took a firm stance before Bethards. "I don't let any damn son of a bitch get away with me," he growled at his enemy.

Not backing down Bethards stiffened. "Brophy, I am no son of a bitch!" he yelled.

By now everyone in the saloon had been alerted to the possibility of trouble. Suddenly a dozen or more revolvers appeared in the crowd as men scuffled around the quarrelling pair. Rushing out from behind the bar the proprietor, John Scott, pushed into the crowd with a knife in one hand and a pistol in the other.

"Get out of here you sons of bitches," Scott yelled. "I won't allow no fighting here!"

In the commotion, friends of Brophy managed to pull him toward the front door and away from Bethards. Before they could escort him all the way out, however, Brophy stopped and turned around. Bethards, for once unarmed, noticed Ruby Hill constable Ed Brannan standing beside him with his six-shooter in his hand. Before Brannan could react, Bethards snatched the gun from his hand.

"Jimmy, you son of a bitch!" Bethards called as he pointed the weapon toward Brophy and squeezed the trigger.

With the crack of the revolver a blue hole instantly appeared in Brophy's forehead. Without a sound he crashed to the saloon floor. Almost immediately after the shot had been fired, Mrs. Bethards and one of the couple's young boys rushed in. With their help Brannan and Scott were able to push Bethards toward the back room, Brannan regaining control of his firearm. While Bethards was being hustled into the back room another shot suddenly rang out. This apparently occurred when a bystander jerked the pistol, which Brophy had managed to draw, out of his hand, causing the gun to discharge. Luckily this bullet buried itself in a saloon fixture causing no harm to flesh and blood.[69] Carried to his cabin James Brophy died at the age of 28 a few hours after being shot.[70]

Taken to his cabin and placed under guard, Bethards was quickly arrested by White Pine County Deputy Sheriff James Mateer, a Bethards family friend who had just paid a social call on the Bethards earlier that day. At first Bethards denied shooting Brophy. After a time, he admitted the deed but claimed self-defense, fearing he would be shot by Brophy or other anti-town lotters, John Scott, Martin Pisante, Carr or Karcher, all having been in the crowd displaying revolvers.

Mateer and Bethards spent a sleepless night as armed men milled around the Bethards cabin until morning. In the morning, Mateer prepared to start Bethards on the road to the county seat at Hamilton. Under the urging of Bethards, Mateer allowed his prisoner to arm himself with a six-shooter until they reached the edge of town. At that point, Bethards relinquished the gun to the deputy.[71] Eventually, Bill Bethards arrived safe and sound at the County Jail in Hamilton where officials lodged a charge of murder against him for the death of James Brophy.

Bethards' trial date was set for February 18, 1873. His attorneys attempted to prove the self-defense theory, Bethards in his own testimony mentioning a number of occasions where Brophy had threatened him.[72] Apparently this tactic proved to have a measure of success, a hung jury being the result. The White Pine court then scheduled a second trial to commence July 7, 1873. This time Bethards luck would fail him.

Bethards second trial came to pass on July 7 in the County Courthouse at Hamilton. On this occasion the County Attorney was able to cast much doubt on most of the defendant's case, including the question of whether Brophy had even been armed during the confrontation.[73] At the conclusion of the four day trial the jury, led by jury foreman Col. J.H. Kerr, brought in a verdict of guilty of murder in the second degree.[74] As a result, Judge William H. Beatty sentenced Bill Bethards to a term of 15 years in the State Prison.[75]

With his wife and family apparently residing in the city of Pioche at this time,[76] William Bethards made his way to his new home in the Nevada State Prison at Carson City. Prison officials received the new inmate on July 28, 1873.[77] The situation proved unfortunate for Bethards in more ways than one. The Nevada penitentiary was no place for a former lawman that had had dealings with some of his fellow convicts in the ways of arrests, etc. More specifically it brought him into contact once again with Thomas Flynn[78] who despised Bethards above all others as a result of Bethards past arrest of the nefarious criminal.

Bethards' days behind the walls of the State Prison must have dragged painfully slow. Two years after his commitment to the institution, in late summer 1875, he began proceedings preparatory to an application to the Governor and Supreme Court of Nevada for a pardon. Under the direction of his attorney and friend Mark M. Gaige, Bethards' application was based on the grounds of:

First: that the facts and circumstances of the case show that the said William H. Bethards has been sufficiently punished for the crime committed if he committed any;

Second: that the facts of the case make it doubtful whether any crime was committed by the said Bethards;

Third: for good behavior during his imprisonment.[79]

A number of Billy Bethards' friends, many of them old friends from his California mining days such as Harry Thornton of San Francisco, O.E. DeLong of Virginia City and *Carson Morning Appeal* editor Harry Mighels, took up the torch and began a campaign in support of the ex-lawman's release. Letters traveled back and forth and to the Board of Pardons promoting the cause.[80] Petitions from the three major points of residence in Bethards' Nevada sojourn, Carson City, Austin and White Pine County, Nevada, were assembled and presented to the pardon board. Signatures included those of Ormsby County Sheriff S.T. Swift and District Attorney William Patterson of Carson City[81]; future County Commissioner T.W. Triplett and County Recorder A.C. McCafferty of Austin[82]; and former White Pine County Sheriff J.D. Patterson, current Sheriff Ed Raum, ex–County Clerk W.T. Hanford, Justice of the Peace and former "town lot league" supporter at Ruby Hill, James Filton, former Bethards employer John Wagner and Deputy Sheriff James Mateer in White Pine County.[83]

January 10, 1876, the pardon board postponed the hearing of Bethards' pardon application to a future sitting.[84] It would be almost two years before they would finally deliberate on his application. In the meantime, the harsh conditions within the state institution began to take their toll on the incarcerated man's health and psyche. In June 1877, Bethards decided to pen a letter to Mark Gaige concerning his thoughts on his case. In it he also revealed his failing health and failing hopes:

Prison June 24,77

Friend Gaige

I recived [sic] a letter from Tennan yesterday and I must say that it was not incuraging [sic] by Enymeans [sic]. I answard [sic] his letter to day whitch [sic] he will show you. I have no doubts now Mark. My opinion is this, if some of the board had made up thare [sic] minds not to vote for my release, But, remain nuteral [sic] in the matter, I think the best policy is for you and the balance of my friends to Consentrate [sic] on some one member that is doubtful, and show some of those points of disadvantage under whitch [sic] I labord [sic] at the time of trial, it might helpe [sic] me, and after all is done that Can be done, and you see then, that I have no show for Pardon nor comutation [sic] no other show than to sink, I think then the act or plan would be to pass it over, dont you think so. I think if it was refused that it would put a prejudice on the Case. I look at it in this lite [sic], But, then I know nothing about it for I have not got an idea above an oister [sic] shell any more. I am worn out half sick all the time with a pain in the brest, [sic] and still I manage [to] keep on my feet with a tereble [sic] Effort [sic]. If I should live that long, I suppose [sic] after the expiration [sic] of fifteen years I will be turned out of hear [sic] broke down without a dollar between [sic] me and the grave not able to work and nothing but starveation [sic] stareing [sic] me in the face, and if I had come under any other Circumstances than whitch [sic] I did I would not mermer [sic], and thare [sic] is but little use anyway as it is I have to face the music, I will look for you down soon. My kind regards to your family, I remain as ever yours truly

Wm. H. Bethards[85]

By mid-1877 the fight for Bethards release had become a fight for pardon on the grounds of poor health. According to Gaige, "Dr. White and Fox [both physicians attached to the Nevada State Prison] will certify that he [Bethards] is unwell and ought to have freedom for health."[86] Despite the work of his many friends, Bethards pessimism in his case proved well founded. The pardon board denied his application on October 8, 1877.[87] So it seemed, the ca. 42-year-old convict faced the prospect of a long stretch of years incarcerated behind the bars of the state prison.

Bethards' health continued to deteriorate. Sometime in early 1878, prison officials took the man's frail constitution into consideration and gave him light duties as steward of the prison kitchen.[88] It was to be here where Bethards and Thomas Flynn would finally clash.

Late on the afternoon of Monday, July 29, 1878, Flynn found himself in his usual predicament, in trouble with prison authorities. Part of his punishment on this day consisted of either cleaning both the kitchen and dining area or hauling water from a pump in the kitchen, reports differ. Be that as it may, his duties found him in the dining room when he spotted Bethards seated at a table eating slices of watermelon. He also spotted a butcher knife with an 11-inch blade left carelessly lying on a cutting block in the kitchen.

Quickly snatching up the knife Flynn made a mad dash toward Bethards. Running head long into the surprised man Flynn landed on top of his victim as the two crashed to the floor. Immediately Flynn began plunging the long blade again and again into Bethards chest and side.

"For God's sake don't murder me!" Bethards screamed as Flynn continued to flail the knife. Stabbed at least seven times, an injury almost completely penetrating his body from front to back, Bethards' wounds began to spurt jets of blood.

"You die there, you son-of-a-bitch!" Flynn yelled, gasping for breath in his murderous exertions. "Once you had a six-shooter pointed at my nose; now I have fixed you!" he shouted just as Captain of the Guard Gounond, attracted by the crowd of yelling inmates pulled him off his dying opponent. Within seconds, Bill Bethards died on the prison dining room floor, sweltering in a pool of his own blood.[89]

As prison guards carted Flynn to his accustomed surroundings in the underground dungeon for another long period of solitary confinement, authorities dealt with the body of their dead convict. Although nothing is known of the whereabouts or disposition of Bethards' own family, his good friend and benefactor Mark Gaige took charge of the body. The day following the killing, services were held in Gaige's Carson City home. Following the service, pallbearers H.J. Mudge, Thomas Condon, Andy Wright and Joseph Brown, followed by a number of carriages of mourners, bore William Bethards last remains to his grave in the local Carson City Cemetery.[90] One of the more poignant aspects of the proceedings proved to be the appearance of a black ex-convict named Jefferson Howard who walked solemnly behind the hearse. Only recently released from the State Prison, Howard had been befriended by Bethards during his incarceration and wished to show his deep respect for his prison pal.[91]

All that was left was for the law to deal with the murderous Flynn. His preliminary hearing took place August 2 at which he received the order to appear for trial in the killing of Bethards.[92] In mid–March 1879, officials brought him forth from his dungeon home to stand trial for murder in the District Court at Carson City.[93] On March 14 the jury found Flynn guilty of murder in the second degree.[94] Eight days later he received a sentence of life in prison.[95]

Two weeks later one visitor to the penitentiary found Flynn looking "vicious, sullen and every inch a murderer. He is kept heavily ironed."[96] Despite this description it would seem prison had a way of mellowing some men. Within ten years, Thomas Flynn would be a candidate for pardon. Acquiring what his victim Bill Bethards had failed to achieve, Flynn received pardon from the Nevada State Prison on July 9, 1889, and walked forth a free man at the age of 49. He had served 18 years, 11 months and eight days in the state lockup.[97]

Billy Bethards friend, *Carson Morning Appeal* editor Harry Mighels, perhaps best summed up Bethards' life when he wrote, following the gunman's funeral:

> Poor Bill! His was a hard fate, hard in respect of his waywardness, his misfortune and his doom. Moralizing is the cheapness and impertinence of self-righteousness under such circumstance as these, and we are not going to sermonize over our dead friend's ashes; but they who are blessed with an education in morals and the gentler way of life, as he, poor fellow, was not; who have home and refinements and the alluring pleasures of the domestic circle, let them not be uncharitable. Rather let them thank God for the pleasant line in which they are cast.[98]

Or, perhaps Mighels' fellow editor at the *Carson Tribune* came even closer to summing up Bethards' existence when he wrote:

> And so, he had received his pardon at the hands of a better board than he applied to on earth. He now knows what of future existence remains to poor, frail humanity, and so let us hope that the sins of his life, probably induced by early training, may be forgiven him. It is better for Bill Bethards that he is dead.[99]

5

Boss Fighter to Political Chief
Leslie Blackburn

When an aged Leslie Blackburn died in Oakland, California, in 1913 most were unaware of the exploits and experiences the man had left on the back trail of his life. Unlike some other veterans of the frontier who were lucky enough to live into the 20th century, Blackburn left very few details of his adventures behind him.[1] Many would have been surprised to learn that the old fellow had been present during the heyday of two of the greatest boom towns of Western legend, Virginia City, Nevada, and Tombstone, Arizona. He had been friends and rubbed shoulders with such famous personalities as Dan De Quille, Mark Twain, Wyatt, Virgil and Morgan Earp and Doc Holliday. Indeed, like the latter individuals, Blackburn had long ago been a shootist and, as it was phrased in the Old West, had "killed his man." With his burying that cool January day in 1913, a man with an untold story to tell had been silenced forever.

Born in New York State ca. 1841, Leslie Fort Blackburn and his young wife Jane early set out for California, arriving in San Francisco possibly as early as 1861 or '62.[2] While in San Francisco, Les, as his friends called him, may have engaged in some aspect of the liquor business. He also probably joined one of the local volunteer fire companies.[3] Here, in early 1863, Blackburn, aged about 21 years, and his young 17- or 18-year-old wife Jane saw the birth of a daughter whom they christened Clara. Shortly, Blackburn would gather up his young family and move to the Comstock in the neighboring silver rich state of Nevada.

Located some 175 miles east of San Francisco, Virginia City, Nevada, by the early 1860s, was in the throes of a silver mining boom centered on the fabulously rich Comstock lode mining district. Having been founded only some three years before, the city had a population of about 3000 people by early 1863.[4] More would be added to this total on a daily basis, including Leslie Blackburn and family.

Upon his entrance into the milieu of Virginia City, Blackburn quickly ingratiated himself into the sporting, saloon, gambling and political cliques of the community. He lost no time in joining one of the Hook and Ladder fire companies. [5]He also worked as a policeman on the Virginia City police force under well-known lawman and personality, Chief of Police Jack Perry, if a story told in later years by former *Virginia City Territorial Enterprise* editor Rollin Daggett can be credited.

According to Daggett, on one occasion Perry wished to be rid of two ne'er-do-wells hanging around the city. After receiving Perry's instructions, Blackburn gathered a number of rocks, tin cans and other garbage, sealed them inside a box slung on a pole and hired the two outcasts to shoulder the valuable package to *Gold Hill News* editor Alf Doten, at that camp, for $5. Blackburn also penned a note to Doten informing him that the two men were check thieves and to send them further down the road with their load. Eventually the pair ended up in the town of Dayton, unable to find their fictitious consignor and told in a final note, "if you can't find the owner keep the box." The two men may have been unhappy with their box of refuse, but Perry and Blackburn were pleased to be rid of them.[6]

Such antics and practical jokes were almost a commodity in the Virginia City of the 1860s. One of Blackburn's friends and drinking companions at this time proved to be a young *Territorial Enterprise* news writer named Samuel Clemens, later to gain fame as humorist and writer Mark Twain. By November 1866, Twain had left Virginia City. He was in the midst of a successful lecture tour at this time and had returned to Nevada to give his presentation at Virginia City and Gold Hill. Following the Gold Hill talk of the evening of Saturday, November 10, Twain and his agent, Denis McCarthy, trudged the mile or so back up the hill to Virginia City. Suddenly, at a high point between the two communities known as the Divide, where a number of robberies and murders had occurred in the past, a group of masked highwaymen stepped out in front of the pair demanding their money and valuables at the point of pistols. Twain, convinced he was in the hands of desperate criminals, gave all he had whereupon, following some jocose banter, the robbers disappeared into the darkness. Twain was convinced he had narrowly escaped with his life until it was later revealed to him that the incident had been a prank and the band was composed of a number of his old chums including Leslie Blackburn, Virginia City Marshall George Birdsall, Pat Holland and a number of others. According to his biographers, the episode, described in some detail in Mark Twain's book *Roughing It*, never quite sat well with the famous author.[7]

Leslie Blackburn always enjoyed a good practical joke. This is evident in another incident often told of him around Virginia City. On one occasion he happened to be strolling down C Street with Comstock personality Pat Holland when the two spotted a street vendor selling watermelons, a "rare and costly" item in the mining camps. Almost immediately Blackburn's brain began to tick and as Mark Twain biographer Albert Bigelow Paine would tell it, Blackburn stated to Holland:

> "Pat, let's get one of those watermelons. You engage that fellow in conversation while I stand at the corner, where I can step around out of sight easily. When you have got him interested, point to something on the back shelf and pitch me a melon."

This appealed to Holland, and he carried out his part of the plan perfectly; but when he pitched the watermelon Blackburn simply put his hands in his pockets and stepped around the corner, leaving the melon a fearful disaster on the pavement. It was almost impossible for Pat to explain to the fruit man why he pitched away a three-dollar melon like that even after paying for it, and it was still more trying, also more expensive, to explain to the boys facing the various bars along C Street.[8]

Virginia City during the 1860s proved to be this aberrant, bizarre combination of jocular hilarity and sudden, brutal violence. Robberies and beatings were common occurrences. Men such as Jack Williams, Sam Brown and Joe McGee kept the early years lively with the song of the pistol and the swish of the Bowie knife. Even as late as 1867, when the aforementioned individuals were long gone to their final reward, the city would often break out into paroxysms of unexpected violence. Such a state caused one local newspaper to grumble in April that year:

> A sort of mania for some kind of muss seems to pervade numerous members of this community just at the present time.... Some of our quietest men, and even a woman or two, have elevated their backs and got on a rampage. It must be some peculiar kind of fighting whiskey they get into them—a whiskey which operates as a sort of letter of marque, commissioning them to sink, burn and destroy, and accordingly out they start, cruising about in regular privateering style, seeking whom they might knock down and drag out.[9]

Left to right, M.A. Williams, Leslie Blackburn, Billy Williams with unidentified Chinese boy, Virginia City, 1867, the year Blackburn went on a binge of gunplay (courtesy Digital Photo Collection, Image #UNRS-P0229-1, Special Collections and University Archives Department, University of Nevada, Reno Libraries).

One of those the newspaper may have been surreptitiously referring to may have been Les Blackburn. For some reason, during mid to late 1867, Blackburn took to drinking in the saloons more than usual and engaging in dustups, causing one newspaper to complain after one such episode, "Blackburn has been doing so much of this same sort of business lately that it is attracting the attention of all good, quiet citizens and we heard it asked last night whether he had not taken out a city license for breaking heads."[10]

Blackburn escalated the violence on the afternoon of the day after Christmas 1867. Blackburn had been drinking heavily all that day and assaulted a Mr. Barnwell at Pipers Opera House earlier in the afternoon. At about 3 o'clock Blackburn crossed D Street and entered Lyons Saloon. Soon he became engaged in an argument with various individuals inside including Pat Lyons, owner of the establishment who was working behind the bar serving drinks. All at once, Blackburn pulled his revolver and pistol-whipped Lyons on the head. Lyons fell to the floor, a large gash in his scalp. The force of the blow having knocked the weapon out of his grasp, Blackburn went behind the bar and picked it up where it had fallen on the floor. Lyons staggered to his feet and headed for the door leading to another room in an attempt to find safety. Aiming his gun, Blackburn fired two shots at the retreating saloon man. Luckily for Lyons both slugs zipped past him and landed in the wall at his side.

Hearing the shots as he walked down D Street, City Jailor McGinnis of the Virginia City police force ran into the saloon and confronted Blackburn. Blackburn presented his pistol at McGinnis in an attempt to shoot again. Reaching out in an attempt to grab the pistol, the webbing of skin between McGinnis's thumb and index finger caught between the hammer and cylinder of the weapon. Thus, the hammer fell on McGinnis's skin and the revolver failed to fire. Finally subduing the shootist, McGinnis, hand bleeding, led him away to the city calaboose.[11]

Brought before City Recorder Bush shortly after, Blackburn was allowed his freedom after posting a $500 bail bond.[12] Although his head wound proved to be of a serious nature, Pat Lyons must have made a full recovery as Blackburn apparently faced no overly harsh consequences as a result of the encounter.[13] What brought on this bout of dissipation and violence remains a mystery. Only a little over three months later he would be involved in another shooting affair, this one resulting fatally to his opponent.

Sometime in the latter months of 1867 a self-proclaimed "shoulder striker" from Montana, one Michael Duane appeared in Virginia City. Duane, a 29-year-old native of Ireland, fancied himself something of a master of the "sweet science" and quickly gained the appellation of "the Montana Boxer."

On the evening of Wednesday, April 15, 1868, Duane, somewhat intoxicated, began telling people he would like to box Jim Cartter, a prominent Virginia City boxer. Later that night, as Duane stood on a street corner talking to Les Blackburn, a well-known friend of Cartter's, Cartter suddenly approached.

"I hear you would like to fight me," Cartter called to Duane.

Looking to be unsure of what to do, Duane simply replied, "No."

"I have a notion to give you one anyhow," Cartter growled as he threw back his right fist as if to strike out at Duane.

Abruptly, Duane turned on his heel and hastened down the street.

A few hours later, early on the morning of the 16th, Duane once again happened to meet Blackburn on the corner of C and Union streets. Without saying a word, Duane pulled a large rock out of his coat pocket and slammed Blackburn in the side of the head. Stunned, Blackburn fell to the sidewalk bleeding from a large laceration on his head.

Walking off down the street a short distance, Duane stood and watched as a number of men came to Blackburn's assistance.

Getting slowly to his feet Blackburn groaned, "Where's the man that hit me?"

Hearing the query, Duane shouted out, "Here I am, follow me if you dare," and turning, disappeared up the street.

After having his head bandaged at the office of Dr. C.C. Green, Blackburn met up with a friend named John Kelly. Making their way down South C Street the pair neared the Crystal Saloon when Blackburn heard someone say, "There is the son of a bitch that is looking for me."

Looking toward the front of the saloon, Blackburn spied Duane reaching into his pocket as if going for a pistol. Quickly snatching his revolver from his belt, Blackburn squeezed off a shot. The slug smacked into Duane's right chest, passed through his lung and lodged near the spine. Ducking, the wounded man attempted to run across the street. Taking aim, Blackburn fired a second shot at the fleeing figure. This projectile deflected off the base of Duane's shoulder blade and perforated the same lung as the first shot.[14]

Duane staggered into Spalding's Saloon almost across the street from the Crystal. At first sitting upon a gas meter inside, he soon lay on the floor. Within six minutes he was dead.

Only one week later the city would be enthralled by the spectacle of the hanging of John Millian for the brutal robbery and murder of a well-known and revered madam named Julia Bulette back on January 20, 1867.[15]

As for Leslie Blackburn, he would find himself released on bail in the Michael Duane killing until his court hearing in August 1868. On Friday, August 17, he received a discharge on the grounds of self-defense.[16]

Some time that year or the next, Blackburn gained employment with Wells Fargo & Co. as one of their detective forces. He garnered mention in the local press for his investigation into the Pancake Mountain stagecoach robbery of late July 1869 near Hamilton in far Eastern Nevada.[17] Some other activities of his back at Virginia City may not have been as exemplary.

By February 1870, Blackburn operated the Alhambra Theater in Virginia City. Here he presented all manner of entertainment acts, theatrical plays and lectures for the enjoyment of the general public at 50 cents a ticket: "Private Boxes $3 and $5. Private entrance to boxes on D Street. The BAR will be stocked with the finest brands of Liquors and Cigars."[18]

In March that year he would associate himself with a rather unsavory character named Johnny Faylor, an itinerant horseman and race speculator. Blackburn was one of those backing Faylor in what was known as a "race against time" in which Faylor proposed to race 50 miles in two hours using no more than 15 horses, $1000 a side being the wager that he would succeed or fail.[19] The race came off at the Carson City racetrack on Sunday, March 27 with Faylor failing to make the time by five minutes.[20] It came out later, however, that Faylor had intentionally thrown the race in a scheme to bilk a heavy better, a faro dealer at Empire, Nevada, named Bright, out of nearly $1000. Faylor, having convinced Bright the event was set up for him to win, then convinced the gambler to place a large bet with a source secretly connected to Faylor. According to the *Carson City Appeal*, "it became apparent after the 25th mile that he [Faylor] was determined to 'chuck' the race. He rode carelessly, let his horses run all over the course, and displayed much awkwardness in his manner of mounting and dismounting."[21] Concerning Faylor's backers, of whom Blackburn was one, the paper continued:

> There was much ill feeling here after the race amongst those who had befriended and trusted Faylor; and it is the general feeling now that he is what is popularly known as a "deadbeat." While we must say that we concur in this opinion, we cannot feel otherwise than that his principal backers and cappers are quite as much to blame as he—more so, if anything; for some of them, gamblers as they are, had the confidence of the public to a very considerable extent and were, in a measure, looked upon as Faylor's endorsers.[22]

Apparently, Johnny Faylor managed to escape the area with a whole skin. Whether or not Les Blackburn knew of Faylor's planned scheme is unknown. It is probably a fact, however, that some looked slightly askance at Blackburn following this incident.

Following a successful run of four or five months, Blackburn closed the Alhambra in mid–June in order to undertake renovations.[23] In the meantime he apparently sold the theater as it would again reopen in July under the management of J.P. Curtis, although Blackburn may have kept an interest in the business.[24]

By mid–1870, Les Blackburn was living in Virginia City's Second Ward.[25] When enumerated on August 6 by census taker P.H.S. Corbett, Blackburn was found residing with his wife Jane and seven-year-old daughter Clara. Also living with them was a 23-year-old man named William Blackburn, like Leslie and Jane, a native of New York, possibly a brother of Leslie.[26] By this time, perhaps at loose ends following the relinquishing of the Alhambra Theater, Blackburn was looking for alternative money-making opportunities. He would find it by hiring out his gun in Virginia City's notorious "water war."

Due to the sudden drying up of various sources, the summer and fall of 1870 found the Virginia City area in a serious water shortage.[27] The situation grew more complicated and dangerous when two concerns, the already established Virginia and Gold Hill Water Co. and the newly formed Peake and Co., began contesting rights and property in Seven Mile Canyon, just east of Virginia City. As was the custom in such situations, the precedent having already been set by the various mining companies of the Comstock, when two monied organizations came into conflict "fighters" were often hired to physically protect interests on the ground. So it would be on this occasion.

Hired by Peake and Co., Blackburn, along with friend and fellow entertainer Robert Lindsay, trooped out to Seven Mile Canyon to take up their posts. Thirty-four-year-old Lindsay, like Blackburn a native of New York State, made a portion of his living as an actor at Piper's Opera House in Virginia City.[28] He had shown his mettle on May 27 of that year when he engaged in a knife fight at Piper's with one Isaac Tamkin.[29] One of the many intriguing characters of Virginia City, Lindsay would later be admitted to the bar and practice law in the wild silver camp.[30]

On the afternoon of Tuesday, October 25, Blackburn, Lindsay and fellow Peake and Co. guard, well-known lawman and gunman Dick Paddock, found themselves lounging around the Peake holdings. Unfortunately for them, they had temporarily laid their firearms aside. Suddenly, they were approached by two rival "fighters," Virginia and Gold Hill men, William Sheik and the notorious shootist Dick Prentice, both armed with pistols.

According to Blackburn, Prentice began arguing with him. When Blackburn dismissed him with a few choice words, Prentice flew into a rage and pulled his pistol from his belt. Before Blackburn could get out of the way, Prentice fired a shot at him. Although the bullet missed him by inches, perforating his coat, in the excitement Blackburn believed he had been shot.

Rushing up, Paddock yelled out to Blackburn, "Are you hit?"

"I believe I am," Blackburn roared, "but I'll get even."

Despite the fact of still facing his antagonist's pointed pistol, Blackburn quickly picked up a large rock and lunged at Prentice. The blow struck Prentice on the side of the head, knocking him to the ground, whereupon Blackburn dived on top of him and continued slamming the rock into his opponent's cranium.

Glancing up from his labors of turning Prentice's head and face into a bloody pulp, Blackburn suddenly spotted William Sheik running toward him, a revolver grasped in his hand. Telling Paddock to commence on Prentice, Blackburn stood up and advanced on Sheik with his trusty rock, while at the same time hollering to Lindsay, "Bob, bring our guns!"

While Paddock and Prentice wrestled on the ground, Blackburn continued to stalk Sheik, Sheik not daring to fire his pistol. Suddenly, the grappling pair rolled down an embankment, Paddock breaking his shoulder in the process. Just as Prentice jumped to his feet, Lindsay appeared, aiming a rifle and firing a shot which failed to hit either Prentice or Sheik. As they fled the scene, Prentice and Sheik answered Lindsay with two or three shots from their pistols. One slug ripped into Lindsay's right leg just above the knee, dropping him to the dirt. With that the fight came to an end.[31]

Eventually, all the participants in the battle would have their wounds tended in Virginia City, the only one to come out relatively unscathed being Leslie Blackburn, save the through shot to his coat.[32] All seem to have avoided any legal implications in the affair and, following the arbitration of the two rival water companies dispute, water soon flowed once again in the region.

These troubles may have disillusioned Blackburn with the Comstock. Very soon after the Seven Mile Canyon fight, he packed up his family and moved to San Francisco. Here he opened the Alhambra Saloon at No. 323 Bush Street.[33] He also renewed his membership with the volunteer firefighting companies of the city. Leslie Blackburn continued to reside in San Francisco for the next ten years.

One cannot help but wonder what Leslie Blackburn's reaction was, at about this time, to a very popular theatrical production which was presented at many of the well-known playhouses throughout the West from Salt Lake City to San Francisco in the 1880s and '90s. The production, entitled *The Phoenix*, was written by veteran actor and playwright Milton Nobles, a native of Michigan. The villain of the play proved to be a ne'er-do-well and all-around reprehensible character Nobles named Leslie Blackburn. Nobles not only produced the performance with his own traveling acting troupe but always played the lead, Carroll Graves, who never fails to vanquish Blackburn, "the heavy villain," in the end.[34]

Milton Nobles had been a resident of Virginia City, Nevada, during the same time as Leslie Blackburn. The 1870 census for Virginia City shows him listed as a 26-year-old "Actor" living in the same general area of the city as a number of other actors, including Blackburn's friend Robert Lindsay.[35] He would have been one of those bohemians who performed at Piper's Opera House and possibly Blackburn's Alhambra Theater as well. Can there be any doubt he knew Blackburn? What dealings did they have? Unfortunately, if Blackburn ever mentioned Nobles' *Phoenix* to anyone his remarks went unrecorded.

After almost a decade in San Francisco, Leslie Blackburn was again ready for adventure. Hearing of all the exciting details surrounding another mining boomtown in the Arizona desert named Tombstone, Blackburn headed for the area possibly as early as 1879.[36]

At this point, beginning to develop the political aspirations which would drive him for the remainder of his life, Blackburn lost no time in cultivating important friendships and joining appropriate organizations in Tombstone. Realizing that the firefighting companies were one of the best places for networking with other like-minded individuals he followed his usual procedure and joined Tombstone's first fire department, Tombstone Engine Co. No. 1, in September 1880. With his experience gained from companies in Virginia City and San Francisco, Blackburn was named foreman of the company. Another member proved to be Wyatt Earp who was named secretary.[37]

In fact, Blackburn became quite friendly with the brothers Earp, Wyatt, Virgil, Morgan and James, early on. At one point he even joined the Earps in backing a well-known foot racer named Ryan traveling through the area. This episode almost ended in a similar fashion to the Johnny Faylor incident of Blackburn's Virginia City days, with the exception that he and the Earps would have been the victims. This time Ryan and his partner were found out beforehand and no money was lost by the prospective betters.[38]

With Cochise County having yet to be created, by late 1880, Tombstone was still a part of Pima County. As a reward for his support in the Sheriff's elections of November 1880, Pima County Sheriff Charles Shibell appointed Blackburn a deputy sheriff on November 24.[39] Four months later, in late March 1881, Arizona Gov. Crawley Dake would also appoint him a deputy U.S. marshal to serve at Tombstone along with the other deputy U.S. marshal of the district, Virgil Earp.[40]

In one of his many roles in the silver camp, Blackburn faced his first major test as foreman of the Tombstone fire company on the afternoon of Wednesday, June 22. Despite the loss to many of the town businesses the local *Tombstone Epitaph* praised the firemen, who, "although not having their apparatus, did good service, and worked like Trojans. Much credit is due them."[41]

On July 5, 1881, it became Deputy U.S. Marshal Blackburn's official responsibility to formally charge Doc Holliday with attempting to rob the U.S. mail.[42] Holliday, a supporter and friend of the Earp clan in the so-called "Earp–Cowboy" feud in newly formed Cochise County, had been arrested for suspected participation in the Drew's Station stagecoach robbery of March 15, 1881.[43] Holliday, most likely totally innocent of the charge, had probably been used as a pawn in the larger Earp–Cowboy conflict and nothing ever came of the charge. In fact, Blackburn would be one of the few in the county to not be drawn in in some form during the conflict. As a result, up to, during and subsequent to the famous O.K. Corral gunfight of October 26 that year, Blackburn managed to stay aloof of the difficulty.

Leslie Blackburn's most active and successful year in Tombstone proved to be 1882. Despite losing his bid for Tombstone City Marshal on January 3, polling 103 votes to winner Dave Neagle's 590 and second-place finisher James Flynn's total of 434, Blackburn was not disillusioned.[44] Soon he would be making his move for control of the Republican Party of Cochise County. In the interim, Blackburn continued with his other duties around Tombstone. In mid–January, in his capacity as deputy U.S. marshal, he arrested John Chenoweth of the Grand Hotel and M. Martin and R. Door, formerly operators of the Palace Saloon on Allen Street, with violating the U.S. revenue laws by selling liquor and tobacco without a license.[45]

Blackburn's talents as a firefighter were again tested on May 26, 1882, when a major fire broke out in the business section of Tombstone. Many business buildings were lost in the conflagration, however, Blackburn and Engine Co. No. 1 managed to help save others.[46]

Occasionally the fighting spirit of the younger Leslie Blackburn of the Virginia City days revealed itself in Tombstone. An example of this occasional factitiousness came about one evening in early August 1882. On this night, Blackburn collided with a member of the Tombstone City Council named Charley Thomas of whom the *Epitaph* declared, "He has been an Ishmaelite, used by a few and despised by everybody."[47] Going on to describe the fight the paper continued:

> About 9 o'clock, while in a maudlin state of intoxication, he [Thomas] entered a saloon on Allen Street and began to abuse the fire department. Foreman Blackburn of the engine company chanced to be a listener, and told the impudent cad to shut his mouth. He declined to notice the admonition, but instead drew back and struck at Mr. Blackburn, but the latter was too quick for him, and instead of giving he received a vigorous blow. Blackburn then properly proceeded to thrash him, and would have made mincemeat of him in a few minutes had not the ever-vigilant police arrived, and Coyle and Kenney hauled them both off to jail. Mr. Blackburn was bailed out instantaneously, and Thomas subsequently secured some parties to give bonds for his appearance today.[48]

Despite being what the newspaper called "an eyesore to the Tombstone body politic," Thomas would continue to dabble in city politics and by 1885 was mayor of the town.

Blackburn soon became one of the leading lights in the Republican Party of Cochise County. He would be responsible, along with a select few, in organizing what was labeled the "Republican Ring," centering the power in Tombstone and largely leaving the rural parts of the county out of the decision-making process.

The first inkling of his sudden power in the party came during the Republican primary meeting held in Tombstone on August 4. Reporting on events the *Epitaph* declared:

> About 2 o'clock it was suddenly noised about that Blackburn had taken the field.... Soon after the earmarks of the "old connubiator" [*sic*] were visible in the contest.... Blackburn sent out his henchmen, and the city was scooped for Republican voters as with a fine-tooth comb.... The ring came out ahead, but not without an eager messenger being sent to Blackburn.[49]

Soon, rumors of a power struggle between Blackburn and former Republican boss Henry C. Dibble became current.[50] Apparently, Blackburn came out victorious if the *Epitaph's* utterances of "Blackburn owns the Republican party of Cochise county" and

"Leslie F. Blackburn ... is, perhaps, at the present time, the most prominent factor in the local Republican politics," are any indications.[51]

In between his political maneuverings, Blackburn continued to perform his duties as a deputy U.S. marshal for the Tombstone area. Traveling to Tucson he arrested a major embezzler named Heinsmmer.[52] In early August, while on a trip to California and visiting the headquarters of the San Francisco Police Department, Blackburn recognized the mugshot of a fugitive from California justice named Edward Terril. Blackburn recognized Terril, an attempted murderer, as a lunch stand attendant in Tombstone's Fountain Saloon. Journeying back to Tombstone, Blackburn recruited Cochise County Sheriff John Behan and the pair quickly placed Terril under arrest. Eventually he was extradited back to California.[53]

Later, on Sunday, September 24, Deputy Blackburn received a visit from famous Indian scout Mickey Free. Free, accompanied by a fellow scout, an Apache Indian named Irish, rode into Tombstone with Quirino Robles. Blackburn accepted Robles into his custody on a charge of selling liquor to Indians.[54]

Back on the political front, an important Republican County committee meeting took place on October 4 in Tombstone. It was an event which may have initiated Les Blackburn's decline in Tombstone. In any event, he would depart shortly after its occurrence.

A number of Republicans outside of Tombstone, known as the "country members," were unhappy with the "Republican Ring's" control of the party in general and Leslie Blackburn's ascension to the throne in particular. At the October 4 meeting a group of country members from Bisbee, led by well-known Wells Fargo detective and former Earp supporter during the Earp–Cowboy feud, Fred Dodge, decided to attend and usurp Blackburn and the Ring.

The meeting quickly degenerated into shouting and cat calling on a grand scale, Blackburn and Dodge clashing on a number of occasions. At one point, Blackburn warned Dodge, "You hadn't better be too saucy," to which Dodge returned, "I'll be as saucy as I damn please." Later the two almost came to blows over a point of motion.

"Shut your damn mouth," Blackburn yelled at Dodge.

"You can't shut it," Dodge shouted back. Blackburn stared at the man. "I'll give you any kind of a game you want," he growled.

Dodge returned his piercing gaze. "You can't give me anything, and the less chin music you give the better," he replied.

Both men moved toward each other in a threatening manner, however, members jumped between them and prevented a physical clash.[55]

In the end Dodge and his clique won the day and managed to win most of their points.

In October 1882, Blackburn, in partnership with N.H. Burdette, opened the Senate Saloon on Allen Street.[56] The decline of his political stature may have been a great disappointment to him though. To be sure, he would not remain much longer in Tombstone.

By spring 1885, Blackburn had relocated to Prescott, Arizona. Here his fractious nature again got him into trouble. According to a report printed in the *Epitaph* of March 23, 1885, he had gotten into a fistfight with one Al Whitney in which he was "badly beaten" and "lying in a very critical condition."[57] The nature or seriousness of his injuries are unknown. He did recover, however, and soon made his way back to California, a political hound once more.

Living in Oakland by 1890, Blackburn was already known as a politician of note.[58] He also supplemented his earnings by working as a bouncer for the pool rooms located on Eighth Street.[59] A man used to wearing many hats, he also later managed to gain an appointment as a deputy sheriff stationed in the County Courthouse.[60]

Blackburn decided to seek appointment as Sergeant at Arms of the California State Senate in November 1894.[61] He proved successful and served in that capacity at Sacramento State Capitol for the following four years.[62]

In late 1897 and mid–1898, Blackburn demonstrated that the fighting Leslie Blackburn of the old Virginia City, Nevada, salad days was not quite dead yet despite having reached his 56th year. On Christmas evening, Blackburn happened to be in the Office Saloon on Eighth Street in downtown Oakland. At length he fell into a disagreement with William "Billy" O'Brien. Apparently, O'Brien felt that Blackburn had reneged on a deal to get him some sort of political appointment. As the argument continued, O'Brien suddenly drew back his fist and struck Blackburn a blow to the face. Parties grabbed both men and attempted to separate them when Blackburn pulled out a keen bladed knife and swiped at his opponent, the blade slicing a furrow in O'Brien's forehead. Friends of the two finally managed to pull them apart and the fracas came to an end.[63] Evidence of legal action as a result of this difficulty is lacking. The animosity between the two politicos continued to simmer.

A little over six months later, on the evening of July 14, Blackburn and O'Brien again collided in the Office Saloon. This time Blackburn upped the ante by pulling his revolver on his enemy. When O'Brien called out that he was unarmed, Blackburn responded for him to "go and arm yourself." However, they were once again separated before any damage could be done.[64] Charged with assault with a deadly weapon, Blackburn would have his case dismissed from the docket on Tuesday, July 26.[65] Not deterred, O'Brien placed another charge against Blackburn, this one for exhibiting a deadly weapon. This charge would float through the courts for months before finally being likewise dismissed in February 1899.[66]

Blackburn lost in his bid for another term as Sergeant at Arms of the California Senate in January 1899.[67] At about this time he began to flex his political muscle and make himself a force to be reckoned with in the Republican Party of Alameda County.

In September 1902, Blackburn and a number of like-minded individuals formed the so-called "Independent Republican Party" within the ranks of the regular party. Surprisingly, one of the leading lights of this faction proved to be Blackburn's old enemy but now staunch friend, William O'Brien.[68] In fact, Blackburn's and O'Brien's relationship had undergone such a complete turnaround that, at one point, Blackburn appeared as a witness in support of O'Brien in a court case involving an accident between O'Brien's wagon and another on an Oakland Street. At the time, Blackburn had been a passenger in O'Brien's wagon.[69]

The formation of the Independent Republican wing proved to be nothing more than a vehicle for Blackburn to promote the candidacy of his political crony and good

5. Boss Fighter to Political Chief

Leslie Blackburn Mausoleum marker, 1840–1913 (courtesy Alfred W. Janske).

friend Henry P. Dalton for the position of County Assessor. In the end, Dalton won his party's nomination and eventually gained election as Alameda County Assessor.[70]

On September 28, 1906, Leslie Blackburn's second wife, Mary, a Michigan native, died in Oakland at the age of 61.[71] When he married her and the fate of his first wife Jane is unknown.

By summer 1910, Henry Dalton had served as County Assessor for the past eight years with his good friend and champion Les Blackburn at his right hand, with all the political power this entailed. That summer, however, the city of Oakland would be rocked when Blackburn and Dalton acrimoniously parted company, Blackburn pressing charges against his former confidant of extortion and bribery. The case would drag on in the Alameda County courts as a cause célèbre for the next year.[72] Dalton was pronounced guilty on July 14, 1911.[73]

At this juncture, Blackburn quietly retired to his home in Oakland. He had fought many fights, both physical and political. He had won some and lost some others. The old frontier veteran finally lost the last one he would ever fight, dying in Oakland of natural causes on July 22, 1913, at the age of 71.[74]

6

A Dedicated Law Man
William McKee

Sudden death by violent means, be it beating, knife or gun, took place with more frequency in Pioche then most any other location in the State of Nevada. In the 1870–1873 time period, at least 31 shooting affairs led to death in Pioche.[1] Of the violent deaths in Nevada listed in Myron Angel's *History of Nevada*, published in 1881, almost 60 percent of all those enumerated for the years 1871 and 1872 took place in Pioche.[2] Most took place within the sporting fraternity. If you kept yourself clear of such doings you were probably fairly safe. However, no one could protect you from the chance occurrence of a random thief on a dark street or stray bullet ripping its way unheeded from one of the frequent gun battles breaking out in Pioche's saloon district. At these times a stouthearted officer of the law was a major asset.

One of those who would attempt, with some effect, to police the rough-and-tumble area through the 1870s and into the 1880s would be a Mississippian of not only stout heart but stout body, named William McKee. McKee would do his part to add to Pioche's death toll. Despite this, his effectiveness as a law officer could not be doubted. In spite of his attainments in keeping the peace, however, William McKee would begin his career in Pioche as just another mining camp gunman.

William L. McKee came into the world somewhere in the state of South Carolina ca. 1833.[3] While still a babe in arms he moved with his family to northern Mississippi. Here the McKee family settled on a farm near Holly Springs, Marshall County. The 1850 census shows young William, listed as 15 years of age, living on the farm with his 46-year-old mother Nancy, 21-year-old brother Milton and two younger brothers, James, 11 and Malcom, aged 8.[4] What became of the boy's father is unknown. Despite the absence of her husband, Nancy McKee would seem to be fairly well set up as she is listed as owning real estate valued at $6500, a substantial amount for the time and place. She also seemed dedicated to giving her children a good education with William, even at the age of 15, being listed as having attended school within the last year. At that time 15 was an age by which many children, especially boys, had long since left the classroom and readers far behind for the labors of the farm.

Exactly when young William left his boyhood home is not of record. Sometime after reaching his majority, however, he said goodbye to his mother and siblings and headed out to seek his fortune in the California gold fields. He was known to have been one of the first miners to work the diggings at Columbia Hill, Nevada County,

California, in the early 1860s.[5] Soon he would be enticed by stories of opportunity in neighboring Nevada Territory.

According to his own recollections, McKee first came to Nevada before statehood, sometime in 1862.[6] His activities and movements are not known, but considering his undertakings in California, chances are he delved into some aspect of Nevada's burgeoning silver mining industry.

By 1869, McKee, in his mid–30s and a frontier veteran of untold experiences and accomplishments, made his first appearance in Lincoln County and the fledgling town of Pioche.[7] He had developed into a large man of substantial girth, tipping the scales at around 240 pounds, in a time when a man was considered hefty at 170 pounds.[8] To honor his ample bulk his friends around Pioche christened him with the pet name "Fat Mac," a moniker McKee not only accepted but reveled in, in the good-natured way it was intended.[9] Everyone soon came to realize that behind the jolly exterior lay a man who could be, and often was, in deadly earnest.

The year of 1870 saw Pioche, named for F.L.A. Pioche, a San Francisco mining financier who had a number of claims in the area, quickly turning into a silver mining metropolis. Two large mining concerns based in San Francisco, the Meadow Valley Mining Co. and Raymond & Ely Mining Co. had moved into the district and began full scale operations. Many other smaller companies did likewise. Pioche itself, soon to be designated County Seat of Lincoln County on February 24, 1871, swiftly became a bustling community in the middle of the desert supporting some 6000 to 7000 inhabitants. A goodly number of these were also attracted to the city's estimated 50–75 saloons, bordellos, dance halls and gambling emporiums. Some came for no other reason than to make as much easy money as quickly as possible while at the same time raise as much hell as possible in Pioche's tenderloin.[10] William McKee would be forced to deal with his share of these ruffians.

Census taker G.R. Megarrigle found the 37-year-old McKee living in Pioche in early August 1870. McKee gave his occupation as "miner" and the value of his real estate as "250 dollars." Also living with him in the same dwelling proved to be a 55-year-old Negro porter from Maryland named H. Johnson.[11] McKee was only months away from his first recorded gunplay. It would not be a stellar performance and would stick in "Mac's" craw for a good time to come.

In October 1870 the Raymond and Ely Company decided to allow two fledgling independent miners, Tom and Frank Newland, the right of way to run a tunnel from their holdings through the Raymond and Ely's Washington and Creole property.[12] Not being much enamored with the, so far, discovered wealth of the Washington and Creole mines, Raymond and Ely officials could see no harm in allowing the Newlands the requested right-of-way.

Unbeknownst to Raymond and Ely, however, in a development the Newlands kept to themselves, the brothers discovered a wealthy silver vein deep in the Washington and Creole holdings estimated to be worth some $300 of silver to the ton of ore.[13] When the Newlands requested a further lease to work their tunnel for 30 days, Raymond and Ely, ignorant of the property's undiscovered riches, could see no harm in granting the request. At the conclusion of the 30-day lease it was estimated the Newland brothers had recovered over $100,000 in high-grade ore.[14] After the 30-day lease had expired, a Raymond and Ely engineer finally ventured into the mine and witnessed the huge silver vein. He was shocked. Now determined not to renew the lease as the Newlands requested, Raymond and Ely were anxious to take over production. The Newlands had other ideas. As one chronicler has put it:

> The Newlands, however, had become used to the idea that this was their mine, and they were disgruntled as hell when they had to leave it. It didn't matter that they didn't own it, nor did it matter that Raymond had given them a chance to make $50,000 a piece in 30 days' time, it only mattered that they were losing it—and this they didn't want to do. Worryingly, they hired a gang of cowboy gunslingers, barricaded themselves in the mine, and refused all entreaties to give it up peacefully.[15]

Although it is debatable how much "cowboying," or "gunslinging" for that matter, William McKee had done up to this point, he proved to be one of the so-called "cowboy gunslingers" the Newlands hired to attempt to hold the rich diggings. Joined by other well known, or soon to be well-known, gunmen like Jack White, McKee trooped out to the Washington and Creole holdings and, along with the Newland brothers and various others, forted up against all comers.[16]

Raymond and Ely were not disposed to brook this situation for long. Accordingly, they hired four of Pioche's most dangerous gunmen, Morgan Courtney, William Bethards, Barney Flood and Michael Casey, to run the Newlands out. This foursome decided to commence operations early on the afternoon of Wednesday, November 9.

In a moment of inspired genius, Courtney and company decided to send a number of bottles of whiskey to the Newland crew along with a card stating that the refreshments were being supplied by supporters. Just who partook of the liquor and how much, if any, William McKee imbibed is unknown. It is stated, however, that by midafternoon many of the Newland man were in various stages of intoxication.

At this point Courtney, Bethards, Flood and Casey unlimbered pistols and charged down the hill into the Washington and Creole fortress with war whoops and revolver fire. Taken totally by surprise the befuddled and confused defenders attempted a brief resistance during which a number of shots were exchanged. During the brief melee defender W.G. Snell received a fatal bullet and a few others less serious injuries before the totally routed Newland men fled the scene leaving Courtney, Bethards, Flood and Casey in charge of the field.[17]

While he managed to exit the battle unscathed, McKee would leave the situation a decided enemy of Morgan Courtney. This would eventually lead to rumors around Pioche of his encouraging Courtney's killing to any like-minded candidate willing to risk his life. In less than two years this state of affairs would lead to another gun battle and establish McKee's reputation as a feared gun handler.

In the interim, William McKee continued his activities in Pioche. In late March 1871, a number of those involved in the November 9, 1870, mine battle had their charges dismissed by the Lincoln County Grand Jury, including William McKee, L.J. Hanchett, Henry Rice, M.H. Lyons, Frank Nichols, Mike Casey, Morgan Courtney, William Bethards, Wythe Walker, James Harrington and everyone else who could be covered with the blanket appellation "John Doe."[18]

Sometime in 1872, McKee gained employment as Lincoln County Road

6. A Dedicated Law Man   73

Superintendent at a salary of $130 per month.[19] Soon he would be working as a lawman in the area and his lifelong career choice would be set in motion.

In the county election held November 5, 1872, Wes Travis gained election to the office of County Sheriff.[20] Upon taking office on Monday, January 6, 1873, Sheriff Travis named his appointments for deputy sheriff's including Undersheriff Joseph R. Hoag and deputies William McKee, J.B. Van Hagan, L.P. Davis and Henry Woodruff. Since Pioche had yet to be incorporated and had no police presence apart from court constables, Travis also appointed McKee and Woodruff night watchmen for the town.[21]

Despite Travis' running a decidedly corrupt administration full of tax manipulation and graft apparently his deputies did their best to operate as efficient officers of the law.[22] McKee lost no time in taking up his duties. On the day of his appointment he, assisted by Deputy Constable George Boyd, arrested two individuals engaged in disturbing the peace of downtown Pioche.[23]

Lincoln County Courthouse, Pioche, Nevada. Known as Lincoln County's $1,000,000 courthouse in recognition of its final cost of construction to the tax payers. McKee would see much activity here in his years in Pioche (courtesy James Hulse Collection, Image #0133 0019, UNLV Libraries Special Collections & Archives, University of Nevada, Las Vegas).

While the local press lamented the constant breaching of the peace, McKee continued to attempt to curtail such activities.[24] On Saturday, January 24, he arrested a man named Lynch passing counterfeit coin at a faro table in a Pioche gaming room.[25] The next day he was instrumental in halting a fight between two Cornishmen on Main Street and arresting the combatants.[26]

Deputy McKee was forced to use his revolver in the line of duty for the first time on the morning of Saturday, March 2. On this occasion two rounders, Thomas O'Brien and Barney Murray, began quarreling in the Mint Saloon. Suddenly O'Brien pulled a revolver and shot Murray in the left breast, the slug exiting below Murray's left shoulder. Running to the scene, Constable George Boyd and Deputy Sheriff Henry Woodruff encountered O'Brien running up Main Street, a revolver in his hand. On being called to halt, O'Brien turned and fired at the officers. Boyd and Woodruff immediately palmed their own revolvers and returned O'Brien's fire. Within seconds, McKee rushed onto the scene and added his own pistol shots to those already speeding toward O'Brien. In the face of this barrage O'Brien, still uninjured, quickly threw down his weapon and surrendered to the officers. At the point of his pistol McKee marched the gunman to the City Jail.[27]

Deputy McKee continued to be active in performing arrests and investigating wanton shooting.[28] Again, on Monday, March 24, he would engage in another dangerous shooting scrape.

That afternoon a Shoshone Indian known as Captain Andy was observed attempting to drag an Indian female out of a cabin on Lacour Street. The rumor was that he wished to kill her for supposed infidelity. Rushing to the scene, McKee attempted to place the furious Shoshone in custody. Breaking free, Captain Andy, carrying a rifle and also armed with a revolver stuck into his waistband, dashed off down the street. McKee attempted to give chase but, perhaps hampered by his ample weight, quickly began to fall behind his quarry.

Commandeering a horse, McKee mounted and galloped after the swift Shoshone. Coming upon Andy about two miles northwest of Pioche, McKee called for him to stop. With that, Andy raised his rifle and fired, the slug missing the lawman. Advancing toward Andy, McKee pulled his revolver and fired four shots at the fugitive. Though one bullet perforated the Indian's shirt none found his body. Throwing down his rifle, Andy grabbed his own revolver and fired back at McKee. McKee later claimed he could hear the slugs whizzing past his head, however, he managed to avoid any injury.[29]

At this point, Capt. Andy suddenly surrendered and McKee triumphantly returned him to Pioche and a cell at the city calaboose. It later became evident that Andy had not intended to kill the squaw but was attempting to return her to her newborn infant whom she had abandoned.[30]

Despite being involved in two dangerous shootings in less than a month, McKee continued to perform his duties undaunted.[31] On Thursday, July 17 he had the distasteful task of arresting a fellow peace officer. That morning Deputy Constable George Boyd entered the Philadelphia Brewery and, intoxicated, drew his revolver on Schustrich, the proprietor of the establishment. Rushing in, McKee disarmed Boyd and escorted him to the jail house. "The conduct of deputy Sheriff McKee was just what it should have been," the local newspaper declared, "and whatever credit is due to an officer for doing his duty, regardless of consequences, is surely due to Mac in this instance."[32]

William McKee's old enemy, gunman Morgan Courtney, had continued to reside in Pioche through the early 1870s. Although there was no love lost between them the pair managed to avoid each other. Suddenly, on August 1, 1873, Courtney was shot dead in Pioche by an itinerant gambler named George McKinney.[33] Though the feud between

McKinney and Courtney seems to have centered around a prostitute named Georgia Syphers, some around town felt that McKee had counseled McKinney in his dispute with Courtney and even encouraged the young sport to use deadly force against the veteran shootist. One of those harboring this opinion proved to be John Manning, a 35-year-old native of Ireland, local rough and professed Courtney supporter.[34] Within a month of Courtney's death, McKee and Manning were destined to have their own encounter on Pioche's Main Street. Only one would walk away from the broil.

During the evening of September 1, Manning and a number of friends, including Jim Hunter and Jimmy Wales, were observed making the rounds of the various saloons, drinking heavily and openly displaying pistols. According to subsequent testimony, Manning was heard to state "that he wanted to find some of Travis' [Lincoln County Sheriff Wes Travis] friends—wanted to kill some son of a bitch.... He also talked about Morgan Courtney ... and said that Fat Mac [McKee], one of Travis' pets, had put up the game for the killing of Courtney."[35]

The following evening, McKee spotted Manning and his cohorts raising a disturbance on Meadow Valley Street. Approaching the group, McKee disarmed Hunter, Wales and a man named O'Brien, Manning having moved off down the street unobserved by McKee. McKee shortly entered Pierson's Saloon closely followed by Jim Hunter who had previously served with McKee as a Lincoln County deputy sheriff. Hunter warned McKee "to look out for Manning, because he blamed him [McKee] for the killing of Courtney."[36]

Early the next morning, Wednesday, September 3, according to later court testimony reprinted in the *Pioche Daily Record*:

> At 8:30 o'clock, James Wales and John Manning, while walking down Main Street, met officer W.L. McKee in front of the "City Club Rooms," third door above Meadow Valley Street. Both Manning and Wales were somewhat under the influence of liquor. Manning said to McKee: "Hold on, Mac, I think you're a friend of the party that killed Courtney." McKee replied: "What have you got to say about it?" Manning answered: "Nothing, Mac, but I don't like officers that murder a man." McKee said: "You are drunk now. Any difference we have had we will settle when you are sober. Go to bed, and when you get sober, I'll talk to you" and laid his hand on Manning's shoulder. Manning replied: "Mac, there's no d-d son of a b-h in this town can make me go to bed. I'll go to bed when I get ready." McKee said that he didn't want to make him go to bed, but that he (Manning) had better take his advice. Other words may have passed between them, but if so, they were not heard. Manning then made a motion as if to draw a weapon, and McKee, being quicker, drew out a self-cocking pistol and fired. Manning quivered for a moment, holding his right hand to his hip, beneath his coat, and then fell on the sidewalk. The only words he spoke were "I'm shot." Wales thinks that he also said, "I'm murdered." Wales drew his pistol, cocked it, and leveled it at McKee, saying, "Mac, don't shoot any more or I'll kill you." McKee said something to the effect that he allowed no one to draw a gun on him, and kept in readiness to defend himself in case Manning should arise, for a short time, and then walked away, and gave himself up at the Sheriff's office. Manning tried to rise several times, but his attempts were ineffectual. He was carried to Bishop & Lee's drugstore. Dr. Lee, who examined the wound, found that the ball had struck him on the left breast bone. It eventually went a little downward, and probably struck one of the blood vessels.[37]

John Manning died a little over an hour after being shot. About another hour later a hastily formed Coroner's Jury decided that Manning "died by a gunshot wound inflicted by W.L. McKee."[38]

The editor of the *Pioche Daily Record* lamented, "People are beginning to think there is something in the atmosphere of Pioche which leads irresistibly to the destruction of human life."[39] Whether it was in the air or in the character of her inhabitants, there is little doubt that Pioche, in the early 1870s, could be a dangerous place.

John Manning's funeral, attended by a substantial crowd of some 150 mourners, took place on the afternoon of the 4th.[40] The next day McKee appeared before Justice J.B. Van Hagan and waved an examination. Bail in the amount of $10,000 was set which was met by a number of the upstanding businessmen of Pioche including O.P. Sherwood, C. Wiedehold and Andy Fife.[41]

Despite being out on bail for the Manning killing, McKee continued with his law enforcement duties. He would be on hand at the time of another of Pioche's notorious shooting scrapes, the shooting death of miner Joe Thomas by mine owner William Rosamurgay on November 2. Hearing the commotion at Wells and Symons Saloon on Meadow Valley Street, McKee and fellow officer Hank Knerr arrived just as Rosamurgay shot Thomas dead. It was simply left for McKee and Knerr to trundle the shooter off to the jail house.[42]

The very next day officers McKee and Knerr stalked and captured a notorious garrotter known as Thomas "Tommy the Headmaker" Williams whom they also lodged in jail.[43]

In early February 1874 the case of William McKee for the shooting death of John Manning back in September of the previous year finally came before the Lincoln County Grand Jury.[44] As was expected, McKee's actions that day were deemed purely in the interest of self-defense and the jury ignored his indictment. Once again, Mac could concentrate solely on his law enforcement duties.

By no means was William McKee all work and no play. He often participated in the social entertainments of the frontier communities as on the evening of February 6 when he performed as doorman and "raiser of the masks" at the fancy dress ball and grand masquerade party held at Brown's Hall and attended by the crème de la crème of Pioche society.[45] Perhaps, still being a bachelor at the age of 40, McKee played the field at these affairs in the hopes of finding a partner to share his life.

McKee employed his revolver again on Thursday, April 30. On this occasion he attempted to arrest a well-known petty thief named Charley "Chicken-thief Charley" Rodds whom he caught in the act of carrying off various articles from another man's cabin. Refusing to obey McKee's command to halt, Rodds took off on the run. Unable to match Rodds foot speed McKee unlimbered his revolver and fired two or three shots at the fleeing criminal. Rodds dropped his load of pilfered items but managed to make his escape unscathed.[46]

Even though the mines had begun to subside somewhat, Pioche continued to display that eruption of sudden violence which had made it renowned on the Nevada frontier. Such proved to be the case on the evening of June 8 when a number of gunshots suddenly erupted out of the small Chinatown located on Lower Main Street. Officers McKee, Knerr and Undersheriff Joe Hoag quickly ventured forth and spent a hectic night sorting out the difficulty, finding one woman injured by a gunshot.[47]

Only two weeks later, Joe Hoag would be seriously wounded when two desperate criminals made their escape from the Lincoln County Jail. Despite Hoag firing his revolver after them the pair, Niconor Rodriguez and George Smock, managed to make their escape.[48] Though suffering a deep laceration to his skull, Hoag was soon up and around once more.[49]

In fact, Hoag would be on hand when he and McKee experienced another close call involving gunfire on the evening of Sunday, July 5. This evening proved to be a rather combative one with a number of scrimmages breaking out through the town. One desperate brawl commenced on Lacour Street, "a couple of fellows pummeling each other around until 'Fat Mac' loomed up in sight, and then they became peaceful very suddenly."[50]

Later that night the peace and quiet of Pioche was again disturbed by a number of pistol shots emanating from the vicinity of Hamilton's Saloon on Meadow Valley Street. Once again, McKee sallied forth, arrested the shooter and was in the act of escorting him to the local calaboose when suddenly, a man named McCann rushed up behind McKee and thrust a revolver barrel into his back. Joe Hoag, in the act of assisting McKee, quickly took in the situation, pulled his own pistol and slammed the barrel into McCann's head. Crashing to the sidewalk, McCann swiftly rose to one knee, aimed his revolver and fired a shot at the lawmen. The slug winged past McKee and struck Hoag in the leg. Quickly, McCann was subdued and dragged off to jail while the unlucky Hoag was again assisted to the offices of Dr. D.L. Deal for treatment.[51]

In September 1874, McKee announced himself as a candidate for Constable of Pioche Township, a position he would win at the November elections while continuing to operate as a deputy sheriff of Lincoln County stationed at Pioche.[52] That October he was instrumental in the investigation of the Hamilton stagecoach robbery which took place about 2 miles outside Pioche. Although the driver of the stage, former Deputy Sheriff James Hunter, one and the same as the man involved in the John Manning affair, was a prime suspect, McKee, in December, eventually arrested a well-known criminal known as "Patsy Marley No. 2" as one of the robbers.[53]

Following the elections of November 3, 1874, the corrupt West Travis would be replaced as Lincoln County Sheriff by Andy Fife, one of those who had paid McKee's bail following the killing of John Manning.[54]

It would be, now as a deputy sheriff under Fife, that McKee would round out the busy year of 1874 by being involved in the investigation of the deaths of a number of whites by renegade Panaca Indians in the remote reaches of Western Lincoln County on the Muddy Reservation near Hiko. Accompanied by fellow Deputy Sheriff McManus, McKee and several others set out in mid–December on the dangerous task of infiltrating the Indian ranks and ferreting out the guilty parties. Although only mildly successful, managing the arrest of only one young Indian, the expedition seemed to end the unrest on the Muddy.[55]

In the summer of 1875, McKee was once again forced to take a life, this time in the line of duty. Encountering James Bass, a 45-year-old black man employed as a freight wagon driver, furiously driving his wagon up Main Street at a breakneck speed on the evening of Saturday, June 26, McKee halted the man and admonished him to slow down. He found the freighter to be slightly intoxicated but convinced him to park his wagon.

"How fast is a man allowed to drive on the streets?" Bass queried after jumping down from his wagon. Before McKee could respond Bass blurted, "I'll drive my horses as fast as I please and where I please," then turned to walk away.

Grabbing him by the shoulders, McKee spun the man around. Ordering Bass back to his wagon, McKee escorted him to the conveyance and told him to move on.

As he drove back down Main Street the way he had come, Bass turned and shook his fist at the lawman.

"You damn son of a bitch," he hollered at McKee. "I'll be seeing you again. I'll go down and get my gun and come back and fix you."

Realizing he may have trouble, McKee recruited officer James Kelly, who happened to be standing nearby, and the pair hastened after Bass' retreating wagon, heading toward Lacour Street where Bass shared a cabin with his wife Levina.

Arriving at the residence a few minutes after Bass, the two lawmen approached the front door just as Bass emerged with a pistol in his hand. Bass fired a wild shot at the startled officers. Jumping back, McKee and Kelly clawed for their own revolvers. Kelly dodged around Bass' parked wagon as the freighter fired another wild shot after him. McKee quickly squeezed off a round which struck Bass in the body before ducking around the corner of an outbuilding.

Now the three combatants fired furiously in a three-cornered battle. One of Bass' slugs plowed along the side of the building McKee had taken shelter behind, showering McKee's face with wood splinters but leaving him uninjured. Kelly emptied his pistol, at which point he then threw the weapon at Bass but failed to hit him. Bass, however, struck at least twice by the lawmen's bullets, suddenly stumbled backwards and pitched onto his back. He would die within 15 minutes of the savage firefight.[56]

The days subsequent to the battle a Coroner's Inquest convened over the remains of James Bass led by coroner Dr. D.L. Deal. They came to the conclusion that the dead man "came to his death from the effects of gunshot wounds inflicted by officers McKee and Kelly, and that such wounds were made while the officers were making an arrest and the deceased was resisting said officers with a fire-arm."[57]

Despite the unfortunate circumstances of having been compelled to take another life, McKee did have other interests which occasionally allowed him to briefly set aside his hectic and dangerous peace officer's duties. Sometime in 1875 he branched out into the cattle business, purchasing a large herd of fine bred cattle which he stocked on a ranch he either bought or leased some miles outside of Pioche in the vicinity of a property known as "Wilson's Ranch."[58] Soon the realities of frontier life in Lincoln County, Nevada, would predominate once again.

In early September, rumors of another large-scale Indian uprising west of Pioche had everyone in an uproar. A large posse of Pioche citizens, including William McKee, Sheriff Andy Fife, *Pioche Record* newspaper editor Pat Holland, W.C. Glissan, Johnny Quillen, Matt Halpin and some 20 or so others headed out on September 5 for the supposed scene of action. The entire episode proved to be highly overblown, a single renegade Indian having shot and killed a miner named Jim Toland. In their wanderings, W.C. Glissan managed to be wounded in a confrontation with some Snake Indians, the offending native being in turn shot and killed by Glissan's son.

Everyone else returned to Pioche unharmed. As McKee told the *Daily Record* on his return, "the Indians on the road and around Shoshone District are all afraid of the white folks, and willing to give up their arms. They have no hesitation in saying that they are peaceable, and that their intentions are such."[59]

Following the brief Indian scare all quickly returned to normal in Pioche. On Thursday, October 14, McKee suffered an unfortunate accident while transporting himself and a lady companion back to town in a buggy. Reaching a rough portion of the road, McKee fortunately had the lady exit the buggy while he drove it through the obstruction. All at once the buggy overturned pitching McKee into the dirt. Although somewhat bruised about the head and one knee McKee's worst injury was probably sustained by his pride. He managed to continue his journey with his lady friend, his new suit of clothes ripped and soiled.[60]

Who the lady was on this occasion is not of record. If she were young Melissa Rudford, the incident failed to deter her as she would marry McKee a little over two months later. William McKee, 42, wed 14-year-old Melissa Rudford on Thursday, December 23, 1875, at Wilson's Ranch.[61] Despite the considerable 26-year age difference between the couple, "Lizzie," a native of the state of Utah, seemed to be happy in her life with her new husband and made him a willing helpmate for the rest of his life.[62]

Now with his bachelorhood finally at an end, McKee continued his law enforcement activities with renewed vigor.[63] He also had a chance to renew his firefighting abilities when, as a member of Protection Hose Company No .2 of the Pioche Fire Department, he helped battle the major fire which broke out in Pioche's commercial district on May 3, 1876.[64] Twenty-one buildings were consumed and some $40,000 in losses incurred before the inferno could be brought under control.[65]

The fire of 1876 added to Pioche's decline. Production in the mines had been gradually declining since 1874. By late 1876 two major producing mining companies in the Pioche area, the Meadow Valley Mining Company and Raymond and Ely Mining Company virtually ceased operations.[66] Pioche would never again see the days of 1870–73.

Despite this decline in fortunes the town could still be a wild and woolly place. One example of this proved to be the early morning hours of Sunday, September 10. As McKee led a malefactor to the lockup the man suddenly grabbed the lawman around the neck and began choking him. Following a desperate struggle, McKee was finally forced to pull his revolver and buffalo the captive in the skull with the barrel before he could drag the now stunned man to the jailhouse.[67]

Feeling the desire to advance in his chosen profession, McKee decided to run for the Democratic Party nomination for sheriff in early October 1876. At the Lincoln County Democratic Convention on October 5 he doubled the vote count of his competitor, J.B. Van Hagan, 24 votes 12, to win the nomination.[68] McKee knew it would be no easy task to win the shrievalty. His Republican opponent for the office in the November elections proved to be George W. Birdsall, a veteran Nevada lawman who had established his reputation for toughness and exemplary law enforcement during the height of the Comstock Lode at Virginia City in the 1860s and had continued that standard during his late residence in Lincoln County, serving in various peace officer positions in and around Pioche.

Whatever trepidations McKee may have felt they were all laid to rest on election night when he defeated Birdsall, 346 votes to Birdsall's 308 to win the office of Lincoln County Sheriff.[69] Independent William Milliken polled a distant third with 92 votes.[70] Although McKee won the election his buggy driving tempered the celebration somewhat. For the second time in a little over a year he again rolled his buggy, this time while returning from Panaca with election results on November 12. Luckily neither he nor his passenger, J.B. Atchison, were hurt in the wreck.[71]

Shortly after taking office, McKee was able to benefit his former boss, ex–Sheriff Andy Fife, by arresting one William Dennis on Thursday, January 17, 1877.[72] Dennis was charged and eventually convicted of stealing over 300 sheep from Fife's ranch in Spring Valley.

What could likely be called the most important case of McKee's first year as Lincoln County Sheriff would be the so-called "Maopa Reservation Murders" case. On Saturday, June 30, four outlaws, led by notorious Pacific Coast criminal Isaac McManus, ventured onto the Maopa Indian Reservation located in far southeastern Lincoln County, along the Utah border. In a dispute with reservation agent B.F. Holland and his employee William Carter the outlaws shot the two men dead. Involved in the apprehension, investigation and prosecution of the gang for the last half of 1877 and into 1878, McKee would ultimately be disappointed when the quartet were eventually acquitted due to lack of evidence.[73]

Most in Lincoln County were pleased with McKee's performance as sheriff. On Saturday, September 14, 1878, the Democratic County Convention for the county again elected him as their nominee for sheriff in the upcoming elections, defeating his deputy Ephraim Turner 30 votes to 15.[74] The vote of the citizenry reaffirmed this confidence and McKee gained reelection as sheriff on November 5.[75]

McKee continued to serve successfully as Lincoln County Sheriff. In October 1879 he and Lizzie took a well-deserved month-long holiday in Salt Lake City. While in the Utah capital McKee almost landed in the calaboose in a rather humorous incident reported in the *Pioche Record* on his return:

> He [McKee] happened to be in a saloon when a fight was started, and imagining that he was at home attending to his duties, he commenced by throwing one individual out in the street. Just then he was caught by the shoulder by some person, and was on the point of letting him have one with his left fist, when on turning he discovered that it was a police man. This put him in mind that he was not on his own stomping ground, so he explained to the Dogberry that he was trying to quell the row, whereupon the police then released him, with an injunction to be careful.[76]

In a day and age when many people relied more on their horse then they did their fellow man, Sheriff McKee was dealt a heart rendering blow in late June 1880. On the 22nd the sheriff's favorite horse, "Baldy," died of what was called "lung fever." Despondent, McKee had Baldy buried on the outskirts of town.[77]

McKee proved he was still in fighting form a month later. On July 22 he chanced to encounter a man named Keyser in a Pioche saloon. Keyser had been heard making threats to release a friend of his who happened to be incarcerated in the County Jail, threatening to perform the act "over the dead body of the sheriff." McKee administered a sound beating to the man, warning him "to leave town within twenty-four hours" or "he would be compelled to bury him." Keyser failed to tarry and shaved a number of hours off the allotted 24 in shaking the dust of Pioche from his boots.[78]

Still feeling the vigor of youth despite his 46 years, in August 1880, McKee again declared himself a candidate for sheriff.[79] He received the Democratic nomination on 27th of September.[80] When the votes were counted in the election of November 2 the seasoned lawman found himself elected to his third term as Lincoln County Sheriff.[81]

After many years out west, following the election campaigning of 1880, William McKee suddenly felt the desire to make a visit to his old boyhood home in Mississippi. Having not seen his mother Nancy and siblings for a reported "26 years," he and Lizzie set out for Holly Springs in late November 1880.[82] Writing back to friends at Pioche on November 30, McKee declared that he "arrived home a few days previous and has been enjoying himself hunting 'possums and turkeys.'"[83] His decision to pay a visit back home at this time would prove most fortuitous. We can only hope his days of hunting and fishing, visiting long neglected loved ones and reliving his boyhood were thoroughly enjoyable and peace providing. As it stood, he would not see old loved ones or home scenes again and would be dead in a little over a year.

Returning to Pioche by mid–January 1881, Lincoln County Sheriff William McKee resumed his duties. All progressed routinely until the morning of Saturday, February 18, 1882. That morning, feeling under the weather, McKee sent for Dr.

Pioche, Nevada, 1885, looking much the same as it did at McKee's death in 1881 (courtesy Nevada Historical Society).

Matthews. Matthews diagnosed him as having a bad case of bronchitis and ordered him to bed. McKee would not be seen on the streets of Pioche again. Day by day his condition worsened. Finally, on the afternoon of Thursday, February 23, Matthews found the sheriff in a desperate state. According to the *Pioche Record*:

> The patient suffered great agony, and Thursday, the doctor seeing that he was strangling to death, as a last resort performed the operation commonly known as laryngotomy. The patient died about half an hour after the operation was performed.[84]

William McKee had done his part to enliven the history of the wild western mining camp known as Pioche. Suddenly, like the snuffing out of a candle, McKee's life and light was extinguished. With the taking over of Pioche pioneer and businessman O.P. Sherwood as sheriff to serve out McKee's unexpired term an era had come to an end.[85]

7

The Fighting Irish
Irish Tom Carberry

Charles Ridgley walked steadily toward "Irish Tom" Carberry who stood in the middle of the intersection of Main and Cedar streets stoically awaiting his adversary. Simultaneously, both men leveled their cocked pistols and squeezed the trigger. The two Colts boomed and spit forth hot lead. Both shots missed their mark. Carberry's bullet splintered the door jam of a saloon behind Ridgley while Ridgley's plowed into the door of a store at Carberry's back. Undaunted Ridgley continued to advance on Carberry. With equal imperturbability, Carberry alertly eyed the other man. Resting the barrel of his revolver on his right forearm Irish Tom took aim and watched Ridgley swiftly walk toward him. When within a few feet of each other the two gunmen fired again. Ridgley's slug narrowly missed Carberry. This time Carberry's aim proved true. The bullet slammed into Ridgley's chest. Pausing only momentarily, Ridgley continued advancing toward his opponent. He was fatally wounded, however, and within a matter of seconds fell dead in the middle of Main Street almost at Carberry's feet.[1]

This was the second man Irish Tom Carberry, coolheaded shootist extraordinaire, had dispatched at almost the same exact spot on Austin, Nevada's Main Street within a year. Though not a formal duel, the fight's informal, duel-like qualities and Carberry's calm resolve mark the encounter. Out of all the known gunfights of the Old West era this most closely resembles the classic Hollywood movie shoot-out. Far from fiction this encounter, and another almost identical gun battle occurring some 12 months before, are actual episodes in the life of Thomas A. "Irish Tom" Carberry, Nevada, gunman.

A native of Cork, Ireland, Carberry arrived on the east coast of America in 1848.[2] Eventually making his way to Sacramento, California, the young adventurer fell in with John Daly, a notorious rough and gunman, and his gang of followers. At length Sacramento lost its appeal and the "boys" looked for greener pastures. The burgeoning mining regions of Nevada provided this opportunity.

Owing its existence to the discovery of rich gold and silver quartz ledges in August 1860 near the California town of Monoville, Aurora was platted out soon after on Gregory Flats.[3] Both California and Nevada claimed the ruckus mining camp until September 1863 when an official border survey placed it some 3 miles inside Esmeralda County, Nevada.[4] By the summer of 1863, Aurora, named for the Greek

Austin, Nevada, 1867, the year of the Carberry-Vance shoot-out (courtesy Digital Photo Collection, Image #UNRS-P1986-12-07, Special Collections and University Archives Department, University of Nevada, Reno Libraries).

god of dawn, had a floating population in the town proper and surrounding area of roughly 10,000 people. The town boasted about 20 stores, a dozen hotels, two local newspapers and a multitude of other businesses. At least 16 quartz mills operated in the surrounding mining area where hundreds of mining claims dotted the mineral rich hills.[5]

Aside from mining, by far Aurora's most conspicuous businesses proved to be the houses of pleasure. That summer of 1863, perhaps the city's most active, there were some 21 saloons, with almost as many gambling joints, dance halls and brothels thrown into the mix. Crime became epidemic. Rowdyism, gunfights and murder were far more common than most of the respectable populace could endure.[6] This state of affairs prompted one Nevada governor to label Aurora "the wickedest town of its size in America."[7] This was exactly the condition that appealed to the Sacramento gang of John Daly, "Irish Tom" Carberry, et al.

Like Carberry, a fellow Irishman, John Daly was already one of the most feared gunmen on the west coast when he and his group moved into Aurora early in 1863. Daly already had four or five deaths to his credit as the result of various shooting scrapes. He would add at least two more to his total during his Aurora career. His cohorts, such as Three-Fingered Jack McDowell, James Sears, William Buckley, Sam Vance, James Masterson and Carberry were no less feared. Although evidence is lacking one source credits Carberry himself for having "been engaged in many shooting scrapes about Aurora and other new mining localities."[8]

The so-called "Daly Gang" quickly came into prominence in Aurora when Daly and his boys hired their guns to the Pond and the Real Del Monte mining companies in their claim disputes on Last Chance Hill.[9] Eventually, through subterfuge,

Daly managed to get one of his own men elected to the office of city marshal. Daly picked for himself the position of deputy city marshal.[10] As a result the gang soon were engaged in graft and kickbacks.

Soon, John Daly began to show his pistol prowess in Aurora. On October 24, 1863, he killed George Lloyd, a former gang member, in a gunfight in the Del Monte Exchange Saloon.[11] Less than two months later, December 9, Daly encountered an enemy named Joe McGee in Carson City. McGee had killed two of Daly's associates in separate shooting scrapes. On this occasion Daly shot McGee dead.[12]

With the election of a new, honest city marshal in January 1864 things began to turn for the Daly gang in Aurora. The incident, which for all intents and purposes precipitated the end of the gang, actually took place back in April 1863. This proved to be the shooting death of gang member James Sears at the hands of an employee of William Johnson following the theft of a horse by Sears.[13] The gang waited nearly ten months but finally managed to corner Johnson on the early morning hours of February 2, 1864. Employing pistols and bowie knives, Daly, McDowell, Buckley and Masterson left Johnson dead in the street in retaliation for Sears' death.[14]

Further excitement followed at the Coroner's Inquest held over William Johnson later that day. While attempting to make his way through the crowd that had gathered at the coroner's office gang member Sam Vance fell into an argument with a citizen named W.F. Watkins. Forthwith, Watkins pulled a revolver and shot Vance in the groin.[15] The intervention of City Marshal Dan Pine probably prevented a riot from breaking out.

These incidents had pushed the limit of what most people in Aurora were willing to endure. Late on the afternoon of the day of the inquest hundreds of citizens met in Armory Hall and formed a vigilance committee. Quickly Daly, McDowell, Buckley, Masterson, Irish Tom Carberry, Sam Vance and various others of Daly's band were rounded up and placed in custody.[16]

The vigilantes bided their time until after the Coroner's Jury had announced their verdict. Then, on February 8, a large squad of vigilantes stormed the Aurora jail. Taking charge of Daly, McDowell, Buckley and Masterson, the mob summarily hung the quartet of murderers from hastily built gallows on Silver Street.[17]

Irish Tom Carberry manifested more luck than his four confederates. Shortly after the hanging he and most of the remaining gang were banished from Aurora. All except Sam Vance, whom the vigilantes allowed to remain in jail to face the official court proceedings for being an accessory after the fact in the killing of Johnson. An opportunity for Vance to make his escape presented itself the evening of March 25 when his three fellow prisoners smashed their way out of the Aurora lockup. Vance, however, perhaps still being bothered by his bullet wound or possibly deciding he was better off being protected by the regularly constituted authorities than falling into the hands of the vigilantes, choose not to avail himself of the opportunity. As the local newspaper put it, "Vance walked leisurely down to Nick Steiner's, took a drink, then went to the courthouse and reported promptly to Sheriff Francis."[18]

Unlike most of his past and future decisions, on this occasion, Vance made a wise choice. Following his trial which commenced on March 28 a jury found the defendant not guilty.[19] Quickly Vance boarded the next stage for Virginia City expressing dire threats against his enemies in Aurora, most notably the editor of the local *Esmeralda Daily Union* newspaper.[20] The *Union* editor, a rather feisty individual named Edwin A. Sherman, warned Vance in the next issue, "Now, most valiant sir, allow us to advise you to 'get cooled down a little' yourself, and should you ever return to Aurora, 'keep cool.' Whenever any person so far loses all self-respect as to get drunk, proclaim himself 'Chief,' defy the officers and insult our citizens he must expect to get the 'benefit' of a notice in the *Union*."[21]

Ultimately Sam Vance never did return to Aurora. In the *Esmeralda Union* of August 10, 1864, Sherman editorialized, "This dangerous class of men ('the Rough'), who for three years have been the terror of this community, have mostly disappeared from our midst." Sherman may have spoken too soon.

Later that summer a few of the old Daly gang did return to Aurora. The most notable of these proved to be Irish Tom Carberry and a large scrapper and political shoulder striker named Bill Pendergast.

At the county elections of September 7, both Carberry and Pendergast worked hard for the election of the People's (Democratic) Party over the Union (Republican) Party. The Union Party managed to squeeze out a narrow majority. Of course, editor Edwin Sherman strongly supported the Union faction stating, "The 'People's Party' mixed up a ticket which was supported by every ruffian and Jeff Davis brawler in town."[22] Sherman, in his unfettered way, went on to single out "Bill Pendergast and Irish Tom—two notorious characters who were run away from Aurora last winter by the Vigilance Committee"[23] as being prominent in the previously mentioned "brawler" class. Carberry and Pendergast did not take kindly to the newspaperman's opinions of them.

On the evening of September 9, a group of roughs led by Carberry and Pendergast confronted Sherman at the corner of Pine and Antelope streets.

"Are you the author of that article?" Pendergast bellowed at Sherman as Carberry and the others stood back, hands on the butts of their pistols.

"Yes, I am," Sherman answered unflinchingly.

With that Pendergast shot out his fist catching Sherman full in the face and bloodying his nose. Reeling, Sherman managed to swing back with a newspaper file stick he had been carrying, breaking the instrument over Pendergast's skull. Before the fight could go any further bystanders managed to pull the pair apart and no further damage resulted.[24]

This proved to be one of the last incidents involving Tom Carberry in Aurora. Soon he would leave town for good. In October 1864 Bill Pendergast would be arrested for causing a disturbance on the streets[25] but soon he too would leave for parts unknown.

Carberry's movements for the next three years are largely unknown. In mid–1867 he made his appearance about 140 miles northeast of Aurora at the new silver mining camp of Austin, Lander County. Situated at an isolated point in the Reese River mining district of central Nevada, Austin was in the midst of a silver boom at the time of Carberry's arrival. Founded in 1863, the town was considered a city with all the conveniences of a major eastern metropolis by 1867. The major settlement in the mineral rich Reese River Valley, Austin was looked on as the base camp of at least 60 mining districts in the Toiyabe Range area of central Nevada.[26]

In Austin, Carberry was reunited with his old friend and former fellow Daly gang member at Aurora, Samuel B. Vance. In the intervening three years since his Aurora days Vance made stops in Virginia City and San Francisco before traveling north to the various Montana mining camps. Arriving in Austin about the same time as Carberry, Vance was willing to renew his friendship with Irish Tom while at the same time engendering a slight rivalry with Carberry for the title of chief gunman in Austin.

While carousing in the various bars and gambling for a living both Carberry and Vance renewed their reputations as dangerous men. The two seemed friendly enough until the hot summer evening of Friday, August 2, 1867. Perhaps engendered by the overabundant use of alcohol, the encounter, the first of two very similar deadly episodes for Carberry, would demonstrate his fatal resolve in a classic gun battle.

Feeling the need to engage in exuberant celebrations a half hour before midnight on this evening, Vance entered the Bank Exchange Saloon on Main Street. He cajoled a number of patrons, including Tom Carberry, to come to the bar and "take a drink." Knowing the reputation of the man all accepted the invitation except Carberry.

"I've had enough," Irish Tom declined and walked toward the side exit stepping out onto the Cedar Street sidewalk.

Vance followed him and again demanded he have a drink with him. For a second time Carberry refused the proffered drink.

Pulling a derringer from his coat pocket Vance hollered to Carberry from the doorway of the saloon, "If you don't drink, I'll take a shot at you."

Turning on his heel and facing Vance, Carberry retorted rather contemptuously, "How big a shot will you take?"

Vance immediately raised the derringer and fired at Carberry just as Carberry jerked out his revolver. Vance's slug whistled wide of his intended victim while, almost instantaneously, Carberry leveled his weapon and squeezed off a shot at Vance. The bullet buried itself in the side of the door near Vance.

At this juncture Police Officer Marshal, who happened to be in the saloon at the time, rushed Vance and threw his arms around him in an attempt to pull him out into the street and end the shooting. In the struggle Vance fell on one knee. Standing his ground and taking deliberate aim Carberry fired again. The slug struck Vance in the lower abdomen. The mortally wounded fighter collapsed to the floor while Austin City Marshal W.H. Knerr rushed up and placed Carberry under arrest.[27]

Carberry waited calmly in the Austin jail until the condition of Vance could be judged. As expected, the wounded rough breathed his last a little over 24 hours after being shot. As a result, officials ordered Carberry to appear before Justice Harmon for a preliminary hearing in the death of Vance the following day, August 4.

The day following the gun battle the editor of the local *Reese River Reveille* felt moved to complain:

> Disorder and crime are on the increase, and there is danger that our town will lose its good name, become as notorious for its evildoers and evil deeds as Aurora, Virginia, Visalia, or the fast towns of Idaho and Montana, and at last disgraced forever by the formation of a vigilance committee.[28]

At the preliminary hearing Justice Harmon decided to release Carberry on the grounds of justifiable homicide following the eyewitness accounts of R.M. Waterhouse, James Leffingwell, City Marshall Knerr and Policeman Marshall.[29]

Despite his release for the Vance shooting Carberry had not quite stepped out of hot water. The very next morning Marshall again brought him before Justice Harmon on a charge of carrying a concealed weapon. On this minor charge Harmon declared the defendant guilty and imposed a fine of $25. This Carberry quickly paid and once again walked the streets of Austin.

Again, he could not seem to stay out of trouble. Although the details are sketchy, lawmen once more arrested Carberry later that same month following some sort of fracas in Austin. Charged with an assault with intent to commit murder the suddenly cantankerous gunman came before Harmon for the third time in less than a month on August 29. As history repeated itself and the examination concluded Harmon dismissed this particular charge against Carberry. This time, however, he ordered the defendant bound over to the next sitting of the District Court on a charge of drawing and exhibiting a deadly weapon. Bail in the sum of $500 was imposed.[30] Whether Irish Tom was able to pay the required amount is not a matter of record.

Arraigned on September 18,[31] Carberry pled not guilty to the charge.[32] Although the court set his trial for September 25, on that day Carberry signed his name to a proposed continuance to enable him time to locate a key witness.[33] Only two days later the trial took place in the Austin County Courthouse. Carberry's luck continued to hold and the jury quickly returned with a verdict of not guilty.[34]

The corner of Main and Cedar streets was quickly gaining a reputation as one of the wildest spots in the unrestrained city of Austin. The local newspaper, the *Reese River Reveille*, grumbled that the "culpable shooting" that went on there was "wanton, criminal mischief" perpetrated by those who "habitually carry weapons concealed in defiance of the law" and that they were used "at random and with the indifference of monkeys."[35]

Whether one of these "monkeys" referred to by the *Reveille* was Irish Tom Carberry couldn't be proven by the record. By any official reports Carberry lived a relatively quiet existence through most of 1868 in Austin's First Ward.[36]

The cause of Carberry's return to the gunfighter mode proved to be the arrival in town of a sport and gunman named Charles Ridgely. Ridgely had already made a name for himself in California and the various mining camps of Idaho and Montana before arriving in Nevada. A cohort of Henry Plummer and other notorious roughs up north, Ridgely himself had killed two or three men in assorted shooting scrapes.[37]

The fact that Ridgely had been a good friend of Sam Vance made him a mortal enemy of Tom Carberry. On several occasions Ridgely had reportedly expressed his desire to several individuals to "get" the killer of Vance.[38]

In July 1868 Ridgley left Austin temporarily to take in the doings of the mining excitement at White Pine in eastern Nevada. In early September, after a two-month absence, he returned to Austin. The stage was now set for Carberry's second deadly encounter on Austin's Main Street.

The two rivals chanced to meet each other on the street late Friday night. Hot words passed between them, but the pair parted before violence could erupt. The next morning, September 5, they came together again on Main Street. Spotting a policeman passing by, Carberry approached him and demanded that he arrest Ridgely for making threats against his life. The officer deferred in Carberry's request. However, he did feel justified in taking Ridgely aside and searching him for concealed weapons. Finding nothing he advised the two to go their separate ways.

Sometime later, Carberry spied Ridgely on the sidewalk. Pulling and cocking his pistol, Irish Tom rushed up to his opponent.

"I'm ready to fight you," Carberry growled. "You abused me last night but I'm ready for you now."

Ridgley threw open his coat. "I'm unarmed," he said.

"Go heel yourself," Carberry answered.

Turning, Ridgley hastily strode over to the International Hotel where he had checked his revolver. Arming himself he quickly returned to the street to encounter a waiting Tom Carberry at the corner of Cedar and Main. An impromptu duel quickly erupted. Following the classic shoot-out, Charles Ridgley lay dead in the dusty street.[39]

Shortly after the fight, City Marshal Knerr arrested Carberry and escorted him to a waiting jail cell.

In its first issue subsequent to the gun battle, the local *Reveille* headlined, "Another Murder" and labeled Carberry, "alias Irish Tom, an individual who, during his stay in Austin, has gained for himself a vile and infamous notoriety." The editor, Oscar L.C. Fairchild, went on to fume:

> This bloody affair, occurring, as it did, in the most populous portion of the town, was witnessed by a large number of the people, who had no time to get out of the way, and were terribly frightened. The marvel is that some innocent passerby was not shot, and we think it about high time that such customers as Carberry, should be made to select some other place besides the corner of Main and Cedar streets wherein to carry on their pistol practice. This makes the second man that this fellow bags near that corner within a year.[40]

Fairchild, like the majority of Austin citizens, was gradually losing patience with the so-called "shooters" and "roughs."

According to the Coroner's Inquest held over the body of Ridgley later on the day of his death, Ridgley's actual name was "James Archie." He was "aged about thirty (30) years" and that his demise was "from a pistol shot discharged from the hands of Thomas Carberry alias Irish Tom."[41]

On the afternoon of the 8th the Lander County grand jury ordered Carberry held to appear before the District Court on an indictment of murder.[42] The next day the court returned a true bill of murder in the first degree against the prisoner.[43]

Once again, Fairchild continued his personal campaign against those who would commit murder in Austin. In the *Reveille* of September 10, he editorialized:

> There are now confined in this county jail no less than three persons on the charge of murder in the first degree, one of whom has been tried, convicted, and sentenced to die.[44] There had scarcely been a term of our District Court in which some capitol offense, generally murder, has not been tried. It is notorious that while venial offenses are of comparatively rare occurrence, those of the capital class are more frequent than in any other county in the state ... the petty thief and the wretched, drunken brawler, are condemned; while the great criminal—the assassins and murderers—are invested with a sort of heroism and excite the lively sympathies of a

considerable part of the people. Human life—the most inestimable of gifts—is held too cheaply.

Fairchild's rant would not have much, if any, effect in the case of Carberry.

On September 11, Carberry was arraigned before the District Court. Through his counsel he entered a plea of not guilty. The court set his trial date for Wednesday the 16th.[45] On that date the accused gunman's attorney presented an affidavit for a continuance in order to locate witnesses. Granting the application, the court remanded Carberry to jail to await the sitting of the District Court in December.[46]

In the meantime, an occurrence at the County Jail in early November served to create a bit of a diversion and take Carberry's mind, for a brief moment, off of his legal difficulties. In the cell next to Irish Tom resided three petty criminals named McCluer, Merritt and Cassanove. On the morning of November 5, County Jailer Bell discovered an attempt by these prisoners to tunnel their way out of their undesirable residence. The trio had made much headway when stymied by the alert jailer. In his report of the incident Bell hastened to add that he "exonerates Carberry from any participation in the attempt to break jail."[47] Carberry, wisely as it would turn out, had more faith in the judicial system's ability, in his mind, to recognize a wronged man.

At the sitting of the District Court on December 14, Carberry's lawyers again filed for continuance on the grounds of being unable to locate key witnesses. For the second time court officials postponed the accused man's trial, this time to the March 1869 term.[48]

The process of selecting jurors for Carberry's trial finally got under way on March 8.[49] With shades of today's complicated jury selection process officials were forced to issue two venires of 50 names before a group of 12 jurymen could be selected. Peremptory challenges by both Lander County District Attorney Henry Mayenbaum as well as Carberry's defense attorneys, David Cooper and George S. Hupp, managed to slim the choices considerably. Another problem that presented itself proved to be the fact that many of the men listed as potential jurors had vacated to the ongoing White Pine mining rush and could no longer be located.[50]

Finally, on March 12, a jury of 12 Lander County citizens was impaneled to decide the fate of Tom Carberry for the taking of Charles Ridgely's life. The panel, composed of Joseph Moss, D. McCracken, G.W. Rutherford, John Ritter, M. McKimmins, D.F. McMin, S.B. Moss, I. Baron, Bart O'Dair, Andrew Nicholson, W.H. Carlyle and A. Steinbach[51] would be put to little inconvenience in the proceedings.

The afternoon of the day of jury selection Carberry's trial went forward. By 3 o'clock both the prosecution and defense had presented their cases for and against the accused's guilt or innocence. Apparently, Cooper and Hupp argued a strong case on their client's behalf. After deliberating about five hours the jury returned with a verdict of not guilty.[52] Irish Tom had once again beaten the rap.

Although Carberry once again enjoyed his freedom there were still those in Austin who held the gunman in contempt. The town had lost its luster for the trouble prone Irishman. A little over two weeks following his acquittal he decided to leave town for better prospects. On March 30 the *Reese River Reveille* in its list of passengers departing Austin via the White Pine Stage enumerates one Thomas A. Carberry as being one of those to migrate east to the new Eldorado in White Pine County.[53]

7. *The Fighting Irish*   91

Aurora, Nevada, 1870, a few months after Carberry's death (courtesy Digital Photo Collection, Image #UNRS-P-2008-01-01, Special Collections and University Archives Department, University of Nevada, Reno Libraries).

The exodus to the camps of White Pine County, about 120 miles east of Austin near the Nevada/Utah boundary, had picked up steam early in 1869.[54] The slump this prompted in Austin probably did not bother Carberry in the least. He located himself in the burgeoning mining camp of Hamilton situated in the southwest portion of the county at the foot of the White Pine Mountains.

In Hamilton, Carberry decided to take a totally unique turn in his life. In mid–June 1869, the Hamilton Board of Trustees hired the gunman as a special policeman on the Hamilton force.[55] The Irishman's courage and proficiency with firearms could not be questioned. Though some may have been surprised at this turn of events others looked on in approval including the editor of the *White Pine Evening Telegram* in nearby Shermantown:

> Appointment—Thos. A Carbery [sic] has been appointed by the Board of Trustees as special policeman. This is an excellent appointment, as Tom is just the man to fill such a position.[56]

By all accounts Carberry made a very efficient officer. His name is often mentioned in the "Recorder's Court" column of the local Hamilton newspaper as making numerous arrests of various lawbreakers throughout that summer.[57] Unfortunately, the fighting Irishman was not destined to enjoy this measure of civic respectability for long.

Carberry's health suddenly began to fail in late summer 1869. The exact nature of his health problems is unknown. It is likely that years of hard living and an intemperate lifestyle had finally taken their toll. He eventually took to his sick bed and died with his boots off in Hamilton on Sunday, September 26, 1869.[58]

The evident respect Thomas Carberry had earned in his brief stay in Hamilton is reflected in the comments of the local *Inland Empire* which stated following his death:

Since his advent in White Pine, or a greater part of the time at least, he had acted as a special officer in this city, and according to all accounts had studiously avoided getting into trouble, of whatever character, and on all occasions. Indeed, those who knew him most intimately say that he had determined never again to participate in difficulties where it was at all possible to avoid them. All we have to say of him is, that if he had faults let them be buried with him. His funeral took place yesterday from Firemen's Hall, and was largely attended. Headed by a band of music, the Police and Fire Departments joined in the procession in full force, added to which was a large number of citizens on foot and in carriages.[59]

Back in Austin the local *Reveille* made note of their former infamous resident's passing as follows:

Death of A Notorious Character—The *Inland Empire* of the 28th instant says that Thomas A. Carberry, familiarly known as "Irish Tom," died at Hamilton on Sunday last after a protracted sickness. Carberry was one of the notorious characters of this coast; one of a numerous class of young men ambitious of a bad eminence. Common report associated his name with deeds of violence and bloodshed. He killed two men in this city. The first instance was that of Samuel B. Vance, who attacked Carberry with a pistol shot; the second was that of Charles Ridgely, and was an informal duel fought in the main street of this city. Carberry was tried and acquitted in both cases. In spite of his lawless life and bloody deeds, Carberry had many friends in this city and elsewhere, who will learn of his death with regret. We knew him personally, and gave him credit for many manly traits. He illustrated the adage, that "the devil is not as black as he is painted." Carberry was a native of Cork, Ireland, and came to the United States in 1848.[60]

Like those more famous personages subsequent to him, Jesse James and Billy the Kid, some averred that Irish Tom did not die when history claims. One old timer even deposed that Carberry actually worked for him at his quartz mill between Bodie, California, and Aurora, Nevada, in 1886.[61] Most assuredly this is simply another apocryphal tale. It cannot be doubted that Irish Tom Carberry died that September day in Hamilton, Nevada. The surprising part is that he died peacefully in bed rather than in a shoot-out with guns blazing.

8

Two Dangerous Men
Jack White and Bob Mellon

Despite its location just over the line in Nevada County, California, the railroad town of Truckee could easily be termed a mere extension of the Nevada mining frontier. Located only about ten miles from the Nevada border near famous Lake Tahoe, Truckee was often a destination point for Nevada travelers. With its readily accessible ties to Reno, Nevada, via the Central Pacific Railroad (C.P.R.R.), Nevadans made the energetic railroad terminus a frequent holiday stop for a busy, entertaining weekend or longer. For those of more earthy tastes Truckee's East Main Street, or "Jibboom Street" as it came to be called, was a must visit. The section's numerous saloons, gambling joints and houses of ill fame could accommodate any number of those brought by the busy C.P.R.R.

Many Nevada sporting men made their excursions to Jibboom Street when things back home in the Silver State got too hot or they simply wished to try their hand at cashing in on the barrels of greenbacks being made in the town's tenderloin. Two of those Nevada sin chasers who would eventually follow the rails to Truckee to test their luck were a pair of dangerous gunmen and fighters named Jack White and Bob Mellon. Whether they knew each other is a moot point although it is likely they were acquainted. Be that as it may, what is known for sure is that both of these Nevada imports would make separate sensations in Truckee that would never be forgotten by the town's residents for decades to come.

Reportedly, Jack White was a native of Illinois, born there in about 1845.[1] One contemporary source described him as "a tall, slender, wiry and 'wild' young man, very dark complexion, and keen, black eyes."[2] Another would genuflect, "He was one of the finest specimens of physical manhood in the country, and, although unusually quiet and diffident, was a man of great personal courage and coolness in danger."[3]

White's first recorded action of note in Nevada came in early November 1870 at the mining boom town of Pioche. At this time, he proved to be one of the army of gunmen hired by Tom and Frank Newland to protect the Newland's dubious interests in the Washington and Creole mine. Barricading their fighters inside the mine workings, the Newland's managed to hold the ground until the afternoon of Wednesday, November 9. At this juncture the rightful owners of the property, the powerful Raymond and Ely Mining Company sent their men, led by renowned shootist Morgan Courtney, into action. Following a lively skirmish in which some 60 shots were fired,

Courtney and company managed to regain the ground for their employers, routing the Newland force.[4]

Although only one man was killed in the short battle, Newland fighter W.G. Snell, many others came away with various injuries. Included in this group was Jack White who managed to escape the field of battle with a painful, though not serious, bullet wound said to have been delivered by another noted gunman representing Raymond and Ely on this day, William "Bill" Bethards.[5] The nature of White's wound is unknown, however, it failed to deter him for long and, following a quick recovery, the young rough was soon mobile once more, despite published stories of his death in contemporary Nevada newspapers.[6]

White dispelled the greatly exaggerated rumors of his death by traveling extensively throughout the Nevada mining camps through 1871 and into 1872. He eventually ended up in Eureka, Nevada, by early 1872.[7] Here he quickly slipped into the sporting milieu of the burgeoning mining town's gambling fraternity which, according to the *Eureka Daily Sentinel*, was a boon to the town's economy:

> Gambling License—the resident sports of Eureka pay about $1500 per month gambling license. There are also about fifty saloons in Eureka which contribute to the State and County funds.[8]

Like most mining communities of the frontier, Eureka at the time contained a certain portion of its population that could be termed "undesirable." The *Sentinel* editorialized after one particularly violent night in February 1872: "we must confess that men so dangerous as several seemed to be whom we saw, should be taken care of, as the unpleasant practice of brandishing pistols and knives in close proximity to innocent men's heads is not agreeable, to say the least."[9]

Jack White found his reality in such conditions as these. He was known to hang out with a desperate crowd and his companions would be those from the "other side of the tracks." If a nefarious act were perpetrated, White often found himself a suspect. Such proved to be the case when, on the evening of Friday, May 3, 1872, the Palisade and Eureka stage was halted and robbed by two men near Mineral Hill, north of Eureka in Elko County. Though the robbers realized little of monetary value in the crime a concerted effort was brought forth to apprehend the thieves.[10]

Based on certain evidence obtained by authorities lawmen consequently arrested White and George Hodge about a week after the hold up, at Shell Creek, some 80 miles east of Eureka, near Ely.[11] On May 12 the stage containing White and Hodge, under the guidance of Elko County Deputy Sheriff Wood, made a stop in Eureka en route to Elko where the prisoners were to be lodged in the County Jail. In a brief interview with the *Eureka Sentinel*, White "appeared to be cheerful, and told us that he and his companion would have no trouble establishing an alibi, as they were stopping at a ranch 30 miles from the scene of the robbery the night on which it occurred."[12]

Jack White knew whereof he spoke. Meeting in late May, the Elko County Grand Jury decided to ignore the charges against White and Hodge due to lack of evidence.[13] Although the local Elko newspaper would comment, "there is no doubt but that the wrong men were taken," it gained report that White's "most intimate friends" were "certain that he committed the robbery with which he was charged."[14] Nonetheless, White left the Elko jail a free citizen once more.

Following his short stint in the Elko hoosegow, White returned to Eureka. As a response to not only his presence, but those of likeminded proclivities moving in the same circles as White, in late June a Eureka vigilance committee, which had been dormant for about a year, reorganized.[15] Subsequent activities of the saloon crowd, including Jack White, would lead one to the conclusion that the organization of a vigilante group may have been justified.

Thursday, July 4, Eureka, as with most towns and cities in the United States, saw much celebrating in honor of America's independence. That evening, White and "Big Alex" Fleming commenced their own celebrations in Fleming's saloon. At length, the pair began to josh an old man known only as "Texas" who was often the butt of the saloon crowds' jokes.

Deciding he had had enough of the two men's ribbing, Texas suddenly pulled out a long-bladed knife and made a lunge at Fleming. Fleming quickly stepped aside. Jack White, who had been standing beside Fleming, was not so lucky. Texas's knife blade entered White's right side, skewering him almost completely through and through before he withdrew it.

Grasping his side, White walked steadily to the bar which he leaned on for support.

"Did the knife strike you," a patron at the bar asked him.

"Yes, it went clear through me," White responded. "And damned if I don't believe he gave it a turn before he pulled it out!"[16]

While Texas was trundled off to jail, White went in search of medical assistance. He spent a number of weeks convalescing from his wound before eventually making a full recovery. At this point he decided to go in search of greener pastures. A vigilante warning may have hastened his decision.

About 245 miles west of Eureka, just over the border in California, sat the bustling railroad town of Truckee. Named after Paiute Indian chief Truckee, who in turn had been named by the whites after his favorite saying, the Paiute word "tro-kay" or "everything's all right," the town of Truckee often attracted Nevada sports looking for a holiday excursion and new surroundings.[17] Located as a major station along the Central Pacific Railroad in 1863, the town soon boasted a number of lumber mills which operated day and night. By 1872 Truckee, located near beautiful Lake Tahoe, supported a population of some 3000 people.[18] Soon one more would be added to the mix.

By about the fall of 1872, now fully recovered from his knife wound suffered in celebration of his country's birthday, Jack White relocated to Virginia City. He first took a job as a laborer, helping to construct the illustrious Sutro Tunnel, which would eventually help drain the Comstock Lode and allow for deeper access to the mineral wealth. This job he held for only two or three months before moving on once more.[19]

By at least the summer of 1873, White appeared in Truckee, California. He made his main habitué in the saloons, gambling dens and brothels located on so-called "Jibboom Street," or East Main Street in the heart of Truckee's Red-Light District. Many of Jibboom streets sin establishments had been started by Virginia City, Nevada, sporting men at the height of the town's founding and the area attracted many a Nevada rough and gambling man.

In the midst of his gambling and saloon cavorting White quickly became enamored with Jennie Williams, one of Truckee's ladies of the evening. Williams operated out of a cabin on Jibboom Street owned by Andy Fugate, a local businessman and tough customer. Fugate owned a number of dwellings in the heart of the tenderloin which he was in the habit of renting out to Truckee's soiled doves on a monthly basis.[20] He and White were destined to clash in a confrontation that would be remembered in Truckee for years to come.

One night early in September 1873, Jack White, in attempting to visit his lover, discovered the door to her cabin locked. With Jennie Williams inside dealing with a customer, White, infuriated, kicked the door in and burst in on the couple, disrupting the culmination of the business transaction. The fact that White had been drinking most of the evening no doubt played a large part in his actions on this occasion.

Andy Fugate took a rather dim view of the proceedings, most notably due to the fact of his property, the cabin door, being damaged. Later that night, Fugate tracked White down and upbraided him severely, warning him to keep clear of his property and barring him from William's cabin. White did not take the chastisement gracefully.

A few days later, on the afternoon of Friday, September 5, White once again defiantly appeared on William's porch. Fugate, who happened to be nearby, spotted him and rushing up, grappled with the man, pushed him off the porch and hollered at him to "get away."

Following an angry exchange of words Fugate, exasperated, growled at White, "Are you heeled?"

Not giving an inch, White defiantly returned Fugate's glare. "No," he growled back.

Fugate swore an oath. "You'd better arm yourself. I'll meet you this evening on the street and settle this difficulty," he shouted back at White.

At this point the two men parted company, neither letting his anger abate in the least.

At around 9 o'clock that night Fugate and a friend, Dave Dodge, were walking down Front Street. As they reached the front of Burkhalter's store a voice behind them called out, "Fugate! I want to see you on business!" Jack White yelled.

Fugate spun around. "Are you heeled?" he came back.

"Yes, are you?" White retorted.

"Yes. Sail in!" Fugate barked.

Both men instantly drew revolvers and began shooting. According to witnesses, Fugate backed to the door of Burkhalter's Store and, his back against the iron door, fired three shots before White answered with one or two of his own. Hit by at least one shot, White staggered off the sidewalk and tumbled into the street, immediately raising himself to one knee.

At this point, Fugate made the mistake of believing his antagonist to be totally incapacitated by his injuries. Jumping ahead, Fugate rushed up to White and, placing the muzzle of his pistol near White's body, fired three more shots into the man.

Incredibly, Jack White was not yet out of the fight. Aiming his revolver at his attacker, who now stood directly in front of him, White jerked off three more shots before falling over onto his side, continually squeezing the trigger of his now empty revolver in an attempt to continue firing.

Shot in the chest, abdomen and groin, Fugate likewise attempted to fire his own now empty revolver by clicking the hammer a few times before falling back onto the sidewalk gasping, "Boys, I'm gone."

Bystanders quickly carried Jack White to Shinn's Pharmacy while others trundled Andy Fugate off to the office of Dr. Curless. Fugate died within minutes. Jack White managed to hang on until seven the following morning before he expired without saying a word to anyone.[21]

The next day a Coroner's Inquest held before Judge Keiser ruled that "the two men had shot each other" and closed the case. Some interesting information came to light when some of the witnesses to the gunfight, including Dave Dodge and Nelson Martin, an employee of Burkhalter's, claimed that a third men had been involved in the desperate battle. Termed a "large man with heavy black whiskers," witnesses reported seeing him fire from a nearby alley and seeing White slump and fall over after his shots.[22] Apparently the inquest decided to ignore this testimony and who the mysterious man was or his motive in the affair remains unknown. Some, however, felt he was a member of Truckee's vigilante committee, the "601." They may have been closer to the truth than realized.

Indeed, Truckee fell into an uproar as a result of the Jack White–Andy Fugate shoot-out which received extensive newspaper coverage throughout Nevada, California and various other major dailies across the United States. As the *Reese River Reveille* of Austin, Nevada, so aptly described the state of affairs in Truckee:

> Lively—Since the late desperate shooting affray at Truckee that town has been indulging in lively times. The hoodlums threaten to burn the town; the *Republican* threatens lynch law and vigilance committees; and even the Chinamen have got the fever, 12 of them having been wounded in a riot amongst themselves on Saturday last.[23]

The *Reveille's* comment "the *Republican* threatens lynch law and vigilance committees" was a hint to a major factor in Truckee's community affairs. Dave Frink, the editor of the *Truckee Republican,* continually filled his newspaper with editorials railing against the criminal element in town and advocating the support of the vigilante presence. One week after the death of White and Fugate another man killed his employer in a wage dispute. Pleading self-defense, the killer was released after a brief hearing.[24] The citizens of Truckee were loath to abide by any more seeming laxity on the part of law enforcement. Many were beginning to come around to the stance that the "bad men," and "bad women" for that matter, needed to be hit and hit hard. The 601 was on the cusp of its popularity.

A little over one year later the vigilantes decided to act. They centered their attention on a group of Jibboom Street ruffians and ne'er-do-wells including Seth McCain, George Brown, Jack Potter, Harry Howard and, like Jack White, another former Nevada fighter named Bob Mellon.[25] It proved to be an affair that would rock Truckee to its very foundations, with the Nevada import, Bob Mellon, in the very eye of the storm.

Robert Mellon's origins and antecedents have, at this point, been lost to history.

He first met the gaze of investigators in May 1864 on the Comstock Lode. That month he appeared on the Storey County District Court criminal calendar charged with an "assault with a deadly weapon with intent to inflict bodily injury."[26] Unfortunately, the causative factor behind this charge as well as the eventual outcome have likewise escaped detection. The least we can say from this is that apparently Mellon was a malefactor early on in his career. He would follow this pattern for at least another ten years.

By 1871, Mellon had migrated to north-central Utah and the copper mining camp of Ophir, about 35 miles southwest of Salt Lake City. Ophir was at the height of its fame as a humming mining town and Mellon most likely tried his hand at winning miners' wages in the local gambling dens.

Mellon's gambling pursuits were interrupted on the morning of Wednesday, October 25, 1871. At about 11:30 that morning he encountered Joseph Flack on an Ophir Street. The pair had been drinking together the night before with no hint of a disagreement between them. Now Mellon demanded to see Flack's belt knife, Flack declined and the pair fell into a heated argument.

All at once Mellon pulled a Colt revolver, cocked the hammer and pointed it at Flack. A bystander reached over and knocked the barrel down toward the ground. Mellon raised the gun once more, at which point it fired. The slug struck Flack in the right chest just below the collarbone. Stunned, the man fell to the sidewalk mortally wounded.[27]

Arrested on a charge of murder, Bob Mellon's case came up in December. At this hearing the gunman managed to gain his release, claiming that his pistol had discharged accidentally at the time of Joseph Flack's death.[28]

Returning to Nevada after beating the Utah rap, Mellon settled in Eureka in spring 1872. Here he most likely was an acquaintance of Jack White who also operated in Eureka at this time. One day in late May, Mellon, for reasons unknown, perpetrated a severe beating on an old man by the name of Hamilton. Arrested by local authorities and brought into Eureka court before Judge Adams on May 27, the judge imposed a fine of $100 on Mellon charging assault.[29]

Perhaps in the same vigilante purge which rid Eureka of Jack White, Bob Mellon also had possibly his first, but by no means last, encounter with a citizen's extra-legal enforcement committee.[30] Leaving Eureka in June or July, by August, the fighting sport landed over 200 miles east at Reno, Nevada. With a seeming mania for committing assaults he beat a young boy "almost to death" in Reno early that month. Later arrested in Virginia City, Mellon's penalty, if any, for this latest pummeling of another human being is not of record.[31]

Mellon's whereabouts for the intervening 13 or 14 months are not evident. If press reports are to be believed, he may have been hanging his hat in Sacramento, California. According to an article in the *Truckee Republican* in late September 1873:

> A telegram from Elko states that a fatal shooting scrape occurred near that place on Sunday morning last [September 28] on the western bound passenger train. The following account is given of the difficulty: three-card monte man named John Kearney, Bob Mellen [sic] of Sacramento, and Tom Wiggins, got into one of two passenger cars containing troops for Benicia [California]. Soon after leaving here Wiggins commenced his manipulations and a sergeant

ordered him to leave the car. Wiggins drew a revolver and refused to leave. The sergeant reached for his revolver, when a private named Harry Thompson stepped between the two to prevent the impending difficulty, and was instantly shot and killed by Wiggins, who threw his revolver out of the window and when arrested produced another that had not been discharged. As soon as the train reached Carlin the commanding officer turned the three criminals over to the civil authorities heavily ironed.[32]

Somehow Mellon managed to extricate himself from this difficulty. If he returned to California after this episode it may have been at about this time that a supposed incident happened which would prove Mellon's mettle in a physical encounter. Although the report seems highly apocryphal, the *Daily Sentinel*, at Mellon's former abode of Eureka, Nevada, seems to hold some stock in the tale. Published over a year after the Elko affair, the *Sentinel* of December 13, 1874, stated:

> Mellon is noted as having killed a man in San Francisco several months ago in a most extraordinary duel. The two men lashed their left arms together with ropes so that they could not possibly become separated. At a given signal each was provided with a Bowie knife and a deadly encounter began. They cut and carved until both were covered with wounds and blood, and one was a corpse. Bob Mellon lived. His face is horribly scarred and disfigured and he delights to boast of his exploit.

If true, and Mellon must have had the facial scars to lend credibility to the account, the man must have had a craw full of sand.

Piper's Opera House, Virginia City, as it looked in 1950. In 1874 Bob Mellon lived a few doors south (courtesy Digital Photo Collection, Image #UNRS-P1641-1, Special Collections and University Archives Department, University of Nevada, Reno Libraries).

By May 1874, Mellon was definitely residing in Virginia City, Nevada, on D Street, just a few doors south of Piper's Opera House, with a "mistress" named Anna Smith. Early on the morning of Thursday, May 14, the pair fell into an argument over matters long since forgotten. Suddenly, Miss Smith picked up a five-shooter revolver and fired a shot at Mellon. The ball punched into Mellon's right breast and, ranging downwards, lodged in his groin. On being summoned to the scene, physicians pronounced the man dangerously, though not fatally, wounded. The wound was probed but the doctors were unable to locate the slug. This, Mellon probably carried in his body for the rest of his life. Although it seemed fairly obvious from the evidence that he had been shot by Anna Smith, Mellon insisted to authorities that he had accidentally shot himself. As a result of this insistence of Mellon's, no consequences devolved upon Smith as a result of the shooting.[33]

Soon after this nearly fatal domestic difficulty Bob Mellon must have shed himself of the pistol packin' Anna Smith. By fall 1874, he made his appearance in Truckee, California. Here he took up with Truckee's most notorious and disreputable female citizen, Carrie "Spring Chicken" Smith.[34] It could not be considered a step up in affairs de amour.

Spring Chicken was a soiled dove with a long history in Truckee. On July 4, 1869, two roughs, George Prior and Jack Whipley shot it out on a Truckee street. Fatally wounded, Whipley died a few days later. Wishing to get some sort of revenge, Whipley's woman, a local madam named Lottie Morton, decided to attack Prior's lover, Carrie Smith. In the melee that followed one of Morton's girls, Emma Butler, snatched a Derringer out of Smith's own pocket and fired. The bullet missed Smith, but grazed Morton in the side. Eventually the fight was broken up, Emma Butler later being convicted on a charge of assault to commit murder and sentenced to an 18-month prison term.[35]

Carrie continued to be a thorn in the side of Truckee tranquility throughout her years in the town, often drunk and disorderly and associating with the tough element. Having long since dumped George Prior by the wayside she quickly took Bob Mellon as her man soon after his arrival in Truckee in the summer or fall of 1874.[36]

Truckee proved to be a most uncongenial location for those of the rowdy mindset at the time of Mellon's appearance. Ever since the White–Fugate gun battle of September 5, 1873, the local vigilantes or "601" as they liked to be called, had been gradually building steam. The reputable citizenry of the town was quickly losing patience with the antics of the Jibboom Street crowd. Vigilantism, inch by inch, slowly gained in popularity.[37]

One of the most vociferous opponents of the criminal class was a man who had the perfect forum to espouse his views. Dave B. Frink, a ca. 40-year-old native New Yorker and editor of the *Truckee Republican* newspaper, saw no need for discretion in his reporting.[38] Often railing against criminality and taking every opportunity to show support for the "601," Frink continually editorialized on the situation and made no bones about his feelings on this state of affairs. Still, the unruly Jibboom Street crowd felt strong. They were still making money in their chosen illegal endeavors. Most people feared to stand up to them. Mellon, Spring Chicken and the rest saw no need for concern. On the contrary, times they were a-changing.

Fourth Crossing of Truckee River. Both White and Mellon would have passed through this crossing many times on their train trips from Nevada to Truckee, California (courtesy Digital Photo Collection, Image #UNRS-P1987-24-54, Special Collections and University Archives Department, University of Nevada, Reno Libraries).

One night in October a group of rowdies created a disturbance in Jerry Payne's saloon on Front Street. One of them, Seth McCain, apparently had some sort of grudge against Payne and wished to exact retribution. Payne's known connection with the vigilantes may have had something to do with McCain's enmity. Although arrested and fined for their antics the roughs remained defiant well into November.[39]

McCain continued to make threats against Payne's safety. A rumor began to make the rounds throughout Truckee that McCain, Bob Mellon and Carrie Smith had even gotten together and hatched a plot to assassinate the saloon keeper. On November 17, Dave Frink ran another of his railing editorials against the ne'er-do-wells titled "Roughs on the Warpath." The vigilantes had come to the end of their patience.[40]

The 601 decided to act on Thursday, November 19. The group delivered notices to a number of the gang inviting them to leave town or suffer the consequences. Seth McCain had been sentenced to the County Jail for 60 days on a charge of disturbing the peace and thus was unable to vacate. Most, however, such as Harry Howard, George Brown and Jack Potter quickly boarded the next train out of Truckee.[41]

A few, most notably Bob Mellon and his paramour Carrie Smith refused to accept the vigilantes offer. According to one historian, the couple even went so far as to send an answering message to the vigilante committee challenging them to "come and get them."[42] One Nevada newspaper later reported that Mellon "had been ordered to leave the place [Truckee], but positively declined to go, thus setting at defiance the mandates of the committee, and swearing meanwhile that he was good for a dozen of them if they persisted in endeavoring to drive him out of town."[43]

The Truckee vigilantes decided to take more aggressive action on the evening of Monday, November 23. Concluding that Mellon and Smith were probably holed up at the saloon of George Hayward on East Main Street, a known hangout of the criminal class, the vigilantes donned hooded masks and trooped forth. Shortly before midnight some 20 to 30 men burst into Hayward's place while others placed themselves at strategic points around the outside of the building to prevent escape. The leader ordered proprietor Hayward to grab a lantern and escort them through the building in order that they may check all the rooms for hidden persons.

At pistol point the startled Hayward led the masked men through a back door of the saloon leading into a hallway off of which were a number of bedrooms. While the vigilantes checked the first bedroom, Hayward turned to face the end of the hall where was located another door leading to the outside, the top panels of which were broken out. All at once Hayward was shocked to see a man suddenly appear at the outside of the door pointing a pistol through the opening presented by the broken-out panels. The vigilante standing nearest to the saloon men also spied the man at the door. Quickly bringing up his revolver the vigilante fired a shot at the man.

"Oh! Oh! Oh!" The man called out, then fell with a thud on the outside of the door.

The concussion of the revolver shot so close to Hayward had snuffed out his lantern. The masked intruders ordered him to re-light it and continue to tour through his premises. The vigilantes would ultimately be disappointed. Following a complete investigation of the building they failed to find Bob Mellon, Carrie Smith or any other wanted person for that matter.

After leaving Hayward's saloon most of the vigilante group moved off toward Front Street. A smaller group went around the building to where the man had fallen at the back door following the revolver shot. One of the group hoisted the man on his shoulder and they followed their comrades to Front Street.

Laying the man on a table inside Hurd's Hall one of their number ran to summon Dr. William Curless. Upon his arrival Dr. Curless found the man dead, the bullet having entered the center of his chest and lodging in the back near the spine. When Curless pulled the hood off the man's head he found the sightless eyes of *Truckee Republican* editor Dave Frink staring up at him.[44]

The people of Truckee were horrified at this latest development. The news quickly flashed through California, Nevada and other Pacific Coast states before making its way across the country. The next day's *Truckee Republican*, put together by Frink's assistant editor and turned out with black bordered columns, simply blared in block letters the column head "DEAD!"

> The Republican is issued to-day to meet a demand on the part of this community, though the task falls heavily upon the person charged with it. D.B. Frink, it's editor and proprietor lies cold in death. No more will his many good qualities of heart and head manifest themselves through the medium of these columns. He was shot dead last night between 11 and 12 o'clock, while engaging in doing what he undoubtedly considered his duty.[45]

The *Sacramento Record* felt moved to comment:

> What strange fatality induced Frink to appear before that broken door and thrust the pistol through the opening is wholly incomprehensible. His three comrades who were assisting in guarding the rear of the house were concealed, as they should have been. Some overruling Providence seems to have decreed that a noble life must be sacrificed to ensure the safety of the community. Frink was ever faithful to Truckee's interest, and if his pure lifeblood was needed to cleanse the town of its foulness, he would willingly have died.[46]

The Coroner Inquest held the day after the tragedy ruled that Frink had come to his death "by a bullet or gunshot wound through the breast, inflicted by the hand of some person unknown to the jury."[47] Though some wanted to believe that he had been shot by Mellon or some other of the nefarious crowd, most realized that editor Frink had been accidentally killed by one of his fellow vigilantes. Mellon and Carrie Smith were likely not even in Truckee on the night of the vigilante raid. Having caught wind of planned developments the pair had decamped for Carson City, Nevada.[48]

The work of the 601 was not over yet. Following the transport of Dave Frink's body to his former home of Nevada City, California, for burial they continued their watchfulness.[49] On Christmas Day one of those banished the month before, Frank Spencer, brazenly returned to Truckee to celebrate the holiday with his father in Frank Rabel's saloon. As he stood drinking at the bar a number of masked men suddenly burst into the establishment. As Spencer turned, he received a shotgun blast which knocked him to the floor. Although left for dead he later managed to recover in the Nevada City hospital. He would give Truckee a wide berth hereafter.[50] For all intents and purposes this proved the last violent act of the Truckee vigilantes. Bob Mellon sat in Carson City blessing his lucky stars that he managed to escape the California railroad town with a whole skin. Despite this he continued unchaste.

Whether Spring Chicken was with him at this time is debatable, but by summer 1875, Mellon had returned to his old haunts around Eureka, Nevada. In August 1875 he involved himself in the embezzlement perpetrated by Eureka saloon keeper Pat Keys. It seems mining boss Henry Kind had entrusted Keys with about $1400 in order to be his agent and cash the miners' checks on payday. Keys, letting temptation get the better of him, absconded with the $1400 and, accompanied by Bob Mellon, headed for the nearby hills on August 6.[51]

Two days later the pair were surprised by Constable Kelley from Eureka at an isolated station near the Spring Valley mines, about 20 miles southwest of Eureka. When ordered to surrender Keys meekly complied. Mellon, however, began to reach for his revolver until Kelley assured him he would kill him if he continued. At this point Mellon complied and the duo were trundled back to town and a bunk at the local jail.[52] Eventually, Keys would be convicted for his greed. Due to the lack of evidence of any complicity on his part, Mellon received a discharge shortly after his arrest.[53]

Mellon continued his rowdyism. On Tuesday, September 21, he and Pete Morris provoked a fight with a Negro named Samuel Mills in a saloon in the "Barbary Coast," Eureka's red-light district. At length Morris picked up an ore specimen from a nearby shelf and hurled it at Mills. The rock struck Mills in the face, as the local newspaper put it, "completely knocking one of his eyes out of his head."[54] Placed in durance vile for the melee both Mellon and Morris received court hearings in the case. Once again Mellon's luck held and he gained his release on the 24th.[55]

As had happened elsewhere, the Eureka citizenry were quickly getting fed up with the rampant lawlessness and defiance of the criminal set. In December 1875 they took a page out of Truckee's book and formed their own vigilance committee which they also termed the "601." Tuesday, December 28, this extralegal organization distributed so-called "tickets of leave" to many of the town's malefactors. Undoubtedly, Bob Mellon, for at least the third time in his career, was the recipient of one of these notices, which, according to the *Eureka Sentinel*, read:

> Eureka, December 28, 1875.
> Mr. ___: Sir—you are hereby commanded to leave Eureka within three (3) days.
> By order of the Executive Committee.
> Remember the fate of those who disobey this command.
>
> 601.[56]

Apparently, Bob Mellon went. Although his movements are unknown for over a year, by early 1877 he was operating in and around Reno, Nevada. Once again accompanied by Carrie "Spring Chicken" Smith, Mellon was one of Reno's notable characters, the newspapers moved to comment:

> Bob Mellon, Spring Chicken, and several other notables who figured so prominently in Truckee two years ago, are hovering around Reno.[57]

Bob Mellon seemed to have an uncanny knack for being in communities that were in the midst of experiencing rashes of criminality and vice. Reno in early 1877 was in the throes of just such conditions. In what must have seemed like a bad case of déjà vu for Mellon, the citizens of Reno formed their own "601" at this time. According to the *Reno Journal*:

> There was quite an excitement among several of the "boys" yesterday [March 7] upon receiving notices from "601" and one or two made some wild threats against the community.
> We felt a couple of weeks ago as though the citizens contemplated such strict measures for ridding Reno of obnoxious characters, but seemingly all notions of such a course had passed away lately. We are mistaken, it appears, and Reno has her "601."
> It is bad when such a state of affairs exists, but times have been pretty rough in Reno lately, and we are not surprised that the people themselves intend to enforce the law.[58]

In what was becoming a tedious and repetitive routine, Mellon departed Reno at the bidding of another vigilance committee. His movements subsequent to his Reno sojourn are somewhat obscure and his trail fades at this point.[59]

Spring Chicken's trail goes almost as cold. Two years before, in February 1875, she, possibly accompanied by Bob Mellon, roistered in Virginia City, Nevada. Thrown in jail on a charge of assault and battery she twice tried to commit suicide in her jail cell. Twice she survived her attempted self-destruction.[60]

Sometime later Smith returned to Truckee. In 1877 she was jailed for grand larceny. Not liking her new lodgings in the Truckee hoosegow, she defiantly set her bed on fire. After the flames were extinguished the judge fined her $30 and sent her back into confinement.[61] This would be Chicken's last press notice. At this juncture, like her former lover Bob Mellon, she disappears from the historical record.

At length, Truckee, like all things, matured, grew old and peaceful and became a tourist stop on the Lake Tahoe circuit. Little do most people realize, while strolling through the town's historic streets, the past rollicking characters in whose footsteps they pre-ambulate. Former Nevada hard cases such as Jack White and Bob Mellon had helped to make Truckee's past vibrate with excitement and action. Their ghosts, perhaps, still haunt the street corners.

9

"Something of a Noted Rogue"
John Burke

In the fall of 1877 John Burke (or Francis Harker as he had renamed himself), was 30 years old. In the previous six years he had experienced his share of hard times and severe conditions. Since at least the age of 23 he had spent all of his time either behind bars or doing his best to keep himself out of the clutches of law enforcement. He had served hard time in three major penitentiaries, the state prisons of both Nevada and Utah as well as his present situation at the federal prison in Detroit, Michigan, known as the Detroit House of Corrections. In addition, he had spent times of various lengths in a number of county jails throughout the Nevada–Utah area.

Likewise, despite the vigilance of authorities, Burke had a series of prison and jail breaks to his credit, escaping at least once from both the Nevada and Utah state facilities as well as various other escapes from local county lockups. Now, on this crisp and cool November 2, 1877, Burke felt his endurance for the Detroit penitentiary had reached its limit. He had gone on the lam from other institutions and he was now determined to do so again. Thus, marshaling all of his ingenuity, the wily convict formed a plan, carried it through and, on this early November day, walked briskly and surreptitiously away from the House of Corrections. This time he hoped to disappear for good.

John Burke was a native Texan of Irish parentage born about 1848 or 1849.[1] Although his early life is not of record he comes more into focus in 1871. Apparently, he settled in Storey County, Nevada, for a time before eventually moving south to Esmeralda County.[2] On August 19, 1871, Burke received a sentence of three years in the Nevada State Prison for manslaughter perpetrated in Esmeralda County.[3]

The incident which resulted in Burke's sentence to the state prison is obscure. Evidence would seem to suggest that it may have come about due to the death of one Robert Wallace at Pine Grove, Esmeralda County, Nevada, who, on December 11, 1870, died as a result of being struck on the head with a bottle during a saloon fracas. This, however, is far from definite.[4] It is known that Burke came close to being lynched by a citizens committee before being spirited away to safety at the jail in Aurora.[5]

Unfortunately, further confusion has been cast on the issue due to a number of chroniclers having mistaken this John Burke for another named John Burke who served a sentence in the Nevada State Prison at around the same time as the Burke dealt with here, but was 20 years his senior.[6] The other John Burke, 43 years of age, and a native of Ireland, had been sentenced to the Nevada State Prison on March 24, 1870, for 40 years from Elko County for the crime of kicking to death a Chinese man named Young Yew at Loray on February 28, 1870.[7] He received an early discharge due to "good behavior and adequate punishment" on August 21, 1871.[8]

The two John Burkes served together in the state penal institution for only two days, the younger being inducted on August 19, two days before his elder namesake received his pardon. The prison Commitment Book describes the 23-year-old Burke:

> John Burke, Texas, sent from Esmeralda for three years (formerly lived in Storey); aged 23; height 5:8 ½; weighs 150; thin face, light hair, blue eyes; three small scars on left knee, and one on inside of right knee, and one on right leg below the knee.[9]

Another contemporary source adds to this description:

> He has a pleasant countenance; playful, expressive, dark blue eyes; a small, laughter-rippled mouth, indicating, in his serious moments, great firmness and decision of character; prominent nose, large ears, dimpled chin, fair complexion, nervous temperament, quick perception; an active mind and an athletic body.[10]

Burke was destined to spend only a month behind the walls of the Nevada State Prison during this, his first induction. Within 31 days he and a number of other desperate convicts would execute one of the most notorious escapes in the history of the Nevada penitentiary.

Around the time of young Burke's entrance into the penitentiary a core of incorrigible inmates began formulating a plan for a major escape. They picked the evening of Sunday, September 17, to make their move. The choosing of this day was not a random selection. Sundays were always designated a non-task day by prison officials. On this day the prisoners were allowed to congregate in a large common area outside of their cells. Also, with all inmates being held inside the prison, it was the practice on Sundays to not post guards on the outside wall turrets. By the 17th the prisoners felt they were ready to implement their plot. A few days before the designated day they let newcomer Burke into their cabal and invited him to come along. He did not need much convincing.

At 6 o'clock that evening, Captain of the Guard Volney E. Rollins entered the common room in anticipation of following the usual procedure of locking the convicts in their own individual cells for the night. Suddenly, after a prearranged signal by one of the inmates, a convict quickly broke a bottle over Rollins' head. Knocked to the floor, Rollins received a sound pummeling from a number of the prisoners before being picked up bodily and thrown into a cell.

Suddenly producing an arsenal of homemade knives, impromptu "slung shots" consisting of socks and trouser pant legs tied up with bits of metal and rocks, and the odd lead pipe or broom handle, the prisoners in on the escape plot, some 30 to 35 men, clambered onto the second tier of cells. With no other prison authorities yet aware of developments the convicts quickly punched and chopped a hole in the lath and plaster ceiling. Gaining the attic, the men ran along through the garret until reaching a point they knew to be just above the personal apartment of Assistant

Warden J.J. Zimmerman, attached to the prisons second floor. Here they hastily punched another hole and began lowering themselves down into Zimmerman's room. Taking a nap at the time, the Assistant Warden received a harsh awakening. Shocked at the sight before him, Zimmerman quickly rolled off his cot and dashed out and downstairs, effectively removing himself from the affair.

Still having met no resistance Burke and his fellow prison mates managed to acquire two or three rifles and a like number of revolvers from a closet in Zimmerman's apartment. Not wasting any time, they now rushed en masse down the staircase leading to the personal apartments of Nevada Lieutenant Governor and State Prison Warden Frank Denver which he shared with his wife and daughter on the main floor under Zimmerman's room.

Entertaining a number of guests at a dinner party at the time, Denver was immediately alarmed at the clamor taking place on the stairwell. Accompanied by Bob Dedman, a lifer whom Denver engaged as his personal waiter, the Warden ran out to the stairs. He was shocked to be greeted by a band of yelling prisoners surging down the stairs toward him. Denver pulled a small derringer from his pocket and jerked the trigger. The slug grazed the abdomen of Frank Clifford, a 29-year-old criminal serving ten years for robbery, who happened to be leading the convict charge. Doubling over and clutching his stomach, Clifford stumbled out through the door. At this point, Dedman grabbed a nearby chair and with a few deft swings knocked a number of prisoners back. With Dedman holding the gang at bay for the time being, Denver rushed into an adjoining room and acquired a large revolver. He returned just in time to see Dedman pummeled to the floor. All at once the convicts rushed Denver. Before he could employ the revolver, the Warden received a blow to the head from a slung shot which sent him crashing to the floor. Losing his grip on the revolver the gun slid along the floor where it was seized by Leander Morton, a 25-year-old train robber serving a sentence of 30 years. Bringing the gun to bear on Denver, Morton fired. The slug struck the dazed Warden in the hip, eventually lodging in his back.[11]

With the Warden vanquished the convicts quickly rushed into the main prison area. Still not having met any resistance, besides that of Warden Denver and trusty Dedman, they broke into the prison armory and, arming themselves with an assortment of rifles, shotguns, revolvers and hundreds of rounds of ammunition, dashed through the main prison building toward the front doors. Finally, they were met by the first guard alerted to the uprising, Francis M. Isaacs. Seeing the prisoners attempting to exit the doors while he stood out in the open in the prison yard Isaacs opened fire with his revolver. In a matter of seconds convict return fire would overwhelm him. Struck in the right knee by one bullet while another pierced his right hip, passed through his body and lodged in his left thigh, Isaacs fell to the ground gravely wounded.

Another guard, John Newhouse, alerted by the gunfire, ran to the scene. He managed to trade a few shots with the convicts before also falling victim to the superior fire of the prisoners. With one slug in the back and another grazing the back of his head, Newhouse fell insensible in the yard.

Reinforcements continued to arrive as two more guards, a Mr. Perasich and Henry Langlois rushed into the prison yard and opened up hot fire on the convicts.

Despite being outnumbered and outgunned by the would-be escapees the resistance of the prison guards had thus far managed to keep the prisoners pinned down inside the main prison building. Soon the hard-pressed guards were joined by Matt Pixley, owner of the nearby Warm Springs Hotel and his bartender C.W. Burgesser. Alerted by the raging gun battle the two men grabbed their pistols and rushed into the prison yard. Creeping close to the wall of the main building, Pixley smashed out a window and began firing at the darting forms within. Attracted by this action of the hotelier a number of convicts turned their guns toward the window and fired. A slug plowed into Pixley's face below the left eye, killing him instantly. As Perasich and Langlois continued to fire, Perasich was struck by a slug in the left hip, the shot traversing his groin and coming to a stop in his thigh.[12] With Perasich now down and Langlois out of bullets the gang of convicts burst forth from the prison building and made a mad dash across the yard toward the main gate. Acquiring this objective, 29 dangerous and desperate prisoners, including John Burke, made their escape and moved as fast as their legs could carry them for freedom.[13] Burke stayed with the majority of the escapees who were seen to head east of the prison and disappear around a ridge. Other smaller groups and individuals broke off from the main party and dashed away in various directions.[14]

Although it was at first felt that the convicts had sustained heavy casualties it soon became evident that their superior numbers and firepower had stood them in good stead. The only damage dealt to them proved to be the grazing shot to Frank Clifford's stomach given him by Warden Denver and another escapee, probably John Jacks, shot in the hand, both minor injuries.[15]

As the state militia, local lawmen and regular citizens posses organized to pursue the prisoners the escapees put as many miles as possible between themselves and the State Prison. About 2 miles from the prison, at a spot on the Carson River called the "Mexican Dam," the largest party of convicts stopped briefly to take stock. Some of them had escaped with shackles and leg irons still attached to their person. At the Dam, tools were obtained and most were able to remove their chains. Quickly moving on, the group further split up. While one contingent headed south toward Silver Peak the other 13 men, John Burke amongst them, crossed the Carson River headed in the direction of the Pine Nut Valley.[16]

Reaching Pine Nut Valley, a further split took place. While seven men went their own way the remaining six, including Burke, Moses Black, Leander Morton, Charles Jones, Tilton Cockerill and the youngest of the escapees, 18-year-old Jack Bedford Roberts, stayed their course toward Esmeralda County. Burke and Jones were familiar with the territory, having lived in the area previously.

At length the group chanced upon the camp of a so-called "Dutch" coal burner. Tying the coal burner up the prisoners ransacked his cabin for supplies and food before appropriating four of his horses and swiftly moving on.[17]

By the evening of the day following the escape the six convicts had crossed the Pine Nut Mountains. By the afternoon of Tuesday, the 19th they had reached the vicinity of Wellington, some 35 miles south of Carson City. Knowing that Capt. Dingman, a former guard at the State Prison who had been instrumental in the shooting deaths of two prisoners attempting to make their escape on December 1, 1870, was now a mail carrier on the road between Wellington and Sweetwater, some of the men, principally Morton and Jones, wished to hover around the road hoping to catch Dingman on his route and exact revenge.

Unfortunately for him, the gang held up 18-year-old Billy Poor, another express rider working his first day on the job. Questioning the youngster about Dingman, Poor told them he would not be along until the next day's run.

According to testimony given later by J.B. Roberts:

> Jones said that they would "cook his [Dingman's] goose," when Morton said, "there, you son of _____, you have let the cat out of the bag!" As they started to take Poor from the road, the helpless boy begged in pitiful tones that his life might be spared, "but," said one of these heartless wretches, while afterwards gloating over the horrible affair, "we didn't give him much time to beg, did we? eh, Morton?" They both shot him; took his clothes and dressed him in one of their convict's suits. Morton took his ring—a plain, gold one—and his boots and gloves. They burned his head, and said that when found "they would think he was some poor convict—."[18]

There are some grounds to suggest that John Burke, at the youthful age of 23, had not yet transformed into the hardened criminal he would become. At this point a further source credits him with a touch of conscience:

> John Burke spoke up at that point. "I don't go a cent on such cold-blooded murders as that," he said. "We'll have the whole country after us. I'm going to leave this crowd." Morton told him to go ahead but wouldn't give him a horse, so Burke stayed.[19]

Apparently, later that day Burke again expressed his distaste for the violence. Once more, according to Roberts:

> A distance further on the road, they passed a house where they saw a man attending milk. Jones wanted to go back, kill him and throw him in the cellar. To this none agreed, and Burke talked a long time against such actions, saying that the country would arm against them and they would all be killed.[20]

Another says that Burke threatened to leave.

"I'll take my rifle and a horse." Burke said.

"Oh no you won't," Morton defied him.

Burke's anger rose. "If any of you bother me, I'll shoot out your guts," he yelled. He then threw a taunt at Morton. "You couldn't kill him [Billy Poor] with one shot. You had to shoot him twice."[21]

Eventually, tempers calmed somewhat and the group moved on.

Following the killing of Poor, the six escapees continued heading south, skirting Sweetwater and Aurora before turning southwest and crossing the California border near Adobe Meadows. By the evening of September 22, the party of fleeing prisoners had reached Monte Diablo Canyon in Mono County, California, just southwest of Mammoth City and about 115 miles from Carson City. Here they decided to camp for the night near Monte Diablo Creek.

On the early morning of Saturday, September 23, almost a week after the mass prison escape, Burke awoke hungry. By necessity of stealth and aloofness the men were able to obtain little, if any, food during their grueling sojourn. This morning Burke, Jones and Cockerill decided to venture up the canyon toward what is now called Convict Lake in search of wild berries for their breakfast. Morton, Black and

Roberts decided to stay in camp. While in the bushes the three men were startled by the sudden sounds of gunfire emanating from the direction of their bivouac.

As they were to learn later, a posse from Benton, California, led by Mono County Deputy Sheriff George Hightower and Wells Fargo agent Robert Morrison had finally tracked the prey to their lair. In the shooting that followed, Morrison and an Indian tracker named Mono Jim would be killed while Roberts sustained wounds that at length led to his capture.[22] Leander Morton's and Moses Black's escapes would only be temporary. Four days later the pair would be captured by another posse near Bishop, California, and eventually met their deaths at the hands of a lynch mob.[23]

At the sound of the firefight, Burke, Cockerill and Jones decided to hastily move out of the area. Soon after leaving Monte Diablo Canyon the trio decided to split up in the vicinity of Round Valley. Burke and Cockerill determined to head east toward the White Mountains and Fish Lake Valley back in Nevada, while Jones resolved on a solo route due south along the Owens River.

Resolving to add further incentive to the hunt for the escaped convicts, on the morning of Monday, September 25, Nevada Governor L.R. Bradley issued a reward notice of $300 for each of a group of ten convicts and $200 each for the remaining 18. Included in the latter grouping was John Burke.[24]

Although up until now it had been hoped that the mail rider, Billy Poor, had not been harmed and only taken hostage, his body was finally discovered on the 29th.[25] This added extra impetus to the pursuit. By October 7, besides the deaths of Black and Morton (which did not become widely circulated until early October), 11 convicts had been recaptured.[26] Up to the end of the first week of October, however, Burke and his partner Cockerill managed to avoid the long arm of the law.

In early October a spurious report gained favor that Burke and Cockerill had killed Charles Jones in a dispute connected with their flight.[27] No body was ever found, however, and indeed, Jones would be declared dead more than once in the subsequent months.[28] As far as the record shows Charles Jones was never retaken and made good his escape.

Rumors were running rampant at this time concerning the whereabouts of the various escapees still at large, not the least of which included John Burke and Tilton Cockerill. On October 6 or 7, a report came in to Carson City that the pair had been shot and killed by a posse at Round Valley.[29] This was demonstrably proven false with the capture of the two convicts on Thursday, October 5.

By the 5th the two men had trudged all the way to the Red Mountains near Silver Peak in Esmeralda County, Nevada. Picking up their trail a posse led by Esmeralda County Sheriff John B. Helm and John Ludwig tracked them into the mountain fastnesses. On a notion by Ludwig that Burke would head for the watering hole he had previously passed with Burke on his initial arrest in late 1870, Ludwig led the posse up a canyon to an old, abandoned icehouse. Catching the posse's movements just before Helm's party came upon them, Burke and Cockerill hastily quit their campsite and dashed into the rocks seeking concealment. A few minutes later Ludwig caught sight of Cockerill's head as he slowly raised up to scan the surrounding area. Quickly, Helm and his posse surrounded the ledge of rock, trained their rifles on the area and demanded the pair surrender. Soon, both Cockerill and Burke, apparently unarmed, popped up from the rocks, hands in the air.[30]

Transported to the jail at Aurora, lawmen soon had reason to fear for the safety of their two prisoners. Aurora citizens, incensed at the killing of mail rider Billy Poor, thirsted for the men's scalps. On the Sunday night following the capture, John Ludwig, one of the jail guards, was approached by a man who offered him and his fellow guards $500 in gold if they would abandon their posts for ten minutes. Of course, Ludwig refused and reported to Sheriff Helm.[31]

This incident and other rumors convinced Helm that Burke and Cockerill would not be safe in Aurora. In the middle of the night, and employing much subterfuge, Helm smuggled the pair out of the Aurora lockup and swiftly headed them toward Carson City. Informed that Helm and his prisoners were headed their way, Deputy U.S. Marshals Augustus Ash and James Slingerland set out to meet them, determined to take charge of the prisoners for the killing of the U.S. mail rider. At first Helm refused to turn the men over to the U.S. Marshals. When assured he would still receive the reward, however, he allowed Ash and Slingerland to deliver the convicts to the Carson City hoosegow on Wednesday, October 11.[32]

The *Daily State Register* of Carson City felt that John Burke's and Tilton Cockerill's situation could be summed up in simple terms:

> First, they will be tried by the United States for robbing the mail by force of arms, and if found guilty will be hanged. Second, they will be tried by the same authority for killing a mail agent or carrier, and if found guilty they will be hanged again. Then they will be turned over to and tried by the State for the murder of Poor, and if found guilty will be hanged a third time. Then again, they will be tried as accessories to the murder of Pixley, and if found guilty they will be hanged the fourth time. And last and least, they will be tried for State Prison breaking and sentenced to prison for from one to ten years.[33]

Little could the *Register* realize that not even one of their prognostications would come to pass.

Despite having had a leg amputated in an attempt to save his life, prison guard Francis Isaacs finally succumbed to his wounds the day following Burke's and Cockerill's arrival back in Carson City.[34] In its verdict of October 13 the Coroner's Jury included the name of John Burke, along with all the other escapees of September 17, as culpable in Isaac's death.[35] The courts would have much to say, all with little result.

Following one postponement, Burke and Cockerill were finally examined in the United States District Court in Carson City on Monday, October 24. The case would seem to have been poorly handled however, as, with no witnesses present, federal authorities decided to relinquish their case against the pair. Later that day the prisoners were turned over to the State of Nevada and relocated to their old home at the State Prison to await developments.[36]

In the intervening months since Burke's recapture three additional escapees had also been collared and returned to Carson.[37] On Thursday, November 9, these three, along with all the other recaptured convicts, those as yet still at large and two prisoners who had been involved in the prison break but failed to make it outside the prison walls, Barney Cosgrove and Dan Taylor, were rewarded with indictments for the death of Isaacs by the convening Ormsby County Grand Jury.[38]

In preparation for trial, Burke and his fellow prisoners mentioned in the Isaacs indictment were transferred to the County Jail. County Sheriff S.T. Swift trooped all his charges into the courtroom two days later to have the indictment read and counsel appointed. Various attorneys took multiple clients including Robert Clarke who agreed to represent John Burke along with fellow prisoners Cockerill, Clifford, Bigelow, Carter and Roth.[39] The group filed back into court again on the 15th at which time, through their lawyers, all entered a plea of not guilty. All legal counsel also demanded a separate trial for each of their clients. Realizing the difficulties and burdens this would place on the court, Judge C.N. Harris refused this particular request, decreeing that the prisoners would be tried as a group.[40]

The trial itself got underway Tuesday, November 21. It proved to be a difficult, almost impossible to manage, task for the prosecution. The most problematic aspect to overcome was the most obvious. How to prove who, amongst the confusion and mayhem of September 17, had actually fired the fatal gunshots that struck Isaacs that day. Most felt the likely candidate, Charles Jones, was not even in the courtroom. Unwilling to convict the whole group on such spurious evidence as presented, the jury came back on the morning of November 26 with a verdict of "not guilty."[41] In its bitter observation the local *Daily State Register* noted sarcastically, "the prisoners were overjoyed, and, as they pinched, punched, nudged, shoved and struck each other, there was a kind of 'Oh, no! It ain't us!' sort of expression on their countenances."[42]

With this fiasco completed there was a good deal of speculation on future action in the killing of Matt Pixley and other charges stemming from the September breakout. Sure enough, two days following the acquittal in the Isaacs case, the Second District Court, realizing it could not expect a different outcome, decided to set aside the indictment against the convicts for the death of Pixley.[43]

With these developments another Nevada newspaper, the *Sentinel* of Eureka, felt just as sarcastic as Carson City's *Register* when it snidely commented:

> Judge Harris, of the Ormsby County District Court, on motion of Counselor Patterson, has set aside the indictment against the convicts for the killing of Matt. Pixley, and the matter is to be submitted to another Grand Jury. But it is hardly probable that those innocent lambs will ever be tried again. Better try the officers of the prison next. There is no question about Lieutenant Governor Denver being guilty of "stunning" Clifford in the abdominal regions at the time of the great break.[44]

Authorities returned Burke and his fellow prison birds to the penitentiary immediately following the dismissal of the Pixley charges. The convicts may have been in the mood for some hijinks and celebration following the dropping of charges against them. Despite being performed in a, perhaps, lighthearted manner, the following incident, reported by the *Carson City Daily State Register* of November 29, 1871, to have occurred on the trip back to the State Prison, may have pointed out three much more serious facts in regard to the prisoners and the prison. The laxity of official security, the convicts' disrespect of that security and, indeed, the convicts' unspoken message that, given the opportunity and the right circumstances, they could launch a half decent escape attempt at any time of the day or night, was plainly evident.

Playful—The eighteen convicts who have recently been on trial in the District Court for the murder of F.M. Isaacs were returned to the state penitentiary yesterday afternoon. They were taken down in two coaches, or rather mud-wagons. In one of the wagons were Clifford, Burke, Flynn, Ryan and four or five others. They were all chained, and each had on a pair of handcuffs when they left the Sheriff's office, but on arriving at the prison Burke had on all the handcuffs, the others having their hands free. They returned to their old quarters reluctantly, but could not resist the temptation to indulge in a little playfulness on the road.

Despite the newspaper's humorous take on the occurrence, it must have given authorities a chilling dose of reality. If so, they did not heed the warning.

The men did stay in their enforced confinement at the penitentiary until early March 1872. At that time, they were all herded back to the County Jail in anticipation of their arraignment on Wednesday, March 6 on charges of prison breaking.[45] Following the pleading of guilty by all hands a postponement of sentencing was requested, supposedly in order to give counsel time to prepare arguments. Acquiescing to the request, Judge Harris set sentencing for the following Monday and Sheriff Swift paraded all his charges back to the County Jail.[46] Unbeknownst to everyone, the convicts had other ideas as to how the situation should play out.

The south wall of the County Jail in Carson City adjoined the neighboring Magnolia Saloon. During the days of their durance vile in the county facility the men held in the cells along this wall, John Burke, J.E. Chapman, J.B. Parsons, William Willis, Thomas Flynn, Thomas Ryan, Thomas Carter, William Russell, George Roth and Frank Clifford began to work on an escape plot. Without attracting the attention of Sheriff Swift or his guards, by toiling during the night and covering their work with blankets, mattresses, etc., the prisoners began removing the floorboards along the back of the two cells on the south wall and tunneling under the wall and into the Magnolia Saloon. Leaving the last bit of tunneling until the night of the planned escape, so as not to be discovered by anyone within the Magnolia, the men accomplished their court delay and settled on the early morning hours of Monday, March 11, to make their move.

Sometime between the hours of 2 a.m., following the closing of the Magnolia, and 5 a.m. Monday morning the desperate convicts went into action. Employing secretly acquired hack saws many took the time to remove only one end of the leg irons, tying the loose end to their belt or waistband. Burke removed his completely and discarded it on the floor of his cell. Completing the tunnel into the saloon the prisoners stole a Faro box containing $100, dashed to the back of the building and escaped out the rear window. At the last minute Chapman decided not to go, stating later, "I got enough of it before," referring to the harrowing ordeal of the September 1871 break. Unfortunately for them, the prisoners in the cells on the opposite side of the hallway were physically unable to participate in the escape and could only watch as their fellow convicts disappeared through the escape tunnel.[47]

While the escapees scampered off in different directions into the bitingly cold March weather the Governor of Nevada was again forced to place a $200 reward on their heads.[48] That evening someone, probably a portion of the escapees, stole two horses from a ranch near Carson City.[49] Two days later, with various posses out scouring the countryside, Sheriff Swift, for some reason taking a special interest in the two criminals, offered an extra $100 reward for Burke and Clifford.[50]

These two, accompanied by George Roth, headed northeast toward Dayton. Near Dayton they managed to steal three horses, along with saddles and blankets.[51] Thus equipped, and managing to elude any pursuit, the trio continued heading east toward the Belmont Mining District, passing through Westgate on the 16th. The *Territorial Enterprise* felt Burke, Clifford and Roth had a good lead on any pursuers, stating, "the convicts have now obtained such a start that they will probably be allowed to work out their own salvation."[52] Salvation would be a long time coming.

By March 28, Burke and his two companions had traveled some 200 miles east to the vicinity of the town of Eureka. At this time, they decided they needed a stake before continuing their journey. It was resolved to waylay the Woodruff & Ennor stagecoach plying between Eureka and Palisade. At about 8 o'clock that Thursday evening the trio of escapees, possibly accompanied by a fourth unidentified individual, halted the stage some 22 miles outside Palisade.[53] Breaking into the Wells Fargo treasure box with an ax the men were somewhat disappointed to find it contained only about $500. Lining up the passengers, except for the one lady passenger who was allowed to remain in the coach, the robbers gathered another $200 along with two or three watches, some jewelry and a small derringer. Then, after rummaging through the various baggage and trunks, the three men cut out two of the stage horses and, absconding with these, galloped off down the road.[54]

Two days later, Saturday, March 30, Deputy Sheriff John Nicholson spied three men standing on the side of the road near Hercules Gap as he rode toward Steptoe Valley. Although he instantly recognized Frank Clifford, who had operated in the area two years previously, Nicholson kept a poker face. Briefly chatting with the men, who inquired of him the distance to the next ranch, Nicholson hastily rode on to the nearest community where he recruited three posse men and rode back to the Gap. Finding the convicts asleep in camp, Nicholson called out for their surrender. Taken by surprise, the men gave up without any resistance.[55]

According to the *Eureka Sentinel*:

> A passenger from Hamilton yesterday informed us that the captured robbers admitted that if they had thought they were recognized by officer Nicholson when first met by him in the evening they should certainly have "doused his glim." One of them [either Burke or Roth] wanted to kill him anyhow as he rode off, to prevent accidents, but Clifford objected.[56]

Transported to Hamilton, the county seat of White Pine County, and placed in the care of Sheriff J.D. Patterson, the prisoners learned that they were almost the last of the escapees to be captured, the only one now still at large being J.B. Parsons.[57] The editor of the *White Pine News* attempted an interview with the trio three days after their capture as they were being held in the White Pine County jail. Clifford and Roth proved quite loquacious; Burke, on the other hand, seemed rather reticent. He claimed his name was Dixon and that he had never been to Texas in his life. The newsman observed:

> All three of the prisoners look as though they had experienced hard times and lived on short rations. The probability is they would have made a fight before being arrested had they not been worn out from traveling, day and night, after leaving the Palisade road.[58]

On Friday, April 5, White Pine County Deputy Sheriff Nicholson and two assistants hustled the prisoners onto the stage for the trip back to Carson City. At the Eureka stage stop a throng of citizens pushed and shoved to get a glimpse of the notorious criminals. Concerned that the crowd may harbor friends of the prisoners looking to perform a rescue, Nicholson and his partners kept a wary eye, shotguns at the ready. After "Big Alec" Fleming, a former State Prison guard, was allowed to present Burke and his fellows with a box of cigars the stage continued on its way to Carson City.[59]

The trip proved notable for two other conspicuous occurrences. At one point in the journey Burke managed to remove one of his shackles and was about to attempt a break when spotted by Deputy Douglas and made to sit still at the point of a gun. Sometime later, at Palisade, Nicholson and his party were met by a group of men led by Elko County Sheriff Ben Fitch. Since the stage robbery had technically occurred in his county, Fitch now demand that the prisoners be turned over to him. A potentially serious confrontation took place between Fitch and Nicholson before the latter finally prevailed and continued on his way.[60] Despite all the drama, Nicholson and his charges finally arrived in the capital on Monday the 8th and once again, Burke, Clifford and Roth were locked behind the bars of their old home at the state penitentiary.[61]

On August 25 another of those who escaped from the state prison in the big break of September 1871, Pat Hurley, was returned to the institution, having been captured in San Francisco.[62] A week and a half later, John Burke, et al., were arraigned in the District Court before Judge Harris on a charge of jailbreaking.[63] All the prisoners entered a plea of guilty the next day.[64] On Saturday the 7th, Harris sentenced Burke to an additional one year, added onto his original sentence, for jailbreaking and another year for the State Prison break of the previous year. All the others received like sentences.[65] Neither Burke, Clifford nor Roth would ever be tried for the Eureka–Palisade stage robbery.

John Burke would spend the next four years of his life confined within the walls of the Nevada State Prison. All went relatively quiet save for one incident in September 1874 when some "thirty or forty" inmates became involved in an elaborate escape plot similar to the 1871 scheme. Luckily, current Warden P.C. Hyman learned of the planned outbreak shortly before its implementation and stymied the affair.[66] Although no names of those involved were released, being a veteran of the prison system and by his past history, it is likely that John Burke was one of those looking for another way out. He would only find it through authorized channels this time.

His sentence having reached expiration, the Nevada State Prison discharged Burke on Tuesday, February 1, 1876.[67] Moving east to the state of Utah the ex-con adopted the alias Francis Harker and drifted through the mining camps.[68] It would seem that once in the clutches of crime, Burke, now Harker, could not redeem himself. Soon he would be up to his old antics once again.

Teaming up with William Willis, another former Nevada State Prison convict and fellow escapee with Burke in the big breakout of 1871, Burke traveled to Millard County, Utah, in late spring 1876. Here, near the Sevier River, late on the evening of Tuesday, May 30, Burke and Willis, who had also taken an assumed name in Utah, now calling himself Ed Bigelow, concealed themselves on the road. Sporting firearms and donning masks the pair halted the westbound Gilmer & Salisbury stage plying between Salt Lake City and Pioche, Nevada. Breaking open the Wells Fargo treasure box and registered mail sacks the robbers found little of value before disappearing into the timber.[69]

Disappointed with the slim pickings, Burke and Willis decided to keep on the road and rob the following day's stagecoach on its way from Salt Lake City to Pioche near Tidwell's Chicken Creek. That excursion proved little better, the two highwaymen obtaining only $25 from a passenger, one dollar of which they returned to him when he told them it was all the money he had.[70] Riding along the road some distance behind the stage, a local man named Roy McBride happened to stumble upon the robbery just as Burke and Willis were preparing to make tracks. Taking in the situation at a glance, McBride unlimbered his gun and opened fire on the robbers as they fled into the darkness, none of his shots taking effect.[71]

Taking up the trail, Gilmer & Salisbury's Fillmore agent, G. Huntsman, stage driver J. Whitbeck, pilot of the first stage robbed, and McBride tracked Burke and his partner to a copse of cedars. Immediately, McBride opened fire on the pair which was returned in kind by the robbers. In the confusion Burke and Willis temporarily managed to elude their pursuers and melt back into the brush.

Deciding they could use reinforcements, Huntsman hurried to the town of Nephi while McBride and Whitbeck continued on the trail of the two robbers. Again, McBride and Whitbeck ran into them near a roadhouse called the Church House. Another gun battle ensued when suddenly Whitbeck's gun jammed and the two-man posse once again had to let the quarry escape.

Eventually three reinforcements from Nephi, Alf McCune, R. Rollins and E. Sparks met up with McBride and Whitbeck. Now strengthened, the posse relentlessly renewed the chase. Four miles down the road toward the mining camp of Tintic, Burke and Willis had again attempted to conceal themselves in the dense cedars. Spotted by the posse, the two men were called on to surrender. Seeing they were now outnumbered, Willis rose up with his hands in the air.

"Your partner must get up too or we will blow you to pieces," McBride shouted.

With that Burke also gave himself up.[72]

The two outlaws were eventually located in the jail at Beaver, Utah, for examination before the U.S. Commissioner's Court on charges of robbing the U.S. mail. On June 6 their hearing gained postponement to June 12 due to nonappearance of witnesses. To everyone's surprise, except possibly those who may have known of John Burke's past history, Burke used the days of grace leading up to the scheduled court date to engineer an escape from the Beaver County Jail. This time, he and Willis were only at large for a few short hours before being recaptured by Beaver County officers.[73]

Authorities decided to relocate Burke and Willis to the more secure confines of the Utah State Penitentiary to await further court action. Only a few days hence, on Thursday, June 22, William Willis and six other state convicts made a daring escape from the Utah pen. Willis managed to make good his escape and was never recaptured.[74]

At this point in its history the Utah State Prison facility was notorious as a porous, insecure establishment. Inmates were continually escaping from its walls at any time of the day or night. Almost one month later, Monday, July 17, Burke decided it was his turn.

That morning, while most of the convicts took their exercise in the prison yard, Burke and cellmate Jack Wiggins, a notorious Nevada/Utah criminal and gunman sentenced to be shot by firing squad for murder, sat, shackled and ironed, in their cell. Burke had been tried June 26 for the armed mail theft and Judge Philip Emerson had sentenced him to a life term at the federal Detroit House of Corrections.[75] Both Burke and Wiggins were considered major flight risks by prison officials, thus their status that hot July day.

At about 11 a.m. one of the guards casually entered Burke's and Wiggins' cell to empty the slop pails. Without warning he was suddenly seized by the two inmates, now free of their irons. Quickly Burke and Wiggins bound and gagged the hapless guard, shut him in the cell and dashed for freedom. Joined by two other inmates in the prison yard, George Brewer and another well-known Utah/Nevada gunman and ne'er-do-well named William "Idaho Bill" Sloan, the four raced for the sheltered southeast corner of the outer wall. Here, seizing a makeshift rope constructed of tied together strips of bedsheets, they somehow managed to fasten the rope to the top of the 20-foot wall and, scaling its height, dropped down on the outside.[76]

The *Salt Lake Tribune* would later be amazed at Burke's and Wiggins' Houdini act in sloughing off their irons:

> But the most singular circumstance is how Wiggins and Harker got their irons off. The former were shackled with very heavy irons, and the latter both shackled and handcuffed, yet both of them had slipped off their shackles without cutting the rivets or otherwise sawing their irons.[77]

Little could they realize that Burke had demonstrated this ability on previous occasions.[78]

Upon their feet striking the soil on the outside of the wall the four men broke into pairs and dashed off in different directions. Brewer and Idaho Bill would make haste and disappear into the countryside. Neither man was caught at this time.[79]

After failing to stop a wagon passing on the road just outside of the prison, Burke and Wiggins held up a second convenience, appropriated the team and thundered off down the road. Alerted to circumstances, Guard A.L. Parrish hastily mounted his horse and galloped after the fugitives. A fair piece down the road Parrish began to gain on the fleeing men, the wagon horses beginning to tire. Unlimbering his Henry rifle, Parrish fired on the pair. Abandoning their fagged-out animals, Burke and Wiggins dashed on foot into the nearby brush.

Taking careful aim, Parrish sent a number of shots into the bush. Suddenly Jack Wiggins appeared out of the timber with his hands above his head, limping badly. Due to a sprained ankle sustained while jumping down from the prison wall he was unable to run any further.[80]

Burke continued his flight with Parrish's rifle balls zinging around him. He had almost made it out of rifle range when a nearby farmer joined the pursuit, road after Burke and eventually brought him back at the point of a rifle.[81]

Utah authorities were not taking any further chances with their desperate inmate. Three days after his escape attempt, U.S. Deputy Marshals Charley Emerson and Marshal Pratt loaded Burke onto a train for the long journey northeast to the federal prison at Detroit, Michigan.[82] As could almost be expected at this point, during the train trip Burke made one futile attempt to slip his bonds and perpetrate another escape.[83] Most likely, much to their great relief, the lawmen managed to see Burke safely to the institution at journey's end.

Operated by the city of Detroit from its inception in 1861, the House of Corrections ran on a fee basis agreement with the federal U.S. government to house federal inmates. Burke's conviction for mail robbery placed him in this category. The prison, located on Detroit's east side near the famous Eastern Markets, housed around 700 convicts at the time of Burke's induction.[84] Its major industry proved to be the manufacture of wooden chairs. It would be over a year before John Burke, alias Francis Harker, would decide he had made his last chair. Not sitting down on the job, on Friday, November 2, 1877, Burke exhibited his major talent and escaped from the Detroit House of Corrections.[85]

Shortly after Burke's escape, House of Corrections superintendent M.V. Borgman, offering a $100 reward for his missing charge, issued the following wanted circular to various law enforcement agencies:

> Escaped from the Detroit House of Correction, on the night of November 2d, the following described person: Francis Harker, 31 years of age, looks to be 35 years of age, has voice and action of a Southerner, being from Texas; he is 5 feet 10½ inches tall, weighs 135 pounds, has light brown mustache, black hair, dark, restless eyes, sharp, long features. Wore when he left, plain gray prison pants, a rubber coat, and dark overcoat. He has an affection of the stomach, by which he is compelled to vomit every little while. He was sentenced from Utah for robbing the United States Mail.

Apparently, Burke's health had begun to suffer as a result of his hectic lifestyle and long incarcerations in various prisons and jails. If the above description is any indication, he looked at least five years older than his true age; he had lost some 15 pounds since his sentence to the Nevada State Prison in 1870; and he had acquired some sort of serious stomach ailment. This failed to inhibit his escape however.

Whether he disappeared into the nearby countryside or lost himself in the metropolis that was Detroit is unknown. One thing is clear. John Burke finally pulled off the ultimate escape. He was never seen again in Detroit or anywhere else that may have had reason to seek his recapture.

Although gone Burke was not forgotten by some in the law enforcement community. As late as the summer of 1878 his case was important enough for famed Wells Fargo Detective Chief James B. Hume to take interest. On July 13, 1878, Hume sent a letter to Carson City Wells Fargo Agent Henry Tickner, seeking his assistance in tracking down the missing fugitive. Reprinted in the *Carson City Morning Appeal* under the headline "Something of a Noted Rogue," Hume wrote:

> Friend Tickner: Herewith I send you a notice of an escape from Detroit Prison. This Francis Harker is a "thoroughbred," an old resident of your Hot Spring prison. His true name is John Burke and was in the "big break" of 1871. After finishing his sentence at Carson, he came to Utah in company with Ed Biglowe [sic], another "big break" fellow, and together, they

committed a series of stage robberies, "going through" the mail as well as our box each time. They were arrested for mail robbery and escaped (I think) from Beaver jail, were recaptured and brought back to Utah penitentiary for safekeeping pending trial. They both escaped from there with Jack Wiggins and others, Bigelow making a clean job of it and has not been caught. Burke, Wiggins and others were retaken. Burke was recaptured and sent to the Detroit House of Correction for life. No one knew of the history of Burke and Bigelow until I came out two years ago. You see by this card that at Detroit they did not take anything like a full description of him. I wish you would get the description from the Carson prison books and if your papers would like to publish it for an item, furnished them the facts of the description and send me copies of papers and I will have them copied into the Utah papers. I think he will work back to the staging country this side of Rocky Mountains. I may be here two weeks yet. Send Brastow Carson papers if they make items about him. Truly, etc.

J. B. Hume.[86]

Despite Hume's efforts, John Burke stayed lost, his future life unknown and unrecorded. The "outlaw Houdini" had performed the ultimate disappearing act.

10

"One of the Worst Men in the Country"
James Harrington

If it proved necessary to compile a top ten of Nevada old west gunslingers, James Harrington would surely be in the top five, if not topping the list. In some eight years of known active involvement in matters of the gun, Harrington conducted himself in a most fearless manner, a fearlessness made deadly with a combination of brutality and offhanded attitude toward human life. It was a combination which made him one of the most feared members of the Nevada mining camp fraternity. Although large in reputation, Harrington, sometimes known as "Little Jimmie," was rather diminutive in physical stature, giving him a most deceptive aura. It might be fair to state that the old axiom, "The lord made man, but Sam Colt made them equal," fits James Harrington to a tee. With a Colt revolver in his hand he proved larger than most.

James W. Harrington had the innate fighting spirit of the Irish, being born on the Emerald Isle sometime in the 1844–1848 time period.[1] At some point he, along with brothers Daniel and Timothy, immigrated to the United States. They eventually settled in the mining regions of Ophir, Toole County, Utah, about 25 miles southwest of Salt Lake City, possibly via Michigan and Montana.[2] It gained rumor that James Harrington killed a man in Montana after a difficulty of some sort.[3] Despite stories, however, he would later claim never to have set foot in the area. Quickly, the Harrington brothers settled into the mining fraternity of the Ophir district, making themselves a force to be reckoned with. James, described at about this time as "a small, spare-made man, below the medium height, but is high tempered, and is ever ready to use weapons on any plausible pretext," soon gained a reputation for toughness.[4] At length the Harrington's became known for their bullying tactics and threats when it came to mine locations and lease lines.

Despite their pug-ugly reputations the Harrington boys always seemed to have high connections in mining and political realms. How this came about has always been somewhat of a mystery. Sometime in 1870, James Harrington tapped into these connections when he relocated to the booming mining town of Pioche, Lincoln County, Nevada, some 200 miles southwest of Ophir, Utah. Here he hired on with wealthy mining moguls William Raymond and John Ely as fixer, trouble shooter and a one-man security force for their burgeoning mining empire developing in the Pioche area. His talents would soon be put to good use.

Early in the fall of 1870, Raymond and Ely gave a temporary, 30-day lease in their Washington and Creole mine to two enterprising brothers named Thomas and Frank Newland. Raymond and Ely were unimpressed with the $30 to the ton of ore property and when the Newlands offered to work the mine for a month in exchange for any profits found, the mine owners agreed. Raymond and Ely were ready to give up on the hole and waited just long enough to see what the Newlands would find.

Lo and behold, when Raymond and Ely foremen Wythe Walker inspected the mine, he discovered the Newlands had uncovered a fabulously wealthy ledge which would eventually go on to yield over $300 to the ton.[5] There was a catch, however. At the end of their 30 days lease the Newlands refused to leave.[6] Not only did they continue working the mine, they also hired a crew of gunmen, including future Pioche law man William McKee and notorious fighter Jack White, to guard the property against any attempts of the owners to retake it.

William Raymond and John Ely felt moved to accept this turn of events for only a week before they decided to take action. Probably with the aid of James Harrington, who moved in the same saloon circles and likely knew all four men, the mining magnets hired four notorious Pioche gunmen, Morgan Courtney, William Bethards, Barney Flood, and Michael Casey, to remove the Newlands and retake the Washington and Creole. The quartet agreed in return for their own 30 days at working the mine.

Courtney, Bethards, Flood and Casey decided to make their move on the afternoon of Wednesday, November 9. After having a few cases of whiskey delivered to the Newlands barricaded fighters in the guise of a gift from the Newlands supporters to their thirsty men, the four waited an appropriate length of time for most of it to be consumed. They then stormed the men forted up in the mine. In the ensuing gun battle one man, W.G. Snell, was fatally shot, while others received nonfatal wounds of various severity, before the Newland men fled the mine.[7] It would not have been in James Harrington's character to have missed a chance to use his revolver and chances are he managed to get off a few shots at the opposition before the fighting ceased.

Shortly after the battle, the Lincoln County Grand Jury indicted Harrington, along with all the other Raymond and Ely fighters, on a charge of "murder as an accessory before the fact."[8] As he did for all of his warriors, William Raymond, along with one A.H. Rutherford, paid Harrington's bail bond of $5000. Harrington did not plan to be around when his court date came to pass. He quickly departed the area, most likely making tracks back to Ophir, Utah, where his brothers gave him sanctuary. As a result, at the December 1870 term of Lincoln County court, Raymond and Rutherford were judged in default and ordered to relinquish their $5000 bond.[9] The two bondsmen would take the matter of the forfeiture back into the courts, eventually receiving a positive judgment in March 1872.[10]

Meanwhile, a new Lincoln County Grand Jury sitting in March 1871 saw the hopelessness of a number of the previous grand jury indictments. On the 27th they voted to ignore the bills against Harrington, Morgan Courtney, William Bethards, Mike Casey and a number of others found as a result of the November 9, 1871, imbroglio.[11] James Harrington would not be out of trouble for long.

Back in Ophir, Utah, one day in early March, around the same time as the Lincoln County, Nevada Grand Jury was dismissing the charges against him, Harrington sat in an Ophir saloon drinking heavily. For reasons unknown he fell into a disagreement with another man by the name of Benjamin James.[12] Without batting an eye, in what one contemporary source would term "without the slightest provocation" and another would call "very little cause," Harrington suddenly palmed his revolver and started shooting.[13] After emptying his pistol into the hapless James's body, he strode up to his fallen victim and beat him over the head with the weapon before being dragged off by stunned bystanders.[14] If not killed instantly, James died soon after being shot.

Arrested by justice of the peace William Barbee, Harrington was slapped into the local lockup to await a court hearing. He almost did not live long enough for one to take place. A number of local citizens, enraged by the wanton killing, banded together and were advocating a lynching, when, eventually, cooler heads prevailed.[15] Turned over to a U.S. Marshal, the lawman transported Harrington to the military base at Camp Douglas, located near Salt Lake City, to await the action of the local Grand Jury in the camp guard house.[16]

Once again, anonymous moneyed individuals stepped in to attempt a rescue of the notorious gunman. Two local attorneys, A. Huggan and V.A. Witcher, were retained to represent Harrington. They did all in their power to obtain their client's release on a legal technicality, presenting a number of points at a hearing in late March.[17] Chief Justice James B. McKean denied the motion, however, and ordered the prisoner held to await further court action.[18]

The Harrington case became somewhat of a cause célèbre around Salt Lake City and the Ophir district. At one point a letter writer, operating incognito, even wrote a missive to the *Deseret News* denigrating Justice McKean for his decision. Most supported McKean, however, the rival *Salt Lake City Tribune* declaring:

> If Judge McKean were now to turn him [Harrington] loose upon the public he would deserve himself to be indicted. Let the *News* get a better case before it again assails the Judiciary for preforming its clear and bounden duty.[19]

Harrington was soon to make discussions of the merits or demerits of his release a moot point.

On the evening of Friday, April 28, with apparent outside assistance, James Harrington and the other four civilian prisoners held in the Camp Douglas guardhouse, escaped. Supposedly having been bribed, the military sentinel on duty unfastened the door and then vamoosed with his charges. Another guard patrolling near the guardhouse suddenly caught a glimpse of the figures swiftly moving through the dim moonlight. Opening fire on them with his rifle, he heard one man shout, "I am shot." All, however, including Harrington, apparently made good their escape.[20]

The *Salt Lake City Tribune* of two days later observed: "Harrington is a notorious desperado, who has been engaged in a number of bloody affrays at Pioche and elsewhere, before he came to East Canyon (Ophir District). Bad as he is, it appears that he has had a number of friends in the mines somewhere who have been working persistently for his release, and there is little doubt that means from that quarter bribed the guard who was instrumental in their escape."[21]

Despite removing himself only some 40 or 50 miles from Salt Lake City, Harrington was never recaptured and never stood trial for the Benjamin James killing. As late as May 1872 his unresolved case was still listed on the Third Judicial District Court docket.[22]

By the summer of 1872, James Harrington, with brothers Daniel and Timothy, had located in the new mining boom camp of Lewiston, situated near Camp Floyd in southeastern Tooele County. Here the boys once again invested in various claims and mining properties. On June 1, 1872, Daniel Harrington managed to get himself appointed as one of the judges in the election for Recorder of the Camp Floyd mining district.[23]

There were also other, more nefarious doings, in the air. According to a letter sent for publication to the *Salt Lake City Tribune*, a Lewiston correspondent huffed, "a rumor was circulated that parties had jumped the Silver Circle Mine but, after inquiry, I find the report unfounded."[24]

The correspondent should have waited a bit longer before pooh-poohing the lot jumping rumor.

On June 4, prominent Lewiston mining speculator and owner of the Silver Circle Mine, L. Pike, accompanied a group of men on an excursion to Salt Lake City.[25] Shortly after, James Harrington moved onto the property, set up camp and claimed the Silver Circle as his own, effectively "jumping" Pike's claim.[26] Upon his return, Pike angrily reported the situation to a local Justice of the Peace.

Swearing out a warrant, the Justice sent a Deputy Sheriff of Toole County to place Harrington under arrest. On being confronted by the deputy, Harrington threatened the man within an inch of his life before declaring his refusal to be arrested.

The Justice next decided to travel to Salt Lake City and obtain a federal warrant from Judge McKean. Apparently having forgotten his prisoner of one year before, McKean simply gave the warrant to a Deputy U.S. Marshal for routine service. The federal lawman met the same defiant Harrington and also retreated under threats of violence.

At some point, an official with more gumption finally managed to place the recalcitrant lot jumper in custody on a charge of resisting an officer in the discharge of his duty and tossed him into the Toole County Jail. According to the *Salt Lake City Tribune*, while Harrington sat in jail:

> Pike went there, sought and obtained an interview with Harrington, told him he was very sorry to see him in that situation, but if he (Harrington) would deed over to him his interest in the Silver Circle mine, he (Pike) would get him out of the scrape, but on being refused he said that, if he would not deed his interest in the claim to him, he (Pike) would employ an attorney to assist the prosecution, and would send him up for two years ... he had both men and money to do it, and would spend $100,000 to accomplish this purpose.[27]

For his time and trouble the Harrington brothers then charged Pike with using threatening language and he was bound over under $1000 bond to appear at the September term of the District Court.[28] Unfortunately, the final outcome of any of these cases is unknown.

The consequences for James Harrington, if any, must have been minor. By fall 1872 he had left the heat of Utah behind and trekked back to Nevada. This time situating himself in the town of Eureka he was rumored to have "figured in a plot to assassinate a sporting man who is still a resident of the Base Range."[29]

The alleged plot obviously having failed, Harrington, by the early winter of 1872, had traveled back to his old stomping grounds at Pioche. It did not take long for the fractious Irishman to get into trouble once again in the mining metropolis.

Although the nature of the charge is not of record, Harrington appeared in Lincoln County District Court on January 11, 1873, indicted for some sort of criminal offense.[30] At this time the court decided to carry the case forward to a future term of the court.[31] Harrington's future actions would guarantee that this particular case would be all but forgotten by authorities.

One o'clock Sunday morning, July 6, 1873, found Harrington drinking with two friends in John H. Lynch's chophouse located on Meadow Valley Street in Pioche. Seated at his table and imbibing with him proved to be two miners, Cornelius "Con" Sullivan, a 32-year-old native of Ireland who had recently come to Pioche via New York and California, who had been a friend of Harrington's back in Ireland before either had come to America; and Edmund O'Neil, 28 years old and a native of Pennsylvania who also came to Pioche by way of California.[32]

At length, the owner of the restaurant, John Lynch, entered his establishment accompanied by Frank Schoonmaker. Trailing at Schoonmaker's heel was his little pet Terrier pup which he prized quite highly. Moving into the building, Lynch led Schoonmaker to a table on the opposite side of the room to that occupied by Harrington, Sullivan and O'Neil. Lynch, born in Ireland and now about 36 years old, had traveled through Oregon and San Francisco, California, before trying his fortunes in Pioche. He had a wife currently residing in San Francisco where he formerly operated a saloon. He had been living in Pioche about two or three years by July 1873.[33]

After a few minutes, Schoonmaker's dog wandered over to Harrington's table. Picking up the animal, Sullivan held it up at arm's length over the table then let it drop. The pup let out a yelp and scampered away.

Noticing this action Schoonmaker jumped up, and went over to check on his pet, closely followed by Lynch.

"What do you mean by hurting my dog," Schoonmaker confronted Sullivan. "When you hurt that dog, you hurt me."

"I did not know whose dog it was," a surprised Sullivan defended himself. "I did not mean to hurt it."

With a look of exasperation O'Neil arose from his chair. "It doesn't matter if the dog is hurt or not," he growled.

"You better not have anything to say about it," Lynch warned O'Neil.

O'Neil glared at Lynch. "You better not either," he said.

Ignoring O'Neil, Schoonmaker said to Sullivan, "As long as you did not intend hurting the dog, we will let the matter drop and have nothing more to say about it."

To this Sullivan agreed and, after paying their bills, the men, including James Harrington, who had thus far remained out of the controversy, headed toward the door.

On the sidewalk in front of the chophouse, O'Neil, disgusted at Sullivan for, in his mind, taking water with Schoonmaker, pointed his finger at him. "You are a damned coward," he said to Sullivan, "apologizing over a dog."

Hearing the remark, Schoonmaker stopped. "What would you have done," he asked O'Neil. "Would you have hurt the dog?"

O'Neil sighed. "No, I wouldn't have hurt the dog," he said.

Attempting to save face in the eyes of his friend, Sullivan then made a disparaging remark about the pup.

With that, Schoonmaker turned and punched Sullivan in the face. While the two men clinched and began to wrestle around in the doorway, Lynch also engaged with O'Neil. After a brief struggle the men separated momentarily before Lynch began to tussle with Sullivan.

"What in the hell do you intend doing with that man!" Harrington hollered, at the same time stepping back, pulling his revolver and firing a shot at Lynch.

Sullivan pushed Lynch away from him when Harrington fired a second shot. "Don't shoot anymore. I'm killed," Lynch gasped as he fell to the sidewalk.

Turning, Harrington began to move away down the sidewalk. Twisting back, he fired a third shot into the group then walked into the arms of Henry Woodruff, a Pioche police officer who had rushed to the scene upon hearing the gunshots.[34]

In a somewhat extraordinary occurrence, investigation later revealed that Harrington's three shots had inflicted five separate wounds, injuring four of the men. Inquiry seemed to reveal that one bullet traversed through Sullivan's left wrist entering Lynch's right shoulder. Another seemed to contact Schoonmaker's side and, without entering the body cavity, passed around under the skin before exiting and striking O'Neil in the hip. The third shot proved to be the most serious, plowing into the head of John Lynch and embedding itself in his brain.[35]

Carried inside his establishment, Lynch was made as comfortable as possible while a physician was summoned. Dr. Bergstein felt the wound was necessarily fatal and Lynch was moved to his rooms to await developments. Surprisingly to most, the gravely wounded man managed to linger, mostly in a state of delirium, for a number of days.[36] Drs. Bergstein, Philson and D.L. Deal, the County Coroner, even attempted a risky trepanning on Lynch's skull in an attempt to relieve the swelling of the brain on the 9th. In this operation a large portion of the frontal bone of the man's skull was removed to ease the compression.[37] All efforts proved hopeless and John Lynch finally succumbed early on the morning of July 11.[38] A coroner's jury called by Dr. Deal eventually placed the death of Lynch on the hands of James Harrington on Monday, July 14.[39] All the others wounded in the affray of the 6th eventually made a full recovery.[40]

Ensconced in overly crowded conditions in the County Jail, Harrington could only bide his time and await his fate. It was probably not a comfortable stay, the local *Pioche Record* reporting on Saturday, July 19, "The Jail—This county institution is brim full.... During such unprecedently [sic] hot weather it must be very unpleasant for so many persons to occupy such a small prison."

Some relief finally came for Harrington in late July when he was able to leave the stifling conditions at the jail to visit the District Court room. Indicted by the Grand Jury, Harrington made his first court appearance on Monday, July 28, to answer murder charges.[41] The State had set aside the prosecution of his earlier indictment from January and could now concentrate solely on this new murder charge.[42] On Saturday, August 2, Harrington came into court and entered a plea of "not guilty" to the charge of murdering Lynch.[43]

Harrington's trial finally commenced on Monday the 18th. Both brothers Daniel and Timothy traveled to Pioche for their sibling's trial and appeared by his side every day of the lengthy proceedings, hiring well-known Pioche attorneys Jesse Pitzer and W.W. Bishop for James' defense.[44]

For six days prosecution and defense attorneys argued Harrington's fate before a standing room only crowd of curious and fascinated Pioche residents. Despite the fact of the two main witnesses for the defense, Harrington's pals Ed O'Neil and Con Sullivan, presenting what amounted to perjured testimony, the weight of evidence proved heavily in favor of the prosecution. After all the witnesses had been called the accused man must have had a feeling of resignation regarding the final outcome.[45]

On the morning of Friday, August 22, lawyers for the prosecution and defense commenced final arguments. Just as defense attorney W.W. Bishop began his final oratory a most curious thing happened, as reported by the *Record* newspaper:

> Just as the eloquent gentlemen seemed to have warmed up thoroughly, the black clouds gathered thick and fast, the lightning flashed and the thunder roared. A suggestion was made that the court had better take a recess; but above the clash of the elements was heard the stentorian voice of the gentleman. "No wonder," he said, "that the heavens grew black, the thunders roared and the lightnings flashed, while the State, represented by eminent counsel, sought to take the life of James Harrington."[46]

Indeed, regardless of Harrington's guilt or innocence, the heavens did open up and release a deluge, flooding Pioche to the tune of some $10,000 worth of damage, many homes and businesses succumbing to the raging waters.[47]

Despite nature's fury, the Harrington trial resumed unabated. Submitted to the jury on Saturday, that august body returned on Sunday morning to declare "the defendant, James Harrington, guilty of murder in the second degree."[48] According to the *Record*, Harrington appeared "weak and exhausted" after the reading of the verdict and "asked for liquor as soon as he was out of the courtroom."[49] "It is a source of congratulation among good citizens," continued the *Record*, "that a verdict of murder in the second degree was obtained.." The paper went on to chastise O'Neil and Sullivan:

> The conviction of Harrington, in the face of the testimony given by O'Neil and Sullivan, is as damaging to their reputation as an indictment for perjury. It cannot be that the jury believed a word said by either of those witnesses, for if their testimony had been credited, an acquittal must have followed.[50]

With his scheduled sentencing being postponed a number of times in order to give his lawyers time to prepare arguments for a new trial, Harrington had time for contemplation as he languished in his jail cell.[51] Developments would soon go to show that he must have contemplated upon how much he desired his freedom. The delays gave him the perfect opportunity to act on these desires.

Asking for a private audience with Lincoln County Sheriff Wes Travis on the evening of Friday, September 5, one of the county prisoners informed him that Harrington was ready to make an escape. Taking a deputy with him into Harrington's cell, Travis found that the convicted murderer had excavated a two and one half by two-foot hole in the back wall of his cell which adjoined an unlocked shed. He was hours away from having a hole large enough to crawl through. The officers found secreted in the cell a crowbar, a cold chisel fashioned from a file and a saw which someone, possibly Harrington himself, had meticulously made by notching the blade of a case knife. It was also discovered that, with this improvised saw, the prisoner had totally cut through the chain attached to his ankle fetter. The sheriff felt that the items employed by Harrington had somehow been smuggled in by parties from the outside. Travis quickly confiscated the items, had Harrington moved to another cell, and ordered him more securely chained.[52]

After more delays, Harrington was finally called to the courtroom again on Tuesday, September 9, to receive sentence. At this time Judge M. Fuller sentenced him to a term of 15 years in the Nevada State Prison.[53] He was reportedly "in much agitation" at the time of his sentencing, "the outward appearances of which he could hardly suppress, even with a strong effort."[54]

Although most of the Pioche citizenry were pleased to have the man convicted and sentenced to a long term in the penitentiary, there were those who wished for something more. The *Record* reflected this feeling when it said of Judge Fuller's decision:

> While we were prompted to accord a word of praise to Judge Fuller for his course in the Howard case [another murder case tried at the same term of court as Harrington's case], we are reluctantly impelled to say that he has not met public expectation in dealing so leniently with one of the worst men in the country—James Harrington—a man who, it is believed by many, killed John H. Lynch for simple wantoness [*sic*].[55]

While Harrington's attorneys placed a petition for a new trial before the court, judicial process, at this point, came to an end for James Harrington. Taking the prisoner in charge, Sheriff Travis escorted him to Carson City and placed him in the State Prison on Saturday, September 13, 1873.[56] Harrington's time behind the walls of the state institution would be far shorter than most could ever have imagined.

Although his conduct during his time inside the penitentiary is not of record, one report which came to light later went far to display Harrington's cunning and active mind:

> [Harrington] was working in the boot makers department and succeeded in manufacturing a boot which he must have expected would be of considerable use to him on future occasions. In the shank was a hollow space, in which he inserted a fine saw and file, both of which had evidently been used, for one morning the Warden happened to strike his hand against one of the bolts of the cell, found that the head came off, being nothing but wax. Harrington had cut away the heads of several bolts and made a good imitation in wax which he covered with lampblack to give them the appearance of iron. When an opportunity of escape presented itself, he expected to drive the bolt out and then makes his exit, probably wearing the same boots in which he had as deftly concealed the file and saw.[57]

While the convict spent his days making boots and planning escapes, his appeal for a new trial sat with the Nevada Supreme Court throughout the remainder of 1873.[58] Although a new trial would not be in Harrington's future, he had his usual abstruse forces, perhaps directed by his brothers, working for his release. Eventually, a petition signed by hundreds of Pioche area residents, later charged to have contained many forged signatures, made its way before the Nevada Parole Board.[59]

Abruptly, after serving only one year, three months and 13 days of his 15-year sentence, Nevada Governor Lewis R. "Broad Horns" Bradley issued Harrington a pardon, supposedly based on his "previous good behavior," in December 1874.[60] Harrington stepped beyond the prison doors the day after Christmas.[61] Gossipmongers quickly spread the tale, probably unfounded, that Bradley had bestowed the gift of freedom on the convict as payback for some sort of political work, presumably of a "shoulder striking" type, performed on behalf of the Governor sometime in the past.[62] Be that as it may, by the new year of 1875, James Harrington had been once again prematurely loosed on the world.[63]

By April 1875, Harrington could be found a resident of Virginia City, working as a watchman at the Consolidated Virginia mill.[64] Sometime previous, his brother Daniel had begun operation of a drinking establishment in the city's saloon district. Another attraction proved to be the presence of the Sullivan family. Recently locating from Pioche, Harrington's old friend Con Sullivan had relocated to Virginia City with his wife and 14-year-old stepdaughter Julia Regan. His 23-year-old brother, John C. Sullivan, would soon follow.[65]

James Harrington's special interest within the Sullivan clan, despite their more than 21-year age difference, was young Julia Regan. He became enamored with the girl and attempted to cultivate a romantic relationship with her, without, at first, much apparent resistance on her part. Her stepfather Con Sullivan and, as they termed each other, "cousin," John, felt differently. They attempted to discourage Julia from any connection with the ex-con. Apparently, John Sullivan and Harrington had clashed on more than one occasion, as far back as their acquaintance in Pioche. Sullivan expressed his fears to friends that Harrington "would murder him sooner or later."[66]

In the spring of 1876, Harrington proposed marriage to Julia Regan. She seems to have accepted, despite the objections of Con and, especially, John Sullivan.[67] According to Julia herself, John went to her and "advised me not to marry [Harrington] because he was a hard case."[68]

Thus, the situation stood until late July 1876. According to James Harrington's story (to which Julia Regan would later object as an outright lie), one day Julia came to him and told him that she had been "seduced" by her stepfather Con Sullivan. As a result, she would not be able to become his (Harrington's) wife. Again, according to Harrington, although upset, he "told her to go to a priest and confess, and that he would make her his wife, notwithstanding what had befallen her."[69]

A day or two later, John Sullivan approached Con and angrily asked him for the loan of a pistol or knife. When Con asked him what for, John said he would die himself or kill Harrington before he would let Julia marry him.[70] Con refused to give him any weapons.

On the morning of Saturday, July 22, Harrington walked to the Sullivan house where he encountered Julia in the yard. As she would later claim:

> He asked me who was in. I told him my mother and Con. He did not say anymore, but went in and appeared to be very angry. He then sat down for a short time and then asked my mother why she did not want to speak to him. My mother said she did not want to speak to him, as there was something else to bother her besides speaking to him, and he said: "May the Lord keep you so." He then asked Con to go down town and both of them went off together[71]

After separating from Con, Harrington encountered John Sullivan on C Street near Dan Harrington's saloon. As James Harrington later told it, "John came up to him and taking him by the shoulder inquired if that was so about the girl. Harrington said he had better ask Con and then go and inquire of his [Con's] stepdaughter."[72] John then left to join Con in Dan Harrington's saloon.

Harrington himself later entered his brother's establishment for a drink where he once again encountered Con and John Sullivan. Almost at once, Harrington and John Sullivan fell into a rancorous shouting match. At length, the pair exited out into C Street where the argument escalated. Harrington suddenly pulled his pistol from his belt but was unable to bring it into play before Con Sullivan jumped between them, grabbed John and dragged him back inside the saloon.

Once inside, John, who had been drinking heavily, raved around the room. "I will go to Harrington if I am cut to pieces," he yelled. Before Con could restrain him the infuriated and slightly tipsy man barged back outside where he again came face to face with Harrington.

Grabbing Harrington's arm Sullivan began pulling on his coat sleeve and imploring him to come back into the saloon for a drink. Although Harrington declined, Sullivan continued to yank on his sleeve and badger him about having a drink with him. Harrington would later claim that he felt the Sullivans were attempting to get him inside where they would look for a chance to assassinate him.

"Let me alone"! Harrington yelled at Sullivan. "You will tear my coat!"

Lashing out with his fist, Harrington landed a punch on John Sullivan's jaw. As Sullivan staggered back, Harrington drew his revolver, placed the muzzle to Sullivan's chest and pulled the trigger. The weapon belched, the bullet tearing Sullivan's heart asunder. Sullivan, dead on his feet, slumped forward, causing himself and Harrington to crash to the boardwalk. With Sullivan laying on top of him, Harrington fired three more shots into his body, two entering the dead man's chest and another piercing his right hip.[73] Pushing his victim's body off of him, Harrington quickly scrambled to his feet and hastened down the street. Hearing the gunfire and seeing a man retreating away from the scene, Officer Merrow, security at the nearby Cowan & Sliter's No. 66 Saloon, who had powers of arrest with the Virginia City police force, ran after the man and arrested Harrington before he could make himself scarce. Escorting Harrington to the County Jail, Merrow turned the gunman over to Storey County Sheriff Thomas Kelly who locked him into a cell.

By evening the word began to drift around the city that the local "601" vigilantes were mobilizing in preparation for a raid on the jail and a neck-tie party for Harrington. Sheriff Kelly spoiled the party, however, when, gaining knowledge of the possible attempt on his prisoner, surreptitiously spirited him onto a late train and transferred him to Carson City.[74]

The news of James Harrington's latest pistol exploits quickly traveled throughout Nevada and the Pacific Coast. In his former home at Pioche the story gained special interest, prompting the *Pioche Record* to editorialize:

> Everyone in Pioche ... remembers the trial of Harrington for killing Lynch; remembers also that it cost the county ten or twelve thousand dollars to convict him even to the extent of having him sent to the Penitentiary, and many of our citizens remember with shame and

indignation at the mockery of law and justice when before the election of '74 a petition was numerously signed for his pardon on the ground of his previous *good behavior* [editor's italics] and sent on to it's successful mission at the State Capitol.... What is the good of spending thousands of dollars to convict a man of wilful, cold blooded murder in Pioche, send him to Carson, and have a worthy Board of Pardons let him go to kill in Virginia's streets by daylight.... We trust for the honor of the State that one of the first acts of the Legislature that assembles next Winter will be the repeal or amendment of the act creating the Board of Pardons. Its abuse is worse than its non-existence.[75]

A harsh denunciation, but a sentiment felt by many.

While sitting in his cell in Carson City, Harrington decided he needed to tell his side of the Sullivan affair. With the acquiescence of officials, he invited a representative of the *Carson City Tribune* to visit him in his cell. The reporter thusly stopped by on Sunday the 23rd and found the shootist "in deep distress, not for the deed committed, but on account of the causes that led to the commission of the murder."

After Harrington emotionally related his meeting and falling in love with Julia Regan, the opposition of Con and John Sullivan to his attentions to their 14-year-old relative and his impressions of the circumstances leading up to the shooting, the *Tribune* scribe concluded:

> Believing, as he says, that the two Sullivans intended to assassinate him, and being crazed with grief, he shot John Sullivan down.
>
> Harrington glories in the act, and says he feels no remorse at all. All he desires is to be hung as soon as possible, as his heart is broken, having lost the only thing he ever loved in the world. He cried and sobbed all the time he was relating the above circumstances, and repeatedly asserted that he plead guilty, and wanted to die as soon as possible.[76]

Over the course of Monday, the 24th, and Tuesday, the 25th, a Storey County Coroner's Jury met to fix the blame of Sullivan's death on Harrington.[77] In the meantime, the local media and citizenry proved fascinated by the case. Another development fed the fires of curiosity on July 27 when none other than young Julia Regan herself sent off a letter to the *Virginia City Chronicle* giving her side of the sordid affair. In part, Miss Regan declared:

> Please give space in one of your columns for a brief statement that I want to make regarding the slander of Harrington against me. It is all false, and a meaner lie was never uttered by man. Harrington is now doing all he can to injure my reputation, and saying all he can to hurt me, because I would not comply with his wishes. He wanted me to leave my mother altogether and not stop with her any more, that he would take full charge of me, and that I would not want for anything. This I refused to do, and he got very angry and said that people were trying to turn me against him, and he said that if people's talk were the means of putting us apart, he would slaughter half a dozen of them and clear out on horseback to the Black Hills.

With the affair still a cause célèbre, authorities felt it safe to return Harrington to Storey County, which was accomplished on August 5.[78] Now the prisoner's long court process could begin. With the preliminaries dispensed with by late September, Harrington's murder trial commenced on December 5.[79] Following the day of testimony and legal arguments the jury returned early on the morning of Wednesday, December 6, 1876, with a verdict of guilty of murder in the first degree.[80] The court set Saturday, December 16, for the day of sentencing.

On the 16th lawmen trooped Harrington back to the Storey County Courthouse to receive his sentence. Asked by Judge Richard Rising if he had anything to say before his sentence was passed, Harrington said only:

> One of his chief witnesses whose testimony would have been of great benefit to him had left town. He did not know why he had done so. There were three other witnesses who were not produced, and there were men on the jury against him, men that heard the shooting and were not forty yards away at the time.[81]

Judge Rising then pronounced the shooting, "a wanton, cruel murder" and sentenced Harrington to be "kept in close confinement until Friday, February 9, 1877," at which time "you, James Harrington, shall be, by the said Sheriff, hanged by the neck until you are dead, and the Lord have mercy on your sinful soul."[82]

Taken back to his cell in the County Jail, Harrington displayed a front of arrogance and indifference toward his fate. According to one source:

> He was greatly given to swaggering and boasting. He said that if he had to die, he would go off like a man. That he was not the kind of a fellow to make any fuss about it. He openly announced that he did not want any priests or preachers around him, and even went so far as to take from an illustrated paper a cut representing the execution of a murderer. He often referred to this ghastly picture, and asked his companions if they thought he would look like that when they swung him off.[83]

Harrington's cell in the County Jail adjoined that of one Peter Larkin, a prisoner sentenced to hang on January 18, 1877, for the killing of a man named Corcoran in Virginia City, August 4, 1875.[84] As the sheriff led Larkin from his cell to meet the hangman, Harrington pressed his face close to the opening in his cell door. Larkin, noticeably affected, prayed as he shuffled along.

"Keep a stiff upper lip, Pete!" Harrington yelled after him. "Don't let the sons of bitches see you weaken! It will be my turn next!"[85]

As his day of execution drew near, however, Harrington's attitude took on a perceptible change. He "became less demonstrative" and at one point even requested that a priest and the Sisters of Charity visit him in his cell in order to pray with him.[86] He need not have worried.

Shortly after his sentencing, Harrington's legal representatives filed an appeal for a new trial with the Nevada Supreme Court based on a number of alleged errors perpetrated during his trial. With this process in effect the condemned man's day of execution gained postponement in early February while the Supreme Court deliberated on the case.[87] Unfortunately, this circumstance would almost cost another man his life.

In early March, Harrington convinced officials at the County Jail, an improvised, insecure structure which had been pressed into service following a fire which had destroyed the previous building, that his heavy ankle shackles impeded his ability to get sufficient exercise. Sympathetic authorities thus removed his more secure shackles, replacing them with a lighter, less confining set. At this point, either with outside aid or his own ingenuity, Harrington obtained a tool with which he was able to pry open his new anklets.

He definitely had outside assistance in his next acquisition, his brothers falling under heavy suspicion. Someone was able to smuggle into him a loaded, self-cocking "Whistler" revolver. On Tuesday, March 6, the day scheduled for the transfer of all the county prisoners to the new jail facility at the recently constructed County Courthouse, Harrington decided it was now or never.

At about 8 o'clock that morning County Jailer Henry Kirch arrived to perform his usual morning routine of escorting the prisoners to breakfast. After unlocking the cell of an inmate named Nelson, he moved to the cell door of Harrington. Just as Kirch unlocked Harrington's cell the desperate man burst forth flourishing his pistol.

Placing the pistol to Kirch's head, Harrington ordered him to "throw up your hands!" Rather than complying, Kirch closed with Harrington and seized the revolver in his left hand. At once a desperate struggle ensued between the two men. Just as Kirch reached with his right hand for his own revolver, while still wrestling with Harrington, Nelson dived into the fray, grabbing Kirch's arm and preventing him from reaching his weapon.

Managing to angle the pistol toward Kirch's body, Harrington squeezed the trigger. The leaden missile slammed into Kirch's left thigh. Luckily for the jailor, he had a money fob in his left pocket filled with $300 worth of gold coins. The bullet failed to enter his leg but left his thigh badly bruised.

With the first shot, Nelson decided to leave the field of fire. Harrington and Kirch, however, continued their life and death struggle. While Kirch called for help at the top of his lungs, Harrington managed to pull the trigger again. This shot flew past the jailor and buried itself in the wall behind the pair.

Gaining a bit more control in the struggle, Harrington fired the pistol a third time. This slug hit Kirch in the right leg, passing in and out through the meaty part of the thigh.

At this point, City Jailor Carpenter, attracted to the scene by Kirch's shouts and the gunfire, rushed up with his pistol drawn. Carpenter immediately fired a shot at Harrington, but fearing he may hit Kirch, fired wide. Running closer, Carpenter fired again. This bullet hit its mark, striking Harrington in the right shoulder, ranging upward and lodging just under the skin.

Though stunned, Harrington continued to struggle with Kirch. Carpenter stepped up to Harrington, placed his revolver to the man's head and fired his third shot. At the last second, Harrington jerked his head to one side. The movement saved his life. The slug missed entering his skull, managing only to blow off his right earlobe, the powder burning the right side of his face.

Realizing his game was up, Harrington released his grip on Kirch, threw his revolver to the floor and ran back to his cell. On his way back to his cell, Harrington passed a table on which sat an empty candle box. Picking up the box he threw it at Carpenter. "Son of a bitch!" he yelled angrily at the City Jailer. Before re-entering his cell, he also passed a stove on which sat a pan of boiling water. This he also tossed at Carpenter. The jailor managed to dodge both objects. Harrington then disappeared into his cell and quietly lay down on his bunk. Quickly, Carpenter stepped over, pulled the door closed and locked him inside.[88]

Despite the events of the morning, Sheriff Kelly decided to go ahead with the prisoner transfer to the new County Jail later that afternoon. All the prisoners were walked through the streets to the new facility, including, as the local newspaper put it, "three [who] wore petticoats and were called women." All, that is, except James

Harrington who, bandaged and bruised, received transport in a covered carriage, closely guarded.[89]

Both Harrington and Kirch rapidly recovered from their wounds.[90] For Harrington it was now a matter of placing all his hopes on the Supreme Court. In this he would be sustained, though many felt he had been given one chance too many. One Nevada newspaper perhaps spoke for a large majority of the populace when it exasperatedly quipped, "If ever a man deserved to pull hemp without a foot-hold Harrington richly deserves such a fate. Turn him loose and he will be true to his nature—a murderer until he shuffles off."[91]

Harrington's hopes, if he had any, proved justified. On Friday, June 1, the Nevada Supreme Court overturned the Storey County District Court's verdict and ordered a new trial for the shootist.[92] The august body based their decision primarily on the fact that during his first trial Harrington had not been allowed to answer the question, "At the moment of the discharge of the pistol at the deceased, did you, or did you not, really believe that you were in danger of losing your life or receiving great bodily harm?"[93]

The *Territorial Enterprise* was outraged. "Could such a result have been foreseen at the time of the murder," the paper howled, "the county would have been saved the expense of even a single trial, and would have incurred only that of a coroner's inquest."[94]

Court action postponed any developments in the James Harrington case until Tuesday, February 12, 1878. At that time the District Court, feeling they would be unable to acquire an impartial jury, ordered a change of venue, sending Harrington to the Washoe County Courthouse at Reno.[95]

Harrington arrived in the Washoe County Jail at Reno just in time to witness the hanging of J.W. Rover on February 19, 1878, for the murder of his business partner I.N. Sharp at Sulphur Springs, Nevada, back on April 18, 1875. According to one contemporary source, Harrington, apparently somewhat obsessed by the subject since he himself had come so close to the noose, "posted himself at the only window from which a view could be obtained and was a close observer of the entire affair."[96]

Harrington languished in the county lockup at Reno until his second trial for the killing of John Sullivan commenced on Monday, May 13. After five days of testimony the jury filed back into the courtroom on the afternoon of Friday, May 17 and declared him guilty of murder in the 2nd degree.[97] With the maximum penalty for 2nd degree murder being life in prison, Harrington and his legal council had finally managed to save his neck from the rope. Eight days later Judge Wright sentenced the convicted man to a term of 20 years in the State Prison.[98]

A reporter for the *Reno Evening Gazette* was allowed a short interview with Harrington following his sentencing. The newsman found that "he did not in his heart feel himself guilty and would commit the same act were he placed under the same circumstances and now regretted that he did not turn loose on some of the rest of them while the iron was hot."[99]

The second trial had cost Storey County $1,691.97 for the privilege of having James Harrington kill someone in their county.[100] Storey County officials probably placed themselves in the same camp as the *Evening Gazette* when it editorialized:

Harrington's record shows him to be anything but a sweet-tempered individual, or an ornamental or a useful member of society, and it is hoped that the udder of official clemency will not again be milked in his interest.[101]

James Herrington entered the Nevada State Prison at Carson City for the second time on Saturday, May 25, 1878.[102] For all intents and purposes, that day ended his career of blood and death, although occasionally his specter would rear its ugly head to remind people of his existence.

Such proved to be the case in October 1878 during a Democratic political rally in Eureka. In his speech as a candidate for political office in the upcoming elections, W.E.F. Deal felt moved to defend Governor Bradley from allegations of political shenanigans in the pardoning of Harrington from the penitentiary in 1874. He rightly concluded that for Bradley to have been involved in a deal with Harrington the plot would also have to have included Judge B.C. Whitman, Judge Belknap and Chief Justice Hawley, all members of the parole board along with Bradley at the time, a most unlikely scenario.[103]

Harrington also made his presence felt in December 1878 when he encountered a reporter for the *Reno Evening Gazette* engaged in a tour of the Carson pen. The scribe reflected on one amidst the convicts:

One dark little man with a deep bright eye and scowling face, was pacing up and down with folded arms and puffing fiercely at a short pipe. This was Harrington, the desperado, who has killed four or five men and been in prison a good part of his life. He is now serving a sentence of twenty years for the cowardly murder of Sullivan in Virginia [City]. The reporter remembered him, having seen him in the Virginia City jail under conviction of murder in the first degree, with little hope of escaping the gallows, which he so richly deserves.

He is thought to have great political influence, and on that he bases a hope for pardon, and the chance to kill somebody else.[104]

Nevada State Prison, 1880. At the time of this photograph James Harrington was behind these walls serving a 20-year sentence for the murder of John Sullivan in 1876 (courtesy Digital Photo Collection, Image #UNRS-P2006-05-059, Special Collections and University Archives Department, University of Nevada, Reno Libraries).

If Harrington had hopes of an early release from his incarceration, this time those hopes would be dashed. He was destined to waste well over a decade of his life within the confines of the State Prison.

It would have been enlightening to have gotten his reaction to the events of March 4, 1879. On that day his old friend/enemy Con Sullivan, the proverbial "innocent" bystander, for the third time in his life, managed to find himself in the midst of deadly gunfire. Receiving his second serious wound in such circumstances when one Taft and Henry Heiff shot it out on a downtown street in Bodie, California, Sullivan again managed to survive his wound.[105]

As for James Harrington, he finally received the pardon he had been longing for in the Summer of 1890. After serving 12 years, two months and 23 days of his 20-year sentence, the 40-something Harrington received his discharge on July 16.[106]

Soon after his release from prison, Harrington moved north to the burgeoning mining region of Wallace, Idaho. Located in the northern portion of the state, Wallace, like Nevada, known for its prodigious silver wealth, was the principal town in the Coeur d'Alene silver mining district. Harrington had gravitated to the raucous frontier atmosphere of the Idaho mining camps. It must have reminded him of the Nevada of the 1870s and he once again reveled in the gritty existence of the saloons and gambling dives.

Early on the morning of Saturday, June 10, 1893, Harrington was drinking in the Gem Saloon at Wallace. In a situation most unusual for him, the day before found him curiously unarmed and he had borrowed a revolver from an acquaintance in possible anticipation of trouble in his carousals. Unfortunately, he failed to familiarize himself with the weapon, a fact that would prove to loom large in his immediate future.

Apparently, Harrington had been bullying a cook at the Gem named R.A. Cunningham. In the course of the evening, Cunningham's dog came snuffling around Harrington's feet, much to the man's annoyance. Feeling disdain for both Cunningham and his hound, Harrington drew back his foot and gave the animal a swift kick in the ribs.

Hearing the dog yelp and seeing it scurry into a corner of the room, Cunningham confronted Harrington concerning the abuse of the dog. Glaring at the cook, the former Nevada convict suddenly pulled his borrowed pistol and, in a show of intimidation, held the weapon across his chest. Nonplussed, Cunningham walked swiftly to the back of the establishment where he armed himself with the revolver he kept in his coat pocket. Thinking he had cowed Cunningham, Harrington was surprised when the man reappeared before him, pistol pointed at him. Once again unlimbering his six-shooter, Harrington attempted to fire. Since he was unfamiliar with the workings of the weapon, the gun failed to discharge. With the delay, Cunningham quickly jerked the trigger firing three bullets into Harrington's body. A few hours after being shot, James Harrington died from his grievous wounds.[107]

As reported in press accounts, those familiar with Harrington's past in Nevada were struck by one glaring coincidence in the circumstances of the man's death. **Many recalled the cause of his shooting John Lynch back in Pioche, Nevada, in the 1870s had stemmed from the ill treatment of a pet dog.** Now the same actions led to Harrington's own death. The irony proved difficult to ignore. Nonetheless, James Harrington had lived by the gun, Now the gun, and the dog, had returned with a vengeance.

11

A Full-Fledged Fighter
George Kirk

The knock on the solid wooden door came heavy and persistent. Startled, George Kirk set down his whiskey bottle. He and his companion for the evening, "Dutch Mary," stared at each other for a few seconds.

Finally, Mary called out, "Who's there?"

"A friend," came the reply.

Leaving Kirk sitting apprehensively in the front room, Mary stepped over to open the door. Before she was able to open it all the way Officer McCready, a policeman on the Virginia City police force, pushed his way inside.

Spotting Kirk sitting in the room nearby, McCready motioned to him. "George, I want you; come along," he said to him.

Kirk took a deep breath. "All right Mac," he said to the lawman whom he had had many encounters with in the past. "I'll come with you."

Getting up from his seat Kirk walked over to McCready who, taking him by the arm, led him out the door. Suddenly, a few feet outside the house, as Kirk conversed with McCready concerning the charges against him, a chorus of shouts emerged from the darkness. As Kirk stood in stunned silence a number of men all at once sprang on him, seizing him by the arms and neck. At that moment George Kirk probably came to the quick realization that, this time, he had tempted fate once too often. Now he must pay the piper.[1]

George B. Kirk was likely a native of Jackson County, Missouri, although the state of Kentucky has also been suggested as his birthing ground.[2] Born about 1836, he would seem to have had a fair education as a later prison record would describe him as being able to read and write.[3] As a teenager, Kirk moved with his family to Bureau County, Illinois, about 105 miles southwest of Chicago.[4] Here, if stories are to be believed, the Kirk family lived a rather illicit existence, being involved in horse theft and rowdyism.[5]

Records do seem to support the allegations leveled against the Kirk family of Bureau County, Illinois, as being less than lawful at times. In September 1851, George W. Kirk, possibly George B. Kirk's father, along with David Kirk, William Reid and Francis Argobright were brought up on charges of "Riot" in Bureau County Circuit Court after an imbroglio involving weapons.[6] Later, in 1860, a Patrick Kirk would be charged in Bureau County court on a charge of "assault with a deadly weapon."[7]

11. A Full-Fledged Fighter

As for young George B. Kirk, he would be long gone from Bureau County by 1860, never to set eyes on it again. By 1856 he undertook the long trek to California. There were tales of his having "killed his uncle before leaving home" and "being hotly pursued by the sheriff of Bureau County" whom "young Kirk shot … and made good his escape."[8] Although no records support these claims it is most probable that the affairs of Kirk or members of his family made Illinois too hot and necessitated the relocation west.

In 1856, George Kirk appeared in the rip-roaring mining camp of Sonora, California, located in the lower northern half of the state, approximately 75 miles southeast of Sacramento, in Tuolumne County. In an area surrounded by other well-known mining camps such as Columbia, Murphy's Camp, Angels Camp, Tuttletown and Chinese Camp, Sonora had already garnered for itself a reputation for violence and sudden death. First located in 1848 after discovery of gold bearing quartz in the area, Sonora would eventually yield some $600 million worth of the precious yellow metal in its long, exuberant history. In its heyday it would also yield up almost one unsolved murder a week, making it a handful for any group of lawmen to attempt to control.[9]

Into this milieu stepped the young 20-year-old George Kirk. Upon his arrival in about 1856 he was described as "an awkward looking, overgrown boy."[10] The editor of the *Union Democrat*, Sonora's local newspaper, who knew him at the time, declared, "We recollect him as a pale, sickly, but industrious boy, kicked and cuffed about at will. Then he was not on the fight."[11] This would soon change. Again, as the *Democrat* so aptly put it, soon

> Kirk began to show signs of the road he had mapped out for the future. Two or three ugly rows served to convince people that he was by no means a safe boy to kick. Then he grew worse daily. Became a lazy loafer and gambler, spent his time in dissipation.[12]

By early 1856, George Kirk gained employment as a dishwasher at the Palace Hotel in downtown Sonora.[13] His extracurricular activities, however, would quickly lead him into trouble.

While drinking in a Sonora resort on Saturday, May 10, 1856, Kirk, for some unknown reason, fell into a disagreement with a man named Eugene Bardende. The difference of opinion quickly led to violence when Kirk unlimbered a "slung shot" loaded with metal and began to beat Bardende with the weapon.[14] Breaking away, Bardende reported to authorities and then sought medical attention for his various wounds. Quickly, Sonora police placed Kirk under arrest and lodged him in jail for safekeeping.

Indicted by the Tuolumne County Grand Jury on a charge of "assault with a deadly weapon with intent to inflict bodily injury upon the person of another," Kirk and his court appointed legal representatives made a number of court appearances in late May and early June. Finally, although complete court transcripts are not available, it appears that, for some reason, the County Attorney decided not to press prosecution and, in early June, Kirk was released on a nolle prosequi.[15]

Although Kirk had caught a lucky break, it would fail to ameliorate his disposition. He continued his carousing and cavorting in the pleasure palaces of Sonora and his violent behavior only escalated.

Early Sunday morning, August 30, 1857, found Kirk in his usual activity, celebrating the weekend in a Sonora dive. In the midst of the revelry he suddenly commenced a disagreement with another celebrant named Otis Holloway. Although later developments would seem to lead to the suggestion that Holloway, rather than Kirk, was the aggressor, Kirk lost no time in pulling a large knife and inflicting a number of lacerations about the person of Holloway.[16]

Arrested and placed in the custody of newly elected Tuolumne County Sheriff John Sedgwick, Kirk awaited the action of the Grand Jury in the County Jail. Sedgwick, taking a liking to the young man and deciding he was simply an unfortunate youth who had taken a wrong turn in life, took pity on his prisoner. He appointed Kirk a trusty of the jail and allowed him the extra liberty of the jail corridors.[17] Future occurrences may have given Sedgwick reason to regret his actions, although he would continue to favor the young man throughout his contact with him.

The Tuolumne Grand Jury eventually brought down a true bill charging Kirk with an "assault with intent to commit murder." Various witnesses, including S.B. Blake, R.P. Malone, H. Patterson and M. Woodruff were subpoenaed and served by Sedgwick and Deputy Sheriff James McFarlane, to appear at Kirk's trial which commenced October 12, 1857, in the County Courthouse.[18] That same day the jury filed back into court and declared Kirk "Not Guilty."[19] George Kirk was once again released.[20]

Following Kirk's acquittal Sheriff Sedgwick, still feeling altruistic toward him, gave him employment as janitor and errand boy around the jail building.[21] All ran smoothly until the morning of Sunday, March 28, 1858.

Conducting his usual weekend celebrations, Kirk entered a billiard room in the "Tigre," the Mexican portion of Sonora. After drinking himself into a state of intoxication he suddenly pulled out his knife and began cutting the cushions on the billiard tables. When the owner of the establishment attempted to get him to desist in his vandalism, Kirk hissed an ominous threat at him and continued in his knife exercise. With that, the Mexican ran to the Sheriff's office and lodged a complaint with Sheriff Sedgwick.

Not expecting any trouble with his recalcitrant ward, Sedgwick entered the pool hall. Spotting Kirk wielding his knife the sheriff approached him in an off-handed manner.

"Here, George, what are you doing?" Sedgwick said to him.

Seemingly startled, Kirk turned toward Sedgwick, at the same time drawing a revolver from his belt.

"Who the hell are you?" Kirk slurred and pulled the trigger. The bullet crashed into Sedgwick's thigh, dropping him heavily to the floor. At this juncture a number of bystanders tackled Kirk and escorted him to the county jail.[22]

Later that day, Deputy Sheriff James McFarlane went before Justice of the Peace William Ford and swore out a complaint against Kirk charging him with assault with an attempt to kill.[23] Although painfully wounded, Sedgwick proved not seriously hurt and, despite being laid up for a few days, soon was back handling his duties at the sheriff's office. Now the court process took over in the life of George Kirk.

Brought to trial on Wednesday, June 16, the proceedings were quick and to the point. That same day Kirk was found guilty of the charges against him.[24] Four days later, on the following Saturday, Judge T.S. Jones sentenced the convicted felon to 5 years in the California State Prison.[25] As a result of this sentence, nine days later, on June 28, Deputy Sheriff James McFarlane transported Kirk, along with Alex Delabash, sentenced to a three-year term for a separate offense, to the State Prison located near San Rafael, a few miles north and across the Bay from San Francisco.[26]

Received at the penitentiary on June 29 as prisoner #1424, Kirk underwent a complete examination by prison officials before donning his new striped prison suit. He is described in the prison record book as a native of Missouri, 22 years of age, with an occupation listed as "Laborer." His physical description is further recorded as follows:

> Height, 5 feet 10¼ inches; Complexion, fair; Color of Eyes, blue; Color of Hair, light. Mole on left forearm, 2 moles on left side hair [sic], mole above left knee, 2 moles above right knee, scar on right hand + wrist, scar on head, small scar back of neck.[27]

Kirk's conduct within the penitentiary is not of record. He felt himself sufficiently punished by summer 1859 however, as, that August, he applied for release with the Governor of California.[28] No pardon was forthcoming. Almost a full year later, on July 23, 1860, the assistant marshal conducting the U.S. federal census found Kirk still incarcerated in the state prison.[29] He seems to have served most, if not all, of his 5 year sentence, being released about December 1863.[30] As one contemporary put it, "the now full fledged [sic] 'fighter' was turned loose upon the community."[31]

Following his regaining of freedom, the now hardened ex-convict, about 27 years of age, decided to seek new surroundings. In 1864 he made his appearance in the frenetic mining town of Virginia City, Nevada.

Prison had failed to alter George Kirk's chosen path in life. With a number of like-minded companions, he soon made himself an object of continued suspicion with the Virginia City police force when it came to petty theft, burglaries, etc. A year after leaving the California State Prison his luck once again ran out.

In the early morning hours of Sunday, November 6, 1864, a Virginia City resident made his way hastily to police headquarters. The man informed officers that an individual was currently under a house on D Street, apparently attempting to break into the residence. Accompanying the man back to the home of Mary Daily, policeman Woodman found someone in the crawl space under the house. Woodman ordered the man to come out. The miscreant, identified as George Kirk, immediately attempted to draw a revolver. Woodman quickly pulled his own revolver and warned Kirk to desist or he would shoot him. With that Kirk shimmied out from under the house, attempting once more to palm his pistol as he was standing up. Woodman overpowered him, however, and disarmed him of a six-shooter and a large case knife. Under the house, officers found a complete set of burglar's tools and a large hole cut into the floor of Daily's bedroom.[32] Kirk quickly found himself behind the bars of the Virginia City calaboose charged with attempted break and enter.

Following a trial early in January 1865, Kirk found himself convicted of "Attempt to commit burglary."[33] On January 3 he was sentenced to serve a term of one year at hard labor in the Nevada State Prison located at Carson City.[34] Two days later

C Street, Virginia City, 1864, the year Kirk was arrested in the city for break and enter (courtesy Digital Photo Collection, Image #UNRS-P1997-06-10, Special Collections and University Archives Department, University of Nevada, Reno Libraries).

authorities delivered Kirk into the hands of Warden Bob Howland. It would be an introduction fraught with recalcitrance on the part of the new inmate.

It took Kirk less than 24 hours to show his displeasure at being shut away in the state correctional institution and a likewise time for Warden Howland to answer the challenge. As recounted later by sources cognizant of the incident:

> Bob [Howland] had then the same reputation for levity that he now enjoys, and when he became Warden the prisoners thought they would have an easy time of it, but were disappointed, as Bob looked well after the discipline of the prison, and not a prisoner escaped during his term of office. George Kirk, a notorious character, was sentenced in 1864 [sic] to imprisonment for highway robbery [sic]. The first morning of his stay in the penitentiary he refused to come out of his cell and "fall in line" with the other prisoners. This is how Howland subdued Kirk: The warden quickly ordered his cell door closed, and the other prisoners were marched "left hand on next man's shoulder" to breakfast. Kirk, in the meantime, was raving, and loudly cursing, and defying the Warden or any other ___ to even try to make him come out, until he felt disposed to. The Warden quickly went to the blacksmith shop, procured a bar of steel about twelve feet long, and had it heated for about four feet on one end to a red heat, and as quietly came back with it to cell No. 5. He again ordered Kirk to come out and "fall in," and was met with the former refusal and violent abuse. The Warden closed the grated door of the cell, and shoved the bar of steel, hot end foremost (which he had now cooled to a dull color), through the bars. Kirk sprang for and grasped it with both hands with a close grip to wrench it from the Warden. With a howl of pain, as it seared the flesh, he dropped it and retreated, cursing with fierce rage. The Warden, without speaking, swayed the hot bar back and forth in the narrow cell, at times wedging Kirk in a corner, searing his limbs with every touch. Kirk howled with mingled rage and torture, now bounding over it, and again under it, striking his head against the top of the cell and falling upon the bar, yelling and screeching like a pandemonium turned loose. At last he realized the helplessness of his position and begged for mercy.[35]

This bit of aggressive discipline managed to settle Kirk for a few days. The temporarily cowed convict, however, was by no means done with his insurrectionist behavior. Next time he would be the one dealing out the dose of strap oil.

11. A Full-Fledged Fighter

In January 1865, Robert Howland decided to resign as warden of the State Prison. As a result, the state appointed his assistant, Alex Hunter, to the warden's office.[36] Wednesday, February 1, was designated as the day for transfer of authority. George Kirk also decided that this would be a perfect day for an escape attempt.

The plans amidst the convicts had been in progress for some days previous. Kirk somehow, possibly with outside assistance, managed to obtain a loaded revolver which he secreted until the evening of the 1st. Although the details are somewhat sketchy, early that night Kirk, along with Edward Donley, Charles Dade, T.H. Miller and a number of other convicts decided to make their move.[37]

As the prisoners made for the outside gate new warden Alex Hunter attempted to intervene. Kirk leveled his revolver and opened fire. A slug plowed into Hunter's left shoulder, dropping him to the ground. Although the wound was serious it was later deemed not life threatening and Hunter would make a slow recovery. Gradually, however, complications set in. Almost a year after his wounding Hunter was forced to travel to San Francisco for medical treatment where he eventually died as a result of the revolver shot.[38]

With Kirk's opening salvo the prison tower guards, now alert to the uprising, opened up with rifle fire on the fleeing convicts. Struck in the body, convict Miller collapsed in the yard.[39] He would die soon after being shot. Kirk and Donley managed to dash out of the prison compound and lose themselves in the gathering dusk. They would prove to be the only two to make their escape. Halted by the guard's withering fire, Dade and the rest were forced to remain within the prison walls.[40]

Donley did not remain free for long. Only a few days after the escape authorities tracked the fugitive to Virginia City where they placed him under arrest. He was quickly returned to the penitentiary.[41]

As for George Kirk, he managed to retain his liberty for over three months. With a reward of $1,000 hanging over his head, issued by Governor Blasdell of Nevada, Kirk made his way to Placer County, California.[42] Lingering in the area of Auburn, a few miles northeast of Sacramento, he attached himself to a gang of petty thieves operating throughout the vicinity. All through that winter, Kirk skulked around Placer County with the pettifoggers, perpetrating various thefts and living by what he could pilfer.

This less than idyllic lifestyle finally came screeching to a halt in early May 1865. Fed up with the continuous round of stealing and criminality the citizens of the village of Stewart Flat, near Auburn, banded together and managed to surround Kirk and four or five of his cronies in their camp. Someone fired a shot and soon a general firefight erupted between the two parties. Driven to the grass with a shotgun charge which peppered his lower back and buttocks, Kirk was captured by the vigilantes.[43]

In a state of great pain from his dangerous wounds, Kirk was carried to Auburn. Here he was turned over to Placer County Sheriff William Sexton who slapped him into a cell before summoning medical aid. At first, Kirk told Sexton his name was Pritchard. After further questioning by the sheriff, however, he finally admitted he was George Kirk and had escaped from the Nevada State Prison in early February.[44]

By mid–May, Nevada Governor Blasdell sent a requisition to his counterpart in California for Kirk to be transported to the Nevada prison to complete his term. Kirk still suffered greatly from his wounds, however, and it was not until May 25 that Sexton finally decided the prisoner was well enough to be transported back to Nevada.[45]

Taking stock of the returned prisoner, the *Carson Daily Appeal* observed:

> George Kirk, who shot Alex Hunter, and then escaped from the State Prison last Winter, and was subsequently arrested in Placer county, Cal., and brought back here, can show more gunshot wounds than any honest man would be likely to carry around with him. The whole front part of his coat is riddled, and both legs of his pantaloons shot away at the bottom. He has some twelve shots in his hip and legs; and Sheriff Smith [Ormsby County Sheriff Timothy G. Smith] says he counted twenty-four shot holes in his clothes.... A halter [noose around the neck] is the only thing that will kill him.[46]

The *Union Democrat*, back in his old abode of Sonora, California, moralized:

> Kirk's career is well-nigh at an end. It has been one of crime and wretchedness, and his present miserable condition—a condemned felon, wounded and dying in a prison cell—is the legitimate result of the course of life he saw fit to adopt when a boy. Drinking, gambling and dissipation have brought their natural fruits.[47]

Although the *Democrat* may have had a legitimate argument in its moral point, the forecasting of Kirk's finish would prove decidedly premature. The young felon still had one final sensation lurking in his future.

Most of the remainder of 1865 Kirk spent convalescing in his prison cubicle, unable to work due to the incapacitating shotgun wounds. Four months later the court process finally kicked in in answer to Kirk's latest exploits.

On September 5, 1865, case #226 was called in Ormsby County District Court charging Kirk, Edward Donley, Charles Dade and another convict named Joseph Wise, jointly with assault with intent to kill Warden Alex Hunter.[48] They also faced a separate indictment of prison breaking.[49] The prosecution found themselves unable to prove one way or the other who had actually pulled the trigger of the gun which had wounded Hunter, though most believed Kirk the culprit. As a result, the four prisoners were able to dodge this particular indictment.

The men were returned to their cells in the penitentiary until Tuesday, March 13, 1866. At this time Sheriff Smith again trooped the quartet before District Judge S.R. Wright to answer to the charge of prison breaking. The four, again jointly charged, entered a plea of "not guilty."[50] Although it would seem, at first glance, to have been an open and shut case, especially in the cases of Kirk and Donley, complications apparently entered into the legalities. Though records are lacking, Kirk and his companions again apparently avoided conviction in the indictment.[51] On Tuesday, March 27, a time span of only a few days after this second trial, George Kirk received his discharge from the Nevada State Prison, his sentence having expired.[52]

Luckily for him, no one from California was waiting at the prison gate to place him under arrest for his actions in Placer County following his February 1865 escape. Kirk would never face charges for those escapades. He was working his way closer to a much more final reckoning.

Soon after his release from prison, Kirk drifted back to Virginia City, still walking with a cane due to his debilitating buckshot wounds of May 1865.[53] Gradually, his health began to improve. He gained employment in the Imperial Mine, a position

Imperial Mine, Virginia City. Following his discharge from prison in 1866 Kirk returned to Virginia City and gained short-term employment at the Imperial (courtesy Digital Photo Collection, Image #UNRS-P0196-1, Special Collections and University Archives Department, University of Nevada, Reno Libraries).

he held for a number of months.[54] At length, however, this job fell by the wayside as his old habits of frequenting the saloons and dance halls and drinking to excess again came to the fore. He became a regular of Virginia City police court on various charges of drunk and disorderly and other petty offences. He also became a suspect in more serious cases of garroting and highway robbery, although the authorities could never pin anything on him for sure.

Kirk managed to acquire a small cabin between C and D streets in Virginia City. This abode quickly became the hangout of a number of Kirk's boon companions, such as Arthur Perkins Heffnan, Tom Laswell, William Willis and Charles McWilliams, all of whom lived hand to mouth off the proceeds of small-time crimes of various sorts.[55]

One of the leading lights of this nefarious group proved to be the aforementioned tri-named Arthur Perkins Heffnan. Heffnan had been born September 26, 1846, aboard the ship *Perkins* en route from New York to the west coast. The ship was transporting the New York Volunteers, an army unit notorious for its collection of New York City toughs and thugs, with whom Heffnan's father was a corporal in Company F. The lad's mother was a sister to the notorious California cutthroat and outlaw Jack Powers, at this time also a member of Company F. Mrs. Heffnan gave the child the first name Arthur, in honor of the helmsman of the ship, a Captain Arthur. She also christened him with the middle name Perkins in memorial to the ship that brought them west.[56]

By his mid–20s Heffnan had done little to commend him to society and much to discourage its approbation. In Virginia City he continued on this road. The proceeds of crime not quite making the grade, at times he also worked as a piano player at Scott's Dance Hall on C Street.[57] This probably only served to bring him closer to the dissipated lifestyle and alcohol to which he was addicted.

On the cool evening of March 5, 1871, Heffnan approached William Smith, a former sailor with the British Navy, talking to some friends in front of the International Hotel. Drawing a pistol, Heffnan's attention was drawn to Smith.

"What do you want?" an intoxicated Heffnan asked Smith.

A bewildered Smith eyed the man. "I don't know that I want anything," Smith replied.

Heffnan raised his pistol to Smith's face. "How do you want it?" he barked. Before Smith could react, Heffnan fired, the ball entering Smith's left eye and coming out at the top of his head. Smith was killed instantly.[58]

Arrested on the scene by a Virginia City police officer, Heffnan, quickly sobering, expressed feeling remorse for his deed. These feelings most likely extended to himself as well. There was a strong vigilante presence in Virginia City at the time. Heffnan probably realized, along with everyone else, that the wanton killing had instantly heightened his profile in the interests of the "601" as the vigilantes had been dubbed. As he sat in his jail cell fretting the consequences of his actions, outside events beyond his control were conspiring to greatly shorten his young life.

Fire was the bane and terror of every frontier community. Many a tinder dry, lumber constructed town had been laid in waste and ruin by the unrelenting flames of conflagration. Thus, when individuals became suspected of the crime of incendiarism the resultant meting out of perceived justice could be very harsh indeed.

Throughout 1870 and into early 1871, Virginia City had been plagued by a series of fires, many suspected to be acts of arson. A few days after Heffnan's incarceration another fire broke out in Piper's Opera House, a Virginia City institution. Fortunately, several men nearby spotted the smoke and managed to douse the flames before much damage was done. At the same time, William Willis, another of the friends of Kirk and Heffnan, was apprehended on the scene reeking of coal oil. He would later admit to attempting to start the fire due to a disagreement he had engaged in with the proprietor of Piper's.

Locked away inside the county calaboose, Willis sweated until the night of March 12. On that evening the aroused vigilantes stormed the jail, apprehended Willis, and, with a rope around his neck, led him to the basement of Piper's, the scene of his intended holocaust. Here, under most persuasive questioning involving a stout rope, Willis managed to confess to almost every crime and hint of fire occurring in Virginia City over the last two or three years.

Of course, he had accomplices, Willis claimed, not the least of which proved to be George Kirk and Arthur Perkins Heffnan, the leaders of an arsonist plot to reduce Virginia City to ashes for spite and perceived wrongs committed against them by "the man." Also named by Willis were Charles McWilliams, Billy Gregory, Tom Laswell and a number of others.[59]

At the end of this ordeal, possibly much to his surprise and definitely much to his relief, Willis received deposit back in his jail cell by the "601," still breathing, perhaps in payment for his information. Willis would go on to serve a number of years in the Nevada State Prison, being involved in the big escape of September 17, 1871. Following his recapture and another eight years of captivity he would finally gain his release on April 14, 1879.

In the meantime, the Vigilance Committee returned to headquarters to debate matters. It soon gained agreement that Heffnan, both an incendiary and a murderer, needed to be dealt with. They picked the early morning hours of Saturday, March 25, to act.

At around 1 o'clock that morning a phalanx of about 80 armed and masked men raided the County Jail building. After a brief struggle with Storey County Sheriff Thomas Atkinson and Undersheriff John Stoner the raiders managed to release Heffnan from his cell. Dragging the criminal up Sutton Avenue to a frame building on the Ophir Mine property at the edge of town, they tossed a rope over a beam protruding over a tramway, attached the other end around Heffnan's neck and swung him off into eternity.[60]

Their point now starkly and poignantly made, the vigilantes, over the next week, issued so-called "tickets of leave" to some dozen other notable ne'er-do-wells, including George Kirk. In most cases these notices to vacate were quickly obeyed. According to the *Gold Hill News* of April 3: "Geo. Kirk and two or three others ordered to leave by the Vigilance Committee, departed from Virginia on the stages last evening."[61]

Many in Nevada applauded the work of Virginia City's extralegal enforcers. The *Pioche Record* in far eastern Lincoln County spoke for a goodly number of citizens when it commented:

> The hanging of Arthur Perkins Hefferman [sic] in Virginia City ... was an act demanded by the people, who had been outraged to such an extent that both life and property were placed in extreme jeopardy. While not sanctioning or approving of Vigilance Committees holding the reins of government where the Courts and law have full sway, we cannot but admit that there are extreme cases in which the popular safety demands that prompt measures be adopted.... One thing is certain ... the recent prompt action of the Vigilantes in Virginia will undoubtedly have a beneficial effect in preventing the "roughs" in our midst from cutting and shooting at pleasure, as they can rest assured that prompt and speedy justice will be meeted [sic] out to them.[62]

Just how much of a "beneficial effect" devolved onto George Kirk is debatable. He gradually developed a defiance toward the vigilantes that led him to be reckless with his well-being.

After leaving Virginia City, Kirk headed down the road to the city of Reno.[63] He only halted here a few days, however, before the Reno citizens committee, aware of his reputation, warned him away. With that, the hounded man decided to head inland to central Nevada and the busy mining metropolis of Eureka. He operated here for almost two months. Inevitably, Eureka's populace eventually got wise to his character of criminality and again, this time from Eureka's own "601" vigilantes, he received a notice to vamoose.[64]

Still fuming at the Virginia vigilantes, Kirk decided to tempt fate and returned to the city on Monday, May 29. Made aware of his presence the "601" sent him a stern warning to leave with all due haste. Deciding he had pushed his luck far enough, the following day, Kirk traveled on to Carson City.[65]

In the capitol, Kirk continually raved against the Virginia City vigilantes to any who would listen and "loudly boasted that all he wanted was to come across some of them."[66]

George Kirk's defiance and hatred eventually got the better of him once again. In mid–July he resolved, or so he told acquaintances in Carson City, to relocate to the Ophir mining district in Utah. Before leaving, however, he wished to collect a trunk and some other personal effects he had been forced to leave in Virginia City back in early April.[67] He settled on Thursday, July 13 as the date of another attempted return to the city which had let him know in no uncertain terms he would be taking his life in his hands if he returned.

Just before boarding the train for Virginia City on the afternoon of the 13th, Kirk conversed with an acquaintance. The man reported later that Kirk said to him in a jocular manner, "Do you think the Vigilantes will hang me if I go to Virginia and stay overnight?"

Answering back in a joking tone the man replied, "Certainly they will. And they ought to."[68]

With that, Kirk let out a laugh and bounded up the train steps. He would have been wise to have taken his friend's joke seriously.

Kirk arrived in Virginia City by 5 o'clock that afternoon. If he had made an attempt to act surreptitiously, kept a low profile and flown under the radar, he most likely would have left the city in a healthy state. Instead, he felt he must defy the vigilantes one more time. As a consequence of this mood, Kirk spent the rest of the afternoon and all that evening moving feely from one dive to another, drinking heavily and threatening the members of the "601."

At about 11 o'clock a man approached Virginia City policeman McCready and demanded Kirk's arrest due to a supposed assault perpetrated on him. McCready tracked Kirk to the home of "Dutch Mary," a notorious Virginia City madam, located on north B Street. As McCready led Kirk out the door in anticipation of taking him to the City Jail, a large group of men attacked the pair from out of the darkness, grabbed Kirk and, pushing him inside a carriage, dashed off down the street.

The vigilantes rushed their prisoner out to the old car track at the Sierra Nevada Mine on the outskirts of the city. Following whatever preliminaries may have been accorded him, the vigilantes bound his legs and feet, tied his hands behind his back and placed a handkerchief over his eyes. Someone obtained a piece of white paper upon which one of the vigilantes scrawled in large letters: "George B. Kirk. Committee. 601." This they pinned to the front of Kirk's shirt. They then tossed a rope over a stringer of the car track, over a deep cut bank. The other end they adjusted around their prisoner's neck. Kirk was then ordered to stand upon the track. He then jumped or was pushed off to his death.[69] Later examination by Dr. Conn would seem to indicate that, his neck not being broken, the 35-year-old George Kirk probably died due to slow strangulation.[70]

Upon being informed of developments by Officer McCready and Dutch Mary, Sheriff Tom Atkinson and his deputy, John Stoner, set out with a posse in an attempt to learn the fate of Kirk. At around 2 o'clock that morning they found Kirk's body slowly twisting in the breeze, suspended by his neck from the side of the Sierra Nevada's unused oar car track.[71]

The corpse was taken to Wilson & Brown's Undertaking Parlor on B Street where, that afternoon, crowds of the curious filed in to view the body of the notorious scamp. In Kirk's pockets were found a costly gold watch, some letters of "no particular import," and a small amount of pocket change.[72]

George Kirk's hanging made headlines throughout Nevada and the Pacific Coast, being picked up by such major dailies as the *Tribune* at Salt Lake City and the *Daily Oregonian* of Portland, Oregon.[73] Eventually, the act of vigilante justice traveled across the country to the East Coast, gaining report in the prestigious *New York Times* on July 25, 1871.

Storey County Coroner S. Symons administered the inquest over Kirk's body four days after his demise, on Monday, July 18. The jury came to the expected verdict that death was the result of "being hung by parties unknown to us."[74] The following day Kirk's body was buried in a pauper's grave in the cemetery north of Virginia City.[75]

Although George Kirk was dead and gone circumstances of his demise lingered for some weeks yet in Virginia City. At the meeting of the Storey County Grand Jury in August 1871, Judge Richard Rising, in his charge to the august body, charged them with the task of ferreting out the murderers of both Kirk and Heffnan. Rising sternly instructed the Jury:

> I informed the last Grand Jury of the formation and existence in this community of a "Vigilance Committee" and the lawless execution by it of Arthur Perkins [Heffnan].
>
> Since the dismissal of that Grand Jury another and still more flagrant outrage and crime has been committed by this same unlawful association of men in the hanging of George B. Kirk, who, I believe, was not even charged with any offense. His life was taken most wantonly; the act was thoroughly lawless and inexcusable, and the parties executing the deed are as guilty of the crime of murder, in the eye of the law, as the assassin taking the life of his victim…. I must call your attention most emphatically to the investigation of these felonies.
>
> It is your duty to strenuously endeavor to discover the perpetrators of these offences, and to present them to this Court for trial.[76]

As expected, the Grand Jury, contrary to Judge Rising, felt justice had been served just fine. In fact, in their report of September 21, 1871, they placed the blame back on the shoulders of the authorities, finding, in the words of the *Gold Hill News*:

> … considerable fault with the Police Department, blaming the police especially in allowing the Vigilance Committee to hang Perkins and Kirk, or never arresting anybody for so doing. As to who this committee were, or in fact anything of importance regarding them, the Jury seems to have been rather oblivious.[77]

Most in Virginia City wholeheartedly concurred. George Kirk was of best use six feet under their feet.

12

A Venomous Desperado
Rattlesnake Dick Darling

"Rattlesnake Dick" was one of the more unusual and eccentric personalities in that aggregation of individuals known as Nevada "roughs" or "fighters." From teen-aged Nebraska homesteader to soldier, blacksmith, miner, railroad brakeman, wife beater, philanderer, outlaw, convict and murderer, Dick lived a life full of adventure and seemingly inevitable degradation. He could severely beat and rob a man without compunction but charm the female members of his Mormon father-in-law John D. Lee's family with apparent ease. He could brutally kill a fellow human being with a pickaxe, then sit down and turn out the most beautiful and intricate treasures in the prison stone cutting shop. When comparing him to other well-known Nevada gunmen, newspaper editor and contemporary Wells Drury would state, "Blue Dick, Rattlesnake Dick, Red-Handed Mike, Cut-Mouth Burke and Mike McGowan, 'the Man-Eater,' were other well-known fighters, but of a lower order."[1] Nevada historian Phillip I. Earl said simply, in referring to Dick and some others, "'Rattlesnake Dick' Darling, characters we would have been better off without."[2] Better off without? Maybe. Nevada history, however, would have been far less interesting without him.

Born ca. 1840 in Kentucky, John Richard Darling, like many another frontier lad, grew up in a hurry.[3] Evidence suggests that by the tender age of 14, when most boys today would be just beginning to set aside the things of childhood, Darling had already left the comforts of home. By at least 1854 he was living the hard scrabble existence of a settler on the barren Nebraska plains. Here he encountered fellow hopeful pioneer, 35-year-old Buffalo, New York, native Erastus F. Beadle (1821–1894).[4] On Friday, June 26, 1857, when the future metropolis of Omaha was merely a "rough and unfinished" collection of clapboard structures along the Missouri River, Beadle recorded in his diary:

> Friday, June 26—By previous engagement, went out to see a claim belonging to "Dick Darling." He made his claim in September 1854. Being still underage, he cannot pre-empt it. Has sold off 160 acres last year. Has talked so much with me about it I agreed to go out and see it.
>
> Dick Darling, the only name I know of for the person, came here before a house, except the "Big Six," was erected.[5] He resides in town in a very small cabin, the only one standing of the first cabins built here. Lives alone and has done for three years in the same cabin. He has got some property, has owned largely here, but sold when he got a fair advance. When he first came to the place, he went up to Saratoga, staked out 160 acres one afternoon, came down and sold his claim for five dollars. Although Dick is under 21 years of age, he is considered one of

the first pioneers and allowed to vote. Is a general favorite, but too much like boys who do not appreciate money. He thinks he can speculate when he gets short and make expenses. Does nothing and spends his money extravagantly. Is here two or three times a day when in town. So much for Dick Darling.

The journey to Darling's claim took them out about ten miles from Omaha, into the Nebraska wilderness. After crossing a small stream on planks, due to the bridge having been washed away after a heavy rain, the pair reached the claim on the west side of Little Papillion Creek. Later that day, Beadle jotted in his diary:

> The log over which Dick was in the habit of crossing [the creek] had been carried away, leaving us in a dilemma about how we should cross. From the top of an elm which hung over the stream, suspended a grapevine. Dick went up this vine to the top of the elm and down the elm which grew on the opposite side, thus landing safely. Not being myself a climber, I concluded to try the stream; accordingly stripped and swam across, which was easy enough, the distance only being about twenty feet.
>
> I found the claim much more valuable than I had supposed. I am trying to make a trade for it. If I do, I shall pre-empt it for my own use. It is not too far from Omaha to suit me. On the claim is a small grove, a number of springs, and a stone quarry. Through said claim runs the Papillion at the east end. And lengthwise, running east is the first stream I have seen in the West with stone bottom. The stream is like our eastern streams—clear and rapid, tumbling along over rocks and pebbles. I was charmed, delighted, with the place, and it was difficult for me to refrain from expressing my admiration. As I was looking with a view of purchasing, I kept silent. The place has advantages but one or two know of. In fact, it has never been examined except from a distance, and only by two or three. We found Indian devices carved in the rock, and on the margin of the stream were otter and wild turkey tracks in great numbers. If I succeed in getting hold of the claim, I will make a thorough examination and report at length.[6]

Apparently, Erastus Beadle never did acquire Dick Darling's claim as he never again mentions it or Darling in his diary. Besides, both he and Darling would soon be gone from Nebraska. In late 1857, Beadle returned to Buffalo, New York, financially disappointed in his western expedition. His fortunes would improve, however, when, in 1860, he and a partner began the publication of a series of cheap fiction books in New York City. The books, dealing with various adventures in the American frontier west, quickly became a phenomenon. Soon, "Beadle's Dime Novels" would make Erastus Beadle a multi-millionaire.[7]

As for Darling—who now used his middle name of Richard, or "Dick," exclusively—by the late 1850s had traveled to the "Far West." If one source is to be believed, the young man quickly joined the outlaw gang of Jim Webster, a notorious bandit who operated in Placer and Nevada counties, California.[8] Webster and his cronies rampaged throughout the countryside for three or four years, engaging in a number of robberies and shooting scrapes before Webster was finally shot to death in 1860.[9]

One of Webster's compadres proved to be a young Canadian outlaw named Richard A. "Rattlesnake Dick" Barter who took over from Webster while he served a prison term in 1857. In later years, Darling was known to have a great admiration for Barter, even appropriating the moniker "Rattlesnake Dick" sometime after Barter's death in a gunfight with lawmen in 1859.[10] Indeed, if Darling were there, this may have been where the reverence for Barter developed, riding with the man on forays throughout the countryside.

Sometime in the early to mid–1860s, Darling, now calling himself "Rattlesnake Dick," drifted over to Utah. Here he ingratiated himself within the Mormon community, specifically the family of prominent Mormon figure and eventual scapegoat, John D. Lee. Lee, a successful rancher, politician, businessman and leader within the Latter-Day Saints church, had been involved in the so-called "Mountain Meadows Massacre" of 1857 in which a party of Arkansas emigrants passing through to California had been slaughtered by a group of Mormons for motives of revenge and politics. Eventually, Lee would pay with his life for this involvement. At the time of his association with Dick Darling, however, this retribution was still over ten years away.

John Lee practiced the Mormon doctrine of plural marriage. He would eventually acquire 19 wives and sire some 67 children. One of these children, a daughter, became enamored with Dick Darling and the couple were married.[11] In later years, Rattlesnake Dick's reputation as a lady's man would almost outstrip his reputation as a notorious outlaw and rough. One newspaper would say of him that he "is said to have been married more times than any man in the United States."[12] Although only two or three of these supposed wives are known, one being John D. Lee's daughter, it would be in Utah where evidence of Darling's philandering nature would come to light.

As can be expected of a man with 19 wives, Lee began having spousal distress during the time of his association with his son-in-law. Unfortunately for Lee, Dick Darling was there to give comfort, not to Lee, but to Lee's wives. According to Lee contemporary and antagonist, Mormon columnist George Armstrong Hicks, one of Lee's wives confessed to her husband that she and all of her "sister wives" had slept with Darling at some point.[13] Granted, Hicks was no fan of John D. Lee and may have been gilding the lily somewhat, however, it would not have been below Rattlesnake Dick's morals to have attempted the feat.

The strain this state of affairs placed on the relationship between Darling, his wife, and her father, John Lee, can only be imagined. It may have played a part, however, in Darling's decision to leave his wife and Utah and head west to the mining camps of Nevada. Eventually, in 1877, 20 years after the event, John D. Lee would be the only Mormon convicted and executed for the Mountain Meadows Massacre of 1857. By that time, Rattlesnake Dick Darling had garnered his own notoriety in the Silver State.

Subsequent to his arrival on the Comstock, in the vicinity of Virginia City, Darling worked for a time in the mines.[14] Tired of sweating underground, on May 31, 1863, he enlisted in Company B, First Battalion, Nevada Volunteer Cavalry under Captain Baldwin at Fort Churchill.[15] With most of the regular army in the east fighting the Civil War, the Nevada Volunteers were organized as a home defense force against the threat of hostile Indian attack.

In the interim, Darling had acquired for himself another wife who balked at living in the Fort Churchill barracks. One day, Rattlesnake Dick beat her within an inch of her life for her obstinacy, gathered up his kit bag and headed out to the Fort.[16]

Deciding he wished to patch things up with his betrothed, one day in mid–September 1863, Darling ventured out to the ranch of Johnson and Floyd, some three

12. A Venomous Desperado 151

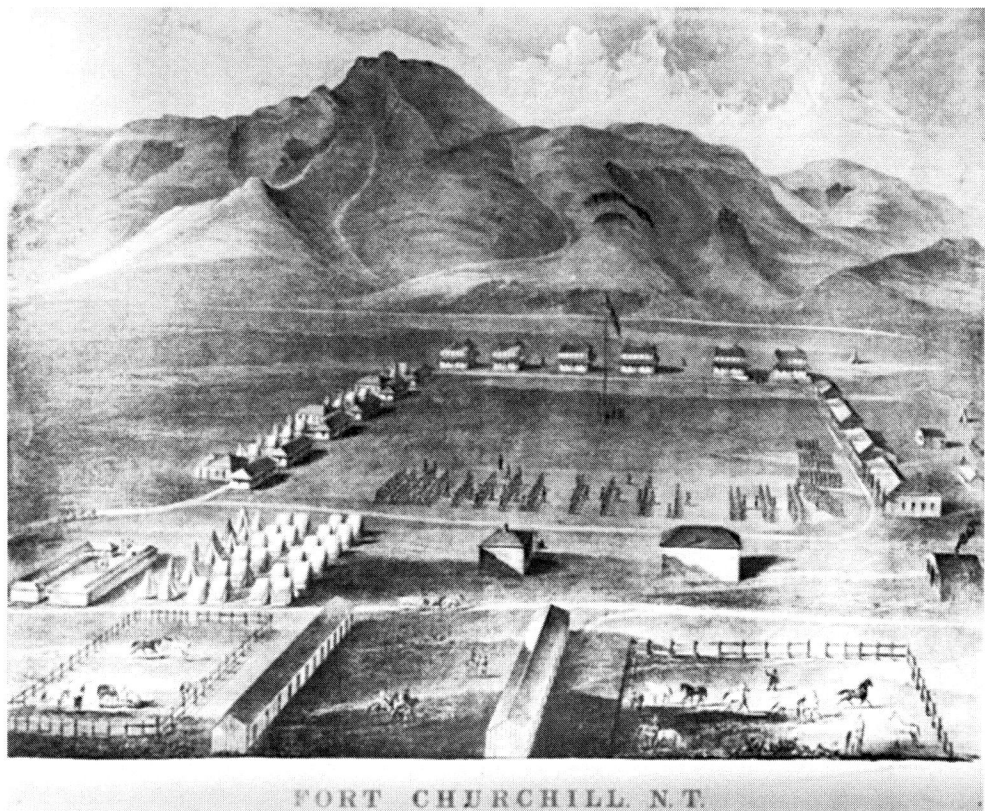

Fort Churchill, 1861. On May 31, 1863, Dick Darling enlisted in Company B, First Battalion, Nevada Volunteer Cavalry and received posting at Fort Churchill (courtesy Digital Photo Collection, Image #UNRS-P0156-1, Special Collections and University Archives Department, University of Nevada, Reno Libraries).

miles from Fort Churchill, where the lady had sought refuge. Mounting the front steps of the ranch house, Darling stopped short when, suddenly, his wife opened the door brandishing a double-barreled shotgun. Swinging the weapon around on him the woman fired both barrels. Peppered in the left breast with buckshot, the seriously wounded man slowly turned and stumbled down the steps. Darling managed to stagger as far as the road before finally collapsing to the ground. Notified of the shooting, Darling's commanding officer in the Volunteers, Captain Baldwin, rushed out with a wagon. Loading his wounded charge into the wagon box he hastened him to the fort infirmary.[17]

The fate of this particular wife is unknown. As for Darling, he eventually recovered from his wounds. Soon, however, he tired of the drudgery of army life. Fort Churchill records list him as having deserted over one year later, on September 24, 1864.[18] Apparently, the search was not too intense for his return.

Undaunted in his dealings with the opposite sex, Darling married again shortly after. Eventually, he and wife Hattie would part company in what was becoming a tiresome tendency. At length, Hattie married again to one James Funk in Austin, Nevada. Dick Darling may have been fortunate he had gotten out when he did. In about 1871, Hattie Funk would be arrested for the murder of husband James. At her subsequent trial she was acquitted and quickly faded from history.[19]

Moving back to the environs of Virginia City, Darling gained employment at one of the mines in the capacity of blacksmith, a vocation which may have been one of his main duties at Fort Churchill and one at which he proved most skilled.[20] Unfortunately, he failed to stick with his lawful employment. Gradually, he began to drift back into unlawful acts of theft and mayhem.

Early in May 1866, Rattlesnake Dick, perhaps settling his affairs with ex-wife Hattie, booked passage on the stage from Austin to Virginia City. During the course of the trip he made the acquaintance of a fellow passenger, a young married lady from Austin. Upon parting company in Virginia City, Darling missed his chance at a dalliance while the young woman missed a valuable watch and a quantity of money.

Virginia City officers arrested Darling for the theft on Monday, May 14.[21] He bided his time in the County Jail until Wednesday. That afternoon, no proof having been developed as to Darling's guilt in the case, Judge Mesick released him.[22] Rattlesnake Dick was just getting started.

Almost two weeks later, Friday, May 25, ranch hand Patrick McCauley came to Virginia City with some $160 in his possession, much of it belonging to his employer for the purpose of buying supplies for the ranch. That morning, McCauley found occasion to stop at the Occidental Saloon on C Street. Here, much to his chagrin, he would have the misfortune of encountering Rattlesnake Dick Darling. According to McCauley's later court testimony:

> I came in Virginia City on Friday last, May 25th, 1866. On the 25th I was going up C Street. I stopped in a saloon. There was a couple of men in there. One of them asked me to take a game. I told them no, I had no time, as I had considerable running around to do. One of the men was in the back room, the other in bar room. After they asked me to take a game, I told them I had not time. I turned round to start off and I was struck on the back part of the head. Soon after I was struck first I came to a little, then I was struck twice again on the back part of the head. That is about all I can tell about it. It happened in forenoon. I had about $160 in gold and silver. When I came to, I had $28 in my pocket loose, the other money I had in a purse in my breast pocket of my coat.... He [Rattlesnake Dick Darling] is one of the men that was in the house at the time, in the bar room, when I was first struck. Cannot say that he hit me first. Cannot say who hit me. My back was turned when I was first struck. I had started out. When I came to myself, I was out in the street and some men talking to me. I told them that I had been pounded over the head and robbed.[23]

Bystanders assisted McCauley to the office of Dr. Bronson while others summoned the law. Upon being notified of events, authorities quickly made Darling their number one suspect.

Later that day, Precinct No. 1 Constable Augustus Ash and Police Chief George Downey learned that McCauley's empty money purse had been found under the bed of Darling's room at the Occidental Lodging House. They also received information that Darling had hastily departed for Ophir City, a mining camp about nine miles east of Virginia City. Tracking their suspect down to a boarding house at Ophir City, Ash and Downey arrested Darling the next day and carted him back to Virginia City, slapping him into the County Jail.[24]

Although he would fail to make any kind of statement on his case for another five years, Darling had a far different story of events that day. Darling would later depose:

> On the 25th day of May, 1866 I was, in company with Patrick McCauley and W.M. Woods, in a saloon on C Street, opposite the Occidental Hotel in Virginia City. Woods had brought me a note that morning from Ophir, stating that a woman wanted to see me for she was very sick and immediately started for Ophir, leaving McCauley and Woods playing cards in the saloon. I arrived in Ophir that afternoon about 3 o'clock and remained all night with a man named Kelly keeping a saloon there. During that night Woods came down from Virginia City and told me he had some trouble with McCauley about cards and that he left to keep from getting into trouble; that he had won one hundred and twelve dollars from him; that McCauley threw a knife at him and he struck him in the head with a bottle and left the saloon. Woods then left the town and I think the state, as he said "it was too hot for him here." The next morning, the 26th, I was arrested by Chief Downey and Augustus Ash of the Virginia police force[sic].[25] Downey told me, after making particular inquiries to the whereabouts of Woods, that if he could find Woods he did not want me, but from appearances was determined, if he could not find Woods, to convict me of the charge.[26]

Three days after the assault and robbery of McCauley, Monday the 28th, Darling, represented by well-known defense attorney and pistoleer Jesse S. Pitzer, appeared in the Justice Court of D.O. Atkinson for a preliminary hearing.[27] Although Darling refused to make any statement regarding the affair because "he never knew a statement to do any good," a number of other witnesses, including McCauley, Occidental Lodging House proprietress Mrs. T. Dirkes, Constable Ash and Occidental Saloon owner Miss Jessie Case, gave testimony. Jessie Case added another angle to the situation when she testified:

> He [McCauley] drank once there [in her saloon]. He paid for the drinks. He first took his purse and held it under the counter and gave me a $20 piece and I told him I could not change it, he said he had some change and put his hand in his pants pocket and gave me a ½ dollar for the drinks. Defendant and another person drank with him. I do not know the name of the other person, but know him by sight. McCauley staid [sic] there some 5 or 10 minutes. He then went out on C Street. Defendant and the other man went out and I then closed my place. The key of the back door I placed in my money drawer. The key of the front door I put in my pocket. I locked the front door. I was gone about one hour. When I returned I found the front door locked. When I went in I found on the knob of the front door inside blood—the back door was just ajar, found quite a quantity of blood in back room. McCauley appeared to me to be sober when he gave me the $20 piece. I gave it to Defendant to go and get changed. McCauley did not tell me he had any change until Defendant returned with the $20 piece. He then told me. I gave it [the $20 piece] to him. When I left the house, I went to the Occidental in room No. 7 to see a sick friend. I did not see McCauley and any person talking together after I left the saloon, did not see him at all after I left the saloon. Did not see Defendant after I left. Defendant said 2 or 3 days before that he was going away but did not say where to.[28]

Judge Atkinson felt that enough evidence pointed to Rattlesnake Dick having something to do with the assault and robbery. He ordered Darling remanded to the County Jail to await trial in the robbery of McCauley.[29]

The court set Darling's trial for the last week in June. His fate rested in the hands of Judge Richard Rising, District Attorney W.W. Bishop, Defense Attorney Jesse Pitzer and a jury composed of J.C. Massel, W.V. Churchill, John McCarty, C.B. Kimbal, J.M. Holiday, W.T. Eaves, A. Caldwell, H.N. Connor, John White, Andrew Whitford and

E. Nye.[30] On Monday, June 25 this venire of 12 of Darling's peers declared him guilty of robbery.

Judge Rising felt that stern punishment was essential in this case. He later wrote:

> I would say that at the time of his [Darling's] sentence many outrages and crimes had been, and were constantly being committed in this city [Virginia City], and to endeavor to create a terror upon evil doers, I imposed upon those convicted, very severe punishments.[31]

With these thoughts in mind, Rising sentenced the convicted robber to a term of 14 years in the Nevada State Prison.[32] Concerning his sentence of Darling, Rising would later explain:

> I sentenced Darling to 14 years on this consideration—It was a severe punishment and probably a much longer term than I would have fixed had this offence been perpetrated at another time.[33]

Darling was on his way to the penitentiary and Pat McCauley probably left the courtroom feeling some sense of vindication. Later evidence would go to show, however, that McCauley himself was far from a man of exemplary character. In the months following Darling's conviction, McCauley would find himself arrested in Eastern Nevada for, as the *Gold Hill News* so aptly put it, "allowing somebody's horse to get between his legs and carry him off."[34]

On Saturday, June 30, Darling was taken in toe by Storey County Sheriff Jacob Clark and deposited in the prison at Carson City.[35] Apparently, on this, his first induction into the State Prison, Darling, on the whole, manifested a favorable character. He would often spend hours of his day chiseling and carving stone in the prison workshop. Almost four years after his entry into the pen, in February 1870, Darling was observed by a correspondent of the *Gold Hill News* placing the finishing touches on a stone "crib-board, very beautifully carved and ornamented."[36] His talents as a craftsman were obvious and perhaps a saving grace to him during his confinement.

One circumstance which may not have benefited him during his incarceration was the unavoidable contact with other men of similar illicit inclinations. It would be here that Darling met, for the first time, one William Chamberlain, a future partner in crime once both were again on the outside.

Chamberlain was a 23-year-old Ohioan working as a stagecoach driver in Elko County.[37] On July 6, 1869, Chamberlain became engaged in a fracas with a man named James Bender at the Crescent Stage Station on the Hill Beachy Toll Road. The confrontation ended in Chamberlain grabbing a gun and shooting Bender to death.[38] In mid-December, Elko County court convicted the young whip of manslaughter. On December 13 the judge sentenced him to a hefty term of 99 years in the State Prison.[39] A few days later, Chamberlain arrived at the pen for, what turned out to be, a much shorter term than which he was originally sentenced. While incarcerated, however, he gained the acquaintance of Rattlesnake Dick Darling. It was destined to be a familiarity of unhappiness for both.

After almost five years behind bars, Darling decided to apply for an early parole with the Nevada Board of Pardons on the grounds of good behavior and his continuing claim of innocence in the McCauley affair. Aided by lawyer T.B. Shamp he also agreed to abide by a stipulation of leaving the State of Nevada if released.[40]

Accordingly, Shamp went to work on behalf of Darling early in 1871. In a statement to the pardon board, the convict said, in part:

> If there was a robbery committed, I knew nothing of it, being in Washoe County at the time. From the statement Woods made to me, I do not believe or think that this man Macauley [sic] was robbed. He was beat out of his money at cards, and then started a difficulty himself in which he was worsted. To be revenged, he entered a charge of robbery against Woods and myself, ... I was not in the town at the time, if I was, I was not in the saloon where the crime is charged to have been committed after 10 o'c. [sic] A.M. of that day. Nor, as I stated before, do I believe he was robbed, for that was a game he practiced himself.[41]

In March 1871, Attorney Shamp managed to collect the signatures of the likes of Gus Ash and George Downey, the two arresting officers in Darling's case; United States Marshal of Nevada George Lammon; Storey County District Attorney William Woodburn; and two of the trial jurors, to a petition advocating Darling's pardon.[42] He even managed to obtain a letter from Judge Richard Rising, the trial judge at Darling's robbery trial, recommending he be released, Rising stating, "He has been confined now 5 years this month, which is, probably, for all purposes a sufficient punishment. If it is proposed to pardon him on the condition that he leaves the State, I can see no objection."[43]

The campaign proved a success. On August 21, 1871, the Board of Pardons granted Darling his release.[44] Some gave him the benefit of the doubt, optimistically hoping that "he will show people yet that he has been more sinned against than sinning."[45] Others, such as the newspaper at Austin, Nevada, where the ex-con had previously lived while married to the alleged murderess Hattie Funk, were somewhat less magnanimous, sniping, "We know nothing of that particular case [the McCauley robbery] but believe upon general principles that the State Prison is a pretty good place for Richard."[46]

Prison officials and lawmen were also cautious in administering Darling's freedom. Less than a month after his release, September 17, 1871, the largest mass prison escape in Nevada history took place when 29 prisoners took forced liberty from the institution. Authorities were positive the former convict had knowledge of the plans of the escape and may even have assisted in some way from the outside. For a number of days after the "emeute" lawmen shadowed Darling, some sources stating at his own insistence, to see if he would implicate himself in the plot.[47]

Soon after his pardoning out, Darling apparently forgot the condition concerning his leaving the State, seemingly, as everyone else had. In fact, according to one contemporary source, Judge William Seawell, who was acquainted with Darling at Dayton, Lyon County, the man still harbored bitter feelings against Judge Rising for sentencing him to such a long term in the prison. As Seawell later wrote, despite Rising's written support of a pardon for the man:

> Shortly after the pardon of Rattlesnake Dick he appeared in the court room at Virginia City while Judge Rising was holding court and that Rattlesnake Dick remained in the room after the audience had gone—Judge R. being still seated on the bench. That Mr. Atkinson [Sheriff Thomas Atkinson] having heard of threats made by Dick against Judge Rising and Mr. A. being apprehensive of trouble gave Judge R. a pistol and proceeded with him out of the court room, leaving Dick in it.[48]

Fortunately, Darling must have decided against a retributive strike against Rising as none was forthcoming. He was far from done with deviltry, however.

Shortly after Darling's pardon, his old pal from the penitentiary, William Chamberlain, had his conviction reversed and he gained his release. The pair partnered up and drifted to Lyon County in the vicinity of Empire, a few miles south of Virginia City. A little over a year after he left the State Prison, Darling, along with Chamberlain and another ne'er-do-well with the theatrical nom de plume of Edwin Booth, decided to fall into highway robbery.

On the evening of Thursday, October 24, Colonel M.N. Stone, a Virginia City attorney and politico, slowly drove his buggy through the cool night air on the road toward Virginia after having taken part in a political rally at Empire City earlier that night. All at once, two masked men stepped in front of his horse and commanded him to halt. Searching Stone's person, the robbers relieved him of a valuable gold watch and chain and $60 in coin. At the conclusion of their heist one of the highwaymen ordered Stone to "drive like hell," which he did, continuing his homeward journey to Virginia City somewhat lighter in pocket.[49]

Stone refused to take the indignity lying down. Upon his arrival back in Virginia City he immediately made a report at the sheriff's office. The next morning, Stone and Deputy Sheriff Ben Lackey returned to the scene of the crime. They found fresh buggy tracks out in the sagebrush pointing toward Carson City. Traveling there, the pair discovered that men answering the descriptions of Rattlesnake Dick Darling and Edwin Booth had rented a buggy on the evening of the hijacking.

Eventually the two sleuths tracked down Darling and escorted him to the Sheriff's Office for questioning. Darling denied any involvement in the robbery but thought he may know where the watch and money were located. He attempted to make a deal with Stone and the lawmen for a reward if he were to recover the items. Not getting anywhere with this line of pursuit, Darling eventually gave up the names of Booth and Chamberlain to the authorities. Eventually, officers had Darling and Chamberlain behind bars.[50] For Chamberlain, this seeming betrayal on the part of Darling placed a loathing in his brain toward his erstwhile partner. This antipathy would fester and grow in his mind for the next eight years and eventually lead to deadly circumstances.

Transported to jail at Silver City, Darling and Chamberlain were soon joined by Booth when lawmen arrested him there on October 30.[51] Following a preliminary hearing on the 30th the trio were held on $3,000 bail and transferred to the Lyon County calaboose at Dayton to await the next sitting of the Grand Jury.[52] According to one newspaper account:

> Dick was in jolly spirits as they rode off in the carriage, saying that it was all right, that he would get bail to-day easy enough. All he was afraid of was getting waylaid [by vigilantes] on the way to jail.[53]

Darling's fears were allayed when he reached Dayton safely. His confidence in obtaining bail, however, was overly optimistic and he stayed locked up. For unknown reasons the charges against Booth were dropped by the State, possibly in exchange for his turning State's evidence and testifying against his two pals.[54] Wednesday,

November 13 saw the commencement of the joint trial of Darling and Chamberlain in the Lyon County District Court at Dayton before Judge William Seawell. Not wasting any time, the following day the jury returned with a verdict of guilty for both men.[55] Two days later Seawell sentenced the pair to terms of ten years in the Nevada State Prison.[56]

The evening of the day they were sentenced, Lyon County authorities shipped Darling and Chamberlain back to the penitentiary, both receiving their second terms in the "big house."[57] The 32-year-old Darling had his occupation listed as "Blacksmith," while Chamberlain gave his employment as "Miner."[58] One pundit felt moved to quip, "It must have seemed to Dick like getting home again, thus to find himself in his old familiar quarters among his numerons [sic] old friends and associates once more."[59]

Darling settled in for another long stretch of drudgery and deprivation of freedom. Prison records note that on September 17, 1874, he engaged in a fight with another prisoner in the prison dining room. At first docked six months good time, three days later Warden P.C. Hyman remitted the lost time back to Darling.[60] Despite this bit of generosity on the part of the Warden, Darling eventually frittered away much of his good time with various minor infractions of the prison rules of conduct.[61] On December 28, 1876, prison officials tossed him into the dungeon for having a long bladed knife in his possession. New Year's Day, 1877 he was let out to celebrate the new year as best he could in the strict confinement of the penitentiary.[62]

Despite the hardships, Darling returned to his hobby of stonework in the prison workshop. Regardless of rumors of his antipathy toward the victim of his criminality, M.N. Stone, for his vigorous work in returning him to the penitentiary, Darling apparently got over his predilection enough in 1875 to gift Stone with a piece of his handiwork. As reported in the local press and reprinted in the *New York Times* on July 4, 1875:

> Yesterday [June 18, 1875] Col. Stone received from Darling a cribbage-board of beautiful workmanship, which he manufactured in prison himself. On one end is carved a picture of a man with a pistol, stopping two horses attached to a buggy, representing the robbery, and beneath it are cut the words, "Darling vs. Stone." On the other end are the words "Stone vs. Darling," and above is a man with a ball and chain attached to his leg, with a mallet and chisel in his hand cutting a block of stone. The cribbage-board is of elegant design and finish, and shows considerable artistic skill on the part of Rattlesnake Dick.[63]

Through the coming years, Darling and his former partner, William Chamberlain, continued to serve out their time together in a state of wary peace. By winter 1880, Chamberlain began making preparations for presenting his case to the Board of Pardons. He managed to receive favorable recommendations from such as Lyon County Judge William Seawell; Lyon County District Attorney John Powell, Jr.; and Constable James Hagar of Hamilton, Nevada.[64] He even garnered a letter of support from robbery victim M.N. Stone.[65] Unfortunately for Chamberlain, Rattlesnake Dick Darling was about to veto Chamberlain's pardon request in a most unexpected way.

At about 10 o'clock in the morning, Thursday, July 1, 1880, both Darling and Chamberlain were toiling in a far corner of the prison stone yard. Suddenly, State Prison bookkeeper Allen Bragg and Lieutenant of the Guards Dan H. Pine were startled by a rattling at the inner gate leading to the inside of the prison building. The two prison officials found Darling leaning on the iron gate.

"There's a dead man out here and I've killed him," Darling said in a matter-of-fact tone.

Upon investigation Bragg and Pine found Chamberlain in the yard lying on his face in a pool of blood, the gore still oozing from five deep head wounds. Apparently inflicted with a pickaxe which lay nearby, the injuries had been perpetrated with such force that the skull on the left side of Chamberlain's head had been laid bare, a portion of the skull bone smashed away. Carried inside to the prison infirmary, Chamberlain, at one point, attempted to speak but was unable to make any sound beyond a gurgle. The mortally injured man died three hours later.[66]

At first, Darling refused to answer any interrogatories regarding the incident. Finally, he told authorities:

> I have expected trouble with Bill for a long time. A few days ago, he said I had been the means of getting him here and he would get even. He acted very strangely and I thought he was looking for a row. This morning we had some words and finally I hit him with the pick. That's about all I have to say, anyhow.[67]

That afternoon Coroner Foster held an inquest over the body of William Chamberlain. At this inquiry, Darling proved more forthcoming, stating:

> I was hewing stone in the remote corner of the yard when Chamberlain refused to do as I told him. I was appointed as a sort of boss [likely a trustee type position] and was held responsible for the work. I told him to do as I said, but he made some back talk and said he wouldn't. I stooped down to take up a pick when I saw him raise his pick to strike me. I raised my hand and caught the point of the pick here. [The witness showed the jurors his right hand which was badly gashed at the base of the thumb and also showed where the point of the pick had penetrated his clothes.] We struggled for the possession of the pick for some time, when he suddenly let go the pick and grabbed up a hammer. Just before he let go, I had gashed him over the eye with it and the blood was streaming from his face. When he raised the hammer, I hit him three or four times on the head pretty quick as I did not have time for a full swing. At the fourth blow he fell and I came in and reported. We were working by ourselves at a point about four hundred feet from the gate.[68]

This last fact stated by Darling, that they had been "working by ourselves" in a "remote" part of the prison yard, proved to be irreducible. With no other witnesses except Darling to tell the tale, authorities were forced to accept his word of the affair. Deeming he had acted in self-defense, Darling was never charged in Chamberlain's death.

Except for a stint of 24 hours in the dungeon for "refusing to work" on May 17, 1881, Darling served the remainder of his prison sentence relatively incident free.[69] Finally, having served almost all of his original ten-year sentence, Darling gained his release from the penitentiary on July 6, 1881.[70]

Whether it proved to be a case of him going back to his old ways almost immediately or more a situation of lawmen being overly vigilant with an ex-con, Darling was in hot water only 17 days after turning his back on the prison walls. Having returned to Virginia City he found himself under arrest by city police on Saturday, July 23 as a suspect in the robbery of Manning's Jewelry Store.[71] Apparently, authorities could pin nothing on the former convict and he was soon released.

At this point, Darling may have decided to seek more anonymous pastures where his name was not quite so notorious. By 1881 this would have been most difficult. Almost everyone in Nevada had heard of the deeds of Rattlesnake Dick.

By February 1882, Darling had relocated south of Virginia City to the booming mining camp of Candelaria, Esmeralda County.[72] Here he came into contact with James Warren, a 29-year-old native Ohioan and small-time gambler, better known throughout the local mining camps by the cognomen "Jimmy Fresh." The two were not strangers to each other. Both had served as inmates together at the Nevada State Prison in the late 1870s to early 1880s, Warren having been sent up for a short term at this time.[73]

Almost immediately, Darling and Warren developed an animosity toward each other. These bitter feelings may have originated back to their days at the State Prison. Whatever the genesis, neither man felt moved to call a truce of peace. Over the course of the next year and a half the pair often encountered each other at the area camps such as Candelaria, Soda Springs and Luning. At these meetings Warren would later claim that whenever Darling saw him "it was anger on his [Darling's] part, always abusing and insulting me."[74]

By the summer of 1883 both Darling and Warren had taken up residence in the town of Hawthorne, the largest community in Esmeralda County, near Candelaria. Warren worked part-time as a baker and house painter when his luck at the card tables was fleeting.[75] Hawthorne being a major rail terminus on the narrow-gauge Carson and Colorado Railroad line, Darling managed to get himself hired as a brakeman on the C. and C.R.R.[76] He often supplemented this income by acquiring odd jobs on construction sites in and around Hawthorne.

Rattlesnake Dick Darling's temperament had failed to abate during his time in Hawthorne. In late July 1883 he engaged in a saloon fracas in Hawthorne with a notorious rowdy and gunman named William "One-eyed Ned" McLaughlin. His nickname of One-eyed Ned had been bestowed on him following a shooting scrape in which a shot had taken out one of his eyes. He had engaged in, at least, three other gun battles, at Clinton, California, and Mill Creek, Nevada, in which he wounded at least three men and was himself peppered with shotgun pellets, before coming to Hawthorne.[77]

The cause of the melee between Darling and McLaughlin is not of record. What is known is that during their confrontation, before Darling could reach his revolver, McLaughlin pulled a knife and slashed Darling in the groin. Bystanders quickly separated the pair before any further damage could be done.[78] The wound to Darling's groin must have been fairly superficial as, within a few days, he would be out and about once again.

Only five or six weeks later, McLaughlin would engage in another gun battle, this time at Sweetwater, Nevada. In this imbroglio, William "Shorty" Cosgrove, a fellow employee with McLaughlin on the Henry Williams ranch, where the fight took place, shot McLaughlin in the hand and chest. In turn Cosgrove was shot and killed by Esmeralda County Deputy Sheriff Edward Moran while attempting to escape across the line into California. Tough as nails, McLaughlin soon recovered and left for parts unknown.[79]

By late August 1883, the feud between Darling and Warren was reaching its boiling point. In Hawthorne, Darling often ruminated in the shop of Mr. Osgood, a Hawthorne businessman and friend. Osgood later reported that Darling "often expressed bitter animosity towards [Warren] and had told him that he had [Warren] scared and meant to do [him] up."[80] Osgood also claimed that Darling told him "he intended to kill [Warren] at the first opportunity."[81]

The situation quickly accelerated to a dangerous level on the evening of Wednesday, August 22. According to the recollections of James Warren, written over seven years later:

> On the evening of August, the 22nd AD 1883 I was sitting in front of the Lake View house in Hawthorne, Esmeralda Co., State of Nevada. Marcadio Briga [a local prostitute and madam] came up and asked me where she could find an officer. I told her that there was two present as James Cardwell and Mr. Comstock were with or near me at the time. She said that Rattle Snake Dick came to her house and kicked the door in. She said she went to the J.P. to get a warrant for his arrest but he would not issue the warrant. Mr. Cardwell + Comstock both said if the J.P. would issue the warrant, they would make the arrest. We all went to the office and asked why he refused to issue the warrant. He told us that the woman was continually bothering him to have someone arrested. He said he was tired such [sic] nonsense and refused to issue a warrant unless the woman would put up the money for court expenses. Then she was told to go home and the officers promised to see that she would be protected. We all left the office and went down town. We separated in front of Comstock's Saloon. I was going to the hotel. I saw Dick coming up the street. He walked up and slapped me on the shoulder and said there was two or three Sons of Bitches that he was going to fill full of holes and that I was one of them. He said I was trying to have him arrested. He said no ___ in town could arrest him. All the time he was talking to me he kept his hand on his pistol. I am satisfied he intended to shoot me then but there was too many men standing near us. He said to me I will see you again you dirty Son ___ and if I find out that you are trying to have me arrested, I will make it damn hot for you. I knew then my life was in danger. I went and borrowed a pistol.[82]

The following morning, Thursday the 23rd, Warren, by accident or possibly by intent, went to Stoner's Hotel for breakfast. It is not known if Warren knew that Darling had taken a job assisting in the remodeling of a back portion of Stoner's Hotel. If Warren knew that Darling was working at Stoner's, a likely fact of common knowledge about town, he may have been planning a premeditated strike against his enemy.

At about 6:30 a.m., Darling, accompanied by James Kerney, a stone mason also working at the Stoner's Hotel project, came up the sidewalk toward the hotel.

"It's too early to go to work," Darling said to Kerney. With that, Kerney walked toward a nearby barber shop while Darling headed to the hotel to check the time.

Inside the hotel bar, Warren walked around in a jittery and "very nervous" manner. He had made remarks to those inside "about someone threatening his life" and said "he expected to get into a little trouble." Keeping his eyes on the window facing the sidewalk, Warren saw Darling approaching the hotel porch. Rushing to the door, Warren pulled his revolver and met Darling on the landing.

"You threatened my life," Warren yelled, at the same time firing his revolver.

The slug crashed into Darling's mouth, shattering teeth and jawbone, before boring through his brain and exiting out the back of his head. Unable to react, Darling died on his feet before crashing face first onto the sidewalk. With his opponent down, Warren fired two more shots into his dead body.[83]

Without hesitation, James Warren sought out Deputy Sheriff James Cardwell and surrendered himself to him. Cardwell took the shooter to the Hawthorne jail to await developments. Later that day coroner and founder of the town, W.A. Hawthorne, assembled a Coroner's Jury to investigate Darling's death. As expected, the jury concluded that Darling came to his death "by the hand of Jas. Warren, who, with a pistol did shoot him in front of Stoner's Hotel."[84]

The *Esmeralda Herald* blared the headline "A Dead Darling" in its next issue, calling the dead man "a tough, hard case."[85] Others were even less generous, the *Sentinel* at Eureka headlining, "Rattlesnake Dick. This Notorious Scrub Comes to a Fitting End," and the *Territorial Enterprise* at Virginia City growling, "No one can regret the taking off of 'Rattlesnake Dick,' for he was not only hardened enough for any deed, but was also very treacherous. 'Jimmy Fresh' did well to make sure of him."[86]

Despite these sentiments, James Warren still had to face the court process in taking the life of another human being. He appeared in court on the 25th for his preliminary hearing in the death of Dick Darling. At this hearing, Justice W.A. Hawthorne, also local Justice of the Peace, ordered Warren held for trial without bail. The accused murderer received transport to the County Jail at Aurora to await his trial.[87]

Warren languished in jail until December 20 when his trial commenced in Esmeralda District Court.[88] Despite a compelling case for self-defense the jury obviously felt there was no shadow of a doubt. Found guilty, James Warren stood up and heard Judge Richard Rising pronounce on him a sentence of 40 years in the Nevada State Prison.[89] After this first conviction was overturned by the Nevada Supreme Court in July 1885, Warren stood trial a second time, this time receiving a much reduced 15-year sentence.[90]

After serving over five years of his sentence, Warren and his legal team began a campaign for a pardon with the Nevada Board of Pardons.[91] The pardon board finally granted the long sought for pardon in January 1892. On the 28th, after serving five years, five months and 26 days of his sentence, James Warren, alias "Jimmy Fresh," walked out of the Nevada State Prison to drift into obscurity.[92]

Unlike Warren, Darling, despite his death, or perhaps because of the manner of his taking off, became somewhat of a legend in Nevada. To this day his deeds and eccentric life are written about and retold around the campfire. Perhaps the *Territorial Enterprise* at Virginia City was right when they quipped after Rattlesnake Dick Darling's death, "'Rattlesnake Dick' had all his rattles before he got his 'button.'"[93]

13

Eureka's Paul Revere
Billy Martin

The anxious rider bent low over the neck of his mount, urging the panting animal to increase its speed with frequent kicks to the ribs. In a movement betraying his determination he pulled his hat down close on his head with one hand while gripping the reins tightly with the other. Glancing over his shoulder, he spat an oath and gritted his teeth. Behind him the source of this mad race roared ever forward, threatening everything before it.

Slowing his snorting mount at every habitation in his path the clarion messenger hollered an alarm to those within before continuing his ride of warning. The enemy quickly gained on his flanks and violently swept everything before it. Having warned many of those along the way the heroic messenger and his exhausted steed finally reached the outskirts of town.

Quickly piling off he ran to the hoist of the Richmond mining works and yelled his forewarning, thus undoubtedly saving many lives of the miners working below ground. The advancing enemy, in all its fury, would soon be upon them.

No, this scene did not take place in the dappled countryside of Massachusetts during the height of the American revolution in 1775, but in the sunbaked, mountainous mining region of Eureka, Nevada, August 14, 1878. The surging enemy was not the red-coated British Army, but the roiling racing flood waters of Pinto Canyon coming to inundate the streets of the lively town. And the fearless messenger, who actually rode a mule on this ride of mercy, did not go by the name of Paul Revere, although some would make the analogy. He proved to be a local Eureka teamster, sometime deputy sheriff and gunman of uneven temperament named Billy Martin.[1]

A native of Cumberland, Maine, born about 1840,[2] William Martin and his wife arrived in the Eureka Mining District of central Nevada in the early to mid–1870s.[3] Although theirs was not a happy union the couple did have one small daughter to brighten their lives.[4] At the time of their arrival the county seat of Eureka, located about 95 miles south of Elko, was a bustling lead/silver mining town of some 4,000 souls.[5] Along with all the modern amenities brought by the mining prosperity came the inevitable down side.

Eureka's reputation bordered at times on profuse violence. The town's overabundance of saloons, gambling dens, houses of ill repute and those who frequented them proved largely responsible for this reputation.

The flash flood of 1878 at the mining camp of Ruby Hill, some 2.6 miles west of Eureka, Nevada (courtesy Digital Photo Collection, Image #UNRS-P1986-22-06, Special Collections and University Archives Department, University of Nevada, Reno Libraries).

Upon his arrival in Eureka County, Martin took up the occupation of teamster. He freighted supplies between the mining camps, timber for mine construction and the man-made charcoal essential for smelter operations. This last item would later loom large in Martin's life.

Although Billy Martin only served sporadically as a Eureka County deputy sheriff, mostly on special occasions, he did see much action against lawbreakers. He proved a habitual posse member, serving whenever he got the chance. It seems he simply enjoyed the thrill of the hunt.

Such an opportunity presented itself in mid–March 1877. On this occasion a friend of Martin's, Josh Alderson, had his house burglarized and a horse stolen from the stables he operated on Main Street in Eureka. Immediately the pair suspected a local cowboy named Stephen H. Winne who had formerly been employed at Alderson's stable. Hesitating only long enough to pack a few supplies for the trail, Martin and Alderson set out after Winne. They tracked their prey for four days before finally cornering him some 150 miles southeast of Eureka in Twin Canyon. Winne quickly surrendered without resistance.

Camping in Twin Canyon overnight the pair planned to begin the return trip to Eureka with Winne the next morning. As Martin broke camp the next day, Winne spotted an opening. Suddenly turning on his heels, he dashed for the nearby brush. Momentarily taken aback, Martin seized the pistol confiscated from the prisoner and squeezed off two or three shots at the retreating figure. Winne managed to keep a whole skin as he disappeared into the undergrowth. Quickly leaping onto his horse Martin galloped off in pursuit. Rapidly gaining on his man, about a mile from camp, Martin called on him to stop. Winne took no heed, continuing to pump his aching legs. Palming his own pistol, Martin fired another shot. The slug struck the fleeing man in the leg, bringing him crashing to the ground.

The evening of March 16, Martin and Alderson rode into Eureka with Alderson's pilfered horse and Stephen Winne in tow. As the *Eureka Daily Sentinel* reported: "they were out on the road six days, but would have remained that number of weeks before coming back without him."[6] Winne faced a term in the State Prison and Billy Martin upheld his reputation as a courageous tracker and man hunter.

Possibly Martin saw himself as an avenger against those who did wrong. If so, he displayed these qualities again on the evening of Friday, July 13, 1878. On this night, he and a number of friends were enjoying a sociable drink and a few hands of poker in Marion Farrell's Saloon located on Main Street in Eureka. Suddenly an intoxicated Italian named Bianca commenced to abuse a young man standing near Martin. Having drawn his pistol once on the object of his wrath, Bianca again pulled his revolver and with a bellow charged the young man. Martin took in the situation in an instant. Jumping up from his chair and swiftly snatching his knife from his pocket he intercepted the raging man. Striking out with the knife Martin plunged the blade into the upper part of Bianca's left arm. Quickly withdrawing the weapon, he struck out again and sunk the cold steel into the Italian's chest just over the heart. Not satisfied with this, Martin pulled the knife free once more and slashing out, drove the blade into his opponent's right side, puncturing a lung.[7]

The fight was now all out of Bianca. Despite his injuries, however, he managed to survive the ordeal. Shortly after this incident, Martin found himself arrested on a charge of assault with intent to kill. The Grand Jury failed to indict him as all of the witnesses to the encounter defended Martin's actions.[8] No doubt he saved the young man's life. It would not be Martin's last confrontation with members of Eureka County's large Italian population.

Only one month after the stabbing affray, August 14, Martin once again came to the defense of his community, jumping on the nearest mount, a sturdy mule, and dashing in front of the foaming flood waters surging toward Eureka, trumpeting a warning. Though some $100,000.00 damage was sustained to buildings and property no lives were lost in the deluge. Billy Martin could take some of the credit for this fortunate outcome.[9]

By the spring of 1879, Martin worked, at least on a part-time basis, as a deputy sheriff under Eureka County Sheriff Mat Kyle. Kyle, a 31-year-old Scotsman born in Ireland,[10] was a fearless officer and preferred his deputies to follow the same course. Men such as Billy Martin; J.B. Simpson, a native of Tennessee[11] and at 29 years of age a veteran peace officer; and Joe Toomey, a handy man with a gun, were in no small measure hired for their ability with firearms and coolness under fire. Again, Martin had a chance to demonstrate these qualities.

On the evening of April 29, the Eureka to Ruby Hill stagecoach had just topped Cariboo Hill near Eureka when it was halted by three masked robbers. After the five passengers had all been relieved of money and valuables the highwaymen ordered the stage to proceed and they vanished into the sagebrush. Apparently, the three then split up. Later only two, John Sullivan and Charles Ennis, surreptitiously arrived on foot back in Eureka. Making their way to John Stewart's stable the pair held the three men inside at gunpoint while they hastily began to saddle two of Stewart's horses. One of the stable hands, John Hoard, managed to back out a side door and began to

Eureka, Nevada, 1878, the year Martin stabbed Bianca in a saloon affray in the city (courtesy Digital Photo Collection, Image #UNRS-P1747-a, Special Collections and University Archives Department, University of Nevada, Reno Libraries).

spread the alarm. Quickly, the stage robbers turned horse thieves mounted up. Bursting out of the stable they galloped furiously down Main Street, passed the Consolidated Mine Works and rapidly disappeared down a canyon on the outskirts of town.[12]

A hastily formed posse consisting of deputy sheriffs J.B. Simpson, Billy Martin, Jim Allen and H.B. McKee lost no time in finding mounts and dashing off after the outlaws. The determined posse doggedly trailed Sullivan and Ennis all night. By dusk next morning they spied a cloud of dust being raised by two horsemen just ahead on the trail. At a point about 28 miles north of Eureka the lawmen chased the robbers into a defile known as Railroad Canyon.

At this point Sullivan and Ennis headed in different directions. Spurring their mounts, the four pursuers hollered for the pair to surrender. Wisely, Ennis obeyed. Sullivan, however, put the spurs to his mount and attempted to drive his horse up the side of the canyon through the sagebrush. Simpson shouted to Martin, who had gained the lead, "knock him off!" Martin raised his rifle and fired. Throwing his arms into the air, Sullivan pitched off his horse. He died within half an hour of being shot.[13]

As Martin stated later at Sullivan's inquest, "could not tell whether the deceased meant to resist; heard the Sheriff's [Simpson's] command to fire, and did so." The coroner's jury decided that the shooting was "justifiable, and that the officers and Billy Martin were entitled to the thanks of the community."[14] Martin had once again come to the aid of his community. His next exploit would be somewhat less laudable in the eyes of some, while others would once again express their gratitude.

The summer of 1879 proved to be a season of much discontent in Eureka, Nevada. This summer the prosperous mining town became infamous for a series of events known collectively as Eureka's "Italian War" or "Coal Burner's War." The labor strife would eventually lead to a major bloodletting. Billy Martin would play a significant part in the tragedy.

An integral part of the mining process, which was the life blood of Eureka, was the smelting down of the ore to remove the valuable elements from the rock which held it. In order to keep the smelter fires burning it was essential to have the man-made charcoal manufactured by the so-called "Charcoal Burners" from the scant supply of timber outside of Eureka. By the summer of '79 these coal burners, mostly native Italians with a few Swiss mixed in, felt themselves grossly mistreated.

In five years, the price the smelter operators were willing to pay for charcoal dropped from 30 cents a bushel to a meager 25 cents. Moreover, this was the amount paid to the teamsters who freighted the coal to the smelters. These same teamsters then paid the coal burners a percentage of this amount. The coal burners also felt they were being cheated by the freighters.[15] One of these freighters proved to be Billy Martin which placed him squarely in the middle of the controversy.

By July radical elements within the Italian community decided to take physical action. Groups of armed coal burners began preventing the loading of wagons. Threats of violence were bandied back and forth. On a number of occasions Sheriff Kyle and his deputies were called out to arrest certain coal burners who had charges preferred against them by certain teamsters.[16] Sheriff Kyle felt strongly enough about the situation to petition the Governor to mobilize the State Militia. This was done by utilizing Eureka's own local company, the Second Brigade of the Nevada Militia.[17] This mobilization would be the extent of their involvement.

Things continued to progress in a downward spiral. Kyle and Simpson most days would be found leading posses to first this coal burning camp then that, searching for rebellious Italians. Despite this, the *Eureka Daily Leader* for August 16 stated: "Mr. Wm. Martin arrived from Alpha and Pine Station this afternoon.... He reports the neighborhood perfectly quiet, and business going on as usual." Although Martin may have found it quiet at Alpha and Pine Stations, just two days later he found another location much hotter.

The *Daily Leader* of August 19, 1879, blared the headlines: "WAR! Battle of Fish Creek. First Bloodshed of the Contest. Five Men Killed and Six Wounded."

The day before, Deputy Sheriff J.B. Simpson found himself on a hill at the coal burners camp of Fish Creek located about 30 miles from Eureka. Together with a posse of heavily armed deputy sheriffs and teamsters Simpson had been called out in order to arrest recalcitrant coal burners engaged in dumping wagon loads of charcoal in the sagebrush and threatening the teamsters. Along with Simpson the posse included Billy Martin, Joe Toomey, Bob Brown, Hank Storey, Marshall Rich, Jim Porter, Lee Jessen and George Smith. They found themselves confronted by anywhere from 75 to 150 angry coal burners armed with everything from guns and revolvers to cleavers and clubs.

Although the facts are somewhat conflicting, it is sure a heated discussion commenced. Suddenly, from which camp is not known, a shot rang out. As Simpson called, "Stand in there, boys!" the shooting became general. It soon became clear that the posse far outweighed the coal burners in fire power. Almost immediately five coal burners, Marcellino Locatelli, 25, Giovanni Pedroni, 22, Tedora Zerli, 28, Italians, and Pompeo Pattini, 35, a leader of the coal burners, and Antonio Canonica, 28, native Swiss, dropped to the ground dead or dying. Another six men fell or staggered away with various gunshot wounds. Not a member of the posse was touched as the coal burners quickly retreated, stampeding into the sagebrush and rocks.[18]

As quickly as it began it was over. Simpson, Martin, et al., managed to gather up a few strikers whom they arrested and carted into the Eureka jail. In a comment which today would be declared decidedly politically incorrect the editor of the *Leader* wrote: "It is the opinion of those who are best acquainted with the fighting qualities of the Italians that this will squelch the coal war effectually, and that the strikers have had all the fighting they want."[19] The Coroner's Jury came to the conclusion that the dead men had come to their deaths "from gunshot wounds, received at the hands of a Sheriff's posse of Eureka County, Nevada while said posse was in discharge of its duty."[20]

One fascinating aspect of the Coroner's Inquest is the testimony of Deputy J.B. Simpson and his amazing recollection of his posse men's weaponry. To quote Simpson:

> I had a Henry rifle and a Navy six-shooter; Bob Brown had a Henry rifle and a Navy six-shooter; Rich had a double-barreled shotgun and a six-shooter; Joe Toomey had a Henry rifle and a Navy six-shooter; Hank Story [sic] had an improved Sharp's rifle and a small Navy six-shooter; Mr. Porter had a double-barreled shotgun and I do not know whether he had a six-shooter or not; Billy Martin had a double-barreled shotgun and I think two six-shooters; Lee Jisson [sic] had a Henry rifle and I don't think he had any pistol; Smith had a Henry rifle and a Navy six-shooter.[21]

A veritable armory! A most formidable fighting force indeed. It is no wonder the fight resulted as it did. For all intents and purposes the "Coal Burners War" came to an end at Fish Creek. All that remained were the legal wrangling's. A number of coal burners were examined on charges of conspiracy and riot. These charges were eventually dropped.[22]

During the progress of the coal burners case, on August 24, Billy Martin and the rest of the posse were arrested on a murder charge preferred by the uncle of Pompeo Pattini. The defendants were immediately released on a bail bond of $5,000 each.

Although most Eurekans supported the posse, there were decenters.[23] The editors of the *Eureka Sentinel* blamed Sheriff Kyle for sending a so-called "shooting-posse" consisting of men such as Martin, Simpson, and Toomey, all three having a gun-fighting reputation.[24] At the preliminary hearing that followed, however, no grounds could be found for binding the group over to the Grand Jury and the case died.[25]

The cycle continued to play itself out when one of the witnesses at the examination of the posse, Dominico Quadro, ended up being arrested immediately following his testimony on September 2. Officials charged him with the attempted murder of Martin and Toomey during the Fish Creek fight.[26] The results of this case are unknown.

Within a month, Martin was in the saddle once again engaged in tracking down a murderer named Lopez. Lopez had managed to escape the Elko jail and headed south with a $250 reward on this head. Being spotted near Eureka, on October 18, Martin and Simpson took up the trail.[27] With these two on his back trail the *Leader* opined: "[Lopez] is sure to be cornered, and if overtaken by the sheriff's deputies will either have to surrender or take the chance of being bullet proof."[28]

After two or three days on the trail, Martin and Simpson managed to get close enough to the fugitive to exchange a few shots with him and capture his horse. Lopez, however, made good his escape on foot. Forced to drop out of the chase due to fatigue and a slight injury, Simpson returned to Eureka. Doggedly, Martin continued the pursuit alone. After having ridden over 100 miles and enduring two days and nights with little food or rest, Martin finally had to give up.[29] Lopez apparently was never captured.

By mid-1880, Billy Martin's personal life had taken a downturn. He and his wife were now divorced. Martin gained custody of his six-year-old daughter but she lived with Mrs. Gus Hymers, a friend of the family.[30] Martin spent more and more time in the saloons of Eureka, drinking to intoxication and quarreling habitually. In a place where most men went armed this was not a life preserving practice.

All Saturday night and into the wee hours of Sunday, May 2, Martin and John Brent visited the various Eureka drinking establishments. Brent, a 38-year-old Wells Fargo express messenger from Wisconsin,[31] and Martin appeared to be on the best of terms. Suddenly, in the Tiger Saloon, the two drinking companions began arguing over $40 Brent had given Martin to hold for him. The quarrel progressed for some time before Brent finally exclaimed, "Billy, I'm no fighter, but I can tell you one thing, I'm a God damn good man."

With this Martin drew his revolver from under his vest and advanced toward Brent. The two men clutched and struggled a few moments before Brent managed to palm his own revolver and fire three quick shots. Two bullets hit the floor. The third caught Martin under the right arm, passed upward and exited under his left ear, breaking his neck in the process. Martin fell flat on his face on the saloon floor, dead before hitting the sawdust.[32]

Many in Eureka were not surprised at the manner of Martin's death. The *Sentinel* commented, "Martin's death in this manner is not unexpected to the majority of those who best knew him as he has been in the habit of showing his revolver frequently upon occasions when intoxicated, and, people knowing that he was an excellent shot, were not expected to take many chances. Martin was a whole-souled man, and many would regret the manner of his death."[33]

Brent, who was said to greatly regret the outcome of the squabble, was arrested on the scene by James Mooney and Dan Patterson, two Eureka policemen.[34] John Brent's preliminary examination came off May 4. All the evidence pointed to it being a simple case of Brent protecting his own life. A verdict of justifiable homicide gave Brent his freedom.[35] By late summer 1880, he still resided in Eureka working as an express messenger.[36] In 1882 he was still working for Wells Fargo when badly wounded in a shooting scrape with Arizona "cowboys."[37]

Martin's funeral took place Monday, May 3, one day after his death. It proved to be a grand affair. A local firefighting company, the Richmond Hose Company, of whom Martin had been a member at one time, took charge of the body. The Eureka

Brass Band playing "a solemn dirge" led him to his final resting place, followed by a large cortege of Eureka citizens. The flags on the various fire houses were lowered to half-mast and the fire bells rang out all during the proceedings.[38]

The bells were like a clarion messenger, peeling out the news of a man's death across the vast countryside of sagebrush and rock. It was reminiscent of a time, some two years before, when a man, in true Paul Revere fashion, had galloped across the same vista of sagebrush and rock, calling out the news of flood waters on the rampage. Like Paul Revere, Billy Martin received the thanks of his friends and neighbors. Unlike Paul Revere, Billy Martin's destiny proved to be a violent life and regretfully, a violent and senseless death.

14

The Ghost of Ely
Hank Parrish

He has been described by both contemporary and latter-day chroniclers as "a bloodthirsty desperado" and "Nevada's worst killer."[1] He may have had a whole career of unlawful acts outside the state of Nevada before arriving in the Silver State in the late 1870s. If so, this has yet to come to light. What is clear is that his course in Nevada was one of blood and death covering over a decade after most Nevada gunmen had seen their time pass into history.

Except for a brief resurgence in the gold mining camps of the early 1900s, Nevada's era of the shootist proved to be the 1860s to late 1870s time period. At this point in time the state exploded in a plethora of silver mining communities, each boasting one, if not more, dangerous gun handlers. Although not arriving in Nevada until the late 1870s and operating through the decade of the '80s, Hank Parrish was a throwback to that earlier epoch.[2] Handling the revolver and the knife with a practiced dexterity, Parrish was definitely a man after his time.

Born in 1840, Henry "Hank" Parrish's place of nativity is in dispute.[3] If we are to believe the 1880 census, Parrish was born a Canadian in the East Coast province of Nova Scotia.[4] The records of the Utah State Prison, however, record his place of origin as Virginia.[5] If allowed a bit of surmising, we could, considering the close proximity of both locations on the eastern seaboard of North America, postulate a Nova Scotia birth and later migration to Virginia. At this writing, however, the matter must remain in doubt.

Another matter of speculation rests with the suggestion of any familial relationship between Hank Parrish and Frank Parrish, the supposed member of Henry Plummer's alleged gang of highwaymen, hung by the Montana Vigilantes in Virginia City, Montana, on January 14, 1864. At least one history claims the pair were cousins who traveled the Wyoming, Idaho, Montana, mining camps together before Frank Parrish's sudden death.[6] Although no evidence seems to support this claim there may be more to the story than is evident at first glance. In their book *Vigilante Victims*, R.E. Mather and F.E. Boswell state, "Glowing reports from a relative—a Methodist-Episcopal clergyman who had opened a bookstore in Salem, Oregon—had lured [Frank] Parrish west."[7] Hank Parrish, as well, apparently had connections to Oregon, later speaking of his two children residing there in 1890.[8] A similar family presence for both men in Oregon is a distinct possibility worth exploring.

Sometime before 1877, according to his own statement, made on his last day on earth in 1890, Hank Parrish married, fathering at least two children. In answer to the accusation that he had abandoned his family, Parrish stated, "My wife has been dead thirteen years; I have two children in Oregon, well fixed."[9] Who the woman was, the manner of her death and the identity and fate of the two children are also concerns lost to history.

By the mid to late 1870s, Parrish, sans family, drifted into Colorado. Although he may have been involved in unlawful activities elsewhere, it is in Colorado where the first hint of Parrish's unlawful bent comes down to us in recorded testimony. During court testimony in 1888 one witness stated that Parrish had been known "in Colorado where he had a racket with a man named Graham."[10] A newspaper report went further when it reported Parrish as "being the party that robbed a bank in Colorado, and shot a man named Major Graham."[11] Parrish's Colorado operations were destined, more than once, to play a part in his later Nevada/Utah troubles. It would not be until he reached the Nevada desert, however, that his violent doings would become widely reported.

Sometime in 1879, Parrish arrived in Eldorado Canyon, Nevada, about 45 miles south of present-day Las Vegas, near the Arizona border, in what was at that time a part of huge Lincoln County. A vast, parched expanse of desert along the Colorado River where temperatures can reach 120 degrees in the summertime, Eldorado Canyon is a forbidding environment. Containing largely rocks, sand, cactus, lizards and rattlesnakes, the Canyon had one other ingredient which insured its invasion by humanity—huge silver deposits.

By 1870 the Eldorado Mining Company had formed and built a new mill on the site to take advantage of the ore garnered from the two main producers, the Techatticup and Queen City mines. In 1879 the Southwestern Mining Company, a Minneapolis, Minnesota, concern, took over the property.[12] By now an active mining camp had developed with the prerequisite saloons, gambling parlors and houses of prostitution. An environment ripe for frontier violence.

Upon Parrish's advent into the Canyon he formed a partnership with another miner named Paddock. The pair entered a mining venture together and worked the nearby ledges. One day Paddock and another miner engaged in a dispute in a local dive. In the exchange of pistol shots Paddock received a serious, though not fatal, wound.

Attempting to escape the consequences of the shooting, Paddock's assailant, who remains unidentified, fled the camp on foot and headed for the Arizona line. When Parrish learned of developments, he and another man mounted horses and galloped out into the desert in an attempt to overtake the fleeing man. Just over the Arizona border, about 18 miles out into the desert, Parrish and his companion came upon the object of their hunt.

Unfortunately for him, the shooter had emptied his revolver in attempting to kill rabbits in order to slake his thirst on their blood. On seeing Parrish and the other man rapidly riding toward him he threw up his hands and shouted that he wished to surrender. Taking no heed, Parrish galloped toward the man, pulling his revolver as he came near. Riding up to the surrendering man, Parrish leveled his

Eldorado Canyon mill buildings. Parrish was one of the first white men to reside and work in this desolate area (courtesy Nevada Historical Society).

revolver at him and deliberately fired five bullets into his body, killing him on the spot.[13]

Most in the Canyon were unconcerned over the death of Parrish's victim, deeming him the aggressor in the wounding of Paddock and feeling he had reaped his just rewards. Though Hank Parrish had established himself as a dangerous man best left alone, he was not overly censured at this point in his Nevada career. Apparently, charges were laid against him in Arizona for this shooting death, however no records exist to show that he ever faced any court action for the deed.[14] Parrish was only beginning his career of shooting in Eldorado Canyon.

In early September 1879, Parrish took part in another shooting scrape in the Canyon. While engaged in a game of cards with one Taylor in a local saloon the pair suddenly began quarreling over some aspect of the play. All at once, Taylor jumped up, at the same time overturning the table, pulling a knife and advancing on Parrish. Palming heavier artillery in the form of his six-shooter, Parrish opened fire on Taylor and, as the *Pioche Record* put it, "commenced to try and fill Taylor with lead pills."[15] Hit twice, one a rather severe wound to the chest, Taylor dropped to the floor. Taken to the post hospital at Fort Mohave, Arizona, the next day, Taylor apparently survived his wounds.[16]

It seems, once again, the community in the Canyon did not censure Parrish too harshly for his shooting of Taylor, possibly feeling Taylor the aggressor. According to the *Record*, "The inhabitants of the canyon exhonorate [sic] Farrish [sic]."[17] A lack of any court records dealing with the shooting suggests that no action was taken against the gunman.

As late as January 1880, the only settled portion of Eldorado Canyon proved to be the camp centered on the Techatticup and Queen City mines. A mere mile or two in any direction, and for countless miles around, was nothing but unexplored, barren, scorched and unclaimed wastelands. Finally, in January 1880, John P. Weaver discovered two paying prospects about five miles southwest of the Techatticup Mine at a location that would come to be known as Knob Hill. Weaver and his brother-in-law, John L. Riggs, would be the first two white men to settle in the area.[18]

One month later, in February 1880, Hank Parrish, along with Hans Godfritzen, James Yocum and Thomas Jennings, followed Weaver's lead and moved into the area. The foursome erected a cabin near Weaver's claim and commenced their own mining venture at what came to be called "1880 Camp."[19]

What became of Parrish's pioneer mining undertaking in the hinterland of the harsh southern Nevada desert is unknown. In September of that year the federal census taker found the 40-year-old "Henry Parish [sic]" working as a mill hand for mining superintendent Richard Knox in the remote fastnesses of Eldorado Canyon.[20] His six-gun would not remain cold for long.

The evening of Monday, February 28, 1881, found Parrish in the saloon of James Greenwood involved in an all-night poker game with Greenwood and "Nigger" Clark, an African American miner in Eldorado Canyon.[21] Besides handling the pasteboards, Parrish imbibed heavily all evening. Gradually, he became more and more surly.

Early the following morning, Tuesday, March 1, the game continued unabated. Sometime between 3 and 4 o'clock that morning, Parrish called on a hand of "ace full on kings." Saloon man Greenwood, a former resident of Pioche and former right fielder with the Pioche Chloriders baseball team, laid down four jacks, beating Parrish's hand. With that, Greenwood reached over and raked in the pot, including $100 of Parrish's hard-earned cash.[22] Without so much as a word or change of expression, Parrish pushed back his chair, stood up, and slowly walked out the front door.

A few minutes later, Parrish again appeared in the front door, this time holding a revolver in each hand. Walking toward Clark he fired a shot. The bullet struck Clark in the body, knocking him to the floor. Greenwood rushed Parrish and grasped his arm. With his unencumbered arm, Parrish pointed his second pistol at Greenwood and squeezed the trigger. The slug perforated Greenwood's arm and lodged in his chest. As Greenwood staggered back, Parrish fired again. The second shot punctured Greenwood's abdomen and he crumpled to the floor. Turning, Parrish ambled out of the saloon and down the road.[23]

Taken to their respective lodgings both Clark and Greenwood had their wounds temporarily dressed and prepared for the trip by steamer down the Colorado River for proper medical treatment at Fort Mohave.

About two hours after the shooting, around 6 o'clock Tuesday morning, Lincoln County Coroner and former county sheriff Andy Fife, who happened to be in EldoradoCanyon on business, stopped by James Greenwood's cabin to take his deposition regarding the shooting before the steamer disembarked. As Fife sat by Greenwood's bedside recording the wounded man's statement, Hank Parrish suddenly appeared in the doorway and strode into the house, again with a revolver in each hand.

In a menacing tone, Parrish told Fife that Greenwood had cheated him at cards, that he wanted his $100 back or Greenwood would "never be taken on the boat alive to be brought down to Fort Mohave for medical treatment unless he returned to him that amount." Unable to see any alternative in the face of the heavily armed man's threatening presence, Fife reached into Greenwood's pocket, counted out $100 and handed it to Parrish. Satisfied, Parrish turned and walked out of the cabin.[24] Though some half dozen men were in the cabin at the time, no one made a move to apprehend the dangerous shootist.[25]

Shortly after this unexpected episode both Greenwood and Clark were assisted onto the waiting steamboat and transported to Fort Mohave. Though both men's lives were feared for initially, their wounds proved not as serious as at first thought and it appears both Greenwood and Clark made a full recovery.[26]

According to the *Pioche Weekly Record* of March 12, 1881: "The shooting caused little or no excitement at the Canyon, and during the day Hank Parrish went back to the mines to work. We are unaware of any preparation being made for the arrest of the shooter." Indeed, none ever would be. In fact, in going back to his job in the mines Parrish was often overheard muttering threats against the life of any man who would dare to attempt his arrest.[27]

The reason for a lack of any attempt to arrest Hank Parrish in the shooting of Greenwood and Clark was both economic and geographic. By early 1881, huge Lincoln County, to which Eldorado Canyon at the time belonged, was nearly bankrupt. Mining, which had been the county's life blood for over a decade, had declined considerably. The situation, as it pertained to the Parrish case, was described best in the *Record* of March 19, 1881:

> Last Saturday Sheriff [William] McKee received a dispatch from John C. King, the Sheriff of San Bernardino County, California, stating that he knew where Parrish was and could and would arrest him if so ordered. Sheriff McKee showed the dispatch to one of our County Commissioners and asked him if the county would pay the expense for the arrest of Parrish and his transportation; if so, he would have the murderer arrested and go after him and bring him to Pioche. The Commissioner said that he had talked with several in regard to the matter, that the expense of trial would be too heavy on the bankrupt county, that they have to pay an attorney $500 for prosecuting the case, and … it was thought that Parrish could not be convicted. The other Commissioners are of the same opinion. We are unaware of the District Attorney having done anything in the matter, and notwithstanding his having received a letter containing the circumstances of the case, he never made complaint and had a warrant issued for the arrest of the shooter as was his duty.

Add to this the fact of Eldorado Canyon being some 180 miles south of the county seat of Pioche in some of the most rugged and forbidding country in the United States and it proved a combination tailor made for Hank Parrish to, literally, get away with murder.

The *Pioche Record* echoed the disgust of many of its fellow Lincoln County residents when, in referring to another former resident of the county who had been arrested in Sanpete County, Utah, for a murder committed there a few months previous, the paper angrily growled, "If [Ike] Mathis had only remained in Lincoln County, Nevada, he never would have been troubled by the officers of the law."[28]

Although any pursuit of him proved nonexistent, Parrish decided to leave Eldorado Canyon to ensure his continued freedom. He soon turned up in Mineral Park, Arizona, at the time the largest community in Mohave County, just over the

Nevada/Arizona border. As was becoming his continuing routine, Parrish eventually quarreled with another Mineral Park resident. Later that same afternoon he came upon his newest enemy laying on the sidewalk along Main Street, passed out from excessive alcohol intake. Picking up a large rock, Parrish was just about to drop it on the sleeping man's head when a miner named Smith noticed Parrish's actions. Quickly pulling a pistol, Smith ordered Parrish to desist or he would shoot him where he stood. Realizing he was at a disadvantage, Parrish tossed the rock aside and slowly backed away. Soon after this incident he left Mineral Park and headed back to Nevada.[29]

Back in Nevada, Parrish returned to the state's deep south mining camps. In mid–August 1882 a rumor drifted north to Pioche that "Hank Parrish has killed another man." In a nutshell, the story claimed that "in a mining locality between Ivanpah, [California] and El Dorado," in Nevada's far southern point "Parrish, took hold of the man's ears that he was quarrelling with and killed him by knocking his head again [sic] the side of a stone cabin."[30] Since one vague newspaper mention is all that is heard of this story, a story may have been the extent of it. The remoteness of southern Lincoln County, however, where reports were scarce and many incidents did not even reach the outside world, leaves open the possibility that it may very well have happened.

At this point in his life, Hank Parrish may have made the decision to live the life of an out and out criminal. From the saloons and sin palaces of the mining camps he apparently gathered around him a gang of cutthroats and ne'er-do-wells. Ranging throughout Lincoln County, Parrish and his cronies began a campaign of dedicated horse and cattle theft from the isolated ranches and stock tenders both north and south.[31]

Sometime in late 1882, someone stole two horses from the Pony Springs ranch of Archibald Stewart north of Pioche. Stewart believed the thieves to be Parrish and his gang of roughs. The rancher reported the crime in Pioche and made an attempt to have Parrish prosecuted. Despite Stewart's efforts, lawmen were unable to find either evidence or Parrish. The case died before it got started.[32] The incident caused an animosity to develop between Parrish and Stewart which may have helped in contributing to developments soon to unfold.

Archibald Stewart was a prosperous freighter in and around Pioche as early as 1868. In 1869 he branched out into the cattle business with his Pony Springs ranch. Amongst his other business dealings, in 1879, Stewart loaned Octavious D. Gass $5,000, using Gass's Las Vegas Ranch, located on the site of the present-day city of Las Vegas, as collateral. In 1881, Gass, a former Arizona legislator when that part of current southern Nevada was a part of Arizona Territory, defaulted on the loan and Stewart took over the property.

In 1882, Stewart decided to move his family, consisting of wife Helen and three children, onto the Las Vegas Ranch. Despite the isolation, the Stewart family prospered, delving into everything from cattle and horses to all manner of grains, fruits, vegetables and wine. A fourth child would be born on the ranch. In the summer of 1884, Helen was pregnant with the couple's fifth child.[33] Unfortunately, Arch Stewart would not live to see the birth of this newest addition to his growing family.

Some miles to the north of the Stewart's Las Vegas Ranch, on the site of present-day North Las Vegas, was the Kiel Ranch, operated by patriarch Conrad "Old Man" Kiel and his five rambunctious sons.[34] Though basically an honest, upstanding rancher, the prosperous Conrad Kiel, possibly due to his adventure seeking sons, was somewhat lax in whom he allowed to frequent his ranch. Thus, the Kiel ranch became something of a hangout and stopping place for numerous characters with a shady reputation. One of these proved to be Hank Parrish. Reportedly, Parrish became quite friendly with the Kiel brothers, especially oldest brother Edwin, and frequently drank and caroused with them in the local saloons and pleasure palaces.[35]

Another aspect thrown into the mix proved to be the dynamic between neighbors Arch Stewart and Conrad Kiel. Kiel, it seems, was a good friend of Octavious Gass and resented the taking over of Gass's ranch by the somewhat overbearing and pompous Stewart. From the start Kiel had been rather cold and unindulgent to his new neighbors, the Stewarts. On the other hand, Archibald and Helen Stewart were less than enamored with the characters frequenting the Kiel place. This feeling was even more pronounced when they learned that one of these characters was none other than Hank Parrish, the purloiner of their horses back in 1882. Events were quickly building to a climax.

Archibald Stewart, taken around the time of his encounter with Hank Parrish (courtesy Helen J. Stewart Collection, Image #0104 0106, UNLV Libraries Special Collections & Archives, University of Nevada, Las Vegas).

Sunday, July 13, 1884, dawned a typically hot summer day in the southern Nevada desert. Arch Stewart was away from the ranch delivering produce to the various area mining camps. Helen Stewart watched over the place while her husband was away. That morning Schuyler Henry, a ranch hand who had been bickering with Stewart over wages, confronted Mrs. Stewart at the ranch house. He demanded she pay him out what he felt he was owed as he was going to quit and leave that day. Mrs.

Stewart refused, telling the man he would have to wait until her husband returned from his freighting trip. Henry flew into a rage. After a few choice epithets directed at Helen Stewart and some other unsavory comments, Henry stomped out to his horse, mounted up, and rode in the direction of the Kiel ranch.

When Arch Stewart arrived back home early that afternoon his wife informed him of Henry's actions and foul language toward her. About 2 o'clock an irate Stewart, armed with a rifle, procured his horse and galloped off to the Kiel spread.

Some four or five hours later one of Kiel's cowboys rode up to the Stewart house and handed Helen Stewart a note. Mrs. Stewart was shocked to read the scrawled, phonetically spelled, missive, "Mrs Sturd send a team and take Mr. Sturd away he is dead. [signed] C. Kiel."[36]

Helen later wrote in her journal:

> I left my little children with Mr. Frazier and went as fast as a horse could carry me. The man that killed my husband [presumably she refers here to Schuyler Henry] ran as I approached. As I got to the corner of the [Kiel] house I said "O where is he, O where is he" and the Old Man Kiel and Hank Parrish said "here he is" and lifting a blanket showed me the lifeless form of my husband. I knelt down beside him, took his hand, placed my hand upon his heart and looked upon his face.[37]

Stewart had been shot in the chest and right side of the head. The left side of his head was caved in as if beaten by some heavy object. Procuring a wagon, Helen had her husband's body transported back to their Las Vegas Ranch. Due to the extreme desert heat she had no choice but to have him buried immediately on the ranch, using doors from the ranch house to fashion an impromptu coffin.

One of the first men to appear at the scene of the shooting proved to be an area resident named J.T. Moore who arrived two days later on the 15th. Conrad Kiel told Moore that neither he nor Parrish were at the ranch at the time of the killing but arrived shortly afterward. According to a report Moore sent to the *Pioche Weekly Record*, Kiel told him:

> It appears that Stewart, on his return from El Dorado Canyon, learned that Henry was at Kiel's. He armed himself, mounted his horse, and taking a circuitous route, came in on the north side of Kiel's ranch, and hitching his horse to a tree behind a cluster of grapevines, proceeded on foot, and when within thirty feet of the house, he was discovered by Henry running in the direction of the door of the house, with his gun in shooting position. Henry, who was sitting by south window (by way, windows and doors were all opened), reached for a shotgun standing against it, and thinking it not loaded, he sprang across the room, took a Spencer rifle from the scabbard, which was leaning against the north window. Stewart fired, missing Henry, who then raised his gun and aimed at Stewart, but his gun missed fire. Seeing that Stewart was about to get in another shot, Henry stepped behind the door, when Stewart placed his gun against the door and fired, the ball passing through the door and grazing Henry's arm. Henry, after recharging his gun, stepped from behind the door, and both parties fired, Henry receiving a flesh wound through the hip, and Stewart being shot through the chest. They both shot again, and Stewart received a shot in the head was instantly killed.[38]

Many did not believe the Henry/Stewart gun duel theory. Some felt Hank Parrish had been the killer of Stewart.[39] Others were of the opinion that at least two different men had been involved in Stewart's death. Rumors circulated that both of the wounds inflicted on Stewart's body seemed to have come from two different caliber firearms. Helen Stewart always believed that her husband's death had been a conspiracy between Conrad Kiel, Hank Parrish and Schuyler Henry. She believed Henry's demonstrations that day on the Stewart ranch were merely a performance to lure Arch Stewart to the Kiel ranch where others, including Hank Parrish, waited.[40]

The great distance between the county seat at Pioche and the southern point of Lincoln County resulted in a slow manifestation of official law. It was almost two weeks before Deputy Sheriff Sam Smith arrived to investigate the death of the prominent rancher. By this time, Hank Parrish had disappeared to parts unknown. Smith did find enough evidence, however, to place both Conrad Kiel and Schuyler Henry in custody and cart them back to Pioche.[41]

In late August, a Lincoln County coroner's jury decided that Kiel, Henry and the absent Parrish should be examined regarding the Stewart death. At the meeting of the Lincoln County Grand Jury in early September that lawful body refused to bring down an indictment for the trio, feeling that Henry had shot Stewart in defense of his own life.[42] Henry and Kiel were released.[43]

Helen Stewart had no further recourse. She continued to operate the Las Vegas Ranch for many years, becoming one of the first pioneers of the city of Las Vegas.[44] Later findings may have proven her theory of her husband's death correct. Ninety-one years later, in 1975, Arch Stewart's grave needed to be excavated and his body relocated due to expansion projects carried on by the city of Las Vegas. Two UNLV anthropology professors, Sheilagh and Richard Brooks, gained permission to examine Stewart's remains before reburial. According to one source, the examination proved that Stewart's head and chest wounds were inflicted by two different firearms.[45] The mystery, however, remains unsolved as to who, Hank Parrish or anyone else, killed Archibald Stewart. His presence on the Kiel ranch on the day of the killing makes Parrish a strong, if not likely, suspect.

Hank Parrish may have felt himself a serious suspect at any rate. At this time, he shifted his base of operations across the border to the southeastern mining camps of Utah. The *Pioche Weekly Record* of November 27, 1886, could just as well have been speaking of him specifically when it editorialized:

> There are 131 prisoners in the Nevada State prison.
> If the swarm of murderers and lawbreakers that have infested Lincoln county and it's Utah boundary for the past few years only had their just deserts, the above count would be much greater. The tract of country in close proximity to the boundary line should be called the "Murderers Paradise." It is so easy to slip over from one side to the other, murder a man and slip back again as innocent as a child, and who is going to the trouble of hunting the murderer up? Echo answers who?

By mid–1887 Parrish had relocated to the Tintic Mining District of Utah and the town of Eureka, some 50 miles south of Salt Lake City. His means of making a living at this time is not of record. He likely worked in the mines when not frequenting the Eureka saloons.

Later in the year another new arrival at the bustling mining town of Eureka proved to be one Enos F. Blancett, a 35-year-old native of Iowa, lately of Durango, Colorado.[46] Blancett, who had operated throughout Colorado and New Mexico and who's "reputation there was bad," arrived in town accompanied by his wife and a notorious gunman named Tom Nance.[47] Blancett walked with the aid of crutches due to a previous ailment or injury, however, this failed to dampen his feistiness in the least. Upon his arrival in Eureka he began the operation of a wood hauling business supplying the area mines.

The instant he learned of Hank Parrish's residence in Eureka, Blancett began telling everyone he came in contact with that Parrish had been involved in a bank robbery back in Colorado and had shot a man named Major Graham. As could be expected, Parrish did not appreciate Blancett's volunteering of information about his past. As a result, the two quickly became deadly enemies.

On the evening of Tuesday, December 20, 1887, Parrish and Blancett were both drinking in McDonald's Saloon in Eureka. At length, Blancett confronted Parrish and, standing in his face, accused him of the Colorado bank robbery and the shooting of Graham. Parrish lashed out and struck Blancett a blow to the head with his fist, knocking the crippled man to the floor. In a rage, Parrish then procured his shotgun and was in the act of shooting the downed man when a bystander, John Watts, stepped up to Parrish and implored him not to shoot. Parrish lowered his weapon and walked away in a huff.

The situation reached its peak the following morning of December 21. According to the later testimony of Tom Nance, he met Blancett on the street that morning. Blancett "said he meant to kill Parrish that day." He also stated "that he would not give himself up and wanted [Nance] to take charge of his property for he didn't know how the matter would end."[48]

Just before noon, Parrish and Blancett again met in McDonald's Saloon. Following an exchange of words, the pair agreed to a duel with shotguns behind the corral of Pat Shea located on the outskirts of town. Accordingly, Blancett went to his residence and armed himself with a shotgun and a revolver. Unbeknownst to him, Parrish, in the meantime, hid himself behind the corner of a house located along the street leading to Shea's corral.

A few minutes later, Blancett limped his way on his crutches up the street toward the corral where he expected to meet Parrish. Without warning, Parrish stepped out of concealment and discharged one barrel of his shotgun toward Blancett. The charge shattered one of Blancett's crutches and he tumbled to the ground.

"You have not got me yet," Blancett yelled as he rolled over and attempted to reach one of his weapons.

Before Blancett could bring a firearm into play, Parrish fired the second barrel of his shotgun. Five buckshot entered Blancett's chest near the heart. Within minutes he was dead.[49]

This time Parrish had no time to make a getaway and found himself locked in the local gaol. He claimed Blancett had fired the first shot and he had then fired in self-defense.[50] This proved impossible, however, when an examination of Blancett's weapons found the revolver fully loaded and both barrels of his shotgun fully charged, no shots having been fired from either.

The local courts found Parrish answerable for the death of Enos Blancett. His trial was set for March 13, 1888, at Provo, Utah.[51] The prisoner stayed in the Eureka jail until February 19, at which time Deputy U.S. Marshal Redfield transported him to the Provo lockup.[52] Abruptly, Parrish's case gained postponement to the next sitting of the court scheduled for October. The reason for this postponement may have been due to the fact of Parrish's key defense witness, Thomas Nance, getting into a shooting scrape of his own the day before Parrish's trial was to begin.

Reports indicate that on the evening of March 12, Nance, intoxicated, went to the barbershop of a Sicilian named Silva La Boa in Eureka for a shave. Nance made some remarks to La Boa to which the barber took offense and ordered Nance out of his place. Nance left, returned with a revolver and, as La Boa ran for his life, fired a shot at the fleeing barber, wounding him in the left arm. Nance ended up in the Provo jail along with Parrish.[53]

As was the usual procedure in Utah at this time for those awaiting trial from the newly settled portions of the state, Hank Parrish found himself transferred to the Utah State Prison to await his court date. Entered on March 22 as prisoner #185 on a murder charge, Parrish's occupation was recorded by officials as "Miner." His age was listed as 47 years, height 5, feet 11 inches with light complexion, blue eyes and light/gray hair. He gave his nativity as "Virginia." He was also recorded as being able to read and write. It was noted that he was a single man and his habits were "intemperate."[54]

Parrish would spend almost seven months behind the walls of the Utah State Prison. Finally, Friday, October 12, probably much to Parrish's great relief, his trial could commence before the 1st District Court at Provo. Both he and his main witness, Tom Nance, who awaited his own court date within the State Prison confines, were taken out and transported to Provo. Nance, strangely enough, since he was supposedly a good friend of the late, lamented Blancett, helped Parrish's cause considerably. He testified to Blancett's previous "bad" character and his declared wish to "kill Parrish that day." After two days of testimony the jury filed back into the courtroom on the 13th and declared Parrish "not guilty."[55] Parrish almost immediately returned to Eureka upon his release.[56]

One Eureka correspondent felt moved to express his opinion on the matter:

> Hank Parrish was acquitted of the murder of Blancett, and returned to Eureka last Sunday. The man Hank killed was a hard citizen, and the world is better off without him, but in view of the fact that the tragedy was the result of a duel, it is difficult to see by what reasoning the jury arrived at a verdict of acquittal when the statutes of Utah hold the slayer in a duel guilty of murder in the first degree.[57]

The correspondent must have forgotten, or was unaware, that Parrish had put a stop to the duel before it could begin by his premeditated ambush murder of Blancett. Many felt either scenario deserved a first-degree murder conviction nonetheless. Be that as it may, Hank Parrish had, once again, gotten away with murder.

By at least late 1889, Parrish had returned to Lincoln County, Nevada. In an interview with a magazine writer in the 1960s, 94-year-old Henry Lee, a former resident of the Pioche area, remembered giving Parrish a ride on his wagon between Panaca and Pioche one day in 1889. In Lee's words:

> He was a real mean looking character. I didn't know he was Hank Parrish at first until he told me, and then I didn't want to know any more. I had heard a lot about him and that was enough. I was just a lad and was quaking in my boots. I drove him straight to Pioche without asking what had happened to his horse.[58]

Sometime before August 1890, Parrish took himself to Royal City, a new mining community about 16 miles north of Pioche. Here he toiled in the mines during working hours and indulged himself at the bars of the saloons during his spare time. His spare time pursuits were to lead to his ultimate undoing.

At about 4:30 Sunday morning on August 3, 1890, Hank Parrish sat at the bar in Jimmie Curtis' saloon in Royal City. Four men, P.G. Thompson, a 36-year-old native of New Jersey; Bob Martin; Harry Hill and an unidentified Chinese man were engaged in a marathon poker game at a nearby table. The game had been in progress since the previous night and was generating much interest. Occasionally, saloon patrons, including Parrish, would pause on their way hither and yon and observe the play. Although it would later be claimed by most that Thompson and Parrish were total strangers to each other, the fact that Thompson had recently arrived in Royal City after a lengthy sojourn in Colorado may point to another Colorado connection with Parrish, a connection not fondly remembered by the Nevada rough.[59] Possibly a connection to his past he hungered to rub out of his mind both literally and figuratively.

At one point, Parrish walked over and, resting his arm on Thompson's shoulder, leaned over to observe the game. Annoyed, Thompson asked him not to lean on him and Parrish returned to the bar. Twice more, Parrish ambled over to the table and leaned on Thompson's shoulder, both times told to cease his actions by the players as he was disturbing the game.

Shortly after the third admonition, with Parrish back at the bar once again, the Oriental was bluffed into folding a club flush. Thompson, Martin and Hill burst into loud laughter which was heard by Parrish. Thinking the poker players were laughing at him, Parrish had a rush of anger.

Walking over to the table, the infuriated man let loose a string of profanities, directed mostly at Thompson. "I don't allow no sons of bitches to laugh at me," Parrish screamed, "and you are a damn cur!" he yelled at Thompson.

Knowing the man's reputation, the poker players hastened to explain to Parrish that they were not laughing at him but at the Chinese man for folding his good hand. As Parrish seemed to accept the explanation and turned to walk away, Thompson added, "I don't give a damn for you and I am no cur."

A minute or so later, as Parrish stood a few feet off, scowling at Thompson, he suddenly reached into his pocket and pulled out a large clasp knife which he opened, fingering the blade. Observed in this action by two other men named Lloyd and McArdle who were acquainted with him, the pair hurried up to Parrish and invited him to the bar for a drink, imploring him to put the knife away. Parrish accepted the drink but refused to put up his knife, standing at the bar with it grasped in his left hand. Parrish's temper was only escalating.

A few minutes later, Parrish, still holding his knife in his left hand, returned to the poker player's table. With a burst of anger, he yelled at Thompson, "You are not only a cur, but a son of a bitch and a bastard!" at the same time slamming his right fist onto the table.

Surprised, Thompson quickly pushed his chair back and sprang to his feet. "I don't want to fight you," he called out just as Parrish's right fist connected with his jaw.

Then, in an arching motion with his left hand Parrish plunged his knife into Thompson's abdomen. With eyes that Thompson would later, on his death bed, describe as "glaring like a mad bull's," Parrish then gave the blade a "wicked twist."

"I don't want to fight you," Thompson gasped a second time as he doubled over in pain, grasping his stomach with his hands.

With the aid of a rush of adrenalin, Thompson managed to spin around and dash out the front door of the saloon and down the street, Parrish at his heels. Unable to overtake the wounded man, Parrish shortly returned to the saloon. Standing in the doorway he shouted after Thompson, "Here, you're a fighter, are you, come back and face me!"

Wandering back to the bar, Parrish growled, "There's another son of a bitch I have stabbed to the heart and he'll go off in the sagebrush and die like the rest of them." He then asked saloon man Jimmie Curtis for the use of his revolver. When Curtis told him he did not have one, Parrish momentarily left the saloon. On returning in a few minutes he confronted Lloyd, "Are you one of the men that is going to lynch me?" he asked, brandishing the bloody knife in his face.

"I never thought of such a thing," Lloyd stammered, relieved when Parrish again exited the saloon.

Out on the sidewalk, Parrish encountered Harry Hill, another of the former poker players. Without warning he slapped Hill's face for, "being one of those lynching sons of bitches."

Returning to the saloon he sought out Curtis once again. Grabbing him by each ear he shook Curtis' head from side to side for, likewise, "being one of the lynching sons of bitches." He then suddenly blurted out to a shocked bystander, "I have killed seventeen men besides Thompson and I have been on trial four times for my life, each time getting acquitted." He then calmly strode out of the saloon.[60]

Sometime later, to everyone's surprise, Parrish returned to Curtis' saloon and sat down at a table, as if waiting for something to happen.

In the meantime, Jimmie Curtis located Thompson bleeding on a Royal City street. He trundled the desperately wounded man into a wagon and speedily drove him to Pioche. After acquiring medical attention for Thompson, Curtis informed Lincoln County Sheriff E.D. Turner of developments. Unable to round up a posse, Turner set out for Royal City alone. Confronting Parrish at Curtis' saloon, Turner placed the seemingly calm man under arrest without any trouble. Turner brought his prisoner back to Pioche and lodged him in the County Jail to await developments in Thompson's condition.

Thompson suffered in agony for five days before finally succumbing to peritonitis on the evening of Thursday the 7th.[61] Parrish would now have to face another murder charge.

Parrish's preliminary examination came off on Saturday the 9th before Justice of the Peace A.A. Young. Following a plea of "not guilty" the prisoner sat wordlessly while the court bound him over without bail to await a Grand Jury indictment.[62] The *Pioche Record* felt

> the evidence for the prosecution was full, and conclusively showed Parish [sic] to be guilty of a cold blooded, dastardly murder, and one for which his neck should stretch in punishment. This

last victim of his cruel and malignant disposition should be the means of effectual [sic] ending Parrish's bloody career.[63]

The Lincoln County Grand Jury found an indictment against Parrish for the murder of Thompson on September 16. His court appointed attorney then moved the court for a change of venue due to the "deep seated prejudice and enmity" against him in the county. No doubt, the attorney was accurate in his appraisal of the situation. The court, however, declined the motion until an effort had been made to empanel a Lincoln County jury. As a result, Parrish's trial was scheduled to commence on Tuesday the 23rd.[64]

On the 23rd only three jurors could be obtained from the city of Pioche and environs. Again, Parrish's council requested a change of venue. The court declined for a second time until a venire of 100 jurors could be summoned from the county at large.[65] As before, the court failed. This venire resulted in only five jurors being obtained. Finally, on Monday, September 29, the Lincoln County court acquiesced to the change of venue and transferred Parrish's case to neighboring White Pine County at the county seat of Ely.[66]

Sheriff Turner and Deputy Sheriff A. Harrison carted Parrish off to Ely, some 100 miles north of Pioche, on October 1 and turned him over to White Pine County officials.[67] His trial was set for Monday, October 13.[68] At 10 a.m. on the 13th the accused murderer sat before Judge Thomas H. Wells, defended by his court appointed attorney O.H. Grey and prosecuted by the team of White Pine County Attorney Major A.B. Treese and Lincoln County Attorney T.J. Osborne, the latter traveling from Pioche especially for the state. Parrish sat nervously throughout the proceedings as such witnesses as James Curtis, Harry Hill, W.C. Lloyd, Bob Martin and Richard McArdle, none in the least friendly to Parrish, gave their testimony. Against such opposition there was little Grey could do. After three days of court proceedings, the jury debated for only a little over an hour before returning with a verdict of guilty of murder in the first degree. The following day, Judge Wells sentenced Parrish to death by hanging, the sentence to be carried out December 13, 1890.[69] With no appeal in the offing, and no money or friends to support his cause, the condemned killer returned to his cell at the County Jail to contemplate his last two months of life.[70]

Hank Parrish had no desire to seek religion or make penance for his dastardly crimes as is so often the case with others in similar circumstances. He often expressed his admiration and homage to the free-thinking American orator and agnostic Robert G. Ingersoll whose philosophy he claimed as his "religion."[71] According to the *Record* he also had no ideas of making things easy on his keepers:

> Parrish was particularly disagreeable and caused great trouble to his guards who are said to have done everything they could for his convenience and comfort, short of turning him loose, taking him up town occasionally, procuring drinks, etc.[72]

He also spent many hours with Ely attorney F.X. Murphy to whom he dictated the story of his life which Murphy planned to publish in book form after Parrish's death.[73] If Murphy succeeded in the publishing endeavor no copies of Parrish's life are known to have survived.

By the first week of December, carpenters were busy at work constructing the gallows from which the condemned man would soon hang.[74] The noise of hammer and saw must have been somewhat unnerving for him. If so, he is not known to have expressed his discomfort.

The eve of his execution Hank Parrish reportedly spent "up until 1:30 o'clock, laughing, smoking and talking incessantly" to White Pine County Sheriff William Bassett, his guards and Ely physician Dr. Campbell, who had seen to the prisoner's health throughout his two month stay in the county hoosegow.[75] Parrish asked someone to find him a copy of the works of Robert Ingersoll but, as the *White Pine News* reported, "in the pious town of Ely, not a copy of those works could be found and that one request could not be granted."[76] In his late night conversations with Dr. Campbell, Parrish apparently admitted to having "killed only three men but [he] had shot three other sons of bitches."[77]

Following a short night of sleep, Parrish arose early on the morning of Saturday, December 13. After a "hearty breakfast," a bath, and attiring himself in a new, dark suit of clothes provided courtesy White Pine County, he met F.X. Murphy. The pair put the final touches on Parrish's life story until about 11:30, at which point Sheriff Bassett entered the cell and read the death warrant to the condemned. Parrish requested of the Sheriff an hour and a half to address the assembled crowd of invited witnesses when he arrived on the gallows to which Bassett agreed.

At this point Dr. Campbell tested Parrish's pulse. He counted 99 beats per minute. "Well Doc, how are they," Parrish laughed.

A few minutes later, as reported by a newsman for the local *White Pine News*:

> As the clock marked 2 minutes of twelve the Sheriff [Bassett] and Deputy [Simpson], the condemned man and physician [Campbell] moved slowly out of the jail, between it and the Court House, and around which canvas was stretched to screen it from public gaze. Parish [*sic*] mounted the scaffold with a firm step and proceeded to the front railing from which he addressed a few rambling remarks to the crowd gathered to witness the execution, which numbered about fifty.[78]

After scanning the crowd Parrish said:

> "I have been charged with a great many crimes. I killed three men, and I was right in doing it. The last man I killed (Thompson), he assisted in stringing me up three times. They say I have a wife and family that I have not treated right. My wife has been dead thirteen years. I have two children in Oregon, well fixed. I am an ignorant man, have always been persecuted, and am innocent of crime. All this will appear in Mr. Murphy's book of my life, and I want you to believe it."[79]

At this point, Parrish abruptly stopped and stepped back onto the trap, having spoken for only about five minutes of his requested 90. The *News* reporter stated that Parrish's remarks concerning Thompson having "assisted in stringing me up," "made many of the spectators looked [*sic*] ashamed for him, especially those who heard the testimony submitted at the trial," concerning Thompson having been a stranger to Parrish previous to the day of the killing. As we have seen, there may be more to this story than at first seems evident.

After shaking hands with Bassett and the others on the scaffold, Parrish stood still while the sheriff tied his hands and feet.

"Tie them tight so they won't slip," Parrish remarked. "How much of a drop have you allowed?" he asked Bassett.

"Six and a half feet," Bassett answered.

Campbell again measured Parrish's pulse. The beat had escalated to 142 strokes per minute. Campbell also noticed a slight trembling of Parrish's lips. Apparently, his coolness was beginning to betray him. Campbell would later state that, in his opinion, Parrish could not have stood on his feet another minute longer.

Quickly, Bassett placed the black hood over Parrish's head, stepped over to the lever controlling the trap door upon which the unfortunate man stood and pulled it back. Parrish's body plummeted downward, stopping short before reaching the ground. Campbell's later examination revealed that Parrish's neck had been cleanly broken causing instant death. The whole process, from leaving the jail to the cutting down of the body had consumed only 12 minutes. At the age of 50 years, outlaw, gunman and killer Hank Parrish was finally dead, the first man to be legally executed in White Pine County.[80]

After being cut down, the body of the notorious killer was taken to the White Pine County Courthouse. Here it lay in state for two hours as a number of the curious filed by to view the corpse, after which the local newspaper stated simply, "it was buried."[81] Just where the burial took place has remained somewhat of a mystery as no gravesite seems to exist in or around Ely. It has been speculated that, due to the frozen ground conditions present in mid–December, someone decided to dispose of Parrish's mortal remains in the basement of a courthouse annex building under partial construction at the time of the hanging.[82] Perhaps that mystery may never be solved.

With Hank Parrish now dead, all that remained for his legacy were the costs incurred in his execution. In late December, White Pine County sent cash strapped Lincoln County a bill for $1569.46, the expenses incurred in the trial and execution. That included $206 for the scaffold, prompting the *Pioche Record* to proclaim, "If this is ours, we ought to have it here ready for future use if required."[83]

Two weeks later the *Record* changed its mind. Even though the *White Pine News* wanted Lincoln County "to take the barbarous thing away at once," the *Record* felt they would never use it as, "even if circumstances here should again justify the use of such a machine we will very likely have to ask our neighbors to do the work for us. The Lincoln County juror will not allow himself to sit on a case where there is much probability of bringing in a verdict which requires a necktie party to carry it into effect so the thing will do us as much good there [White Pine County] as here."[84] Apparently the gallows stayed in Ely, its ultimate fate unknown.

Despite the fact of Hank Parrish's mortal death on the gallows at Ely in 1890 he continues to live on metaphorically throughout his old stomping grounds. In 1918 Nevada/Utah pioneer Peter Gottfredson garnered newspaper headlines and brought the desert killer back to public consciousness when he presented a piece of the rope used to hang Parrish to the Utah State Historical Society where it apparently remains to this day.[85]

Up to the present day the local Pioche, Nevada, theater group continues to perform plays dealing with Hank Parrish and his hanging.[86] It has even been suggested that, if the conditions are just right and the spirits are willing, you may be lucky enough to see Parrish's ghost floating through the corridors of the old White Pine County Courthouse.[87]

Despite all the sensation, perhaps the most poignant aspect of Hank Parrish's demise took place 215 miles south of Ely back in 1890. On the day of Parrish's hanging, Helen Stewart at Las Vegas, made note of the event in her journal. Under the notations mentioning the death of the man she always believed responsible for her husband's killing, Mrs. Stewart drew two heavy underlines to emphasize the words. "Dec. 13,1890. Hank Parrish hung today." Perhaps, at least in her mind, justice, if not vengeance, had been served.[88]

Helen Stewart in later life (courtesy Helen J. Stewart Collection, Image #0104 0114, UNLV Libraries Special Collections & Archives, University of Nevada, Las Vegas).

Epilogue

by Elmer D. McInnes

Men like Hank Parrish were already an anachronism in Nevada by the time of his hanging in 1890 and had been for almost 15 years. The heyday of the Nevada gunfighter, ca. 1855–1875, had been witness to the death of many of them. It also marked the death of many a Nevada mining town, the breeding ground of the deadly "fighters." These camps had a habit of explosive early growth with the discovery of the precious metal—in Nevada usually silver—raucous, short years, or even months, of frenetic activity, then, with the petering out of the hotly sought-after auriferous treasure, the sudden decamping of citizenry and death of the town. With them went the "sports," the ladies of the evening and the gunmen. Barring a short resurrection with the advent of a gold rush in the Nevada of the early 1900s, the age of the Nevada gunfighter died as well.

Men like Dick Prentice, Dick Paddock, James Harrington and Billy Martin would not be seen again, nor the times and conditions that produced them. Some who lived through those times, and possibly experienced some of the violence, may have been glad to see the phenomenon pass. For us, looking back from the 21st century, however, we can perhaps be forgiven for a feeling of nostalgia and wish for a time machine in which to travel back to the Virginia City of the 1860s or Pioche of the 1870s. To be sure, it may be a wish laden with ignorance to how things "really were." An ignorance to the hardships, the often-deplorable living conditions, the sometimes gritty and horrific violence. But a wish nonetheless tinged with the adventure and romanticism of a bustling Nevada mining camp and a chance to meet a George Kirk or Irish Tom Carberry in passing on the street.

In my Nevada research I have come to the conclusion that the "Silver State" is one of the most neglected and fertile grounds for the discovery of unknown and active Old West outlaws, lawmen and gunmen. I have researched some 30 to 35 Nevada shootists and so-called "fighters," any one of whom could have made an excitement filled chapter in this book. My aim in writing this volume, and hopefully one or two more future volumes presenting more Nevada characters, has been to, hopefully, give Nevada its place in the field of gunfighter chronicling. Although Nevada has been neglected when compared to other Old West hotbeds of frontier gunmen such as Kansas, Texas, or Oklahoma, I hope this book will be the means of creating interest in the gun handlers and wild mining camps of the state. The lives waiting to be discovered will make the effort extremely worthwhile.

Chapter Notes

Chapter 1

1. Federal Census of the United States, 1870, Treasure City, County of White Pine, State of Nevada, enumerated 13 day of June 1870, p. 39, Dwelling #777: Coleman, Thomas, Age: 39, Male, White, Occupation: City Marshal, Value of Personal Estate, $600, Place of Birth: Ireland, Father of Foreign Birth, Mother of Foreign Birth.
2. *Ibid.* If Coleman's age of 39 in the 1870 census is accurate that would calculate to a birth year of 1830 or 1831.
3. Secrest, William B., *California Badmen*, Quill Driver Books/Word Dancer Press, Inc., Sanger, California, 2007, p. 4.
4. *Ibid.*; Boessenecker, John, *Gold Dust & Gunsmoke*, John Wiley & Sons, Inc., New York, 1999, pp. 306–307.
5. *Pioche Daily Record*, May 10, 1873.
6. *Stockton Independent*, no date, reprinted in Bancroft, Hubert Howe, *The Works of Hubert Howe Bancroft, Volume XXXVI, Popular Tribunals, Vol. 1*, The History Company, Publishers, San Francisco, California, 1887, p. 609.
7. *Ibid.*
8. *Sacramento Daily Bee*, April 1, 1862. In his testimony following the fight George Lloyd said, "some months ago [I] had some words with Coleman."
9. *Sacramento Daily Bee*, March 22, 24, 27, April 1, 2, 1862; McGrath, Roger D., *Gunfighters, Highwaymen & Vigilantes*, University of California Press, Berkeley, California, 1984, p. 88. All quotes taken from original court testimony reprinted in the *Sacramento Daily Bee*.
10. *Sacramento Daily Bee*, March 24, 1862.
11. *Ibid.*
12. *Ibid.*
13. *Ibid.*, March 25, 1862.
14. *Ibid.*
15. *Ibid.*, March 24, 26, 1862.
16. *Ibid.*, March 27, April 1, 2, 3, 1862. We are indebted to the local *Sacramento Daily Bee* for their detailed coverage of the testimony resulting from the fight on the Sacramento wharf. Because of it we are able to reconstruct the gun battle almost shot for shot. We can also blame them, however, for a misconception which has plagued the Tom Coleman story from that day to the present. In transcribing George Lloyd's testimony at the inquest of his brother in its issue of, perhaps appropriately, April 1, 1862 the *Bee* mistakenly reported Lloyd as testifying: "am in the habit of carrying a knife and six-shooter; had lent my knife at nine o'clock to *Coleman* [authors italics], my brother-in-law," the newspaper mistakenly transposing Coleman's name for Callaghan, it being abundantly clear by reading the rest of the testimony that Callaghan is George Lloyd's brother-in-law and the man to whom he had lent his knife. This slip has led to the misconception, perpetuated in some circles over the last century and a half, of Coleman being a brother-in-law to the Lloyd brothers, from perhaps the earliest mention, the *Daily State Register*, Carson City, Nevada, March 20, 1871, to wit, "We beg leave to make a few corrections [referring to a report published in the *Virginia City Territorial Enterprise*] Coleman was a brother-in-law to the Loyd [sic] brothers," to latter day treatments of the story, i.e., Hegne, *Virginia City Rascals & Renegades*, "George Lloyd was killed by Thomas Coleman, his own brother-in-law." p. 18.

This whole situation has led to an even more complicated misperception of there being two different Thomas Colemans, one a Lloyd brother-in-law and one not, i.e., *Stockton* (California) *Independent*, no date, reprinted in Bancroft, *Popular Tribunals*, p. 610, "The silver excitement took over to the vicinity of Aurora, George Lloyd, Johnny Daly, Jimmy Sears, and the other Thomas Coleman, who was a brother-in-law of the Lloyd's, but who had nothing to do with the steamboat business."

A detailed reading of the available material makes it quite evident that the California and Nevada incidents dealing with a Thomas Coleman, before his death in 1871, are relating to one and the same individual.

17. *Sacramento Daily Bee*, September 17, 1862.
18. *Ibid.*; McGrath, Roger D., *Gunfighters, Highwaymen & Vigilantes*, pp. 88–90; Bancroft, Hubert Howe, *Popular Tribunals*, p. 609.
19. Bancroft, Hubert Howe, *Popular Tribunals*, p. 609; McGrath, Roger D., *Gunfighters, Highwaymen & Vigilantes*, p. 90.
20. Bancroft, Hubert Howe, *Popular Tribunals*, pp. 609–610; McGrath, Roger D., *Gunfighters, Highwaymen & Vigilantes*, p. 90.
21. *Eureka Daily Sentinel*, April 1, 1871; *Daily*

State Register (Carson City), March 29, 1871; Bancroft, Hubert Howe, *Popular Tribunals*, p. 610; McGrath, Roger D., *Gunfighters, Highwaymen & Vigilantes*, p. 90; Hegne, Barbara, *Virginia City Rascals & Renegades*, Nevada Pioneer Series, Sparks, Nevada, 2000, p. 18; Angel, Myron, *History of Nevada*, Thompson & West, Oakland, California, 1881, reprint Howell-North, Berkeley, California, 1958, p. 345. Some sources seem to suggest that Tom Coleman was at least suspected of the McGee killing. Due to circumstances this seems highly unlikely. The most likely candidate seems to be stagecoach robber Al Waterman.

22. Bancroft, Hubert Howe, *Popular Tribunals*, p. 610.

23. *Ibid.*; McGrath, Roger D., *Gunfighters, Highwaymen & Vigilantes*, p. 90; Angel, Myron, *History of Nevada*, p. 345.

24. *Stockton Independent*, no date, quoted in Bancroft, Hubert Howe, *Popular Tribunals*, p. 610.

25. *Eureka Daily Sentinel*, April 1, 1871.

26. McGrath, Roger D., *Gunfighters, Highwaymen & Vigilantes*, pp. 92–101.

27. Baker, Stanley, *Nevada Ghost Towns and Mining Camps*, Howell-North Publishing, Berkeley, California, 1970, pp. 166–167.

28. *Reese River Reveille* (Austin), April 21, 1864; Secrest, William B., *California Badmen*, pp. 52–53.

29. *Reese River Reveille* (Austin), April 21, 1864; Secrest, William B., *California Badmen*, p. 53.

30. *Reese River Reveille* (Austin), April 11, 1871.

31. *Ibid.*, April 21, 1864.

32. *Ibid.* Wow! Either Wilson was a duelist himself or he had a rather overblown case of hero worship and misplaced romanticism.

33. Secrest, William B., *California Badmen*, pp. 54–61.

34. *Reese River Reveille* (Austin), July 19, 1864.

35. *Gold Hill News*, December 29, 1866.

36. Cerveri, Doris, *Nevada: A Colorful Past*, Dave's Printing & Publishing, Sparks, Nevada, 1975, p. 21.

37. *White Pine Evening Telegram* (Shermantown), June 11, 1869.

38. *Daily Inland Empire* (Hamilton), June 26, 1869.

39. *Nevada Ghost Towns*, http:www.ghosttowns.com/states/nv/treasurecity.htm, accessed May 23, 2005.

40. *Daily Inland Empire* (Hamilton), June 26, 1869.

41. *White Pine News* (Treasure City), no date, reprinted in *Mountain Champion* (Belmont), February 6, 1869.

42. *Daily Inland Empire* (Hamilton), June 8, 1869; *White Pine Evening Telegram* (Shermantown), June 8, 1869; *Virginia City Territorial Enterprise*, June 9, 1869.

43. See Chapter 3.

44. *Eureka Daily Sentinel*, September 29, 1880; *Pioche Weekly Record*, September 25, 1880.

45. *Daily Inland Empire* (Hamilton), June 15, 1869; *White Pine Evening Telegram* (Shermantown), June 14, 1869.

46. *Daily Inland Empire* (Hamilton), June 24, 1869.

47. *Ibid.*, July 15, 1869. Fitzpatrick, Lamb, Murphy and Donohue would eventually be released on $1,000 bail. Mitchell was held pending the meeting of the next Grand Jury.

48. *Daily Inland Empire* (Hamilton), July 22, 1869.

49. Federal Census of the United States, 1870, Treasure City, County of White Pine, State of Nevada, enumerated 13 day of June, 1870, p. 39, Dwelling #778. In an apparent boarding house situation along with James Clancy, a 30-year-old saloon keeper: Flood, Barney, Age 40, Male, White, Occupation: Miner, Place of Birth: Ireland, Father of Foreign Birth, Mother of Foreign Birth.

50. *Daily Inland Empire* (Hamilton), August 8, 1869.

51. *Ibid.*, August 3, 1869.

52. *Ibid.*; *White Pine Evening Telegram* (Shermantown), August 4, 1869.

53. *Daily Inland Empire* (Hamilton), August 14, 1869.

54. *Ibid.*, August 15, 1869.

55. *Ibid.*, August 26, 1869.

56. See Chapter 4.

57. *Daily Inland Empire* (Hamilton), October 24, 1869.

58. *Ibid.*, November 25, 1869. Coleman is reported as transporting a prisoner named Donovan to the county sheriff at Hamilton in a capacity of deputy sheriff.

59. *Daily Inland Empire* (Hamilton), December 18, 1869; *Reese River Reveille* (Austin), December 21, 22, 1869.

60. *Daily Inland Empire* (Hamilton), December 19, 22, 1869.

61. *Ibid.*, April 1, 1870.

62. *Nevada Ghost Towns*, http://www.ghosttowns.com/states/nv/treasurecity.htm, accessed May 23, 2005.

63. *Daily Inland Empire* (Hamilton), October 23, 1870. Coleman is listed in the Registered Voters list, Township No. 3, Treasure City.

64. *White Pine News* (Treasure City), February 27, 1871, reprinted in *Virginia City Territorial Enterprise*, March 3, 1871.

65. *Ibid.*

66. *Ibid.*

67. *Ely Record*, March 1, 1871, reprinted in *Daily State Register* (Carson City), March 4, 1871; *Reese River Reveille* (Austin), February 28, 1871; *Gold Hill News*, February 27, 1871; *Elko Independent*, March 4, 1871; *White Pine News* (Treasure City), February 27, 1871, reprinted in *Virginia City Territorial Enterprise*, March 4, 1871; Angel, Myron, *History of Nevada*, p. 350.

68. *Virginia City Territorial Enterprise*, March 3, 1871.

69. *Daily State Register* (Carson City), March 29, 1871.

70. *Ibid.*; *Eureka Sentinel*, April 1, 1871; *Virginia City Territorial Enterprise*, March 28, 1871.

71. 7th District Court, Lincoln County, Nevada, Case No. 1652, The State of Nevada vs. Barney Flood, Morgan Courtney, Michael Dolan, Indictment for Murder, December term A.D. 1871.

72. Writ of Arrest, District Court of the 7th Judicial District, State of Nevada, County of Lincoln, March 13, 1872.

73. Writ of Habeas Corpus, District Court of the 7th Judicial District, State of Nevada, County of Lincoln, Application of Morgan Courtney, March 13, 1872; State of Nevada vs. Morgan Courtney, Instruction to Jury, April 5, 1872.

74. Earl, Phillip I., "Violent Life of a Nevada Badman," *Quarterly of the National Association and Center for Outlaw and Lawman History*, Vol. XII, No. 3, Winter 1988, p. 10.

75. *Pioche Daily Record*, October 15, 1872.

76. *Ibid*.; Application of Michael Dolan for Habeas Corpus, 7th Judicial District, County of Lincoln, State of Nevada, October 14, 1872.

77. *Pioche Daily Record*, November 24, 1872; *Eureka Sentinel*, November 26, 1872.

78. *Pioche Weekly Record*, September 25, 1880; *Eureka Sentinel*, September 29, 1880. Referring to Dolan as "alias Billy Farrell," the *Record* said of him: "Although a quiet man, Farrell was a desperado and well-known on this Coast. He was connected in the job put up which resulted in the killing of Tom Coleman here in '71... Up in Idaho, prior to his coming to Pioche, he was mixed in with several of the cold-blooded jobs up in mining camps in that Territory."

79. *Pioche Daily Record*, May 10, 1873.

80. *Pioche Cemeteries*, http://files.usgwarchives.net/nv/lincoln/ccmctcrics/piochecem.txt, accessed August 28, 2010.

81. See Chapter Seven.

82. *Reese River Reveille* (Austin), May 22, 1873. The fight, taking place in Austin's Cosmopolitan Saloon on Wednesday, May 21, involved a dispute between two gamblers named James Wilson (no known relation to editor Wilson) and Joseph Noon. Wilson received one shot which went through his hand and entered his groin. He survived the wound. Noon exited the fight unhurt.

Chapter 2

1. Prentice's initials have also been reversed as D.W. in some sources. What the W. stood for is not known. His surname has also been spelled Prentisse and Prentise.

2. Drury, Wells, *An Editor on the Comstock Lode*, Farrar & Rinehart, Incorporated, New York, 1936, pp. 75, 174.

3. *Eureka Daily Sentinel*, January 18, 1878.

4. *Gold Hill News*, February 9, 1864.

5. *Ibid*.

6. *Ibid*., May 4, 1864.

7. *Ibid*., May 5, 1864.

8. *Virginia City Territorial Enterprise*, April 11, 12, 17, 1870.

9. *Ibid*., August 31, 1870.

10. *Ibid*., April 17, 1870.

11. *Ibid*., August 31, October 22, 1870.

12. *Ibid*., September 9, 10, 1870.

13. Federal Census of the United States, 1870, Virginia City, Storey County, State of Nevada, enumerated August 12, 1870, p. 94: Dwelling #10, Family #9, Sheek, Wm., Age 32, Male, White, Occupation: Miner, Value of Personal Estate: $1,000, Place of Birth: Canada, Father of Foreign Birth, Mother of Foreign Birth. Sheek, Matilda, Age 30, Female, White, Occupation: Keeping House, Place of Birth: Ireland. Perkins, Arthur, Age, 27, Male, White, Occupation: Gambler, Place of Birth: California. Sheik's name is also spelled Sheek, Sheiks and Sheeks in various sources. Shortly before the big fight, on October 13, 1870, he saved an apparent suicide, one George Crane, from drowning in a water tank. Sheik would fight a gun battle with Pat Quinn on C Street, Virginia City, on Friday, November 4, 1870. No one was injured. Again, on C Street, Wednesday, September 11, 1872, he fought another pistol duel with Billy Nolan. He would also exit this fight uninjured. In the summer of 1880, Sheik was working as a mill hand in the Shell Creek Valley, White Pine County, Nevada. *Virginia City Territorial Enterprise*, October 13, November 4, 5, 1870; *Gold Hill News*, September 11, 1872; *Eureka Sentinel*, September 14, 1872; Federal Census of the United States, 1880, Shell Creek Valley, County of White Pine, State of Nevada, Super. Dist. No. 81, Enum. Dist. No. 57, p. 4.

14. See Chapter 5.

15. Robert Lindsay was an actor at Virginia City's famous Piper's Opera House. On May 28, 1870, he had been badly cut by one Isaac Tamkin in a fight at Piper's. *Gold Hill News*, May 28, 1870.

16. *Virginia City Territorial Enterprise*, October 26, 1870; *Daily Inland Empire* (Hamilton), October 29, 1870.

17. *Virginia City Territorial Enterprise*, October 26, 28, 1870; *Daily Inland Empire* (Hamilton), November 1, 1870.

18. *Virginia City Territorial Enterprise*, November 4, 1870.

19. *Gold Hill News*, February 22, 1872; *Virginia City Territorial Enterprise*, February 23, 1872.

20. *Gold Hill News*, February 21, 1872; *Virginia City Territorial Enterprise*, February 22, 1872; *Reese River Reveille* (Austin), February 24, 1872; *Eureka Sentinel*, February 25, 1872. Quotes taken from newspaper accounts.

21. *Gold Hill News*, February 21, 1872; *Virginia City Territorial Enterprise*, February 22, 1872.

22. *Gold Hill News*, February 23, 1872.

23. *Ibid*., February 22, 1872; *Virginia City Territorial Enterprise*, February 23, 1872.

24. *Gold Hill News*, February 23, 1872; *Virginia City Territorial Enterprise*, February 24, 1872.

25. *Virginia City Territorial Enterprise*, March 3, 1872.

26. *Gold Hill News*, October 8, 1874; Earl, Phillip I., *This Was Nevada, Volume II, The Comstock Lode*,

Nevada Historical Society, Reno, Nevada, 2000, p. 53.
  27. *Gold Hill News*, October 8, 1874.
  28. *Ibid.*, T.F. Smith testimony at Coroner's Inquest.
  29. *Ibid.*, October 5, 1874, testimony of G.W. Werk, Coroner's Inquest.
  30. *Ibid.*, testimony of Harry Foster, Coroner's Inquest.
  31. The best account of the fight can be pieced together from testimony contained in the Coroner's Inquest, Monday, October 5 and Thursday, October 8, 1874, and reprinted in the same day's issues of the *Gold Hill News*. Also see, *Reese River Reveille* (Austin), October 5, 6, 1874; Earl, Phillip I., *This Was Nevada*, pp. 53–55; De Quille, Dan, *The History of the Big Bonanza*, American Publishing Company, Hartford, Connecticut, 1877, pp. 454–460; Drury, Wells, *An Editor on the Comstock Lode*, pp. 73–75.
  32. *Gold Hill News*, October 8, 1874.
  33. *Ibid.*, October 5, 1874.
  34. *Ibid.*
  35. *Ibid.*, October 8, 1874; *Reese River Reveille* (Austin), October 13, 1874.
  36. *Gold Hill News*, October 9, 1874.
  37. *Ibid.*, October 8, 1874; *Reese River Reveille* (Austin), October 10, 1874.
  38. *Gold Hill News*, October 8, 1874.
  39. *Ibid.*, October 15, 21, 1874.
  40. *Ibid.*, October 27, 1874.
  41. Drury, Wells, *An Editor on the Comstock Lode*, pp. 165, 176.
  42. The term "chief" developed in the mining camps of the Old West as a designation for a certain rough, fighter or gunman who had displayed his mettle by killing one or more rival "fighters" in personal encounters and whom all others of the class in his location held in a certain degree of fear and respect.
  43. Drury, Wells, *An Editor on the Comstock Lode*, p. 174.
  44. *Ibid.*, pp. 175–176.
  45. *Ibid.*, p. 177.
  46. *Eureka Daily Sentinel*, January 16, 1878.
  47. *Ibid.*, January 18, 1878.
  48. *Ibid.*, January 19, 1878; *Virginia City Territorial Enterprise*, January 18, 1878, reprinted in *Ward Weekly Reflex*, January 26, 1878.
  49. For Markey's history and activities see McGrath, Roger D., *Gunfighters, Highwaymen & Vigilantes*, University of California Press, Berkeley, California, 1984, pp. 115, 120, 177, 184, 204, 209–210, 213, 230, 244.
  50. *Virginia City Territorial Enterprise*, November 2, 1880; *Reno Evening Gazette*, November 2, 1880; *Eureka Daily Sentinel*, November 3, 1880; McGrath, Roger D., *Gunfighters, Highwaymen & Vigilantes*, p. 210; Drury, Wells, *An Editor on the Comstock Lode*, p. 165.
  51. *Reno Evening Gazette*, November 2, 1880; *Eureka Daily Sentinel*, November 3, 1880.
  52. Drury, Wells, *An Editor on the Comstock Lode*, pp. 165–166. Although Drury is unsure of the exact date, he terms it "about ten years later" following the Eugene Markey/Prentice fight.
  53. Drury, Wells, *An Editor on the Comstock Lode*, pp. 165–166.
  54. *Ibid.*, p. 165.

Chapter 3

  1. DeArment, Robert K., *Knights of the Green Cloth*, University of Oklahoma Press, Norman, Oklahoma, 1982, p. 298 quoting the *Gold Hill News*, January 2, 1877.
  2. Federal Census of the United States, 1870, State of Nevada, County of Storey, Virginia City, Dwelling #4, Family #5. Paddock is listed as 32 years of age in 1870. *Daily Territorial Enterprise*, January 11, 1877. At the time of his death the Coroner's Inquest judged Paddock to be "aged about thirty-nine years."
  3. *Eureka Daily Sentinel*, January 7, 1877, reprinted from the *Virginia City Chronicle*, January 4, 1877.
  4. *Ibid.*
  5. *Virginia City Union*, March 7, 1865.
  6. *Ibid.*, March 4, 7, 1865.
  7. DeArment, Robert K., *Knights of the Green Cloth*, pp. 295–306; Angel, Myron, ed., *History of Nevada*, Arno Press, New York, 1973, reprinted ed., p. 357.
  8. *Virginia Daily Union*, December 10, 1864.
  9. *Ibid.*, February 9, 1864.
  10. *Ibid.*, July 8, 1864.
  11. *Ibid.*, September 8, 1864.
  12. *Ibid.*, October 18, 1864.
  13. *Ibid.*, March 29, 1865. On March 28, Fire Warden Paddock arrested a homeowner for having a short stovepipe located too close to the eaves of his house.
  14. *Ibid.*, May 20, 24, 1865.
  15. *Ibid.*, May 31, 1865.
  16. *Ibid.*, November 9, 1865.
  17. *Ibid.*, November 8, 1865.
  18. *Ibid.*, March 3, 1866. What trouble existed between the pair is unclear but Ballou ended the exchange of insults by slapping Sheppard's face. Sheppard then drew his pistol, presented it in the apparently unarmed Ballou's face and backed him into the Capital Saloon. As Ballou yelled out, "stop him, he is going to shoot me!" Sheppard fired. The slug caught Ballou in the forehead just above the left eye. Ballou died within moments. Sheppard, quickly arrested, faced a murder indictment, however, the results of this case are unknown.
  19. *Ibid.*, March 5, 1866.
  20. Perhaps named in honor of Paddock's dead friend Ben Ballou.
  21. Federal Census of the United States, 1870, State of Nevada, County of Storey, Virginia City, Dwelling #4, Family #5.
  22. *Virginia Daily Union*, January 9, 1866.
  23. *Ibid.*, March 6, 8, 15, 1866. M.R. Williams was elected Chief Engineer.

24. *Ibid.*, April 4, 1866.
25. *Ibid.*, June 18, 1866.
26. *Daily Territorial Enterprise*, July 9, 13, August 7, 1867, are a few of many like examples.
27. *Ibid.*, August 7, 1867: McGinnis, City Jailer, reported 108 as the whole number of arrests for the month of July, as follows: Assault and battery, 8; murder, 1; carrying concealed weapons, 3; drunk and asleep on the sidewalks, 36; disturbing the peace, 20; contempt of court, 1; accessory to murder, 1; vagrancy, 8; abuse of animals, 1; petty larceny, 5; assault with intent to kill, 1; for safe keeping, 1; fighting, 10; assault with deadly weapons, 4; violation of city ordinances, 8; arrests made by regular force: Chief Edwards, 3; Captain of Police, 9; Officer Highbee, 7; Officer Cartter, 10; Officer Paddock, 27; Officer Hardy, 5; Jailer McGinnis, 7. Arrest made by special force: Officer Harmon, 5; Officer Daley, 4; Officer Brinton, 5; Officer Kelly, 8; Officer Wright, 4; Officer Kerrin, 1; Officer Johnson, 2; Constable Ash, 2; Deputy Constable Lackey, 4; Deputy Constable Leemey, 4; Officer Hawkins, 1.
28. *Ibid.*, July 28, 1868.
29. A native of Hungerford, Ontario, Canada, Williams had started back home to Canada only a few days before his death. Having reached San Francisco, he received a telegram to return to Virginia City to tie up some business matters. He was scheduled to have started for home again the day after his death. Williams' dog followed the body when it was carried from the scene of the shooting and, in an agitated state, licked the blood from his chest and whined continually.
30. *Daily Territorial Enterprise* (Virginia City), July 28, 1868. The case that precipitated the whole incident proved to be the theft of $105 and a silver pocket watch from under the mattress of a man's bed by Russian Pete.
31. *Daily Reese River Reveille* (Austin), June 19, 1869.
32. Federal Census of the United States, September 19, 1870, State of Nevada, County of Storey, Virginia City, Dwelling #4, Family #5: Paddock, R., Age 32, Miner, born Ireland; Paddock, Anna B., Age 26, keeps house, born England; Paddock, Benj., Age 4, born Nevada; Paddock, Rich. Jr., Age 2, born Nevada; Paddock, Mary, Age 2/12, born Nevada; Draper, W. Age 37, born Ohio. For some reason Dick Paddock is listed twice in the 1870 census. Three houses before the Paddock family dwelling Paddock is listed as a resident in an apparent boarding house. Perhaps Paddock was visiting someone at the boarding house of Paul and Laura Barrow during the visit of census taker P.H.S. Corbett and ended up being listed in both places.
33. *Ibid.*, Dwelling #5, Family #6; Hughes, Thos., Age 29, miner, born Ireland; Hughes, Mary, Age 31, keeps house, born Ireland; Bascum, John, Age 31, Teamster, born Ohio.
34. *Daily Territorial Enterprise* (Virginia City), October 22, 1870.
35. Dick Prentice was a notorious Virginia City gunman. His escapades would stretch well into the 1880s.
36. Lindsay was a professional actor at a theater in Virginia City.
37. *Daily Territorial Enterprise* (Virginia City), October 26, 1870.
38. *Ibid.*, October 28, 1870.
39. *Eureka Daily Sentinel*, March 7, 1873.
40. *Ibid.*
41. *Ibid.*, March 28, April 17, 1874.
42. *Ibid.*, January 15, 1875, one example of daily ad.
43. *Ibid.*, July 25, 1874.
44. *Ibid.*, June 11, 1874.
45. *Ibid.*, September 17, 1874.
46. *Ibid.*, October 8, December 4, 1874.
47. *Daily Territorial Enterprise* (Virginia City), February 25, 1875.
48. *Eureka Daily Sentinel*, February 25, 1875.
49. By May 1875, Dick Paddock's ad for the Eureka Saloon disappears from the local *Eureka Daily Sentinel*.
50. *Eureka Daily Sentinel*, January 3, 1877.
51. *Ibid.*, May 27, 1875. The *Sentinel* reported the last ballot as standing at 7 to 4 for conviction.
52. *Ibid.*, January 3, 1877.
53. *Daily Territorial Enterprise* (Virginia City), October 13, 1876. Another member of the militia company was R.H. Lindsay the actor and Paddock's former fellow Parke & Co. guard during the Virginia City water war of 1870. At the Guard's annual target shooting contest held October 12, 1876, Lindsay proved to be one of the better shots in the company finishing among the top eleven marksmen. Paddock and Lieutenant Hughes proved to be two of the worst, Paddock being two misses away from winning the so-called "Leather Medal," the award given to the marksman with the lowest score.
54. *Eureka Daily Sentinel*, January 3, 1877. In discussing the death of Paddock, the paper says: "Paddock leaves a wife and three children—boys."
55. *Daily Territorial Enterprise* (Virginia City), September 9, 1876.
56. *Ibid.*, January 3, 4, 9, 1877; *Eureka Daily Sentinel*, January 3, 4, 1877.
57. *Daily Territorial Enterprise* (Virginia City), January 4, 1877.
58. *Ibid.*, January 9, 1877.
59. *Ibid.*, January 3, 1877.
60. *Ibid.*
61. *Ibid.*, January 4, 1877.
62. *Eureka Daily Sentinel*, January 18, 1878. Prentice is called "the man who killed five men at Waller's Defeat shaft of the Justice, three years ago" and "considered the best fighter in Nevada."
63. *Daily Territorial Enterprise* (Virginia City), January 4, 1877.
64. *Ibid.*
65. *Ibid.*, January 5, 1877; *Eureka Daily Sentinel*, January 5, 6, 1877.
66. *Daily Territorial Enterprise* (Virginia City), January 6, 1877; *Eureka Daily Sentinel*, January 7, 1877.

67. *Daily Territorial Enterprise* (Virginia City), January 9, 1877.
68. *Ibid.*, January 7, 9, 1877. The *Enterprise* commented: "we have no space for particularization as to the various merits of the performers, but the professional will scarcely deem it invidious if we mention the excellence of the amateur impersonation of the character of Admiral Kinston by Bob Lindsay."
69. *Ibid.*, January 9, 11, 1877.
70. *Ibid.*, October 8, 1879; *Eureka Daily Leader*, October 9, 1879.

Chapter 4

1. *Carson Morning Appeal*, July 30, 1878.
2. *Ward Weekly Reflex*, August 3, 1878.
3. At the time of his entrance into the Nevada State Prison in 1873 officials recorded Bethards' age as 38, thus giving him a birth year of about 1835. *Biennial Report of the Warden of the Nevada State Prison, for the Years 1873 and 1874*, Table No. 1, Showing the number of convicts received at the Nevada State Prison during the year 1873, p. 19.
4. *Biennial Report of the Warden of the Nevada State Prison, for the Years 1873 and 1874*, Table No. 1, Showing the number of convicts received at the Nevada State Prison during the year 1873, p. 19; *Biennial Report of the Warden of the Nevada State Prison, for the Years 1877 and 1878*, Table No. 10, Showing the number of deaths in the Nevada State Prison during the year 1878, p. 50; Federal Census of the United States, 1870, Pioche City, County of Lincoln, State of Nevada, dwelling #31; *Carson Morning Appeal*, July 30, 1878.
5. *Carson Morning Appeal*, July 30, 1878.
6. Just how many children Bethards and his wife produced is unknown. Testimony at his 1873 trials for the killing of James Brophy would seem to suggest multiple children, one a young boy old enough to handle firearms in the year 1873.
7. *Carson Daily Appeal*, May 20, 1865.
8. *Ibid.*, July 4, 1865.
9. *Ibid.*, August 4, 1865.
10. *Ibid.*, August 9, 1865.
11. *Ibid.*, January 23, 1866.
12. *Ibid.*, February 28, 1866.
13. *Ibid.*
14. *Ibid.*, March 4, 1866.
15. *Ibid.*, February 12, 1867.
16. *Ibid.*
17. *Ibid.*, February 13, 1867.
18. *Ibid.*, February 26, 1867.
19. *Ibid.*, March 26, 1867.
20. *Ibid.*, April 2, 1867.
21. *Ibid.*, April 10, 1867.
22. *Ibid.*
23. *Daily Reese River Reveille* (Austin, Nevada), May 13, 1868.
24. *Ibid.*, May 27, 1868.
25. *Ibid.*, May 30, 1868.
26. *Ibid.*, June 8, 1868.
27. *Ibid.*, July 23, 1868.
28. *Ibid.*, July 29, 1868. The council appointed John H. Emory to replace Bethards.
29. *Daily Inland Empire* (Hamilton, Nevada), October 24, 1869.
30. *Ibid.*, January 26, 1870. The other man mentioned proved to be one Charles F. McIntyre, another local lawman.
31. *Ibid.*, December 28, 1869. Apparently, Cartwright accused Howard of reneging on the payment of his rent for the building in which Howard had located his drinking establishment in Hamilton called Howard's Sample Rooms. While both were drinking in Howard's place located on Main Street, early on the evening of December 26, an argument broke out. This disagreement culminated with Howard drawing a pistol and shooting Cartwright in the head, killing him instantly.
32. *Ibid.*, February 24, 1870.
33. *Ibid.*, February 26, 1870.
34. *Ibid.*, March 9, 1870.
35. *Ibid.*, February 24, 1870.
36. *Biennial Report of the Warden of Nevada State Prison, for the Years 1879 and 1880*, Tenth Session of the Nevada Legislature, 1880, Table No. 15, Showing the Number of Convicts in the Nevada State Prison December 31, 1880, p. 56: Name: Thomas Flynn, alias Matt Rafferty; Age: 30; Nativity: Ireland; County Sent From; White Pine; Crime: Grand Larceny, Term of Sentence: 5 years, Attempt to rob, 2 years, Burglary, 9 years, Prison breaking, 1 year, Prison breaking, 10 years, Murder in the second degree, Life; Date of Committal, August 29, 1870; Trade or occupation, Laborer.
Biennial Report of the Warden of Nevada State Prison, For the Years 1889 and 1890, Table No. 5, Showing the number of convicts pardoned during the year 1889, p. 99.
37. *Ibid.*
38. *The Daily Inland Empire*, in reporting Flynn's testimony in its issue of February 24, 1870, misspelled his name "Flinn."
39. *Elko Independent*, March 12, 1870.
40. *Ibid.*, July 27, 1870.
41. Federal Census of the United States, 1870, Pioche City, County of Lincoln, State of Nevada, Dwelling #31: Bethards, Wm.; Age, 21 (*sic*); Profession, Silver Miner; Place of Birth, Del. Although about 35 years of age, for some reason Bethards age is mistakenly listed as "21" by the census taker. The absence of Bethards' family can probably be explained by his leaving them at home in Treasure City during his Pioche sojourns.
42. *Eureka Daily Sentinel*, August 3, 1878.
43. *Biennial Report of the Warden of Nevada State Prison, for the Years 1879 and 1880*, Tenth Session of the Nevada Legislature, 1880, Table, No. 15, Showing the Number of Convicts in the Nevada State Prison, December 31, 1880, p. 56.
44. *Daily Inland Empire* (Hamilton), October 19, 1870.
45. Owned by two mining entrepreneurs named W.H. Raymond and John Ely.
46. Gracey, Charles, "Early Days in Lincoln

County," *Nevada Historical Society First Biennial Report*, 1908, p. 110.

47. Higgs, Gerald B., *Lost Legends of the Silver State*, Western Epics, 1976, p. 119.

48. Gracey, Charles, "Early Days in Lincoln County," p. 110.

49. *Ibid.*, pp. 110–111; Higgs, Gerald B., *Lost Legends of the Silver State*, pp. 119–120.

50. Gracey, Charles, "Early Days in Lincoln County," p. 111; Higgs, Gerald B., *Lost Legends of the Silver State*, p. 120.

51. *Elko Independent*, November 16, 1870; *Territorial Enterprise* (Virginia City), November 16, 1870; Gracey, Charles, "Early Days in Lincoln County," p. 111; Higgs, Gerald B., *Lost Legends of the Silver State*, p. 120.

52. *Elko Independent*, November 16, 1870; *Territorial Enterprise*, November 16, 1870.

53. *Ibid.*

54. Higgs, Gerald, B., *Lost Legends of the Silver State*, p. 120.

55. "Chief" was the title often bestowed upon the primary gunman of a particular Nevada mining camp in the 1860–90 time period.

56. Higgs, Gerald, B., *Lost Legends of the Silver State*, p. 120.

57. *Daily State Register* (Carson City), December 31, 1870.

58. *Ibid.*, April 4, 1871. It would be an all-star line-up on the Lincoln County docket that April and a wholesale release. Besides Bill Bethards ten other Pioche fighters would also have their indictments ignored by county officials including L.J. Hanchett, Henry Rice, M.H. Lyons, W.L. McKee, John Doe (a designation given an unidentified individual), Frank Nichols, Mike Casey, Morgan Courtney, Wythe Walker and James Harrington. Four of the released besides Bethards (McKee, Casey, Courtney and Harrington), either already were, or would go on to become, well known Nevada gunmen.

59. *Ward Weekly Reflex*, August 3, 1878.

60. Only six days after the Washington and Creole Battle two other Pioche mining operations, the Caledonia and the Overman Companies, fought a battle over disputed ground. The situation became so serious that a vigilante committee was formed in Pioche in the summer of 1871 and five cases of Henry rifles were shipped to the town for the vigilantes to use. *Territorial Enterprise*, November 19, 1870; *Eureka Daily Sentinel*, June 24, 28, 1871; *Daily State Register*, June 28, 1871.

61. Thompson and West, *History of Nevada*, 1881, Oakland, California, reprint Howell-North, Berkley, California, 1958, p. 656.

62. *Eureka Sentinel*, August 10, 1872.

63. The State of Nevada vs. William H. Bethards, Eighth Judicial District Court of the State of Nevada, County of White Pine, July 7, 1873 (second trial), testimony of John C. Scott, continued in Wm. H. Bethards application for pardon file.

64. *Ibid.*, testimony of James Filton; State of Nevada vs. W.H. Bethards, February 18, 1873 (first trial), testimony of Frank Alman and Wm. H. Bethards, contained in Wm. H. Bethards application for pardon file.

65. *Ibid.*

66. *Ibid.*, testimony of Ed Brannan.

67. State of Nevada vs. W.H. Bethards, February 18, 1873, testimony of Frank Alman.

68. The State of Nevada vs. William H. Bethards, Eighth Judicial District Court of the State of Nevada, County of White Pine, July 7, 1873, testimony of John C. Scott.

69. The State of Nevada vs. William H. Bethards, Eighth Judicial District of the State of Nevada, County of White Pine, July 7, 1873; State of Nevada vs. W.H. Bethards, February 18, 1873; *Eureka Sentinel*, November 7, 1872; *Gold Hill Evening News*, November 11, 1872.

70. *Gold Hill Evening News*, November 11, 1872.

71. The State of Nevada vs. William H. Bethards, Eighth Judicial District of the State of Nevada, County of White Pine, July 7, 1873, testimony of William H. Bethards.

72. The State of Nevada vs. William H. Bethards, February 18, 1873, testimony of William H. Bethards.

73. The State of Nevada vs. William H. Bethards, Eighth Judicial District Court of the State of Nevada, County of White Pine, July 7, 1873.

74. *Ibid.*, Judgment.

75. *Ibid.*; *Biennial Report of The Warden of Nevada State Prison, for the Years 1873 and 1874*, p. 19.

76. Seven months after her husband was sent to the State Prison, Mrs. Bethards gained mention in a local item of the *Pioche Daily Record* concerning her attendance at a "Grand Masquerade and Fancy Ball" held in Pioche. Interestingly, also listed as attending were a Mrs. O.P. Sherwood and Mrs. Wm. Sherwood. If these were any relation to the John Sherwood killed by Billy Bethards in Carson City in 1867 it would seem to suggest that the Sherwood family continued to hold friendly relations with Mrs. William Bethards at least. *Pioche Daily Record*, February 8, 1874.

77. *Biennial Report of the Warden of the Nevada State Prison, For the Years 1873 and 1874*, Table No. 1, Showing the number of convicts received at the Nevada State Prison during the year 1873, p. 19: Name, Wm. H. Bithards [*sic*]; Age, 38; Nativity, Delaware; County from where sent, White Pine; Crime, Murder, second degree; Term of sentence, 15 years; Date of Committal, July 28, 1873; Trade or occupation, Miner.

78. According to Flynn at his subsequent trial for the killing of Bethards he had been born in Ireland where he received five years of schooling. He lived the life of a sailor until 1867 when he appeared in the Idaho mines. In 1869 he moved to Nevada where he worked as a mine guard for the Hidden Treasure Mining Company at White Pine County. Involved in the mass breakout at the Nevada State Prison in 1871 and at least one other attempted escape, Flynn, at the time of Bethards' arrival, was serving a total of five separate terms for five convictions vis: Grand

Larceny, five years; attempt to rob, two years; Burglary, nine years; and two counts of prison breaking one and ten years, respectively, for a total aggregate sentence of 27 years. Described by one contemporary source as looking "vicious, sullen and every inch a murderer" the 33-year-old Flynn was a troublesome convict who spent much of his time in the prison dungeon serving solitary confinement for various infractions. *Carson Morning Appeal*, March 14, 1879; *Reno Evening Gazette*, April 2, 1879, *Biennial Report of the Warden of Nevada State Prison, for the Years 1879 and 1880*, Tenth Session of The Nevada Legislature, 1880, Table No. 15, Showing the Number of Convicts in the Nevada State Prison, December 31, 1880, p. 56.

79. Pardon Application of Wm. H. Bethards, notice of M.M. Gaige to Hon. Fred N. Cole, Dist. Judge and J.B. Barker, Dist. Atty., White Pine Co., Nev., September 1875.

80. Pardon application of Wm. H. Bethards, various letters in pardon file. DeLong wrote to Gaige, "I am willing to do everything in my power for Bethards without any charge." Jonas Seely, to the Board of Pardons, stated in part, "If there be such a thing as earning pardon by repentance, good conduct and determination to lead a virtuous life, then Bethards has earned one in my opinion."

81. Pardon Application of Wm. H. Bethards, Petition requesting pardon to the Honorable, The Board of Pardons of the State of Nevada, Carson City, Ormsby County.

82. *Ibid.*, Austin, Lander Co., Nevada.

83. *Ibid.*, Hamilton, White Pine Co., Nevada.

84. Pardon Application of Wm. H. Bethards.

85. Wm. H. Bethards to "Friend Gaige," June 24, 1877, letter contained in Wm. H. Bethards application for pardon file.

86. Note contained in Wm. H. Bethards application for pardon file.

87. Pardon Application of Wm. H. Bethards.

88. *Eureka Daily Sentinel*, March 13, 1879.

89. *Ibid.*, August 3, 1878; *Reno Evening Gazette*, July 31, 1878; *Carson Morning Appeal*, July 30, August 3, 1878; *Ward Weekly Reflex*, August 3, 1878; *Esmeralda Herald* (Aurora), August 3, 1878; *Biennial Report of the Warden of Nevada State Prison for the Years 1877 and 1878*, Ninth Session of The Nevada Legislature, 1879, Table No. 10, showing the number of deaths in the Nevada State Prison during the year 1878, p. 50, also Report of Attending Physician.

90. *Carson Morning Appeal*, July 31, August 3, 1878.

91. *Ibid.* Howard was a former resident of Pioche who had served a term in the prison for killing a professional gambler in a dispute over a card game. He was a former Union Soldier and veteran of the Civil War who, during an attempted escape by other prisoners on one occasion, stood by Warden Batterman and helped protect Captain of the Guard Matthewson who had been shot and wounded in the arm.

92. *Carson Morning Appeal*, August 3, 1878.

93. *Ibid.*, March 13, 14, 1879; *Eureka Daily Sentinel*, March 13, 1879.

94. *Carson Morning Appeal*, March 14, 1879; *Reno Evening Gazette*, March 14, 1879.

95. *Carson Morning Appeal*, March 23, 1879; *Biennial Report of the Warden of Nevada State Prison, for the Years 1879 and 1880*, Tenth Session of the Nevada Legislature, 1880, Table No. 15, Showing the Number of Convicts in the Nevada State Prison, December 31, 1880, p. 56.

96. *Reno Evening Gazette*, April 2, 1879.

97. *Biennial Report of the Warden of Nevada State Prison, for the Years 1889 and 1890*, Table No. 5, Showing the number of convicts pardoned during the year 1889, p. 39; Pardon of Thos. Flynn, State of Nevada, Office of the Board of Pardons, Recorded, July 12, 1889.

98. *Carson Morning Appeal*, July 31, 1878.

99. *Eureka Daily Sentinel*, August 3, 1878, quoting the *Carson Tribune*.

Chapter 5

1. Historian Paula Mitchell Marks said of Blackburn, "Despite the fact that he was also a deputy sheriff and collector [in Tombstone, Arizona], Blackburn remains a shadowy figure." Marks, Paula Mitchell, *And Die in the West*, William Morrow and Company, Inc., New York, 1989, p. 302.

2. Federal Census of the U.S., 1870, Virginia City, County of Storey, State of Nevada, p. 84, enumerated August 6, 1870: Dwelling #4, Family #1; Blackburn, L.F., Age: 29; Male; White; Occupation: Melodeon Keeper; Place of Birth: New York. Blackburn, Jane, Age: 25; Female; White; Occupation: Keeps House; Place of Birth: New York. Blackburn, Wm., Age: 23; Male; White; Place of Birth: New York. Blackburn, Clara, Age: 7; Female; White; Place of Birth: California; Attended school within the last year. Wm. Blackburn may have been Leslie's brother.

3. Shillingberg, Wm. B., *Tombstone, A.T.: A History of Early Mining, Milling, and Mayhem*, The Arthur H. Clark Company, Spokane, Washington, 1999, pp. 155, 165.

4. Angel, Myron, *History of Nevada*, Thompson & West, Oakland, California, 1881, reprint Howell—North, Berkeley, California, 1958, p. 572.

5. Shillingberg, Wm. B., *Tombstone, A.T.*, p. 155. Shillingberg says of Blackburn's entry into Tombstone, "He brought with him experience as a fire department volunteer at both Virginia City and San Francisco."

6. Daggett, R.M., "Brisk Days on the Comstock," *San Francisco Morning Call*, August 6, 1893.

7. Twain, Mark, *Roughing It*, American Publishing Company, Chicago, Illinois, 1872, Chapter LXXIX; Paine, Albert Bigelow, *Mark Twain: A Biography*, Harper & Brothers, New York, 1912, Chapter LV, "Highway Robbery"; Powers, Ron, *Mark Twain: A Life*, Free Press, New York, 2005, pp. 166–167; Kaplan, Fred, *The Singular Mark Twain*, Doubleday, New York, 2003, pp. 165–166. Some sources claim Twain and McCarthy were riding in a coach when the mock robbery occurred. This is highly unlikely,

however, as Virginia City and Gold Hill were only a mile, or a little less, apart. Most everyone walked or at the very least rode horseback between the two communities. Twain himself, in *Roughing It,* says they were walking.

8. Paine, Albert Bigelow, *Mark Twain: A Biography*, Chapter XXXVIII.

9. *Virginia City Territorial Enterprise*, April 5, 1867.

10. *Ibid.*, December 27, 1867.

11. *Ibid.*

12. *Ibid.*

13. *Ibid.*, December 28, 1867.

14. *Ibid.*, April 17, 1868; *Carson City Daily Appeal,* April 17, 1868; Angel, Myron, *History of Nevada,* p. 348.

15. *Virginia City Territorial Enterprise,* April 25, 1868.

16. *Ibid.*, August 18, 1868.

17. *Daily Inland Empire* (Hamilton), July 31, 1869.

18. *Gold Hill News*, June 7, 1870.

19. *Daily Inland Empire* (Hamilton), March 27, 1870.

20. *Ibid.*, March 31, 1870.

21. *Carson City Daily Appeal*, March 29, 1870, reprinted in *Daily Inland Empire* (Hamilton), April 1, 1870.

22. *Ibid.*

23. *Gold Hill News*, June 6, 7, 8, 13, 1870.

24. *Ibid.*, July 2, 1870; Federal Census of the U.S., 1870. In the census enumerated on August 6, 1870, Blackburn is listed as a "Melodeon Keeper."

25. *Virginia City Territorial Enterprise*, October 23, 1870, "List of Registered Voters, Second Ward, Blackburn, L.F."

26. Federal Census of the U.S., 1870, Virginia City, County of Storey, State of Nevada, p. 84.

27. *Virginia City Territorial Enterprise*, April 17, August 11, 12, 31, October 22, 1870.

28. Federal Census of the U.S., 1870, Virginia City, County of Storey, State of Nevada, p. 126: Dwelling #2, Family #2 [apparent boarding house situation], Lindsay, Robert, Age: 34; Male; White; Occupation: Actor; Place of Birth: New York.

29. *Gold Hill News*, May 28, 1870.

30. *Ibid.*, December 16, 1870.

31. *Virginia City Territorial Enterprise*, October 26, 1870; *Daily Inland Empire* (Hamilton), October 29, 1870.

32. *Virginia City Territorial Enterprise*, October 28, 1870; *Daily Inland Empire* (Hamilton), November 1, 1870.

33. *Gold Hill News*, December 16, 1870.

34. *Salt Lake City Herald*, November 15, 1884; *Salt Lake City Democrat*, September 26, 1885; *San Francisco Call*, October 15, 1895.

35. Federal Census of the U.S., 1870, Virginia City, County of Storey, State of Nevada, p. 126: Nobles, Milton; Age: 26; Male; White; Occupation: Actor; Place of Birth: Michigan.

36. An article in the *Tombstone Epitaph* of February 18, 1888, reproduced from the *Missouri Republican,* relates a story in which Blackburn is mentioned as chief of the Tombstone fire department in 1879.

37. Shillingberg, Wm. B., *Tombstone, A.T.,* pp. 154–155.

38. *Kansas City Star*, no date, reprinted in the *Salt Lake City Herald,* May 24, 1903.

39. Young, Roy B., "Robert Havlin Paul, Frontier Lawman," *Western Outlaw Lawman History Association Journal,* Vol. XIII, No. 3, Fall 2004, n. 28, p. 53; Shillingberg, Wm. B., *Tombstone, A.T.,* pp. 165, 167; Roberts, Gary L., *Doc Holliday: The Life and Legend,* John Wiley & Sons, Inc., Hoboken, New Jersey, 2006, p. 136.

40. Shillingberg, Wm. B., *Tombstone, A.T.,* p. 167; Marks, Paula Mitchell, *And Die in the West,* p. 302.

41. *Weekly Tombstone Epitaph,* June 27, 1881, reprinted in Parsons, George W., *A Tenderfoot in Tombstone: The Private Journal of George Whitwell Parsons: The Turbulent Years: 1880–82,* ed. Lynn R. Bailey, Westernlore Press, Tucson, Arizona, 1996, pp. 238–246.

42. http://www.legendsofamerica.com/we-lawmanlist-b.html., accessed September 22, 2010.

43. Roberts, Gary L., *Doc Holliday,* pp. 141–158.

44. *Tombstone Epitaph,* January 4, 1882; Roberts, Gary L., *Doc Holliday,* p. 234; DeArment, Robert K., *Deadly Dozen: Forgotten Gunfighters of the Old West, Volume 3,* University of Oklahoma Press, Norman, Oklahoma, 2010, p. 110–111; Shillingberg, Wm. B., *Tombstone A.T.,* p. 295.

45. *Tombstone Epitaph*, January 16, 1882.

46. Shillingberg, Wm. B., *Tombstone, A.T.,* pp. 327–328; Martin, Douglas D., *Tombstone's Epitaph,* University of New Mexico Press, Albuquerque, New Mexico, 1951, pp. 129–132.

47. *Weekly Tombstone Epitaph*, August 5, 1882.

48. *Ibid.*

49. *Ibid.*

50. *Ibid.*, August 12, 1882.

51. *Ibid.*, September 2, 23, 1882.

52. *Ibid.*, August 12, 1882.

53. *Ibid.*, August 12, 19, 1882.

54. *Ibid.*, September 30, 1882.

55. *Ibid.*, October 7, 1882. Dialogue taken from the *Epitaph's* report of the meeting.

56. *Weekly Tombstone Epitaph,* July 1, October 28, 1882.

57. *Ibid.*, March 23, 1885.

58. *San Francisco Morning Call,* September 24, 1890. In a report concerning Blackburn's filing suit against an actress named Esther Williams for $100 he claimed she owed him, the *Call* designates him "Leslie Blackburn, a politician."

59. *San Francisco Morning Call,* October 11, 1892, May 22, 1893.

60. *Ibid.*, October 11, 1892, May 22, August 6, 1893.

61. *Ibid.*, November 25, 1894, January 7, 1895.

62. *Ibid.*, January 8, March 17, 1895, January 3, 4, 5, March 18, 1897; http://www2.senate.ca.gov/portal/site/SENSergeant/SENSergeantNavHistory.

63. *San Francisco Morning Call*, December 26, 1897.
64. *Ibid.*, July 15, 26, 1898.
65. *Ibid.*, July 27, 1898.
66. *Ibid.*, February 11, 1899.
67. *Ibid.*, December 14, 1898, January 1, 1899.
68. *Ibid.*, September 27, 1902.
69. *Ibid.*, December 21, 1904.
70. *Ibid.*, October 3, 4, 5, 1902.
71. *Ibid.*, September 29, 1906.
72. *Ibid.*, August 4, 5, 7, 9, 14, November 10, 11, 12, 16, 19, 29, 30, December 14, 1910, July 15, 1911.
73. *Ibid.*, July 15, 1911.
74. Shillingberg, Wm. B., *Tombstone, A.T.*, p. 361.

Chapter 6

1. www.sincitywebhosting.com/wintimes/pioche/history; Angel, Myron, *History of Nevada*, Thompson & West, Oakland, California, 1881, reprint, Howell—North, Berkeley, California, 1958, pp. 349–352.
2. Angel, Myron, *History of Nevada*, pp. 350–351.
3. *Pioche Weekly Record*, February 25, 1882; Federal Census of the United States, 1850, County of Marshall, State of Mississippi, enumerated on September 20, 1850; Federal Census of the United States, 1870, Pioche City, County of Lincoln, State of Nevada, enumerated on August 3, 1870, p. 3; Federal Census of the United States, 1880, town of Pioche, County of Lincoln, State of Nevada, enumerated June 1 and 2, 1880, p. 1, Enum. Dist. No. 27. Out of the three censuses the only one to throw doubt on an approximate birth year for McKee of 1833 is the 1850 census in which he is listed as 15 years old.
4. Federal Census of the United States, 1850, County of Marshall, State of Mississippi, enumerated on September 20, 1850: Dwelling #191; Family #191; Nancy McKee; Age, 46; Female; Value of Real Estate, $6,500; Place of Birth, S.C. Milton M. McKee; Age, 21; Male; Occupation, Farmer; Place of Birth, S.C. Wm. M. (*sic*) McKee; Age, 15; Male; Place of Birth, S.C.; Attended School Within the last Year. James D. McKee; Age, 11; Male; Place of Birth, Miss.; Attended School Within the last Year. Malcolm M. McKee; Age, 8; Male; Place of Birth, Miss.; Attended School Within the last Year.
5. *Pioche Weekly Record*, February 25, 1882.
6. Angel, Myron, *History of Nevada*, p. 671.
7. *Ibid.*
8. *Pioche Weekly Record*, June 25, 1880.
9. *Pioche Daily Record*, September 4, 1873; July 7, 1874; DeArment, Robert K., *Deadly Dozen: Forgotten Gunfighters of the Old West, Volume 3*, University of Oklahoma Press, Norman, Oklahoma, 2010, p. 315, n. 21.
10. Angel, Myron, *History of Nevada*, pp. 477–478, 487; Baker, Stanley, *Nevada Ghost Towns and Mining Camps*, Howell-North, Berkeley, California, 1970, pp. 291, 296; Higgs, Gerald B., *Lost Legends of the Silver State*, Western Epics, 1976, pp. 116–118.
11. Federal Census of The United States, 1870, Pioche City, County of Lincoln, State of Nevada, Page No. 3, enumerated on August 3, 1870: Dwelling #42; McKee, Wm. L.; Age, 37; Male; White; Occupation, Miner; Value of Real Estate, 250; Place of Birth, S.C. Johnson, H.; Age, 55; Male; Col.; Occupation, Porter; Place of Birth, Md.
12. Two contemporary newspapers term the Raymond and Ely holdings as the "Banner and Creole" mines. However, Charles Gracey, the former chief engineer for Raymond and Ely and who should have been in a position to know, later termed the disputed property the "Washington and Creole." Gracey, Charles, "Early Days in Lincoln County," *Nevada Historical Society First Biennial Report*, 1908, p. 110.
13. Gracey, Charles, "Early Days in Lincoln County," p. 110; Higgs, Gerald B., *Lost Legends of the Silver State*, Western Epics, 1976, p. 119.
14. Higgs, Gerald B., *Lost Legends of the Silver State*, p. 119.
15. *Ibid.*
16. For James Harrington see Chapter 10.
17. Gracey, Charles, "Early Days in Lincoln County," pp. 110–111; Higgs, Gerald B., *Lost Legends of the Silver State*, pp. 119–120; *Ely Record*, no date, reprinted in *Elko Independent*, November 16, 1870; *Virginia City Territorial Enterprise*, November 16, 1870.
18. *Ely Record*, March 30, 1871, reprinted in *Daily State Register* (Carson City), April 4, 1871.
19. *Pioche Daily Record*, November (unknown date), 1872.
20. Angel, Myron, *History of Nevada*, p. 478.
21. *Pioche Daily Record*, January 7, 1873.
22. Angel, Myron, *History of Nevada*, pp. 479–480; Higgs, Gerald B., *Lost Legends of the Silver State*, p. 121.
23. *Pioche Daily Record*, January 7, 1873.
24. See: *Pioche Daily Record*, January 18, 1873, "On the War Path," "Shooting in the Streets," February 4, 1873, "Reckless Use of Firearms."
25. *Pioche Daily Record*, January 27, 1873.
26. *Ibid.*, January 28, 1873.
27. *Ibid.*, March 2, 1873. Apparently, Murray's wound, though serious, did not prove fatal.
28. See: *Pioche Daily Record*, March 6, 1873, "Officer McKee"; March 13, 1873, "The Shooting at the Floral Mill."
29. *Pioche Daily Record*, March 25, 1873.
30. *Ibid.* The fate of Captain Andy is unknown.
31. During this period McKee's name is continually mentioned in the local *Pioche Daily Record* for his many arrests of ne'er-do-wells and other official duties, i.e.: April 8, May 10, May 17, June 2, 1873.
32. *Pioche Daily Record*, July 18, 1873.
33. *Ibid.*, August 2, 3, 5, September 11, 12, 14, 17, 18, 19, 1873.
34. *Ibid.*, September 4, 1873.
35. *Ibid.* Taken from testimony presented at the inquest over the body of John Manning.
36. *Ibid.*
37. *Ibid.*
38. *Ibid.* The jury was composed of W.H.

McKillip, James Simmons, A.D. Jones, A.M. Colwell and Jesse Beene.

39. *Pioche Daily Record*, September 4, 1873.
40. Ibid., September 5, 1873.
41. Ibid., September 6, 1873. Others contributing to McKee's bail were James W. Wright, E. Hamilton, Henry Phillips, George C. Johnston, S.C. Barnes, John Roedre, G.H. Fish, H. Manning (no relation to John Manning), G.R. Alexander, Peter Harrison, C.H. Light, J.R. Clark and H. Ward.
42. *Pioche Daily Record*, November 4, 1873. William Rosamurgay would eventually be convicted of the Thomas killing and sentenced to 15 years in the Nevada State Prison. Angel, Myron, *History of Nevada*, p. 351.
43. *Pioche Daily Record*, November 9, 1873.
44. Ibid., January 29, 1874.
45. Ibid., February 6, 1874. The entertainment for the evening proved most interesting with John Oliphant and Samuel Mitchell performing as violinists and Charley Bello, better known as "Long Haired Charley," taking up the base viol. Bello would shoot gambler John Galvin in Pioche on April 14, 1874. After moving to Ward, Bello would be killed in another shooting affair with gambler Johnny Leonard on April 1, 1877. *Pioche Daily Record*, April 15, 16, 1874; *Pioche Weekly Record*, April 7, 1877; *Virginia City Territorial Enterprise*, April 6, 1877.
46. *Pioche Daily Record*, May 2, 1874.
47. Ibid., June 9, 1874.
48. Ibid., June 21, 1874.
49. Ibid., June 24, 1874.
50. Ibid., July 7, 1874.
51. Ibid. The fate of McCann is unknown.
52. *Pioche Daily Record*, September 17, 1874.
53. Ibid., October 28, December 13, 1874.
54. Angel, Myron, *History of Nevada*, p. 478.
55. *Pioche Daily Record*, December 17, 1874.
56. Ibid., June 27, 29, 1875.
57. Ibid., June 29, 1875.
58. Ibid., July 31, 1875.
59. Ibid., September 8, 10, 12, 1875.
60. Ibid., October 15, 1875.
61. Ibid., December 24, 1875.
62. Federal Census of the United States, 1880, the town of Pioche, County of Lincoln, State of Nevada, enumerated on the 1st & 2nd days of June 1880, Page No. 1, Enum. Dist. No. 27: Dwelling #14; Family #14; McKee, William L.; White; Male; Age, 46; Occupation, County Sheriff; Place of Birth, S. Carolina; Father Born, N. Carolina; Mother Born, S. Carolina. McKee, Lizzie; White; Female; Age, 19; Occupation, Keeping House; Place of Birth, Utah; Father Born, U.S., Mother Born, U.S.
63. *Pioche Daily Record*, February 3, 18, 22, 1876; *Pioche Daily Record*, April 13, 1876, reprinted in *Eureka Daily Sentinel*, April 19, 1876. McKee is mentioned in the newspapers continuously throughout 1876 for various arrests including, in April 1876, the arrest of Gilbert Roycroft, a notorious pedophile.
64. *Pioche Daily Record*, May 4, 1876; *Pioche Weekly Record*, February 25, 1882.
65. *Pioche Daily Record*, May 4, 1876.
66. Baker, Stanley, *Nevada Ghost Towns and Mining Camps*, p. 296.
67. *Pioche Daily Record*, September 12, 1876.
68. Ibid., October 6, 1876.
69. *Pioche Tri-Weekly Record*, November 19, 1876; Angel, Myron, *History of Nevada*, p. 478.
70. *Pioche Tri-Weekly Record*, November 19, 1876.
71. *Pioche Daily Record*, November 14, 1876.
72. *Pioche Weekly Record*, January 20, 1877.
73. Ibid., July 7, 14, 21, 28, August 11, September 29, October 13, 29, December 15, 28, 1877; *Ward Semi-Weekly Reflex*, July 12, 29, August 2, 1877; *Ward Weekly Reflex*, October 7, 1877; *Reno Evening Gazette*, July 25, 30, 1877; *Morning Appeal* (Carson City), July 26, 1877, January 5, 1878. McManus's three companions were Charles Newman, Jesse Sloan and William Dean. Before coming to Nevada, Isaac McManus, a 27-year-old native of Arkansas, had been involved in the shooting of a lawman named Titchenal at Santa Ana, Los Angeles County, California. Wounded in the shoulder by a shotgun blast in the fight with Holland and Carter, McManus, before his capture, reportedly "tramp[ed] through the wilderness, his arm ... full of maggots, which he was constantly taking out with a stick." Reportedly, Jesse Sloan, apparently sometime in 1878, was killed, along with another prisoner named Tutle, by Lincoln County Deputy Sheriff Mark Moore while attempting to escape the lawman somewhere in Utah. Moore himself was a somewhat notorious character. After leaving his job in the Lincoln County Sheriff's Office he became an active horse thief in southern Lincoln County and western Utah. On September 5, 1880, Moore fought a desperate gun battle with Jose Ascerano at Harshaw, Arizona, in which both men were desperately wounded, but both may have survived. In an interview conducted with Sheriff William McKee in Carson City by the *Morning Appeal* on January 29, 1879, McKee stated "... that McManus, Sloan and Newman—three out of four of the Maopi (sic) murderers—have been killed. Dean, the fourth man, is said to be living on a ranch near Los Angeles." *Pioche Weekly Record*, July 28, 1877, May 29, September 11, 18, 25, 1880; *Morning Appeal* (Carson City), January 30, 1879; *Reno Evening Gazette*, July 25, 1877; *Ward Weekly Reflex*, October 5, 1878.
74. *Pioche Weekly Record*, September 21, 1878; Federal Census of the United States, 1880, the town of Pioche, County of Lincoln, State of Nevada, enumerated on the 1st & 2nd days of June 1880, Enum. Dist. No. 27: Dwelling #190; Family #191; Turner, Ephriam D.; White; Male; Age, 47; Occupation, Deputy Sheriff; Place of Birth, Tennessee; Father Born, Tennessee; Mother Born, Tennessee. Turner, Kate; White; Female; Age, 21; Wife; Occupation, Keeping House; Place of Birth, Minnesota; Father Born, Wisconsin; Mother Born, Wisconsin. Turner, Charles D.; White; Male; Age, 4; Son; Place of Birth, Nevada. Turner, Dela U.; White; Male; Age, 2; Son; Place of Birth, Nevada.
75. Angel, Myron, *History of Nevada*, p. 478.

76. *Pioche Weekly Record*, October 25, 1879.
77. *Ibid.*, June 25, 1880.
78. *Ibid.*, July 24, 1880.
79. *Ibid.*, August 14, 1880.
80. *Ibid.*, October 2, 1880. McKee beat out Sam D. Smith, 26 votes to 19.
81. Angel, Myron, *History of Nevada*, p. 478.
82. *Pioche Weekly Record*, November 20, 1880.
83. *Ibid.*, December 11, 1880.
84. *Ibid.*, February 25, 1882. The online encyclopedia, Wikipedia, describes laryngotomy as "the surgical operation of cutting into the larynx ... Laryngotomy is an important procedure in assisting respiration when the upper part of the airway has been obstructed." http://en.wikipedia.org/wiki/Laryngotomy.
85. *Pioche Weekly Record*, March 11, 1882.

Chapter 7

1. *Reese River Reveille* (Austin), September 5, 1868.
2. *Ibid.*, September 30, 1869. The *Daily Inland Empire* (Hamilton), September 28, 1869.
3. Baker, Stanley, *Nevada Ghost Towns and Mining Camps*, Howell-North, Berkeley, California, 1970, p. 466; Ashbough, Don, *Nevada's Turbulent Yesterday*, Westernlore Press, Los Angeles, California, 1963, pp. 123–124; McGrath, Roger D., *Gunfighters, Highwaymen & Vigilantes*, University of California Press, Berkeley, California, 1984, pp. 1–2.
4. Baker, Stanley, *Nevada Ghost Towns and Mining Camps*, p. 466; Ashbough, Don, *Nevada's Turbulent Yesterday*, p. 129; McGrath, Roger D., *Gunfighters, Highwaymen & Vigilantes*, pp. 65–66.
5. Baker, Stanley, *Nevada Ghost Towns and Mining Camps*, p. 466; Ashbough, Don, *Nevada's Turbulent Yesterday*, pp. 124–131; McGrath, Roger D., *Gunfighters, Highwaymen & Vigilantes*, pp. 7–11.
6. McGrath, Roger D., *Gunfighters, Highwaymen & Vigilantes*, pp. 11–16.
7. *Ibid.*, p. 11. Roswell K. Colcord, a later Nevada governor, as a young man had been a miner and prospector in the Aurora area during its heyday.
8. Angel, Myron, ed., *History of Nevada*, Arno Press, New York, 1973 reprint of 1881 edition, p. 348.
9. McGrath, Roger D., *Gunfighters, Highwaymen & Vigilantes*, p. 87.
10. *Virginia Daily Union*, February 14, 1864; McGrath, Roger D., *Gunfighters, Highwaymen & Vigilantes*, p. 88.
11. *Virginia Daily Union*, February 14, 1864; McGrath, Roger D., *Gunfighters, Highwaymen & Vigilantes*, p. 90; Angel, Myron, ed., *History of Nevada*, p. 345.
12. Angel, Myron, ed., *History of Nevada*, pp. 344–345; McGrath, Roger D., *Gunfighters, Highwaymen & Vigilantes*, p. 90.
13. McGrath, Roger D., *Gunfighters, Highwaymen & Vigilantes*, p. 86; Angel, Myron, ed., *History of Nevada*, p. 422; Ashbough, Don, *Nevada's Turbulent Yesterday*, p. 131.
14. *Virginia Daily Union*, February 3, 5, 1864; McGrath, Roger D., *Gunfighters, Highwaymen & Vigilantes*, pp. 90–91; Angel, Myron, ed., *History of Nevada*, p. 422; Ashbough, Don, *Nevada's Turbulent Yesterday*, pp. 131–132.
15. *Virginia Daily Union*, February 5, April 3, 1864; McGrath, Roger D., *Gunfighters, Highwaymen & Vigilantes*, p. 91; Angel, Myron, ed., *History of Nevada*, p. 422.
16. *Virginia Daily Union*, February 5, 14, 1864; McGrath, Roger D., *Gunfighters, Highwaymen & Vigilantes*, pp. 92–94; Angel, Myron, ed., *History of Nevada*, p. 423.
17. *Virginia Daily Union*, February 14, 1864; McGrath, Roger D., *Gunfighters, Highwaymen & Vigilantes*, pp. 94–97; Angel, Myron, ed., *History of Nevada*, p. 423; Ashbough, Don, *Nevada's Turbulent Yesterday*, p. 132.
18. *Esmeralda Daily Union* (Aurora), March 26, 1864. D.G. Francis was sheriff of Esmeralda County.
19. *Ibid.*, April 1, 1864; McGrath, Roger D., *Gunfighters, Highwaymen & Vigilantes*, p. 99.
20. *Esmeralda Daily Union*, April 16, 1864.
21. *Ibid.*
22. *Ibid.*, September 9, 1864.
23. *Ibid.*
24. *Ibid.*, September 10, 1864; McGrath, Roger D., *Gunfighters, Highwaymen & Vigilantes*, pp. 66–67.
25. *Esmeralda Daily Union*, October 15, 1864.
26. Baker, Stanley, *Nevada Ghost Towns and Mining Camps*, p. 167.
27. *Reese River Reveille*, August 3, 5, 1867; McGrath, Roger D., *Gunfighters, Highwaymen & Vigilantes*, p. 99; Angel, Myron, ed., *History of Nevada*, p. 348. Many writers, beginning with Myron Angel in his *History of Nevada* first published in 1881, have confused Irish Tom Carberry's first gunfight in Austin against Sam Vance with his second of a little over a year later against Charles Ridgley, fought in almost the same location in downtown Austin and in similar circumstances to the first.
28. *Reese River Reveille*, August 3, 1867.
29. *Ibid.*, August 5, 1867.
30. *Ibid.*, August 29, 1867.
31. *Ibid.*, September 18, 1867.
32. *Ibid.*, September 23, 1867.
33. District Court of Sixth Judicial District, State of Nevada, County of Lander, State of Nevada vs. Thomas A. Carberry, Application for Continuance, September 25, 1867.
34. *Ibid.*, verdict, September 27, 1867; *Reese River Reveille*, September 27, 1867.
35. *Reese River Reveille*, January 6, 1868.
36. *Ibid.*, April 20, 1868. "Carbery [sic], T.A." is listed on the official list of Registered Voters of the City of Austin as a resident of the First Ward.
37. *Ibid.*, September 11, 1868; Mather, R.E., and F.E. Boswell, *Gold Camp Desperadoes*, History West Publishing Company, San Jose, California, 1990, pp. 170–175.
38. *Reese River Reveille*, September 11, December 14, 1868, March 13, 1869.

39. *Ibid.*, September 5, 1868, March 13, 1869; Mather, R.E., and F.E. Boswell, *Gold Camp Desperadoes*, pp. 174–175.

40. *Reese River Reveille*, September 5, 1868.

41. *Ibid.*, September 7, 1868. Later the *Reveille* would change "Archie" to "Archer."

42. *Ibid.*, September 8, 1868.

43. *Ibid.*, September 9, 1868.

44. This unfortunate individual proved to be a young 18-year-old named Rufus B. Anderson who had shot and killed Noble Slocum following a dispute in Austin on May 5, 1868. At his legal execution held in Austin on October 30 of the same year the crowds of witnesses were shocked when, after the first attempt to hang Anderson, the noose slipped, landing the young man on the ground in a heap beneath the gallows trap door. Hauled back up onto the scaffold, Anderson again plummeted to the ground when the improperly tied noose again slipped off his neck. The revolted crowd of witnesses had almost decided to rush the platform and end the terrible scene being enacted in front of them by rescuing the tortured Anderson before a third attempt finally succeeded in suspending him between heaven and earth. Still, the poorly tied noose failed to break his neck, however, and the poor fellow finally had to slowly strangle to death before the ordeal could be brought to a close.

Besides Tom Carberry and Anderson, the third individual accused of murder residing in the county jail at this time was one Robert Elliott. Elliott killed Stephen Richards in Austin on May 19, 1867, following what were described as "hasty words." Angel, Myron, ed., *History of Nevada*, pp. 347, 348.

45. *Reese River Reveille*, September 11, 1868.

46. *Ibid.*, September 16, 1868.

47. *Ibid.*, November 6, 1868.

48. *Ibid.*, December 14, 1868.

49. *Ibid.*, March 8, 1869.

50. *Ibid.*, March 10, 1869.

51. *Ibid.*, March 12, 1869.

52. *Ibid.*, March 13, 1869; District Court of Sixth Judicial District, State of Nevada, County of Lander, State of Nevada vs. Thos. A. Carberry, verdict, March 13, 1869.

53. *Reese River Reveille*, March 30, 1869.

54. Baker, Stanley, *Nevada Ghost Towns and Mining Camps*, p. 167.

55. *White Pine Evening Telegram* (Shermantown), June 16, 1869.

56. *Ibid.*

57. *The Daily Inland Empire* (Hamilton), July 21, 1869, and various previous and subsequent issues.

58. *Ibid.*, September 28, 1869; *Reese River Reveille*, September 30, 1869.

59. *The Daily Inland Empire* (Hamilton), September 28, 1869.

60. *Reese River Reveille*, September 30, 1869.

61. Davis, Sam P. Ed., *The History of Nevada*, Elms Publishing Company, Reno, Nevada, 1913, pp. 237–238.

Chapter 8

1. *Virginia City Chronicle*, September 8, 1875, reprinted in *Truckee Republican*, September 9, 1873. A few days after his death the *Chronicle* reported that White was 28 years old when he died, making his birth year ca. 1845.

2. *Eureka Daily Sentinel*, October 24, 1873.

3. *Virginia City Chronicle*, September 8, 1873, reprinted in *Truckee Republican*, September 9, 1873.

4. Gracey, Charles, "Early Days in Lincoln County," *Nevada Historical Society First Biennial Report*, 1908, pp. 110–111; Higgs, Gerald B., *Lost Legends of the Silver State*, Western Epics, 1976, pp. 119–120; *Ely Record*, no date, reprinted in *Elko Independent*, November 16, 1870; *Virginia City Territorial Enterprise*, November 16, 1870.

5. *Ely Record*, no date, reprinted in *Elko Independent*, November 16, 1870; *Virginia City Chronicle*, September 8, 1873, reprinted in *Truckee Republican*, September 9, 1873. Subsequent to White's death the *Chronicle* stated, "He was once shot on Treasure Hill [Pioche, Nevada] by Bill Bethards."

6. *Virginia City Territorial Enterprise*, November 19, 1870. The *Enterprise* reported, erroneously as it turned out, "The *Inland Empire* [of Hamilton, Nevada] is informed that Jack White, who was wounded in the late fight at Pioche, died at that place the morning after the fight."

7. *Eureka Daily Sentinel*, May 14, 1872. There is some confusion in the Jack White story as the result of there being two other men with the same name operating in Nevada at this same time. One Jack White was a prominent miner and president of the Miner's Union in both Gold Hill and White Pine. Another of the identical moniker had been a policeman on the Hamilton, Nevada, police force in 1870 who gained some notoriety, leaving for the east in the Fall of 1870. *Eureka Daily Sentinel*, May 14, December 1, 1872, October 24, 1873.

8. *Eureka Daily Sentinel*, December 14, 1871.

9. *Ibid.*, February 8, 1872.

10. *Ibid.*, May 5, 1872.

11. *Ibid.*, May 12, 14, 1872.

12. *Ibid.*, May 14, 1872.

13. *Elko Independent*, June 1, 1872.

14. *Ibid.*; *Virginia City Chronicle*, September 8, 1873, reprinted in *Truckee Republican*, September 9, 1873.

15. *Eureka Daily Sentinel*, June 21, 1872.

16. *Ibid.*, July 6, 1872; *Virginia City Chronicle*, September 8, 1873, reprinted in *Truckee Republican*, September 9, 1873.

17. Meschery, Joanne, *Truckee, An Illustrated History of the Town and its Surroundings*, Rocking Stone Press, Truckee, California, 1978, p. 16.

18. *Ibid.*, pp. 31–57; Ficklin, Marilou West, *Showdown at Truckee*, Western Book/Journal Press, Reno, Nevada, 1997, pp. 21–28.

19. *Virginia City Chronicle*, September 8, 1873, reprinted in *Truckee Republican*, September 9, 1873.

20. *Ibid.*; Ficklin, Marilou West, *Showdown at Truckee*, p. 65.

21. *Truckee Republican*, September 6, 1873, reprinted in *Eureka Daily Sentinel*, September 9, 1873; Ficklin, Marilou West, *Showdown at Truckee*, pp. 65–67. Quotes taken from report of the incident in the *Republican* plus commentary in *Showdown at Truckee* by Marilou West Ficklin.

22. Ficklin, Marilou West, *Showdown at Truckee*, pp. 66–67.

23. *Reese River Reveille* (Austin), September 11, 1873.

24. Meschery, Joanne, *Truckee, An Illustrated History*, p. 63.

25. *Ibid.*; Ficklin, Marilou West, *Showdown at Truckee*, p. 71.

26. *Gold Hill News*, May 2, 1864.

27. *Salt Lake City Tribune*, October 26, 1871, reprinted in *Reese River Reveille* (Austin), October 28, 1871. The *Tribune* called Mellon's victim Joseph "Flax."

28. *Eureka Daily Sentinel*, December 16, 1871.

29. *Ibid.*, May 28, 1872.

30. *Ibid.*, August 6, 1872, December 13, 1874.

31. *Ibid.*, August 6, 1872.

32. *Truckee Republican*, no date, reprinted in *Reese River Reveille* (Austin), October 2, 1873.

33. *Gold Hill News*, May 14, 1874, reprinted in *Reese River Reveille* (Austin), May 16, 1874; *Virginia City Chronicle*, May 14, 1874, reprinted in *Pioche Daily Record*, May 19, 1874; *Eureka Daily Sentinel*, May 19, 1874.

34. Whether Carrie Smith had any connection to Bob Mellon's previous companion Anna Smith or the identical last name was a simple coincidence is unknown.

35. Ficklin, Marilou West, *Showdown at Truckee*, p. 33.

36. Meschery, Joanne, *Truckee, An Illustrated History*, p. 63.

37. Ficklin, Marilou West, *Showdown at Truckee*, pp. 57, 58, 67, 72–76.

38. *Truckee Republican*, November 24, 1874.

39. Ficklin, Marilou West, *Showdown at Truckee*, pp. 71–73.

40. *Ibid.*, pp. 73, 190.

41. *Ibid.*, pp. 72–73; Meschery, Joanne, *Truckee, An Illustrated History*, p. 63.

42. Meschery, Joanne, *Truckee, An Illustrated History*, p. 63.

43. *Eureka Daily Sentinel*, December 13, 1874.

44. *Truckee Republican*, November 24, 1874; Ficklin, Marilou West, *Showdown at Truckee*, pp. 73–75; Meschery, Joanne, *Truckee, An Illustrated History*, p. 64.

45. *Truckee Republican*, November 24, 1874.

46. *Sacramento Record*, no date, reprinted in *Truckee Republican*, December 12, 1874.

47. *Truckee Republican*, November 24, 1874.

48. *Ibid.*, December 12, 1874; *Eureka Daily Sentinel*, December 13, 1874.

49. *Nevada Transcript* (Nevada City, California), November 27, 1874, reprinted in *Pioche Daily Record*, December 3, 1874.

50. *Truckee Republican*, December 26, 1874, reprinted in *Gold Hill News*, December 28, 1874; Ficklin, Marilou West, *Showdown at Truckee*, p. 79; Meschery, Joanne, *Truckee, An Illustrated History*, p. 64.

51. *Eureka Daily Sentinel*, August 10, 1875, January 5, 1876.

52. *Ibid.*, August 10, 1875.

53. *Ibid.*, January 5, 1876.

54. *Ibid.*, September 22, 1875.

55. *Ibid.*, September 22, 23, 24, 25, 1875. The fate of Pete Morris is unknown.

56. *Eureka Daily Sentinel*, September 29, 1875.

57. *Truckee Republican*, no date, reprinted in *Eureka Daily Sentinel*, February 21, 1877.

58. *Reno Journal*, March 8, 1877, reprinted in *Eureka Daily Sentinel*, March 9, 1877.

59. If he moved back to Sacramento, California, he may have been the Robert Mellon who petitioned the city to grant him a license to operate a saloon in June 1894. *Sacramento Daily Record-Union*, June 14, 1894. There seems to have been another Robert Mellon in Sacramento at this time who was a prominent businessman and went by the title "Dr." He may have been the petitioner in this case.

60. Ficklin, Marilou West, *Showdown at Truckee*, pp. 82–83.

61. *Ibid.*, p. 115.

Chapter 9

1. *Report of the Warden of the Nevada State Prison, For the Years 1871–1872*, List of Prisoners, pp. 8–9. The *Warden Report* lists Burke as 23 years old upon his sentence to the State Prison in August 1871.

2. *Daily State Register* (Carson City), September 27, 1871. "Reward Notice."

3. *Report of the Warden of the Nevada State Prison, For the Years 1871–1872*. List of Prisoners, pp. 8–9.

4. Newspaper searches for the time and place proved inconclusive. In his *History of Nevada*, "Homicide and Some of its Causes," published in 1881, Myron Angel presents an exhaustive listing of the killings perpetrated in Nevada, 1846–1881. For 1869 and the first half of 1871, up to the time of Burke's trial and conviction, he lists no deaths occurring in Esmeralda County. His listing for 1870, however, lists two Esmeralda County homicides. On August 23 one Glasset shot and killed William Thompson in a difficulty at Pine Grove. The second death took place on December 11, 1870. Quoting the *History*: "December 11. Robert Wallace was killed, by being struck on the head with a bottle, at Pine Grove. *Name of murderer not given*" (author's italics). Depending on the thoroughness of Angel's listings, this is the only possibility that may reveal John Burke's first recorded infraction of the law. Angel, Myron, *History of Nevada*, Thompson & West, Oakland, California, 1881, reprint, Howell-North, Berkeley, California, 1958, pp. 348–349.

5. *Daily State Register* (Carson City), October 11, 1871.

6. Hume, James B., and John N. Thacker, *Wells, Fargo & Co., Report of Losses from Stagecoach and Train Robbers, 1870 to 1884*, 125th Anniversary edition, ed. R. Michael Wilson, Stagecoach Books, Las Vegas, Nevada, 2007, p. 143, "Harker, Francis—alias 'John Burke.' Nativity, Texas; Age, 45 years." O'Dell, Roy, "Mass Prison Break-Out at Carson City," *The English Westerners' Society Tally Sheet*, Autumn 1992, Volume 39, Number 1, p. 5, "John Burke was a Texan of 23, 5' 8" in height he weighed about 150 pounds. He was fair skinned with blue eyes, and a most desperate character. *On February 28, 1870, he was reputed to have killed a chinaman named Yung Yew at Elko, Nevada*" (author's italics). This, of course, was the other, older John Burke.

7. *Elko Independent*, March 9, 16, 19, 23, 1870; *Daily Inland Empire* (Hamilton), March 26, 1870; *Second Biennial Report of the Warden of Nevada State Prison, 1869 and 1870*, "Whole Number of Prisoners Received During My Administration," "No. 82, Jno. Buck [sic], Age, 45, Ireland, Murder, second degree, Elko, March 24, 1870, Forty Years, Miner." Federal Census of the United States, 1870, Carson City Township, County of Ormsby, State of Nevada, enumerated on 23rd of June 1870: (Prisoners within the Nevada State Prison). Burk [sic], John; Age, 45; Male; White; Occupation, Laborer; Place of Birth, Ireland. Angel, Myron, *History of Nevada*, p. 349, "1870. February 28. Yung Yew was killed by John Burke at Elko [sic]. He was kicked to death."

8. *Eureka Daily Sentinel*, December 5, 1872; *Daily State Register* (Carson City), August 22, 1871.

9. *Daily State Register* (Carson City), September 27, 1871.

10. Ibid., November 23, 1871.

11. Despite a long convalescence Warden Frank Denver would eventually recover from his wounds. On October 4, 1871, Bob Dedman was given a full pardon for his act of heroism in protecting Warden Denver and his family. *Daily State Register* (Carson City), October 5, 1871.

12. All of the wounded prison guards, save Francis Isaacs, eventually made a full recovery.

13. Along with John Burke, those who managed to make their escape, along with ages and prison terms, were: Frank Clifford, 29, ten years; J.B. Roberts, 18, ten years; Pat McCue, 35, seven years; David Lynch, 24, three years; Elijah Ingram, 38, twenty years; E.B. Parsons, 29, twenty years; Thomas Heffron, 35, Life; William Russell, 31, six years; George Roth, 23, thirty-five years; Edward Bigelow, 29, five years; Chris C. Blair, 29, five years; J.G. Watson, 26, twenty-five years; Thomas Flynn, 31, fifteen years; Charles Jones, 22, ten years; Tilton P. Cockerell, 38, twenty-two years; Pat Hurley, 32, five years; John Squires, 38, twenty-three and one half years; Marion Pruitt, 21, five years; William Willis, 24, twenty-one years; J.E. Chapman, 26, eighteen years; Leander Morton, 25, thirty years; Tim McNamara, 30, thirteen years; William Forrest, 22, five years; Daniel Baker, 24, thirty years; Thomas Carter, 25, ten years; John I. Jacks, ---, seven years; Moses Black, 34, seven years; Thomas Ryan, 26, ten years. Others were involved in the escape attempt but failed to make it out of the prison yard. *Daily State Register* (Carson City), September 19, 1871; *Report of the Warden of the Nevada State Prison, for the Years 1871-1872*, List of Prisoners, p. 8, List of Prisoners Who Escaped in the Emeute of September 17, 1871, p. 15.

14. Various sources, to a greater or lesser degree, deal with the escape. These are: *Daily State Register* (Carson City), September 19, 1871; *Gold Hill News*, September 18, 19, October 26, 31, November 4, 1871; *Virginia City Territorial Enterprise*, September 19, 1871; *Reese River Reveille* (Austin), September 18, 19, 20, 23, 25, 1871; *Eureka Daily Sentinel*, September 23, 1871; *Elko Independent*, September 23, 1871; *Carson City News*, August 21, 1910; Williams, George, III, *The Murders at Convict Lake*, Tree By The River Publishing, Riverside, California, 1984, pp. 4–11; Bristow, Allen P., "Break Out!" *Old West*, Winter 1998, Vol. 35, No. 2, pp. 26–28; O'Dell, Roy, "Mass Prison Break-Out at Carson City," *The English Westerners Society Tally Sheet*, Autumn, 1992, Volume 39, Number 1, pp. 1–3; Chalfant, W.A., *Gold, Guns & Ghost Towns*, Stanford University Press, Stanford, California, 1947, pp. 132–135.

15. *Virginia City Territorial Enterprise*, November 3, 1871.

16. *Reese River Reveille* (Austin), October 12, 1871; *Daily State Register* (Carson City), September 21, 1871; Williams, George, III, *The Murders at Convict Lake*, p. 12

17. *Reese River Reveille* (Austin), October 12, 1871; *Daily State Register* (Carson City), September 21, 1871; Williams III, George, *The Murders at Convict Lake*, p. 12.

18. *Reese River Reveille* (Austin), October 12, 1871.

19. Garrigues, George L., "Convicts on The Loose," *Wild West*, October 1998, p. 57.

20. *Reese River Reveille* (Austin), October 12, 1871.

21. Williams, George, III, *The Murders at Convict Lake*, pp. 25–26.

22. *Reese River Reveille* (Austin), September 26, October 12, 1871; Williams, George, III, *The Murders at Convict Lake*, pp. 17–22; Garrigues, George L., "Convicts on The Loose," pp. 57–58; Bristow, Allen P., "Break Out!" pp. 29–30; O'Dell, Roy, "Mass Prison Break-Out at Carson City," p. 6.

23. *Reese River Reveille* (Austin), October 12, 1871; *Daily State Register* (Carson City), October 5, 1871; *Virginia City Territorial Enterprise*, October 8, 1871; Williams, George, III, *The Murders at Convict Lake*, pp. 17–22.

24. *Daily State Register* (Carson City), September 27, 1871; *Reese River Reveille* (Austin), September 26, 1871; *Virginia City Territorial Enterprise*, September 27, 1871.

25. *Reese River Reveille* (Austin), September 29, 30, 1871; *Daily State Register* (Carson City), September 26, 30, 1871; *Elko Independent*, September 30, 1871.

26. *Daily State Register* (Carson City), September 29, October 4, 6, 1871; *Virginia City Territorial Enterprise*, September 28, 29, 30, October 7, 1871. Those retaken proved to be Thomas Flynn, Frank Clifford, E.B. Parsons, John Squires, J.E. Chapman, George Roth, William Willis, Thomas Carter, Edward Bigelow, Pat McCue and J.B. Roberts.

27. *Daily State Register* (Carson City), October 6, 7, 10, 1871; *Reese River Reveille* (Austin), October 6, 1871.

28. *Reese River Reveille* (Austin), December 23, 1871. The *Reveille* printed a report from a Mr. George Slawson that Jones was killed in a gun battle with Francis F. Armistead sometime in December 1871 in the San Joaquin country, California. Again, no body was ever produced. A tantalizing report gained print as late as December 16, 1874, in the *Gold Hill News* that Jones had finally been arrested in Iowa. This report faded away almost as quickly as it appeared and no more is known of this reported arrest.

29. *Daily State Register* (Carson City), October 10, 1871.

30. *Ibid.*, October 11, 1871.

31. *Ibid.*; *Virginia City Territorial Enterprise*, October 11, 1871.

32. *Daily State Register* (Carson City), October 11, 1871; *Virginia City Territorial Enterprise*, October 11, 1871; *Reese River Reveille* (Austin), October 12, 1871.

33. *Daily State Register* (Carson City), October 11, 1871.

34. *Reese River Reveille* (Austin), October 5, 1871; *Virginia City Territorial Enterprise*, October 14, 1871.

35. *Daily State Register* (Carson City), October 14, 1871.

36. *Ibid.*, October 15, 24, 1871.

37. *Ibid.*, October 26, 1871; *Gold Hill News*, October 26, 30, 31, November 4, 1871. These three were Thomas Ryan, William Russell and the negro Marion Pruitt.

38. *Daily State Register* (Carson City), November 10, 1871.

39. *Ibid.*, November 11, 12, 15, 1871.

40. *Ibid.*, November 15, 16, 21, 1871.

41. *Ibid.*, November 22, 23, 24, 25, 28, 1871; *Virginia City Territorial Enterprise*, November 24, 26, 28, 1871; *Gold Hill News*, November 28, 1871.

42. *Daily State Register* (Carson City), November 28, 1871.

43. *Ibid.*, November 29, 1871; *Eureka Daily Sentinel*, December 2, 1871.

44. *Eureka Daily Sentinel*, December 2, 1871.

45. *Daily State Register* (Carson City), March 7, 1872.

46. *Ibid.*, March 10, 1872.

47. *Ibid.*, March 12, 1872; *Virginia City Territorial Enterprise*, March 12, 1872; *Eureka Daily Sentinel*, March 15, 1872; *Humboldt Register* (Winnemucca), March 16, 1872; Hume, James B., and John N. Thacker, *Wells, Fargo & Co., Report of Losses*, ed. R. Michael Wilson, p. 144.

48. *Daily State Register* (Carson City), March 12, 1872; *Virginia City Territorial Enterprise*, March 12, 1872; *Humboldt Register* (Winnemucca), March 16, 1872.

49. *Daily State Register* (Carson City), March 13, 1872.

50. *Ibid.*, March 14, 1872.

51. *Ibid.*, March 15, 1872; *Virginia City Territorial Enterprise*, March 15, 1872; *Gold Hill News*, March 15, 1872.

52. *Virginia City Territorial Enterprise*, March 20, 1872, reprinted in *Daily State Register* (Carson City), March 21, 1872.

53. It was later decided that the fourth "man" was a dummy propped up in the bushes to give the appearance of an extra gun hand.

54. *Eureka Daily Sentinel*, March 30, 1872; *Humboldt Register* (Winnemucca), April 6, 1872; Hume, James B., and John N. Thacker, *Wells, Fargo & Co. Report of Losses*, ed. R. Michael Wilson, pp. 85–86.

55. *White Pine News*, April 2, 1872, reprinted in *Eureka Daily Sentinel*, April 4, 1872; *Daily State Register* (Carson City), April 4, 1872; *Reese River Reveille* (Austin), April 3, 1872; *Humboldt Register* (Winnemucca), April 6, 1872; Hume, James B., and John N. Thacker, *Wells, Fargo & Co. Report of Losses*, ed. R. Michael Wilson, p. 87.

56. *Eureka Daily Sentinel*, April 4, 1872.

57. Thomas Carter had been apprehended two days after fleeing the County Jail, Tuesday, March 12. *Daily State Register* (Carson City), March 13, 1872; *Virginia City Territorial Enterprise*, March 13, 1872; *Humboldt Register* (Winnemucca), March 16, 1872. Thomas Flynn was caught the same day. *Virginia City Territorial Enterprise*, March 14, 1872. William Russell and Thomas Ryan were captured the following day. *Daily State Register* (Carson City), March 14, 1872; *Virginia City Territorial Enterprise*, March 14, 1872. William Willis gave himself up on the evening of Saturday, March 16. *Virginia City Territorial Enterprise*, March 19, 1872.

58. *White Pine News*, April 4, 1872, reprinted in *Gold Hill News*, April 8, 1872.

59. *Eureka Daily Sentinel*, April 6, 1872.

60. *Daily State Register* (Carson City), April 9, 1872.

61. *Ibid.*

62. *Ibid.*, August 27, 1872.

63. *Ibid.*, September 5, 1872.

64. *Ibid.*, September 6, 1872.

65. *Ibid.*, September 8, 1872.

66. *Ibid.*, no date, reprinted in *Gold Hill News*, September 1, 1874.

67. *Biennial Report of the Warden of the Nevada State Prison, for the Years 1875 and 1876*, Table No. 7, Showing the number of convicts discharged from the Nevada State Prison by expiration of sentence during the year 1876, p. 28; *Carson City Morning Appeal*, July 17, 1878.

68. Some sources have suggested that Francis Harker was his true name and John Burke an alias. This is made highly doubtful, however, when considering a letter from no less an authority than the

redoubtable Wells Fargo Chief of Detectives James B. Hume to the Wells Fargo agent at Carson City, Henry Tickner, where Hume states, "This Francis Harker is a 'thoroughbred,' an old resident of your Hot Springs prison. His true name is John Burke and was in the 'big break' of 1871." *Carson City Morning Appeal*, July 17, 1878.

69. Hume, James B., and John N. Thacker, *Wells, Fargo & Co. Report of Losses*, ed. R. Michael Wilson, pp. 144–145.

70. *Ibid.*, p. 145; *Pioche Daily Record*, June 7, 1876.

71. *Pioche Daily Record*, June 8, 1876.

72. *Ibid.*; Hume, James B., and John N. Thacker, *Wells, Fargo & Co. Report of Losses*, ed. R. Michael Wilson, pp. 145–146.

73. Hume, James B., and John N. Thacker, *Wells, Fargo & Co. Report of Losses*, ed. R. Michael Wilson, p. 146.

74. *Ibid.*, p. 146.

75. *Ibid.*; *Salt Lake City Daily Tribune*, July 1, 1876.

76. According to the *Salt Lake City Tribune*, "How they got the slips of blankets fastened to the top of the wall, which is some twenty feet high, is something of a mystery, but it is thought that they stood one upon the other's shoulders and that the lightest man was thus enabled to mount the wall and tie the strips, by which the others were enabled to follow him." *Salt Lake City Daily Tribune*, July 18, 1876.

77. *Salt Lake City Daily Tribune*, July 18, 1876.

78. Such as the hijinks of late November 1871 back in Carson City.

79. William "Idaho Bill" Sloan would continue his nefarious activities before supposedly being killed in Wyoming in July 1881. Hume, James B., and John N. Thacker, *Wells, Fargo & Co. Report of losses*, ed. R. Michael Wilson, pp. 284–285.

80. Jack Wiggins would eventually miss his date with the firing squad and continue his depredations before meeting his fate.

81. *Salt Lake City Daily Tribune*, July 18, 1876.

82. *Ibid.*, July 20, 1876.

83. Hume, James B., and John N. Thacker, *Wells, Fargo & Co. Report of Losses*, ed. R. Michael Wilson, p. 146.

84. *Illustrated Guide and Souvenir of Detroit*, http://cc.bingj.com/cache.aspx?q=detroit+house+of+correction+1878&d=472801182037.

85. *Carson City Morning Appeal*, July 17, 1878. There is some confusion and debate on the actual dates of Burke's incarceration and escape from the House of Corrections. From the records and newspaper articles in my collection these are my conclusions.

86. *Carson City Morning Appeal*, July 17, 1878.

Chapter 10

1. *Biennial Report of the Warden of the Nevada State Prison, for the Years 1873 and 1874*, Table No. 1, Showing the number of convicts received at the Nevada State Prison during the year 1873, pp. 18–19: Name: James Harrington; Age: 27; Nativity: Ireland; County from where sent: Lincoln; Crime: Murder, second degree; Term of sentence: 15 years; Date of committal: Sept. 13, 1873; Trade or occupation: Miner. *Ibid.*, Table No. IX, Showing the number of convicts pardoned during the year 1874, p. 29: Name: James Harrington; Age: 30; Nativity: Michigan [*sic*]; County from where sent: Lincoln; Crime: Murder, second degree; Term of sentence: 15 years; Date of committal: Sept. 13, 1873; Date of discharge: Dec. 26; Time served: 1 year 3 months 13 days. *Biennial Report of the Warden of Nevada State Prison for the Years 1877 and 1878*, Table No. 7, Showing the number of Convicts received at the Nevada State Prison during the year 1878, p. 46: Name: James Harrington; Age: 30; Nativity: Ireland; County sent from: Washoe; Crime: Murder in 2d degree; Term of sentence: 20 years; Date of committal: May 25, 1878; Trade or Occupation: Miner. Federal Census of the United States, 1880, County of Ormsby, State of Nevada, State Prison, enumerated on the _ day of June 1880, Page No. 21, Supervisor's Dist. No. 81, Enumerator's Dist. No. 39: Name: Harrington, Jas. W.; White; Male; Age: 32; Prisoner; Single; Occupation: Miner; Place of Birth: Ireland. The *Warden's Report* of 1873 lists Harrington's age as 27, giving him a birth date of ca. 1846. On his release in 1874 his age is recorded as 30, translating to a birth year of ca. 1844. Both the *Warden's Report* of 1878, giving an age of 30, and the census of 1880, giving an age of 32, translate into a birth year of ca. 1848. They all agree on Ireland as his place of birth, except for an odd notation in the *Warden's Report* of 1874 listing his birthplace as "Michigan."

2. *Biennial Report of the Warden of the Nevada State Prison, for the Years 1873–1874*, Table No. 1, Showing the number of convicts received at the Nevada State Prison during 1873, pp. 18–19.

3. *Virginia City Territorial Enterprise*, July 23, 1876.

4. *Pioche Daily Record*, July 8, 1873.

5. *Ibid.*, May 21, 1873.

6. Gracey, Charles, "Early Days in Lincoln County," *Nevada Historical Society First Biannual Report*, 1908, p. 110; Higgs, Gerald B., *Lost Legends of the Silver State*, Western Epics, NP, 1976, p. 119.

7. *Ely Record*, no date, reprinted in *Elko Independent*, November 16, 1870; *Virginia City Territorial Enterprise*, November 16, 1870; Gracey, Charles, "Early Days in Lincoln County," pp. 110–111; Higgs, Gerald B., *Lost Legends of the Silver State*, pp. 119–120.

8. The State of Nevada vs. James Harrington, 9th Judicial District Court, Lincoln County, Nevada, 1870.

9. The State of Nevada against James Harrington, Indictment for Murder as an accessory before the fact, 9th Judicial District Court, Lincoln County, Nevada, December term, 1870.

10. The State of Nevada vs. James Herrington, A.H. Rutherford and W.H. Raymond, Seventh

District Court, Lincoln County, Nevada, December Term, 1871; The State of Nevada vs. James Herrington, W.H. Raymond and A.H. Rutherford, Seventh Judicial District Court, Lincoln County, Nevada, March Term, 1872.

11. Lincoln County, Nevada, Grand Jury Special Report, March 27, 1871; *Ely Record*, March 30, 1871, reprinted in *Daily State Register* (Carson City), April 4, 1871.

12. *Salt Lake City Tribune*, May 2, 1872.

13. *Ibid.*, April 9, 1871; *Reno Evening Gazette*, May 25, 1878.

14. *Reno Evening Gazette*, May 25, 1878.

15. *Salt Lake City Tribune*, April 19, 1871.

16. *Ibid.*, April 20, 1871.

17. *Ibid.* Huggan and Witcher attempted to prove that the Harrington arrest warrant was faulty because (1) it had been directed to a United States Marshal, the marshal having no jurisdiction; (2) the place of imprisonment is not stipulated; and (3) the prisoner was ready to answer the charge, but the court refused to act.

18. *Salt Lake City Tribune*, April 20, 1871.

19. *Ibid.*, April 19, 1871.

20. *Ibid.*, April 30, 1871.

21. *Ibid.*

22. *Ibid.*, May 2, 1872. Harrington's indictment for the first-degree murder of Benjamin James is listed on the same court calendar, in May 1872, as some other historically interesting cases involving such high-power Mormon personalities as Brigham Young, Orson Hyde, Hosea Stout and the notorious William A. Hickman, charging them with the alleged murders of various Gentiles stretching back a number of years. Chief Justice James McKean, the same jurist who refused to set James Harrington free, was said to be bound and determined to prosecute the Mormon hierarchy. Like Harrington in the James case, however, Young, et al. would never stand trial on these charges. Hilton, Hope A., *"Wild Bill" Hickman and the Mormon Frontier*, Signature Books, Inc., Salt Lake City, Utah, 1988, pp. 124–128.

23. *Salt Lake City Tribune*, June 6, 1872.

24. *Ibid.*

25. *Ibid.*

26. *Ibid.*, July 31, 1872. There can be no doubt that this is the same James Harrington whose story we are chronicling. One year later, after Harrington's shooting of John Lynch and others at Pioche, Nevada, in July 1873, the *Salt Lake City Tribune* commented: "The *Pioche Record* of the 8th contains full particulars of the recent shooting affair at that place, from which it appears that the shooting was done by one, James Harrington, whom from the description given, we should judge to be the same Harrington who figured as 'bully' and 'lot jumper' at Ophir about a year ago." *Salt Lake City Tribune*, July 14, 1873.

27. *Salt Lake City Tribune*, July 31, 1872.

28. *Ibid.*

29. *Eureka Sentinel*, July 18, 1873.

30. Lincoln County Judicial District Court, State of Nevada vs. James Harrington, January 11, 1873.

31. *Pioche Daily Record*, January 12, 1873.

32. *Ibid.*, July 8, August 22, 1873. Although the *Record* claimed Sullivan had originated in New York, in his testimony during Harrington's trial for the death of Lynch, Sullivan stated: "I have known Harrington about twenty years; knew him in Ireland," thus making it likely that Sullivan first entered the U.S. at New York, staying there for a time before moving on.

33. *Pioche Daily Record*, July 8, 1873.

34. *Ibid.*, July 8, August 19, 20, 21, 22, 1873. Quotes taken from court testimony at Harrington's trial re: the death of John Lynch.

35. *Ibid.*, July 8, 1873.

36. *Ibid.*, July 9, 10, 11, 1873.

37. *Ibid.*, July 10, 1873.

38. *Ibid.*, July 12, 1873.

39. *Ibid.*, July 12, 13, 15, 1873.

40. *Ibid.*, July 11, 19, 1873. The most seriously wounded of the remaining three, Ed O'Neil, who was shot in the hip, would be bedridden for a number of weeks before he regained his mobility.

41. *Pioche Daily Record*, July 29, 1873.

42. State of Nevada, vs. James Harrington, District Court, Seventh Judicial District, Lincoln County, State of Nevada, August Term, A.D. 1873.

43. *Ibid.*

44. Jesse Pitzer was himself an experienced shootist, having at one time even exchanged shots with well-known Nevada gunman Dick Paddock.

45. State of Nevada vs James Harrington; *Pioche Daily Record*, August 19, 20, 21, 22, 1873. O'Neil's and Sullivan's main thrust was to prove there had been more than three shots fired and that Lynch himself employed a pistol in the fight thus making it possible that, not only had some of the wounds been inflicted by him but, more importantly, Harrington had been acting in self-defense. O'Neil and Sullivan were literally the only ones within hearing of the battle to hear more than three shots fired. This line was most assuredly perjured evidence.

46. *Pioche Daily Record*, August 23, 1873.

47. *Ibid.*, August 23, 24, 1873.

48. State of Nevada vs James Harrington; *Pioche Daily Record*, August 24, 26, 1873.

49. *Pioche Daily Record*, August 26, 1873.

50. *Ibid.*

51. *Ibid.*, September 3, 7, 1873; State of Nevada vs James Harrington.

52. *Pioche Daily Record*, September 6, 1873. Daniel and Tim Harrington must have been strong suspects in the affair as they visited their brother almost every day at the County Jail.

53. *Pioche Daily Record*, September 10, 1873; State of Nevada vs James Harrington.

54. *Pioche Daily Record*, September 10, 1873.

55. *Ibid.*

56. *Biennial Report of the Warden of the Nevada State Prison, for the Years 1873 and 1874*, p. 19.

57. *Eureka Daily Sentinel*, February 9, 1877.

58. *Pioche Daily Record*, November 6, December 18, 1873.

59. *Ibid.*, July 24, 1876; *Reno Evening Gazette*, May 25, 1878.

60. *Pioche Daily Record*, July 24, 1876.

61. *Biennial Report of the Warden of the Nevada State Prison, for the Years 1873 and 1874*, Table No. IX, Showing the number of convicts pardoned during the year 1874, p. 29.

62. *Eureka Daily Sentinel*, October 25, 1878. This source states that the so-called "political services" rendered by Harrington for Bradley took place during the election of 1874. This makes no sense as the election of 1874 took place on November 3, Harrington not being released from prison until December 26 that year. Unless, of course, it is meant to infer that the work was done by Daniel and/or Timothy Harrington, or agents on their behalf, in return for James' release.

63. Another claimed episode in the life of James Harrington which can be debunked at this time is his supposed involvement in the Eldorado Canyon riot. Many sources, including Mary G. Stano's, "Duel at El Dorado" in *True West* magazine and W.A. Chalfant in his book *Gold, Guns & Ghost Towns*, which likely both derive from the earlier paper by early Nevada pioneer John L. Riggs published in 1912, have Harrington traveling to the Eldorado Canyon area. Located in what was then Lincoln County, near present day Las Vegas, Eldorado Canyon was another of Nevada's fledgling mining booms. These accounts have Harrington being hired, along with a former Nevada prison bird named Jim Jones and a rowdy character named William Piette, as "lot jumpers" by mine owner John Nash. As the tale is told, Nash planned to double-cross his hired "fighters" by withholding payment after they had completed their task. Realizing Harrington's reputation, however, Nash supposedly paid him in full and Harrington left the area. At length, Nash, using subterfuge, managed to turn Jones and Piette against each other. The whole affair ended in a violent shooting affray in which Jones and a local miner named Tom King, were killed and Piette was seriously wounded.

Nash, Jones and Piette were real characters and the gun battle did happen. However, as can be seen by the contemporary news reports in the *Pioche Daily Record* (which, of course, do not mention Harrington in any way), the shooting took place on April 8, 1874. At this time James Harrington had been incarcerated since the Pioche fight of July 6, 1873, was still incarcerated in the Nevada State Prison and would not be released for another eight- and one-half months. *Pioche Daily Record*, April 22, 24, 1874; Riggs, John L., "The Reign of Violence in El Dorado Canyon," *Third Biennial Repot of the Nevada Historical Society*, State Printing Office, Carson City, 1913, *The Nevada Observer*, April 27, 2006, accessed February 2, 2011, www.nevadaobserver.com; Stano, Mary G., "Duel at El Dorado," *True West*, December, 1989, Vol. 36, No. 12, pp. 54–57; Chalfant, W.A., *Gold, Guns & Ghost Towns*, Stanford University Press, Stanford, California, 1947, pp. 154–162.

64. *Carson City Tribune*, July 24, 1876, reprinted in *Pioche Daily Record*, July 29, 1876; *Virginia City Territorial Enterprise*, July 23, 1876. In an interview with the *Tribune* in July 1876, Harrington said he had "lived in Virginia City fifteen months."

65. Although Con Sullivan's stepdaughter and John Sullivan would call each other "cousin" evidence seems to suggest that Con and John were brothers.

66. *Eureka Daily Sentinel*, July 28, 1876.

67. *Carson City Tribune*, July 24, 1876, reprinted in *Pioche Daily Record*, July 29, 1876; *Reno Evening Gazette*, May 16, 1878.

68. *Reno Evening Gazette*, May 16, 1878.

69. *Carson City Tribune*, July 24, 1876, reprinted in *Pioche Daily Record*, July 29, 1876.

70. *Reno Evening Gazette*, May 16, 1878.

71. *Virginia City Evening Chronicle*, July 28, 1876, reprinted in *Pioche Daily Record*, August 3, 1876.

72. *Carson City Tribune*, July 24, 1876, reprinted in *Pioche Daily Record*, July 29, 1876.

73. *Ibid.*; *Virginia City Territorial Enterprise*, July 23, 1876; *Reno Evening Gazette*, May 16, 1878.

74. *Virginia City Territorial Enterprise*, July 23, 1876.

75. *Pioche Daily Record*, July 24, 1876.

76. *Carson City Tribune*, July 24, 1876, reprinted in *Pioche Daily Record*, July 29, 1876.

77. *Virginia City Territorial Enterprise*, July 25, 1876; *Eureka Daily Sentinel*, July 28, 1876.

78. *Virginia City Territorial Enterprise*, August 6, 1876.

79. *Ibid.*, September 4, 22, December 5, 1876.

80. *Ibid.*, December 6, 1876.

81. *Ibid.*, December 17, 1876. What Harrington was saying these men could testify to is not clear.

82. *Virginia City Territorial Enterprise*, December 17, 1876.

83. *Gold Hill News*, no date, reprinted in *Eureka Daily Sentinel*, February 16, 1877.

84. Angel, Myron, *History of Nevada*, Thompson & West, Oakland, California, 1881, reprint, Howell-North, Berkeley, California, 1958, p. 353.

85. *Reno Evening Gazette*, May 22, December 17, 1878.

86. *Gold Hill News*, no date, reprinted in *Eureka Daily Sentinel*, February 16, 1877.

87. *Virginia City Territorial Enterprise*, January 30, February 8, 1877; *Pioche Weekly Record*, February 17, 1877; *Eureka Daily Sentinel*, February 9, 1877; *Gold Hill News*, no date, reprinted in *Eureka Daily Sentinel*, March 1, 1877.

88. *Virginia City Territorial Enterprise*, March 7, 1877; *Reno Evening Gazette*, March 7, 1877.

89. *Virginia City Territorial Enterprise*, March 7, 1877.

90. *Ibid.*, March 18, 1877.

91. *Ward Semi-Weekly Reflex*, April 29, 1877.

92. *Virginia City Territorial Enterprise*, June 2, 7, 1877; *Carson City Morning Appeal*, June 15, 1877.

93. *Virginia City Territorial Enterprise*, June 7, 1877.

94. *Ibid.*, June 28, 1877.

95. *Reno Evening Gazette*, February 13, 1878; *Esmeralda Herald*, February 16, 1878.

96. *Reno Evening Gazette*, February 20, 1878.

97. *Ibid.*, May 15, 16, 17, 18, 1878.

98. *Ibid.*, May 25, 27, 1878; *Carson City Morning Appeal*, May 26, 1878; *Reno Journal*, no date, reprinted in *Ward Weekly Reflex*, June 1, 1878.

99. *Reno Evening Gazette*, May 25, 1878.

100. *Ibid.*, June 21, 1878.

101. *Carson City Morning Appeal*, May 26, 1878.

102. *Biennial Report of the Warden of Nevada State Prison, for the Years 1877 and 1878*, Table No. 7, Showing the number of Convicts received at the Nevada State Prison during the year 1878, p. 46.

103. *Eureka Daily Sentinel*, October 25, 1878.

104. *Reno Evening Gazette*, December 17, 1878.

105. *Carson City Morning Appeal*, March 4, 1879. Taft was killed in the fracas.

106. *Biennial Report of the Warden of Nevada State Prison, for the Years 1889 and 1890*, Table No. 6, Showing the number of convicts pardoned during the year 1890, p. 40.

107. *Carson City Morning Appeal*, June 16, 1893; *White Pine News* (Treasure City), June 24, 1893; *Wood River Times* (Hailey, Idaho), June 12, 1893; *Idaho Semi-Weekly World* (Idaho City), June 13, 1893; *Weiser Signal* (Idaho), June 15, 1893.

Chapter 11

1. Scene and dialogue taken from various contemporary accounts of the incident, principally the *Gold Hill Evening News*, July 14, 1871.

2. The inquest resulting from his death found that Kirk "was a native of Jackson County, Missouri." The 1860 census and the California State Prison agreed with the Missouri decree, as did an article in the *Gold Hill News*, although the *News* said "Fayette County, Missouri." Later the *News* would claim Kentucky as his birthplace. The *Daily State Register* and Nevada State Prison records also agree on Kentucky as his state of origin. *Gold Hill Evening News*, July 14, 15, 18, 1871; *Daily State Register* (Carson City), July 15, 1871; *Annual Report of the Warden of the Nevada State Prison, for the Fiscal Year Ending Dec. 31, 1866*, J.S. Crosman, Warden, Joseph E. Eckley, State Printer, Carson City, Nevada, 1867, Tabular Statement, Showing the Names and Number of Prisoners on January 1st, 1866, and all that Have Been Received Since That Date, Properly Classified, and Disposition Made of Them: No. 7; Name of Prisoner, G. Kirk; Age, 25, Nativity, Kentucky; Crime, Attempt to commit burglary; County sent from, Storey; Date of Sentence, Jan. 6, 1865; Duration of Sentence, 1 year; Occupation, Miner; Educational Abilities, Read and Write; Discharged by Expiration of Sentence, March 27, 1866. Federal Census of the United States, 1860, Cortemadero Township, County of Marin, State of California, Post Office of San Rafael, enumerated on 23rd day of July 1860, p. 78: State Prison; Family No., 1858; Name, George Kirk; Age, 24; Male; Occupation, Laborer; Place of Birth, Mos.; atp. To murder. California State Prison records: #1424; Name of Convict, Geo. Kirk; Nativity, Missouri; Crime, Aslt. With intent to commit murder; When Received, June 29, 1858; Term of Sentence; 5 years; County Sent from, Tuolumne; Age, 22; Occupation, Laborer; Height, 5 feet 10 ¼ inches; Complexion, Fair; Color of Eyes, Blue; Color of Hair, Light.

3. The ruling of age at his inquest, as well as ages listed in the 1860 census and California State Prison all work out to a birth year of 1835 or 1836. Kirk is listed in the Nevada State Prison records as being able to read and write, a talent held in common with a majority of the prisoners. *Gold Hill Evening News*, July 18, 1871; Federal Census of the United States, 1860; California State Prison Records; *Annual Report of the Warden of the Nevada State Prison, for the Fiscal Year Ending Dec. 31, 1866*.

4. *Gold Hill Evening News*, July 14, 15, 1871; *Daily State Register* (Carson City), July 15, 1871.

5. *Gold Hill Evening News*, July 14, 15, 1871; *Daily State Register* (Carson City), July 15, 1871.

6. State of Illinois, Bureau County, Circuit Court, The People vs William Reid, George Kirk, et al., September–October 1851. No disposition of the case is recorded.

7. State of Illinois, Bureau County, The People vs Patrick Kirk, August–September 1860.

8. *Gold Hill Evening News*, July 14, 15, 1871; *Daily State Register* (Carson City), July 15, 1871.

9. Baxter, George, "Sonora, City of Screaming Murder," *The West*, July 1965, Vol. 3, No. 2, pp. 38–40, 56–58.

10. *Gold Hill Evening News*, July 15, 1871.

11. *Union Democrat* (Sonora, California), no date, reprinted in *Reese River Reveille* (Austin), June 20, 1865.

12. *Ibid.*

13. *Union Democrat* (Sonora, California), July 22, 1871.

14. Court of Sessions, Tuolumne County, The People of the State of California against G.B. Kirk, June Term, 1856.

15. *Ibid.* A nolle prosequi is the legal term (after the Latin—to be unwilling to pursue) for an entry on a document of legal action stating that the prosecutor or plaintiff will proceed no further in a certain legal case.

16. Court of Sessions, Tuolumne County, The People of the State of California against George Kirk, October Term, 1857.

17. *Daily State Register* (Carson City), July 15, 1871.

18. Court of Sessions, Tuolumne County, The People of the State of California against George Kirk, October Term, 1857; Writ of Subpoena, State of California, Tuolumne County, ss. S.B. Blake, R.P. Malone, October 12, 1857; ss. H. Patterson, M. Woodruff, October 10, 1857.

19. Court of Sessions, Tuolumne County, People, etc., vs George Kirk, Verdict, October 12, 1857.

20. County Jail Book, Tuolumne County, Record of prisoners in the Tuolumne County Jail, George Kirk, Discharged, October 12, 1857.

21. *Daily State Register* (Carson City), July 15, 1871.

22. *Union Democrat* (Sonora, California), April

3, 1858; *Daily State Register* (Carson City), July 15, 1871; *Gold Hill Evening News*, July 15, 1871.

23. County Jail Book, Tuolumne County Jail, George Kirk, committed to answer the charge of assault with attempt to commit murder, March 27 (*sic*), 1858; State of California, County of Tuolumne, Case #44, The People vs George Kirk, Complaint, March 28, 1858.

24. Court of Sessions, Tuolumne County, The People vs George Kirk, June Term, 1858; The People vs George Kirk, Verdict, June Term, 1858.

25. Court of Sessions, Tuolumne County, The People vs George Kirk & Alex Delabash, Return Order for Sheriff, June Term, 1858; County Jail Book, George Kirk, Sentenced, June 19, 1858.

26. Court of Session, Tuolumne County, The People vs George Kirk & Alex Delabash, Return Order for Sheriff, June Term, 1858; County Jail Book, George Kirk, Sent to State Prison, June 28, 1858.

27. California State Prison Records, #1424, George Kirk, June 1858.

28. "To all whom it may concern," notice of application for pardon by George B. Kirk, G.T. Martin, County Judge, et al; State of California, Tuolumne County, Geo. S. Evans, County Clerk, certification of intention of George B. Kirk to apply for pardon.

29. Federal Census of the United States, 1860.

30. Hegne, Barbara, *The Nevada Vigilante Hangings, Virginia City, Carson City, Dayton, Aurora, "601,"* Nevada Pioneer Series, Reno, Nevada, 2000, p. 29.

31. *Daily State Register* (Carson City), July 15, 1871.

32. *Gold Hill News*, November 7, 1864; *Union Democrat* (Sonora, California), December 17, 1864.

33. State of Nevada against George Kirk, Edward Donley, Joseph Wise and Charles Dade, District Court of the Second Judicial District of the State of Nevada, Ormsby County, September Term, 1865; *Annual Report of the Warden of the Nevada State Prison, For the Fiscal Year Ending Dec. 31, 1866.*

34. State of Nevada against George Kirk, et al., September Term, 1865; *Annual Report of the Warden of the Nevada State Prison, For the Fiscal Year Ending Dec. 31, 1866.*

35. *Eureka Daily Sentinel*, no date, reprinted in Angel, Myron, *History of Nevada, 1881*, Thompson & West, Oakland, California, 1881, reprint Howell—North, Berkeley, California, 1958, p. 546; Penrose, Matt R., *Pots O'Gold*, A. Carlisle & Co. of Nevada, Reno, Nevada, 1935, pp. 75–77.

36. *Reese River Reveille* (Austin), February 4, 1865; *Daily State Register* (Carson City), July 15, 1871.

37. Edward Donley had been convicted on November 10, 1863, for a robbery with violence in Storey County, Nevada and sentenced to a ten-year term in the penitentiary. Charles Dade was convicted on January 9, 1865, for a burglary in Ormsby County and sentenced to a term of two years in the State Prison. District Court Case #226, Second Judicial District of the State of Nevada, Ormsby County, September Term, 1865, The State of Nevada against George Kirk, Edward Donley, Joseph Wise and Charles Dade, Assault with intent to kill.

38. *Gold Hill Evening News*, July 14, 1871; *Daily State Register* (Carson City), July 15, 1871.

39. T.H. Miller, alias Tom Mitchell, was a well-known malefactor from Sacramento, California, where he had been convicted of robbery on more than one occasion. At one time he was even suspected of having killed a principal witness in one of his cases. *Sacramento Union*, no date, reprinted in *Reese River Reveille* (Austin), February 27, 1865.

40. *Lyon County Sentinel* (Dayton), February 4, 1865; *Reese River Reveille* (Austin), February 4, 1865; *Daily State Register* (Carson City), July 15, 1871; *Gold Hill Evening News*, July 14, 1871; District Court Case #226, State of Nevada against George Kirk, et al., Assault with intent to kill, September 1865.

41. *Lyon County Sentinel* (Dayton), February 11, 1865. The *Sentinel*, alike with other contemporary sources, called Donley "Donnery" in its coverage of the men's exploits. A more official record, however, the District Court case #226, in which he is charged along with Kirk, Wise and Dade, with assault with intent to kill in September 1865, clearly shows that his name was Donley.

42. *Union Democrat* (Sonora, California), May 13, 1865; *Carson City Daily Appeal*, May 26, 1865.

43. *Auburn Stars and Stripes*, no date, reprinted in *Reese River Reveille* (Austin), May 5, 1865; *Sacramento Union*, no date, reprinted in *Union Videte* (Camp Douglas, Utah), May 19, 1865; *Union Democrat* (Sonora, California), May 13, 1865.

44. *Auburn Stars and Stripes*, no date, reprinted in *Reese River Reveille* (Austin), May 5, 1865.

45. *Carson City Daily Appeal*, May 26, 1865.

46. *Ibid.*, June 7, 1865. On December 12, 1867, Timothy G. Smith, Sheriff of Ormsby County, would be shot and killed while attempting the arrest of Thomas Riley.

47. *Union Democrat* (Sonora, California), no date, reprinted in *Reese River Reveille* (Austin), June 20, 1865.

48. District Court Case #226, State of Nevada against George Kirk, et al., Assault with intent to kill, September 1865. Joseph Wise was convicted July 11, 1864, on a charge of Grand Larceny. He was a native of England, 26 years old in 1865. Nevada State Prison records list his occupation as "Sailor." He would receive a sentence of two years and finally be released May 19, 1866. *Annual Report of the Warden of the Nevada State Prison, for the Fiscal Year Ending Dec. 31, 1866.*

49. The State of Nevada against George Kirk, Edward Donley, Joseph Wise and Charles Dade, District Court of the Second Judicial District of the State of Nevada, Ormsby County, September Term, 1865, Indictment, Prison Breaking.

50. *Carson City Daily Appeal*, March 14, 1866.

51. The State of Nevada against George Kirk, et al., District court of the Second Judicial District of the State of Nevada, Ormsby County, March Term, 1866, Prison Breaking (a very limited record group).

52. *Annual Repot of the Warden of the Nevada State Prison, for the Fiscal Year Ending Dec. 31, 1866.*

53. *Virginia City Territorial Enterprise*, no date, reprinted in *Gold Hill Evening News*, July 15, 1871.
54. *Ibid.*
55. *Gold Hill Evening News*, July 14, 1871; Hegne, Barbara, *The Nevada Vigilante Hangings*, p. 20. Heffnan's surname has also been rendered as Heffernan, Hefferman, Hefforan and Heffnerman in various sources. I have decided to go with Heffnan, the spelling of the contemporary *Gold Hill Evening News*, who seemed to have the most reliable information on the man.
56. Bancroft, Hubert Howe, *Popular Tribunals, Vol. 1, The Works of Hubert Howe Bancroft*, Volume XXXVI, The History Company Publishers, San Francisco, California, 1887, p. 617.
57. Hegne, Barbara, *The Nevada Vigilante Hangings*, p. 20.
58. *Ibid.*, pp. 20–21; Bancroft, Hubert Howe, *Popular Tribunals, Vol. 1, The Works of Hubert Howe Bancroft*, Volume XXXVI, p. 617.
59. *Gold Hill Evening News*, March 25, 1871; Hegne, Barbara, *The Nevada Vigilante Hangings*, pp. 22–23.
60. *Gold Hill Evening News*, March 25, 1871.
61. *Ibid.*, April 3, 1871.
62. *Pioche Daily Record*, April 2, 1871, reprinted in *Gold Hill Evening News*, April 5, 1871.
63. *Daily State Register* (Carson City), July 15, 1871, reprinted in *Gold Hill Evening News*, July 15, 1871.
64. *Ibid.*; *Gold Hill Evening News*, June 2, 1871.
65. *Gold Hill Evening News*, June 2, 1871.
66. *Ibid.*, July 14, 1871.
67. *Ibid.*
68. *Daily State Register* (Carson City), July 15, 1871, reprinted in *Gold Hill Evening News*, July 15, 1871.
69. *Gold Hill Evening News*, July 14, 1871.
70. *Ibid.*, July 18, 1871.
71. *Ibid.*, July 14, 1871.
72. *Ibid.*
73. *Salt Lake Tribune*, July 24, 1871; *The Daily Oregonian* (Portland, Oregon), July 22, 1871.
74. *Gold Hill Evening News*, July 18, 1871.
75. *Ibid.*
76. *Ibid.*, August 8, 1871.
77. *Ibid.*, September 22, 1871.

Chapter 12

1. Drury, Wells, *An Editor on the Comstock Lode*, Farrar & Rinehart, Incorporated, New York and Toronto, 1936, p. 165.
2. Earl, Phillip I., http://dmla.clan.lib.nv.us/docs/dca/thiswas/thiswas37.htm, Department of Cultural Affairs, *This Was Nevada*, "Comstock Lode Featured in New Book," accessed April 26, 2005.
3. Sources, including the *Pioche Weekly Record*, September 1, 1883, claimed Darling's nativity as Kentucky and his age as 43 years at his death in that year. The inquest held over Darling following his death in 1883 and reported in the *Esmeralda Herald* (Hawthorne), August 25, 1883, concurs. This agrees with other sources such as the 1880 federal census: County of Ormsby, State of Nevada, enumerated June 1880, Page No. 21, Supervisory Dist. No. 81, Enumeration Dist. No. 39, State Prison: Name: Darling, John; White; Male; Age: 40; Married; Occupation: Blacksmith; Prisoner; Place of Birth: Kentucky. Also, the Warden's Report of 1866, the year of Darling's first induction into the Nevada State Prison: *Annual Report of the Warden of the Nevada State Prison, for the Fiscal Year Ending Dec. 31, 1866*. J.S. Crosman, Warden, Joseph E. Eckley, State Printer, Carson City, Nevada, 1867: Tabular Statement, Showing the Names and Number of Prisoners on January 1st, 1866, and all that have been Received since that Date, Properly Classified, and the Disposition made of them: No. 27, J.R. Darling; Age, 25; Nativity, Kentucky; Crime, Robbery; County sent from, Storey; Date of Sentence, June 30, 1866; Duration of Sentence, 14 years; Educational Abilities, Read and write.
4. Beadle's Nebraska adventure is chronicled in, Bristow, David L., *A Dirty, Wicked Town: Tales of 19th Century Omaha*, Caxton Press, Caldwell, Idaho, 2002, pp. 7–42.
5. The "Big Six" was amongst one of the first businesses built in Omaha, a general merchandizing store. Bristow, David L., *A Dirty, Wicked Town*, p. 3.
6. Beadle, E.F., http://members.aol.com/oldnebraska/index.htm, "To Nebraska in 1857, A Diary of E.F. Beadle," accessed April 26, 2005.
7. Bristow, David L., *A Dirty, Wicked Town*, p. 25.
8. *Truckee* (California) *Republican*, no date, reprinted in *Eureka Daily Sentinel*, September 2, 1883.
9. Boessenecker, John, *Gold Dust & Gunsmoke, Tales of Gold Rush Outlaws, Gunfighters, Lawmen, and Vigilantes*, John Wiley & Sons, Inc., New York and Toronto, 1999, pp. 241–244.
10. *Ibid.*, pp. 244–249.
11. *Carson City Morning Appeal*, July 2, 1880; *Virginia City Territorial Enterprise*, August 24, 1883.
12. *Carson City Morning Appeal*, July 2, 1880.
13. Hicks, George A., *Family Record and History of George A. Hicks*, ed. Maud Hicks Lewis, self-published, 1938, pp. 42–43.
14. *Virginia City Territorial Enterprise*, August 24, 1883.
15. Earl, Phillip I., *This Was Nevada, Volume II, The Comstock Lode*, Nevada Historical Society, Carson City, Nevada, 2000, p. 117.
16. *Ibid.*; *Virginia City Evening Bulletin*, September 15, 1863.
17. *Virginia City Evening Bulletin*, September 15, 1863.
18. Earl, Phillip I., *This Was Nevada, Vol. II*, p. 117.
19. *Reese River Reveille* (Austin), no date, reprinted in *Eureka Daily Sentinel*, August 26, 1871.
20. Earl, Phillip I., *This Was Nevada, Vol. II*, p. 117.
21. *Gold Hill News*, May 15, 1866.
22. *Ibid.*, May 17, 1866.
23. State of Nevada vs. John Richard Darling,

charge of robbery, Justice Court preliminary hearing, May 28, 1866.

24. *Ibid.*; *Gold Hill News*, May 30, 1866.

25. Ash was not a member of the Virginia City police force but a precinct constable allied with the Justice Court.

26. Statement of John R. Darling, of the Nevada State Prison, on application to the Hon. Board of Pardons for pardon, 1871.

27. State of Nevada vs. John Richard Darling, charge of robbery, Justice Court preliminary hearing, May 28, 1866.

28. *Ibid.*, testimony of Miss Jessie Case.

29. *Ibid.*, ruling of Justice D.O. Atkinson.

30. Notice of intent to apply for pardon of John R. Darling, alias "Rattlesnake Dick," to Wm. Woodburn, District Attorney, Storey County, March 1871.

31. Richard Rising to Frank Denver, June 17, 1871.

32. *Ibid.*; *Annual Report of the Warden of the Nevada State Prison, for the Fiscal Year Ending Dec. 31, 1866*; *Eureka Sentinel*, December 5, 1872.

33. Richard Rising to Frank Denver, June 17, 1871.

34. *Gold Hill News*, August 22, 1871.

35. *Ibid.*, June 30, 1866; *Annual Report of the Warden of Nevada State Prison, for the Fiscal Year Ending Dec. 31, 1866*.

36. *Gold Hill News*, February 16, 1870.

37. *Second Biennial Report of the Warden of Nevada State Prison*. 1869 and 1870, Whole Number of Prisoners Received During My Administration [Lieutenant Governor and Warden Frank Denver]: No. 71; Name of Prisoner, Wm. Chamberlain; Age, 23; Nativity, Ohio; Crime, Murder Second deg.; County Sent From, Elko; Date of Sentence, Dec. 13, 1869; Duration of Sentence, Ninety-nine years; Occupation, Stage-driver, Education, Read & write.

38. Angel, Myron, *History of Nevada*, Thompson & West, Oakland, California, 1881, reprint, Howell-North, Berkeley, California, 1958, pp. 348–349.

39. *Report of the Warden of the Nevada State Prison, for the Years 1871–1872*, List of Prisoners, pp. 6–7.

40. Petition to the Hon. The Board of Pardon Commissioners of the State of Nevada, 1871.

41. Statement of John R. Darling of the Nevada State Prison, on application to the Hon. Board of Pardons for pardon, 1871.

42. To the Hon. The Board of Pardon Commissioners of the State of Nevada, Petition re: pardon for John R. Darling, 1871.

43. Richard Rising to Frank Denver, June 17, 1871.

44. *Report of the Warden of the Nevada State Prison, for the Years 1871–1872*, Prisoners Discharged from January 9, 1871, to January 1, 1873, p. 12; Office of Nevada State Prison, Carson, Nev., Mar. 10/81, John R. Darling; *Daily State Register* (Carson City), August 22, 1871; *Eureka Sentinel*, December 5, 1872; *Gold Hill News*, August 22, 1871.

45. *Gold Hill News*, August 22, 1871.

46. *Reese River Reveille* (Austin), no date, reprinted in *Eureka Daily Sentinel*, August 26, 1871.

47. Dolan, Trent, "The Great Carson City Prison Escape of 1871," http://www.nevadaappeal.com/aps/pbcs/dll/article?AID=/20081012/NEWS/110129991/, accessed November 11, 2010.

48. William Seawell to James Warren, December 19, 1890.

49. *Gold Hill News*, October 25, 1872; Convis, Charles L., *Outlaw Tales of Nevada*, Globe Pequot Press, Guilford, Connecticut, 2006, p. 33.

50. *Virginia City Chronicle*, June 19, 1875, reprinted in *New York Times*, July 4, 1875, *Gold Hill News*, October 28, 1872; *Reese River Reveille* (Austin), October 31, 1872; Convis, Charles L., *Outlaw Tales of Nevada*, pp. 33–35.

51. *Gold Hill News*, October 31, 1872.

52. *Ibid.*

53. *Ibid.*

54. Convis, Charles L., *Outlaw Tales of Nevada*, p. 34.

55. *Gold Hill News*, November 12, 15, 1872; *Daily State Register* (Carson City), November 15, 1872.

56. *Daily State Register* (Carson City), November 17, 1872; *Nevada State Journal* (Reno), November 23, 1872; Office of Nevada State Prison to Hon. Board of Pardons, Prison Record of John R. Darling, March 10, 1881; *Biennial Report of the Warden of Nevada State Prison, for the Years 1879 and 1880*, pp. 53, 56.

57. *Gold Hill News*, November 18, 1872; *Nevada State Journal* (Reno), November 23, 1872; *Biennial Report of the Warden of Nevada State Prison, for the Years 1879 and 1880*, pp. 53, 56.

58. *Biennial Report of the Warden of Nevada State Prison, for the Years 1879 and 1880*, pp. 53, 56.

59. *Gold Hill News*, November 18, 1872.

60. Office of Nevada State Prison to Hon. Board of Pardons, Prison Record of John R. Darling, Conduct Record, March 10, 1881.

61. *Ibid.* Numerous times over the next ten years, Darling would be docked good time credits or locked in his cell for such infractions as "talking in dining room" or "Disobediance" [*sic*].

62. *Ibid.*

63. *Virginia City Chronicle*, June 19, 1875, reprinted in *New York Times*, July 4, 1875.

64. W. Seawell to W.C. Chamberlain, March 17, 1880; John Powell, Jr., to Honorable Board of Pardons, 1880; James Hagar to Honorable, the Board of Pardons, January 28, 1880. Hagar had worked as an employee, with Chamberlain, for the stage company in 1871 and, in referring to Chamberlain, said he was, "always a good hard working and honest man."

65. M.N. Stone to W.C. Chamberlain, March 2, 1880.

66. *Carson City Morning Appeal*, July 2, 1880; *Biennial Report of the Warden of Nevada State Prison for the Years 1879 and 1880*, Report of Attending Physician, Table No. 11, Showing Number of Deaths For 1880, p. 53.

67. *Carson City Morning Appeal*, July 2, 1880.

68. *Ibid.*

69. Office of Nevada State Prison to Hon. Board of Pardons, Prison Record of John R. Darling, Conduct Record, March 10, 1881.

70. *Ibid.*; *Biennial Report of the Warden of Nevada State Prison, for the Years 1881 and 1882*, Table No. 3, Showing the Number of Convicts discharged from the Nevada State Prison by expiration of sentence during the year 1881, p. 40.

71. *Ward Weekly Reflex*, July 23, 1881.

72. *Candelaria True Fissure*, no date, reprinted in *Esmeralda Herald* (Aurora), February 4, 1882.

73. Federal Census of the United States, 1880, County of Ormsby, State of Nevada, enumerated June 1880, Page No. 21, Supervisory Dist. No. 81, Enumeration Dist. No. 39, State Prison: Name: Warren, Jas.; White; Male; Age, 27; Single; Occupation, Waiter; Place of Birth, Ohio.

74. James Warren to The Hon. Board of Pardons, November 18, 1890.

75. *Biennial Report of the Warden of Nevada State Prison for the Years 1883 and 1884*, Table No. 2, Showing the number of convicts received at the Nevada State Prison during the year 1884, p. 36: Name: James Warren, alias Jimmy Fresh; Age: 33; Nativity: Ohio; County Sent From: Esmeralda; Crime: Murder second degree; Term of Sentence: 40 years; Date of Commitment, January 9; Trade or Occupation: Baker & painter.

76. *Virginia City Territorial Enterprise*, August 24, 1883.

77. *Ibid.*, August 29, 1883.

78. *Ibid.*; *Esmeralda Herald* (Aurora), September 8, 1883; *Sacramento Daily Record-Union*, August 29, 1883.

79. *Esmeralda Herald* (Aurora), September 1, 8, 1883; *Sacramento Daily Record-Union*, August 29, 1883; *Virginia City Territorial Enterprise*, August 29, 1883.

80. W.F. St. John to James Warren, December 27, 1890.

81. *Ibid.*

82. James Warren to The Hon. Board of Pardons, November 18, 1890.

83. *Ibid.*; *Esmeralda Herald* (Aurora), August 25, 1883; *Pioche Weekly Record*, September 1, 1883; *Eureka Daily Sentinel*, August 25, 1883; *Virginia City Territorial Enterprise*, August 24, 1883. All quotes taken from contemporary sources.

84. *Esmeralda Herald* (Aurora), August 25, 1883.

85. *Ibid.*

86. *Eureka Daily Sentinel*, August 25, 1883; *Virginia City Territorial Enterprise*, August 24, 1883.

87. *Esmeralda Herald* (Aurora), September 1, 1883.

88. *Ibid.*, December 15, 22, 1883.

89. *Biennial Report of the Warden of Nevada State Prison for the Years 1883 and 1884*, Table No. 2, Showing the number of convicts received at the Nevada State Prison during the year 1884, p. 36. The prison record shows his date of commitment as January 9, 1884.

90. Earl, Phillip I., *This Was Nevada, Volume II, The Comstock Lode*, p. 118.

91. James Warren to The Hon. Board of Pardons, November 18, 1890; James Warren to Hon. Richard Rising, notice of application for pardon, September 29, 1891; James Warren to G.M. Bowler, notice of application for pardon, September 29, 1891; Petition to The Honorable, The Board of Pardons of The State of Nevada, 1891; James Warren to B.F. Curler, notice of application for pardon, November 19, 1890.

92. *Biennial Report of the Warden of Nevada State Prison for the Years 1891 and 1892*, Table No. 6, Showing the number of convicts pardoned during the year 1892, p. 41.

93. *Virginia City Territorial Enterprise*, September 4, 1883.

Chapter 13

1. Angel, Myron (Ed.), *History of Nevada*, Thompson &West, Oakland, California, 1881. Reprint, Arno Press, New York, 1973, p. 441; *Eureka Daily Sentinel*, August 15, 1878.

2. *Eureka Daily Leader*, May 3, 1880; *Eureka Daily Sentinel*, May 4, 1880. Both sources state that Martin was 40 years of age at the time of his death in May 1880. Although William Martin could not be found in the 1850 or 1860 federal census conducted in Cumberland, Maryland, an interesting possibility remains. In the 1860 census, dwelling 68, family 68, is a family headed by one Thomas Martin, 25 years old. Included in this family is a William N. or H. "Pani," 20 years old, the exact age Billy Martin would have been in 1860. Did William Pani, taken in by the Martin family, assume the Martin name before heading west? Of course, this can only be conjecture, but an interesting possibility.

3. Martin's early life is unknown. In Robert K. DeArment's book, *Knights of the Green Cloth*, University of Oklahoma Press, Norman, Oklahoma, 1982, pp. 309, 314, DeArment mentions a well-known professional gambler named William J. "Billy" Martin who operated in the Cheyenne, Wyoming, area in the late 1860s to early 1870s time period. Again, whether this is the Billy Martin of Nevada or not would be pure speculation at this point.

4. *Eureka Daily Sentinel*, May 4, 1880.

5. Earl, Phillip I., "Nevada's Italian War," *Nevada Historical Society Quarterly*, Vol. 12, No. 2, Summer 1969, p. 53. The count as of 1873.

6. *Eureka Daily Sentinel*, March 17, 1877.

7. *Ibid.*, July 13, 1878.

8. *Ibid.*, July 17, 1878.

9. *Ibid.*, August 15, 1878; Angel, Myron, ed., *History of Nevada*, p. 441. The cause of the flood proved to be a tremendous cloud burst which dumped torrents of water on the mountains surrounding Eureka. The waters poured down the sides of the mountains into the canyons below. That from Pinto Canyon joined streams from other canyons a few miles before reaching Eureka and sent a torrent down the town's Main Street. Much damage was sustained. However, unlike a similar flood which had

hit Eureka in July 1874 and which had claimed 14 lives, no lives were lost in the 1878 flood. The *Eureka Daily Sentinel* reports many near losses of life and harrowing escapes of Eureka citizens.

10. Federal Census of the U.S., June 4, 1880, State of Nevada, County of Eureka, Eureka, Dwelling #165, Family #144, Kyle, Matthew. Also listed is Kyle's 21-year-old wife Ella born in California, a four-year-old daughter, Jennie, born in Nevada and a one-and-a-half-year-old son, listed simply with the initial "L," also born in Nevada.

11. *Ibid.*, Dwelling #214, Simpson, J.B. Simpson lived in an apparent boarding house with various other individuals including, Ed McSorley, a 46-year-old saloon keeper, Auguste Hintze, also a saloon keeper, aged 41; Chas. Graham, another saloon keeper, 33 years old; C.U. Aiken, a 45-year-old carpenter, a 26-year-old miner named R. Athorn, etc.

12. *Eureka Daily Leader*, April 30, 1879.
13. *Ibid.*, May 1, 1879.
14. *Ibid.*, May 1, 1879.
15. Earl, Phillip I., "Nevada's Italian War," *Nevada Historical Society Quarterly*, Vol. 12, No. 2, Summer 1969, pp. 47–87. Earl gives a good analysis of the coal burners origins and society as well as events leading up to, during and subsequent to the so-called "war."
16. Earl, Phillip I., "Nevada's Italian War," pp. 65–71; *Eureka Daily Leader*, July 21, 1879.
17. Earl, Phillip I., "Nevada's Italian War," pp. 66–68; *Eureka Daily Leader*, August 11, 1879; Angel, Myron (Ed), *History of Nevada*, Arno Press, New York, 1973 (reprint edition), p. 438. The militia would play no part in future events of the conflict.
18. *Eureka Daily Leader*, August 19, 20, 21, 22, 23, 25, 26, 27, September 2, 3, 1879; Earl, "Nevada's Italian War," pp. 71–77.
19. *Eureka Daily Leader*, August 19, 1879.
20. *Ibid.*, August 20, 21, 1879.
21. *Ibid.*, August 21, 1879.
22. *Ibid.*, August 22, 23, 25, 26, 1879; Earl, Phillip I., "Nevada's Italian War," pp. 77–82.
23. Angel, *History of Nevada*, p. 438.
24. Earl Phillip I., "Nevada's Italian War," p. 72.
25. *Eureka Daily Leader*, August 25, September 2, 3, 1879; Earl Phillip I., "Nevada's Italian War," p. 78.
26. *Eureka Daily Leader*, September 2, 1879.
27. *Eureka Daily Sentinel*, October 18, 1879.
28. *Eureka Daily Leader*, October 20, 1879.
29. *Ibid.*, October 24, 27, 1879.
30. *Eureka Daily Sentinel*, May 4, 1880. The former Mrs. Martin eventually moved to Dayton, Nevada, where she married her brother-in-law's killer.
31. Federal Census of the U.S., June 4, 1880, State of Nevada, County of Eureka, Eureka, Dwelling # 130, Family #108, Brent, John E. A.
32. *Eureka Daily Leader*, May 3, 1880; *Eureka Daily Sentinel*, May 4, 1880.
33. *Eureka Daily Sentinel*, May 4, 1880.
34. *Eureka Daily Leader*, May 3, 1880.
35. *Ibid.*, May 4, 5, 1880.

36. Federal Census of the U.S., June 4, 1880, State of Nevada, County of Eureka, Eureka, Dwelling #130, Family #108, Brent, John E.A.
37. *Esmeralda Herald*, February 11, 1882.
38. *Eureka Daily Sentinel*, May 4, 1880; *Eureka Daily Leader*, May 3, 1880.

Chapter 14

1. *Eureka Daily Sentinel*, March 10, 1818; "Hank Parrish—Nevada's Worst Killer," *Western Frontier*, January 1978, p. 5.
2. Hank Parrish's surname is just as often spelled "Parish" in contemporary accounts. I have decided to use the two-r spelling for continuity.
3. Federal Census of the United States, 1880, Eldorado Canon [sic], County of Lincoln, State of Nevada, enumerated September 29, Page No. 6, Supervisor's Dist. No. 81, Enumeration Dist. No. 27: Dwelling #16; Family #22; Name, Parish [sic], Henry; White; Male; Age, 40; Occupation, Works in Mill; Place of Birth, Nova Scotia; Father Born, Nova.; Mother Born, Nova. State of Utah, State Archives and Records Service, Utah State Prison, Admission Records. The records of the Utah State Prison agree with the 1880 census within a year or less, depending on Parrish's actual birth date, by recording his age as 47 in 1888.
4. Federal Census of the United States, 1880.
5. State of Utah, Utah State Prison, Admission Records.
6. "Nevada's Worst Killer," *Western Frontier*, January 1978, p. 5.
7. Mather, R.E., and F.E. Boswell, *Vigilante Victims*, History West Publishing Company, San Jose, California, 1991, p. 62.
8. *Ely News*, December 14, 1890, reprinted in *Salt Lake City Tribune*, December 17, 1890; *Nevada State Journal* (Reno), December 17, 1890.
9. *Ely News*, December 17, 1890, reprinted in *Salt Lake City Tribune*, December 17, 1890; *Nevada State Journal* (Reno), December 17, 1890.
10. *Utah Enquirer* (Provo), October 16, 1888.
11. *Provo American*, no date, reprinted in the *Pioche Weekly Record*, December 31, 1887.
12. Riggs, John L., "The Reign of Violence In El Dorado Canyon," *The Nevada Observer*, April 27, 2006, from the *Third Biennial Report of the Nevada Historical Society*, State Printing Office, Carson City, Nevada, 1913, pp. 95–107, http://www.nevadaobserver.com/Reading%20Room%20Documents/The%20Reign%20of%20Violence%20El%20Dorado%20Canyon%20(1913).htm, accessed February 2, 2011. Today Eldorado Canyon is in Clark County.
13. *Pioche Weekly Record*, October 25, 1890.
14. *Ibid.*
15. *Ibid.*, September 6, 1879.
16. *Ibid.*; *Reno Evening Gazette*, September 9, 1879.
17. *Pioche Weekly Record*, September 6, 1879.
18. Riggs, John L., "The Reign of Violence In El Dorado Canyon."

19. *Ibid.*

20. Federal Census of the United States, 1880, Eldorado Canon [*sic*], County of Lincoln, State of Nevada.

21. The date of the shooting is in dispute. The *Pioche Weekly Record* of March 12, 1881, said the incident took place early on the morning of March 1. A letter from Lincoln County to the *Eureka Daily Sentinel*, reprinted in the issue of March 10, 1881, and dated March 6 stated that the shooting happened, "Three days ago," or March 3.

22. For Parrish's losing and Greenwood's winning hands see *Pioche Weekly Record,* March 12, 1881. For Greenwood's baseball playing see *Eureka Daily Sentinel*, March 12, 1881.

23. *Pioche Weekly Record*, March 12, 1881, October 25, 1890; *Eureka Daily Sentinel*, March 10, 1881; *Nevada State Journal* (Reno), March 11, 1881.

24. *Pioche Weekly Record*, March 12, 1881; *Eureka Daily Sentinel*, March 10, 1881; *New York Tribune*, March 11, 1881.

25. *Pioche Weekly Record*, March 12, 1881.

26. *Ibid.*, March 19, 1881; *Ward Weekly Reflex*, March 26, 1881; *Eureka Daily Sentinel*, March 12, 1881.

27. *Eureka Daily Sentinel*, March 10, 1881; *Omaha* (Nebraska) *Daily Bee*, March 26, 1881; *New York Tribune*, March 11, 1881.

28. *Pioche Weekly Record*, March 12, 1881.

29. *Ibid.*, October 25, 1890.

30. *Ibid.*, August 12, 1882.

31. "Hank Parrish—Nevada's Worst Killer," *Western Frontier*, January 1978, p. 5; George, Cowboy, "Hank Parrish, Gunfighter, Horsethief, Murderer," www.sincitywebhosting.com/pioche, accessed April 15, 2011; Wilson, R. Michael, "Where is Henry 'Hank' Parrish Buried?" www.wildwesttales.com/stories/hank_parrish.htm, accessed April 15, 2011.

32. Evans, K.J., "The First 100, Part 1: The Early Years, Helen Stewart (1854–1926), 'The First Lady of Las Vegas,'" http://www.1st100.com/part1/stewart.html, accessed April 13, 2011; George, Cowboy, "Hank Parrish, Gunfighter, Horsethief, Murderer," Wilson, R. Michael, "Where is Henry 'Hank' Parrish Buried?"

33. Nevada Women's History Project, "Women's Biographies, Helen J. Stewart," http://www.unr.edu/nwhp/bios/women/stewart.htm, accessed April 13, 2011; Evans, K.J., "The First 100, Part 1: The Early Years, Helen Stewart (1854–1926), 'The First Lady of Las Vegas.'"

34. The Kiel name has also been spelled "Kyle" and "Keil" in various sources although Kiel is the correct spelling. As a result, Kyle Canyon near present day Las Vegas is spelled incorrectly while Kiel Way, a street in current North Las Vegas, is spelled correctly. Lillis, Maggie, "Misspelling of Kiel name remains a mystery in canyon's christening," http://www.viewnews.com/2011/VIEW-Jan-04-Tue-2011/CentennialHill/41089547.html., accessed April 13, 2011.

35. "Hank Parrish—Nevada's Worst Killer," *Western Frontier*, January 1978, p. 5.

36. Wright, Frank, *Nevada Yesterdays*, Stephens Press, Las Vegas, Nevada, 2010, Chapter One; Nevada Women's History Project, "Women's Biographies, Helen J. Stewart"; Evans, K.J., "The First 100, Part 1: The Early Years, Helen Stewart (1854–1926), 'The First Lady of Las Vegas'"; Flinchum, Robin, "Flashback, Murder One," *Las Vegas Life*, May 2000, http://www.lvlife.com/2000/05/flashback/story01.html, accessed April 25, 2005.

37. Nevada Women's History Project, "Women's Biographies, Helen J. Stewart."

38. *Pioche Weekly Record*, July 26, 1884.

39. *Reno Evening Gazette,* July 24, 1884; *Sacramento Daily Record-Union*, July 28, 1884.

40. *Pioche Weekly Record*, August 21, 1884.

41. *Ibid.*; Flinchum, Robin, "Flashback, Murder One."

42. *Pioche Weekly Record*, September 6, 1884.

43. Conrad Kiel operated his ranch prosperously until his death in 1894. Following the patriarch's death his sons continued the ranching operation. On October 11, 1900, two of the Kiel brothers, Edwin and William, were found shot to death on the Kiel ranch property. Ironically, the discoverers of the bodies proved to be Helen Stewart's second husband, Frank Stewart (no relation to her first husband), and Helen's son Will. At the time the coroner's jury ruled the deaths a murder/suicide, deciding that Edwin had shot William, then turned the gun on himself. So it stood for 75 years. In 1975 the city of North Las Vegas acquired a portion of the old Kiel Ranch, including the historic Kiel family cemetery, in an expansion project. It proved necessary to relocate all the bodies in the Kiel cemetery and thus excavations took place. Before the bodies were reinterred Sheilagh and Richard Brooks, two anthropologists affiliated with the University of Nevada–Las Vegas, received permission to examine the bodies of Edwin and William Kiel. The Brooks' decided that the wounds on the two men were inconsistent with a murder/suicide. They came to the conclusion that Edwin and William Kiel were probably murdered by some other individual or individuals. One suspect speculated upon is Hiram Stewart, the son of Archibald and Helen Stewart, in revenge for the murder of his father on the Kiel Ranch. Nothing has been proven, however. Akita Dad & Akita Mom, "Murder in the Desert," http://www.geocaching.com/seek/cache_details.aspx?ID=44205, accessed April 13, 2005; Flinchum, Robin, "Flashback—Murder One"; Nevada Women's History Project, "Women's Biographies—Helen J. Stewart"; Lillis, Maggie, "Misspelling of Kiel name remains mystery in canyon's christening."

44. Helen Jane Wiser was born April 16, 1854, in Springfield, Illinois, and raised in Galt, California. She married Archibald Stewart, a native of Dublin, Ireland, born in 1835, on her birthday, April 16, 1873. They had three children before moving to the Las Vegas Ranch, one more at the ranch, and Helen was pregnant with their fifth child when Archibald was killed in 1884. Helen proved a successful rancher after her husband's death, being the largest

landowner in Lincoln County by 1890. She became the first postmaster of Las Vegas in 1893. In 1903 she married her second husband, ranch foreman Frank Stewart, no relation to Archibald. By 1916, Helen lived in the burgeoning city of Las Vegas, built on land donated by Helen from part of her ranch holdings. She was elected to the school board and became the first woman to sit on a jury in newly organized Clark County, which had been carved out of Lincoln County. Helen Stewart became an authority on the history of the area and garnered the appellation, "First Lady of Las Vegas." Helen Stewart died at the age of 71 in Las Vegas on March 6, 1926. Nevada Women's History Project, "Women's Biographies, Helen J. Stewart"; Evans, K.J., "The First 100, Part 1: The Early Years, Helen Stewart (1854–1926), 'The First Lady of Las Vegas.'"

45. Land, Barbara and Myrick Land, *A Short History of Las Vegas*, University of Nevada Press, Reno, Nevada, 2004, pp. 32–34; Flinchum, Robin, "Flashback—Murder One"; Akita Dad & Akita Mom, "Murder in the Desert."

46. *Provo* (Utah) *American*, no date, reprinted in *Pioche Weekly Record*, December 31, 1887.

47. *Daily Utah Enquirer* (Provo), October 16, 1888. Tom Nance was a participant in the so-called "San Juan County War" of New Mexico/Colorado in the early 1880s in opposition to Ike Stockton and his followers. He would be involved in a number of gun battles and killings before his brief sojourn in Utah. Eventually, Nance would end up being kicked to death in a drunken saloon brawl in Holbrook, Arizona, on September 20, 1892. DeArment, Robert K., *Deadly Dozen, Forgotten Gunfighters of the Old West*, Volume 3, University of Oklahoma Press, Norman, Oklahoma, 2010, pp. 162–198; Rasch, Philip J., "Tom Nance A Dangerous Man," *Real West*, March 1979, No. 162, Vol. 22, pp. 25, 49, 52–53.

48. *Daily Utah Enquirer* (Provo), October 16, 1888. Testimony of Thomas Nance at Parrish's trial for murder.

49. *Ibid.*, December 23, 1887, February 21, 1888; *Provo American*, no date, reprinted in *Pioche Weekly Record*, December 31, 1887. Quote taken from contemporary newspaper reports.

50. *Provo American*, no date, reprinted in *Pioche Weekly Record*, December 31, 1887.

51. *Daily Utah Enquirer* (Provo), March 2, 1888.

52. *Ibid.*, February 21, 1888.

53. *Ibid.*, March 16, 1888.

54. State of Utah, State Archives and Records Service, Utah State Prison, Admission Records, 1888, Henry Parrish.

55. *Daily Utah Enquirer* (Provo), October 16, 1888.

56. *Ibid.*, October 23, 1888.

57. *Ibid.*

58. "Hank Parrish—Nevada's Worst Killer," *Western Frontier*, January 1978, p. 50.

59. The *Pioche Weekly Record* of August 9, 1890, reported that Thompson had only just arrived in Royal City via Aspen, Colorado.

60. The best sources for the Thompson killing are *Pioche Weekly Record*, August 9, October 25, December 20, 1890; *Salt Lake Tribune*, October 23; *White Pine News* (Ely), December 14, 1890, reprinted in *Salt Lake Tribune*, December 17, 1890. Also see Frederick, Donna C., "Hank Parrish from Pioche!" January 2000, http://www.robertwynn.com/ParrishH.htm, accessed April 15, 2011; Wilson, R. Michael, "Where is Henry 'Hank' Parish Buried?"

61. *Pioche Weekly Record*, August 9, 1890. For Turner's arrest of Parrish see *Fitchburg Sentinel* (Fitchburg, Massachusetts), October 12, 1896.

62. *Pioche Weekly Record*, August 16, 1890.

63. *Ibid.*

64. *Ibid.*, September 20, 1890.

65. *Ibid.*, September 27, 1890.

66. *Ibid.*, October 4, 1890.

67. *Ibid.*

68. *Ibid.*, October 11, 1890.

69. *Ibid.*, October 18, 25, 1890; *Salt Lake Tribune*, October 23, 1890.

70. *Pioche Weekly Record*, December 13, 1890.

71. Robert G. Ingersoll (1833–1899), was a Civil War veteran, politician, attorney, and orator whose ideas on humanism, agnosticism and free thought have influenced generations of intellectuals. His lectures would attract standing room only crowds of rapt listeners and his many writings are considered classics of importance and merit still studied to this day. http://en.wikipedia.org/wiki/Robert_G._Ingersoll.

72. *Pioche Weekly Record*, December 20, 1890.

73. *Ibid.*, December 6, 20, 1890.

74. *White Pine News* (Ely), December 6, 1890.

75. *Ibid.*, December 13, 1890, reprinted in *Pioche Weekly Record*, December 20, 1890.

76. *Ibid.*

77. *Ibid.*

78. *Ibid.*

79. *Ibid.*

80. The best sources for the lead up to and hanging of Hank Parrish are *ibid.*.; *White Pine News* (Ely), December 14, 1890, reprinted in *Salt Lake Tribune*, December 17, 1890.

81. *White Pine News*, December 13, 1890, reprinted in *Pioche Weekly Record*, December 20, 1890.

82. Wilson, R. Michael, "Where Is Henry 'Hank' Parish Buried?"

83. *Pioche Weekly Record*, December 27, 1890.

84. *Ibid.*, January 20, 1891.

85. *Salt Lake City Telegram*, January 23, 1918.

86. Lloyd, Lisa C., Lincoln County Deputy Clerk to author, May 14, 2003.

87. Wilson, R. Michael, "Where is Henry 'Hank' Parish Buried?"; White Pine Middle School, "White Pine County History—White Pine County Courthouse," http://www.whitepine.k12.nv.us/WhitepineMSHistory/WPC%20courthouse%20shawn.htm, accessed April 25, 2005.

88. Nevada Women's History Project, "Women's Biographies—Helen J. Stewart."

Bibliography and Source List

Books

Angel, Myron, ed., *History of Nevada*, Thompson & West, Oakland, California, 1881, reprint, Howell-North, Berkeley, California, 1958.

_____. *History of Nevada*, reprint, Arno Press, New York, 1973.

Ashbough, Don, *Nevada's Turbulent Yesterday*, Westernlore Press, Los Angeles, California, 1963.

Baker, Stanley, *Nevada Ghost Towns and Mining Camps*, Howell-North, Berkeley, California, 1970.

Bancroft, Hubert Howe, *The Works of Hubert Howe Bancroft, Volume XXXVI, Popular Tribunals, Vol. 1*, The History Company, Publishers, San Francisco, California, 1887.

Boessenecker, John, *Gold Dust & Gunsmoke*, John Wiley & Sons, Inc., New York, 1999.

Bristow, David L., *A Dirty, Wicked Town: Tales of 19th Century Omaha*, Caxton Press, Caldwell, Idaho, 2002.

Cerveri, Doris, *Nevada: A Colorful Past*, Dave's Printing & Publishing, Sparks, Nevada, 1975.

Chalfant, W.A., *Gold, Guns & Ghost Towns*, Stanford University Press, Stanford, California, 1947.

Convis, Charles L., *Outlaw Tales of Nevada*, Globe Pequot Press, Guilford, Connecticut, 2006.

Davis, Sam P., ed., *The History of Nevada*, Elms Publishing Company, Reno, Nevada, 1913.

DeArment, Robert K., *Deadly Dozen: Forgotten Gunfighters of The Old West, Volume 3*, University of Oklahoma Press, Norman, Oklahoma, 2010.

_____. *Knights of the Green Cloth*, University of Oklahoma Press, Norman, Oklahoma, 1982.

De Groot, Henry, *The Comstock Papers*, The Grace Dangberg Foundation, Reno, Nevada, 1985.

De Quille, Dan, *The History of The Big Bonanza*, American Publishing Company, Hartford, Connecticut, 1877.

Drury, Wells, *An Editor on The Comstock Lode*, Farrar & Rinehart, Inc., New York, 1936.

Earl, Phillip I., *This Was Nevada, Volume II, The Comstock Lode*, Nevada Historical Society, Reno, Nevada, 2000.

Ficklin, Marilou West, *Showdown at Truckee*, Western Book/Journal Press, Reno, Nevada, 1997.

Hegne, Barbara, *The Nevada Vigilante Hangings, Virginia City, Carson City, Dayton, Aurora, "601,"* Nevada Pioneer Series, Reno, Nevada, 2000.

_____. *Virginia City Rascals & Renegades*, Nevada Pioneer Series, Sparks, Nevada, 2000.

Hicks, George A., *Family Record and History of George A. Hicks*, ed. Maud Hicks Lewis, Self-Published, 1938.

Higgs, Gerald H., *Lost Legends of The Silver State*, Western Epics, 1976.

Hilton, Hope A., *"Wild Bill" Hickman and the Mormon Frontier*, Signature Books, Inc., Salt Lake City, Utah, 1988.

Hume, James B., and John N. Thacker, ed., R. Michael Wilson, *Wells, Fargo & Co. Report of losses from Stagecoach and Train Robbers, 1870 to 1884*, 125th Anniversary edition, Stagecoach Books, Las Vegas, Nevada, 2007.

Kaplan, Fred, *The Singular Mark Twain*, Doubleday, New York, 2003.

Land, Barbara, and Myrick Land, *A Short History of Las Vegas*, University of Nevada Press, Reno, Nevada, 2004.

Lyman, George D., *The Saga of The Comstock Lode, Boom Days in Virginia City*, Charles Scribner's Sons, New York, 1949.

Marks, Paula Mitchell, *And Die in The West*, William Morrow and Company, Inc., New York, 1989.

Martin, Douglas D., *Tombstone's Epitaph*, University of New Mexico Press, Albuquerque, New Mexico, 1951.

Mather, R.E. *Vigilante Victims*, History West Publishing Company, San Jose, California, 1991.

Mather, R.E., and F.E. Boswell, *Gold Camp Desperadoes*, History West Publishing Company, San Jose, California, 1990.

McGrath, Roger D., *Gunfighters, Highwaymen & Vigilantes*, University of California Press, Berkeley, California, 1984.

Meschery, Joanne, *Truckee, An Illustrated History of the Town and its Surroundings*, Rocking Stone Press, Truckee, California, 1978.

Neider, Charles, ed., *The Selected Letters of Mark Twain*, Harper & Row, Publishers, New York, 1982.

Paine, Albert Bigelow, *Mark Twain: A Biography*, Harper & Brothers, New York, 1912.

Parsons, George, W., ed., Lynn R. Bailey, *A Tenderfoot in Tombstone: The Turbulent Years: 1880-82*, Westernlore Press, Tucson, Arizona, 1996.

Penrose, Matt R., *Pots O'Gold*, A. Carlisle & Co. of Nevada, Reno, Nevada, 1935.

Powers, Ron, *Mark Twain: A Life,* Free Press, New York, 2005.

Roberts, Gary L., *Doc Holliday: The Life and Legend,* John Wiley & Sons, Inc., Hoboken, New Jersey, 2006.

Secrest, William B., *California Badmen,* Quill Driver Books/Word Dancer Press, Inc., Sanger, California, 2007.

Shillingberg, Wm. B., *Tombstone, A. T.: A History of Early Mining, Milling, and Mayhem,* The Arthur H. Clark Company, Spokane, Washington, 1999.

Twain, Mark, *Roughing It,* American Publishing Company, Chicago, Illinois, 1872.

Williams, George, III, *The Murders at Convict Lake,* Tree by The River Publishing, Riverside, California, 1984.

Wright, Frank, *Nevada Yesterdays,* Stephens Press, Las Vegas, Nevada, 2010.

Magazines and Periodicals

Baxter, George, "Sonora, City of Screaming Murder," *The West,* Vol. 3, No. 2, July 1965.

Bristow, Allen P., "Break Out!" *Old West,* Vol. 35, No. 2, Winter 1998.

Earl, Phillip I., "Nevada's Italian War," *Nevada Historical Society Quarterly,* Vol. 12, No. 2, Summer 1969.

_____. "Violent Life of a Nevada Badman," *Quarterly of the National Association and Center for Outlaw and Lawman History,* Vol. XII, No. 3, Winter 1988.

Garrigues, George L., "Convicts on the Loose," *Wild West,* October 1998.

Gracey, Charles, "Early Days in Lincoln County," *Nevada Historical Society First Biennial Report,* 1908.

"Hank Parrish: Nevada's Worst Killer," *Western Frontier,* January 1978.

O'Dell, Roy, "Mass Prison Break-Out at Carson City," *The English Westerner's Society Tally Sheet,* Volume 39, Number 1, Autumn 1992.

Rasch, Philip J., "Tom Nance: A Dangerous Man," *Real West,* Vol. 22, No. 162, March 1979.

Riggs, John L., "The Reign of Violence in El Dorado Canyon," *Third Biennial Report of the Nevada Historical Society,* State Printing Office, Carson City, 1913.

Smith, Grant H., "The History of The Comstock Lode, 1850–1920," *University of Nevada Bulletin,* Vol. XXXVII, No. 3, July 1, 1943.

Stano, Mary G., "Duel at El Dorado," *True West,* Vol. 36, No. 12, December 1989.

Young, Roy B., "Robert Havlin Paul, Frontier Lawman," *Western Outlaw Lawman History Association Journal,* Vol. XIII, No. 3, Fall 2004.

Newspapers

Carson City Daily Appeal
Carson City Morning Appeal
Carson City News
Daily Inland Empire (Hamilton)
Daily Oregonian (Portland, Oregon)
Daily State Register (Carson City)
Daily Utah Enquirer (Provo, Utah)
Elko Independent
Ely Record
Esmeralda Herald (Aurora)
Eureka Daily Leader
Eureka Daily Sentinel
Fitchburg (Massachusetts), *Sentinel*
Gold Hill Daily News
Humboldt Register (Winnemucca)
Idaho Semi-Weekly World (Idaho City)
Lyon County Sentinel (Dayton)
Mountain Champion (Belmont)
Nevada State Journal (Reno)
New York Times
New York Tribune
Omaha Daily Bee
Pioche Daily Record
Pioche Tri-Weekly Record
Pioche Weekly Record
Reese River Reveille (Austin)
Reno Evening Gazette
Sacramento Daily Bee
Sacramento Daily Record-Union
Salt Lake City Democrat
Salt Lake City Herald
Salt Lake City Telegram
Salt Lake City Tribune
San Francisco Morning Call
Stockton (California) *Independent*
Tombstone (Arizona) *Epitaph*
Truckee (California) *Republican*
Union Democrat (Sonora, California)
Union Vedette (Camp Douglas, Utah)
Virginia City Chronicle
Virginia City Daily Union
Virginia City Evening Bulletin
Virginia City Territorial Enterprise
Ward Semi-Weekly Reflex
Ward Weekly Reflex
Weekly Tombstone (Arizona), *Epitaph*
Weiser Signal (Idaho)
White Pine Evening Telegram (Shermantown)
White Pine News (Ely)
White Pine News (Treasure City)
Wood River Times (Hailey, Idaho)

Public Records

Application of Michael Dolan for Habeas Corpus, 7th Judicial District, County of Lincoln, State of Nevada, October 14, 1872.

Biennial Report of The Warden of the Nevada State Prison, 1866, 1869–1870, 1871–1872, 1873–1874, 1875–1876, 1877–1878, 1879–1880, 1881–1882, 1883–1884, 1889–1890, 1891–1892.

California State Prison Records, #1424, George Kirk, June 1858.

County Jail Book, Tuolumne County, Record of prisoners in the Tuolumne County Jail, George Kirk, Discharged, October 12, 1857; Attempted murder commitment, March 27 [sic], 1858; George Kirk sentenced, June 19, 1858; sent to State Prison, June 28, 1858.

Court of Sessions, Tuolumne County, The People of the State of California against G. B. Kirk, June Term, 1856; October Term, 1857; Verdict, October 12, 1857; June Term, 1858; Verdict, June Term, 1858.

District Court Case #226, Second Judicial District of the State of Nevada, Ormsby County, September Term, 1865, The State of Nevada against George Kirk, et al., Assault with intent to kill; Indictment, Prison Breaking.

District Court of Sixth Judicial District, State of Nevada, County of Lander, State of Nevada vs Thomas A. Carberry, Application for Continuance, September 25, 1867; verdict, March 13, 1869.

Federal Census of the United States, 1850, Marshall County, Mississippi.

Federal Census of the United States, 1860, Marin County, California.

Federal Census of the United states, 1870, Lincoln County, Ormsby County, Storey County, White Pine County, Nevada.

Federal Census of the United States, 1880, Eureka County, Lincoln County, Ormsby County, White Pine County, Nevada.

Lincoln County, Nevada, Grand Jury Special Report, March 27, 1871.

Lincoln County Seventh Judicial District Court, State of Nevada vs James Harrington, January 11, 1873; August Term, 1873.

Notice of intent to apply for pardon of John R. Darling, alias "Rattlesnake Dick," to Wm. Woodburn, District Attorney, Storey County, March 1871.

Office of Nevada State Prison, Prison Record of John R. Darling, 1881.

Pardon Application of Wm. H. Bethards, September 1875.

Pardon of Thos. Flynn, State of Nevada, Office of the Board of Pardons, July 12, 1889.

Petition to the Hon. the Board of Pardon Commissioners of the State of Nevada, re: pardon application of John Darling, 1871; Statement of Darling, 1871.

7th District Court, Lincoln County, Nevada, No. 1652, The State of Nevada vs Barney Flood, Morgan Courtney, Michael Dolan, Indictment for Murder, December Term, A. D. 1871.

State of California, County of Tuolumne, Case #44, The People vs George Kirk, Complaint, March 28, 1858.

State of Illinois, Bureau County, Circuit Court, The People vs William Reid, George Kirk, et al., September–October 1851.

State of Illinois, Bureau County, The People vs Patrick Kirk, August–September 1860.

State of Nevada against George Kirk, et al., District Court of the Second Judicial District of the State of Nevada, Ormsby County, March Term, 1866, Prison Breaking.

State of Nevada against George Kirk, et al., September Term, 1865.

State of Nevada vs James Harrington, 9th Judicial District Court, Lincoln County, Nevada, December Term, 1870.

State of Nevada vs James Harrington, A. H. Rutherford and W. H. Raymond, Seventh District Court, Lincoln County, Nevada, December Term, 1871; March Term, 1872.

State of Nevada vs John Richard Darling, charge of robbery, Justice Court preliminary hearing, May 28, 1866.

State of Nevada vs Morgan Courtney, Instruction to Jury, April 5, 1872.

State of Nevada vs W. H. Bethards, February 18, 1873.

State of Nevada vs William H. Bethards, Eighth Judicial District Court of the State of Nevada, County of White Pine, July 7, 1873.

State of Utah, State Archives and Records Service, Utah State Prison, Admission Records, Henry Parrish, 1888.

Statement of John R. Darling of the Nevada State Prison, on application to the Hon. Board of Pardons for pardon, 1871.

"To all whom it may concern," notice of application for pardon by George B. Kirk; State of California, Tuolumne County, Geo. S. Evans, County Clerk, certification of Kirk intention to apply for pardon.

Writ of Arrest, District Court of the 7th Judicial District, State of Nevada, County of Lincoln, March 13, 1872.

Writ of Habeas Corpus, District Court of the 7th Judicial District, State of Nevada, County of Lincoln, Application of Morgan Courtney, March 13, 1872.

Writ of Subpoena, State of California, Tuolumne County, ss. S. B. Blake, R. P. Malone, October 12, 1857; ss. H. Patterson, M. Woodruff, October 10, 1857.

Correspondence

James Hagar to Honorable, the Board of Pardons, January 28, 1880.

James Warren to B. F. Curler, November 19, 1890.

James Warren to G. M. Bowler, September 29, 1891.

James Warren to the Hon. Board of Pardon, November 18, 1890.

James Warren to Hon. Richard Rising, September 29, 1891.

John Powell, Jr., to Honorable Board of Pardon, 1880.

Lisa C. Lloyd, Lincoln County Deputy Clerk to author, May 14, 2003.

M. N. Stone to W. C. Chamberlain, March 2, 1880.

Richard Rising to Frank Denver, June 17, 1871.

W. Seawell to W. C. Chamberlain, March 17, 1880.

W. F. St. John to James Warren, December 27, 1890.

William Seawell to James Warren, December 19, 1890.

Websites

Akita Dad & Akita Mom, "Murder in the Desert," http://www.geocaching.com/seek/cache_details.aspx?ID=44205.

Beadle, E. F., "To Nebraska in 1857, A Diary of E. F. Beadle," http://members.aol.com/oldnebraska/index.htm.

California Senate History, http://www2.senate.ca.gov/portal/site/SENSergeant/SENSergeantNavHistory.

Cowboy George, "Hank Parrish, Gunfighter, Horsethief, Murderer," www.sincitywebhosting.com/pioche.

Dolan, Trent, "The Great Carson City Prison Escape of 1871," http://www.nevadaappeal.com/apps/pbcs.dll/article?AID=/20081012/NEWS/11012991/.

Earl, Phillip I., Department of Cultural Affairs, "This Was Nevada, Comstock Lode Featured in New Book," http://dmla.clan.lib.nv.us/docs/dca/thiswas/thiswas37.htm.

Evans, K.J., "The First 100, Part 1: The Early Years, Helen Stewart (1854–1926), 'The First Lady of Las Vegas,'" http://www.1st100.com/part1/stewart.html.

Finchum, Robin, "Flashback, Murder One," *Las Vegas Life*, May 2000, http://www.lvlife.com/2000/05/flashback/story01.html.

Frederick, Donna C. "Hank Parrish from Pioche!" January 2000, http://www.robertwynn.com/ParrishH.htm.

Illustrated Guide and Souvenir of Detroit, http://cc.bingj.com/cache.aspx?q=detroit+house+of+correction+1878&d=472801182037.

Legends of America, http://www.legendsofamerica.com/we-lawmanlist-b.html.

Lillis, Maggie, "Misspelling of Kiel Name Remains Mystery in Canyon's Christening," http://www.viewnews.com/2011/VIEW-Jan-04-Tue-2011/CentennialHill/41089547.html.

Nevada Ghost Towns, http://www.ghosttowns.com/states/nv/treasurecity.htm.

The Nevada Observer, www.nevadaobserver.com

Nevada Women's History Project, "Women's Biographies, Helen J. Stewart," http://www.unr.edu/nwhp/bios/women/stewart.htm.

Pioche Cemeteries, http://files.usgwarchives.net/nv/lincoln/cemeteries/piochecem.txt.

Sincity, www.sincitywebhosting.com/wintimes/pioche/history.

White Pine Middle School, "White Pine County History—White Pine County Courthouse," www.whitepine.k12.nv.us/WhitepineMSHistory/WPC%20courthouse%20shawn.htm.

Wikipedia, "Laryngotomy," http://en.wikipedia.org/wiki/Laryngotomy; "Robert G. Ingersoll," http://en.wikipedia.org/wiki/Robert_G._Ingersoll.

Wilson, R. Michael, "Where is Henry 'Hank' Parish Buried?" www.wildwesttales.com/stories/hank_parrish.htm.

Index

Numbers in ***bold italics*** indicate pages with illustrations

Adams, Judge 98
Alderson, Josh 163–164
Allen, Jim 165
Alman, Frank 52
Anderson, Richard 38–39
Angel, Myron 3, 70; see also
  History of Nevada
"Archie, James" see Ridgley,
  Charles
Argobright, Francis 136
Arick, Mayor 32
Arthur, Captain 143
Ash, Augustus 35, 111, 152–153,
  155
Askew, Dan 27
Atchison, J.B. 80
Atkinson, D.O. 153
Atkinson, Thomas 26–27, 145,
  146, 155
Aurora, Nevada 2, 8, ***9***, 83–86,
  91, 111
Austin, Nevada 2, 9–11, 47, 83, ***84***,
  86–90

Baldwin, Captain 150–151
Ballou, Ben 33–34, 192n18
Barbee, William 122
Bardende, Eugene 137
Barker, James 45
Barnwell, Mr. 60
Baron, I. 90
Barter, Richard A. "Rattlesnake
  Dick" 149
Bartlett, W.H. 39
Bass, James 77–78
Bassett, William 184
Beadle, Erastus F. 148–149
Beatty, William H. 38, 54
Behan, John 67
Belknap, Judge 134
Bell, Jailor 90
Bender, James 154
Bergstein, Dr. 125
Bethards, Mrs. 46, 53–54
Bethards, William H. 14, 43–***44***,
  45–57, 72, 94, 121; Brophy,
  James, killing of 52–54; death
  of 56–57; Griffin, Edward,
  shooting at 44–45; McFarland,
  battle with 52; Sherwood, John,
  killing of 46–47; Washington
  and Creole, battle of 49–51
Bianca, Italian 164
Bigelow, Ed see Willis, William
Billy the Kid 92
Birdsall, George W. 59, 79–80
Bishop, W.W. 126, 153
Black, J.L. 42
Black, Moses 108–110
Blackburn, Clara 58, 63
Blackburn, Jane 58, 63
Blackburn, Leslie Fort 22,
  36–37, 58–59, ***60***, 61–69; Duane,
  Michael, killing of, 61–62;
  Lyons, Pat, shooting at 60–61;
  O'Brien, William, knifing of 68;
  "Water War," battle of 63–64
Blackburn, Mary 69
Blackburn, William 63
Blackwell, H.B. 20–21
Blake, S.B. 138
Blancett, Enos F. 178–180
Blasdell, Governor 141
Bodrow, Lew 11
Booth, Edwin 156
Borgman, M.V. 118
Boring, S.W. 12
Boswell, F.E. 170
Boyd, George 73, 74
Bradley, Lewis R. "Broad Horns"
  110, 128, 134
Bradshaw, E.S. 10
Bragg, Allen 157–158
Brannan, Ed 52–54
Brent, John 168
Brewer, George 117
Briga, Marcadio 160
Bright, faro dealer 62
Bronson, Dr. 152
Brooks, Richard 178
Brooks, Sheilagh 178
Brophy, James 52–53
Brown, Bob 166–167
Brown, George 97, 101
Brown, John 25
Brown, Joseph 56
Brown, Sam 60
Buckley, William 84–85
Bulette, Julia 62
Burdette, N.H. 67
Burgesser, C.W. 108
Burke, John 105–119; McBride,
  Roy, shot at by 116; Parrish, A.L.,
  shot at by 117; prison break out
  106–110
Burke, John (elder) 105–106
Bush, City Recorder 61
Butenop, H. 42
Butler, Emma 100
Byron, Joseph 12

Caine, Michael 25–26
Callaghan, Patsey 6–8
Calswell, A. 153
Campbell, Dr. 184–185
Canonica, Antonio 167
Captain Andy 74
Carberry, Thomas A. "Irish Tom"
  18, 83–92, 187; Ridgley, Charles,
  killing of 83, 88–90; Vance,
  Samuel, killing of 87
Cardwell, James 160–161
Carlyle, W.H. 90
Carpenter, Jailor 132
Carr, anti-town lotter 54
Carson City, Nevada 8, 9, 37,
  43–47, 54, 56, 62, 111–113, 115,
  127, 129–130, 145–146, 156
Carter, Thomas 113
Carter, William 80
Cartter, Jim 61
Cartwright, James 48
Case, Jessie 153
Casey, Michael 50–51, 72, 121
Cassanove, criminal 90
"Cela" 48–49
Chamberlain, William 154,
  156–158
Chapman, J.E. 113
Chenoweth, John 66
"Chileno George" 47
Churchill, M.V. 153
Clapp, Dr. 7
Clapp, Justice 51
Clark, Jacob 154
Clark, John 38–39
Clark, "Nigger" 173–174
Clarke, Robert 112
Clarkson, Officer 32
Clemens, Samuel see Twain, Mark

221

Index

Clifford, Frank 107–108, 112, 113–115
"Coal Burner's War" 166–167
Cockerill, Tilton 108–112
Coleman, Thomas 5–18, 35, 189n16; death of 16–17; Llyod, George, killing of 8; Mulligan, Billy, duel with 10–11; Sheehan, John, shooting of 14–15; "wharf runners," battle of 5–7
Comstock, Mr. 160
Comstock Lode 2
Condon, Thomas 56
Conn, Dr. 146
Connor, H.N. 153
Cooper, David 90
Corbet, P.H.S. 63
Corcoran (killing) 131
Cosgrove, Barney 111
Cosgrove, William "Shorty" 159
Courtney, Morgan 16–17, 50–51, 72, 74–75, 93, 121
Coyle, Officer 66
Cunningham, R.A. 135
Curby, Officer 38
Curless, William 97, 102
Curtis, J.P. 63
Curtis, Jimmie 181–182, 183

Dade, Charles 141, 142
Daggett, Rollin 58
Daily, Mary 139
Dake, Crawley 65
Daley, Officer 38
Daley, Peter 42
Dalton, Henry P. 69
Daly, John 8–9, 83–86
Darling, Hattie see Funk, Hattie
Darling, John Richard "Rattlesnake Dick" 148–161; Chamberlain, William, killing of 157–158; Darling, Mrs., shot by 150–151; McLaughlin, William, knifed by 159; Warren, James, killed by 160–161
Darnes, J. 37–38
Davenport, Judge 21
Davis, Dr. 10–11
Davis, L.P. 73
Deal, D.L. 77, 78, 125
Deal, W.E.F. 134
Dedman, Bob 107
Delabash, Alex 139
DeLong, O.E. 55
Dennis, "El Dorado Johnny" 32
Dennis, William 80
Denver, Frank 107, 112
De Quille, Dan 58
Detroit House of Corrections 105, 117, 118–119
Dibble, Henry C. 66
Dingman, Capt. 108–109
Dirkes, T. 153
Dodge, Dave 96–97
Dodge, Fred 67
Dolan, Michael 12, 16–17, 191n78
Doliff, Al 51
Donahue (injured miner) 15

Donahue, John 13
Donley, Edward 141, 142
Door, R. 66
Doten, Alfred **26**, 27, 59
Douglas, Deputy 115
Downey, George 152–153, 155
Drury, Wells 19, 28–29, 30
Duane, Michael 61–62
Dunican, James 10
Dunn, John 25
Dunn, Peter 39
"Dutch Mary" 136, 146

Earl, Phillip I. 148
Earp, James 65
Earp, Morgan 58, 65
Earp, Virgil 58, 65
Earp, Wyatt 58, 65
Eaves, W.T. 153
Ely, John 120–121
Emerson, Charley 118
Emerson, Philip 117
Ennis, Charles 164–165
Eureka, Nevada 2, 37, 94, 95, 98, 103–104, 114, 123, 162–164, **165**, 166–169
Eureka Sentinel 161, 164, 167

Fairchild, Oscar L.C. 89–90
Farrell, Marion 164
"Fat Mac" see McKee, William L
Faylor, Johnny 62–63, 65
Fife, Andy 76, 77, 78, 80, 173–174
Filton, James 55
Finley, James 51
Fitch, Ben 115
Fitzpatrick, Frank 13
Flack, Joseph 98
Flarety, John 13
Fleming, "Big Alex" 95, 115
Fleming, John 21
Flood, Barney 13, 15–17, 50–51, 72, 121
Flynn, James 66
Flynn, Thomas 48, 49, 54–57, 113, 195n78
Ford, William 138
Foster, Coroner 158
Foster, Harry 25–26
Fox, Dr. 56
Francis, Sheriff 85
Frazier, Mr. 177
Fredericks, F. 42
Free, Mickey 67
Fremont, John C. 1
Frink, Dave 97, 100–103
Frisbie, Mr. 44–45
Fugate, Andy 96–97
Fuller, M. 127
Funk, Hattie 151–152, 155
Funk, James 151–152

Gaige, Mark M. 54–55, 56
Gass, Octavious D. 175, 176
Gilmer, Judge 7
Gilpatrick, James 47
Glen, Officer 40
Glissan, W.C. 78

Glissan (son of W.C.) 78
Godfritzen, Hans 173
Gold Hill, Nevada 11, 12, 21–25, 59
Gold Hill News 27, 28, 59, 145, 147, 154
Gottfredson, Peter 185
Gounond, Captain of the Guard 56
Gracey, Charles 49–51
Graham, Major 171, 179
Graves, Carroll 64; see also *The Phoenix*
Gray, James 47
Green, C.C. 62
Greenwood, James 173–174
Gregory, Billy 144
Gregory, Deputy Sheriff 35
Grey, O.H. 183
Griffin, Edward 44–45
Grosh, E. Allen 2
Grosh, Hosea 2

Hagar, James 157
Hall, Dr. 24
Halpin, Matt 78
Hamilton, Nevada 2, 11, 12, 54, 91–92, 114, 157
Hamilton (old man) 98
Hampton, J.C. 42
Hanchett, L.J. 72
Hanford, W.T. 55
Harker, Francis see Burke, John
Harkin, Tom 23–24, 25, 26–27
Harmon, Justice 87–88
Harrington, Daniel 120, 123, 126, 128, 129
Harrington, James W. 72, 120–135, 187, 207n62, 207n63; Cunningham, R.A., killed by 135; jail guard, shot at by 122; James, Benjamin, killing of 121–122; Kirch, Henry, battle with 131–132; Lynch, John, killing of 124–125; Sullivan, John C., killing of 128–130; Washington and Creole battle 120–121
Harrington, Timothy 120, 123, 126
Harris, C.N. 112, 113, 115
Harrison, A. 183
Haswell, Deputy Sheriff 45
Hawley, Chief Justice 134
Hawthorne, W.A. 161
Haynes, P. 10
Hayward, George 101–102
Heath, Dr. 22
Heffnan, Arthur Perkins 143–145, 147
Heffnan, Mrs. 143
Heiff, Henry 135
Helm, John B. 110–111
Henry, Schuyler 176–178
Hestres, E. 24, 27
Hicks, George Armstrong 150
Hightower, George 110
Hill, Harry 181–182, 183
Hill, John F. 24–25
Hill, "Russian Pete" 34–35

Index

History of Nevada 3, 70; *see also* Angel, Myron
Hoag, Joseph R. 73, 76–77
Hoard, John 164
Hodge, George 94
Hodges, D.F. 42
Holiday, J.M. 153
Holland, B.F. 80
Holland, James 45
Holland, Pat 59, 78
Holliday, Doc 58, 65
Holloway, Otis 138
Holmes, Coroner 27
Howard, Harry 97, 101
Howard, Jefferson 56
Howard, Samuel P. 48, 194n31
Howland, Bob 140–141
Hubbel, Isaac 24
Huggan, A. 122
Hughes, Jim 5
Hughes, Thomas 12, 24, 29, 35, 38–40
Hume, James B. 118–119
Hunt, Laurence 47
Hunter, Alex 141, 142
Hunter, Jim 75, 77
Huntsman, G. 116
Hupp, George S. 90
Hurley, Pat 115
Hyman, P.C. 115, 157
Hymers, Mrs. Gus 168

Iby, Officer 38
Ingersoll, Robert G. 183–184
Ireland 5, 13, 23, 25, 31, 48, 75, 83, 92, 105, 106, 120, 124, 164
Irish (Apache Indian Scout) 67
"Irish Tom" *see* Carberry, Thomas A.
Irwin (White Pine County Sheriff) 14, 48
Isaacs, Francis M. 107, 111–112, 113
"Italian War" *see* "Coal Burner's War"

Jacks, John 108
Jackson, J.P. 24
James, Benjamin 122, 123
James, Jesse 92
Jennings, Thomas 173
Jessen, Lee 166–167
"Jimmy Fresh" *see* Warren, James
Johnson, H. 71
Johnson, William 85
Jones, Charles 48, 108–110, 112
Jones, T.S. 139

Kane, John 51
Karcher (anti-town lotter) 54
Kearney, John 98
Keiser, Judge 97
Kelley, Constable 103
Kellogg, George F. 24–25, 27
Kellogg, William 25–27
Kelly, James 78
Kelly, John 62
Kelly, Thomas 129, 132
Kenney, Officer 66

Kerney, James 160
Kerr, J.H. 54
Keys, Pat 103
Keyser, Mr. 80–81
Kiel, Conrad "Old Man" 176–178
Kiel, Edwin 176, 214n43
Kimbal, C.B. 153
Kind, Henry 103
King, John C. 174
Kirch, Henry 132–133
Kirk, David 136
Kirk, George B. 136–147, 187; death of 146; Holloway, Otis, knifing of 138; prison escape of 141; Sedgwick, John, shooting of 138–139; vigilantes, battle with 141
Kirk, George W. 136
Kirk, Patrick 136
Knerr, Hank 76, 87, 88, 89
Knox, Richard 173
Kyle, Mat 164, 166–167

La Boa, Silva 180
Lackey, Ben 20, 156
Lamb, Pat 13
Lammon, George 155
Langlois, Henry 107–108
Larkin, Peter 131
Laswell, Tom 143–144
Lawrence, Charles M. 42
Leconey, John 12
Lee, Dr. 75
Lee, Henry 180
Lee, John D. 148, 150
Leffingwell, Jim 10, 88
Leonard, Peter 14
Lewis, Gus 47
Lindsay, Robert 22, 36–37, 41, 63–64
Lloyd, Edward "Ned" 6–8
Lloyd, George 6–9, 85
Lloyd, Thomas 6
Lloyd, W.C. 181–182, 183
Locatelli, Marcellino 167
Lopez, murderer 167–168
Ludwig, John 110–111
Lynch, John H. 124–125, 129
Lyons, M.H. 72
Lyons, Pat 61

Macintosh, Police Officer 7
Malone, R.P. 138
Manning, John 75–76, 77
Marcuse, James 12
Markey, Eugene 29–30
Marshal, Police Officer 87–88
Martin, Bob 181, 183
Martin, M. 66
Martin, Nelson 97
Martin, William 162–169, 187, 212n2; Bianca, knifing of 164; Brent, John, killed by 168; "Charcoal Burners War," battle of 166–167; Lopez, shooting at 167–168; Sullivan, John, killing of 164–165; Winne, Stephen, shooting of 163–164

Massel, J.C. 153
Masterson, James 84–85
Mateer, James 54, 55
Mather, R.E. 170
Mathis, Ike 174
Matthews, Dr. 81–82
Mayenbaum, Henry 90
McArdle, Richard 181, 183
McBride, Roy 116
McCafferty, A.C. 55
McCain, Seth 97, 101
McCann (pistol shooter) 77
McCarthey, Justin 14
McCarthy, Denis 58
McCarty, John 153
McCauley, Patrick 152–155
McCluer (criminal) 90
McCluskey, Mike 11, 12, 17
McCracken, D. 90
McCready, Officer 136, 146
McCune, Alf 116
McDonald, Robert 29, 39, 40
McDougal, J. 38
McDowell, Three-Fingered Jack 84–85
McEwen, Arthur 28
McFarland, Mr. 52
McFarlane, James 138–139
McGee, Joe 6–8, 60, 85
McGinnis, City Jailer 61
McGowan, Mike 148
McKean, James B. 122, 123
McKee, H.B. 165
McKee, James 70
McKee, Lizzie *see* Rudford, Melissa
McKee, Malcom 70
McKee, Milton 70
McKee, Nancy 70, 81
McKee, William L. 70–82, 121, 174; Bass, James, killing of 77–78; Manning, John, killing of 74–76; McCann, battle with 77; O'Brien, Thomas, battle with 73–74; Rodds, Charley, shooting at 76; Washington and Creole, battle of 71–72
McKimmins, M. 90
McKinney, George 74–75
McLaughlin, William "One-eyed Ned" 159
McManus, Deputy Sheriff 77
McManus, Isaac 80, 199n73
McMin, D.F. 90
McWilliams, Charles 143–144
Meadows, William 42
Megarrigle, G.R. 71
Mellon, Robert 93, 97–104; Flack, Joseph, killing of 99; San Francisco, killing in 99; Smith, Anna, shot by 100
Merritt (criminal) 90
Merrow, Officer 129
Mesick, Judge 152
Mighels, Harry 55, 57
Miller, T.H. 141
Millian, John 62
Milliken, William 80

224 Index

Mills, Samuel 103
Minear, A.P. 24
Mitchell, John 13
Mono Jim 110
Mooney, James 168
Moore, J.T. 177
Moran, Edward 159–160
Morgan, John 51
Morris, Pete 103
Morrison, Robert 110
Morrow, Policeman 24
Morton, Dr. 10–11
Morton, Leander 107–109
Morton, Lottie 100
Moss, Joseph 90
Moss, S.B. 90
Mudge, H.J. 56
Mulcahy, Sheriff 35
Mulligan, Barney 10
Mulligan, Billy 5, 10–11, 18
Mulligan, Jerry 30
Murphy, Dan 13, 14
Murphy, F.X. 183–184
Murphy, Thomas 27
Murray, Barney 40, 74

Nance, Tom 179–180, 215n47
Neagle, Dave 66
Nelson (inmate) 132
Nevada State Prison 43, 48, 49, 54–56, 105–108, 115, 127–128, **134**, 135, 139, 139–142, 144, 154–155, 157–158, 159, 161
Newhouse, John 107
Newland, Frank 49–51, 71–72, 93–94, 121
Newland, Tom 49–51, 71–72, 93–94, 121
Nichols, Frank 72
Nicholson, Andrew 90
Nicholson, John 114–115
Nobles, Milton 64–65; see also *The Phoenix*
Nye, E. 154

Oakland, California 17, 58, 68–69
O'Brien, Thomas 74
O'Brien, William "Billy" 68
O'Connell, Peter 19–20
O'Dair, Bart 90
Ogden, Peter S. 1
O'Neil, Edmund 124–126
O'Reiley, H.J. 20–21
O'Rourke, Patrick 23–24
Osborne, T.J. 183
Osgood, Mr. 160

Paddock, Anna 34, 37, 38, 40
Paddock, Benjamin 34, 37
Paddock, Mary 34, 37
Paddock (miner) 171–172
Paddock, Richard 12, 13, 22, 29, 31–42, 63–64, 187; death of 38–42; Hill, Peter, killing of 34–35; Peel, Langford, battle with 31–32; Pitzer, Jesse, battle with 33; "Water War," battle of 35–37

Paddock, Richard, Jr. 34, 37, 42
Paine, Albert Bigelow 59
Parrish, A.L. 117
Parrish, Frank 170
Parrish, Henry "Hank" 3, 170–186, 187; Blancett, Enos, killing of 178–180; fugitive, killing of 171–172; Graham, Major, shooting of 171; Greenwood and Clark, shooting of 173–174; hanging of 183–186; Stewart, Archibald, killing of 175–178; Taylor, shooting of 172; Thompson, P.G., killing of 181–183
Parsons, J.B. 113, 114
Patchen, C.H. 10
"Patsy Marley No. 2" 77
Patterson, Counselor 112
Patterson, Dan 168
Patterson, H. 138
Patterson, J.D. 48, 55, 114
Patterson, William 55
Pattini, Pompeo 167
Payne, Jerry 101
Pedroni, Giovanni 167
Peel, Langford "Farmer" 31–32
Pendergast, Bill 86
Pennison, William 34
Perasich, Mr. 107–108
Perry, Jack 58–59
Peters, Patrick 27
Philson, Dr. 125
The Phoenix 64–65; see also Nobles, Milton
Pierson, John 20–21
Pike, L. 123
Pine, Dan H. 85, 157–158
Pioche, F.L.A. 71
Pioche Daily Record 76, 78, 79, 82, 126, 127, 145
Pioche, Nevada 2, 15, **16**, 17, 48–51, 70–72, **73**, 74–80, **81**, 82, 93–94, 120–121, 124–126, 180, 182, 185, 187
Piper's Opera House 42, 60, 63, 65, **99**, 100, 144
Pisante, Martin 54
Pitzer, Jesse S. 33, 126, 153
Pixley, Matt 108, 111, 112
Plummer, Henry 88, 170
Poor, Billy 109, 110, 111
Porter, Jim 166–167
Potter, Jack 97, 101
Powell, John, Jr. 157
Powers, Jack 143
Pratt, Marshall 118
Prentice, "Waller Defeat" see Prentice, W.H. "Dick"
Prentice, W.H. "Dick" 19–30, 36–37, 40, 63–64, 187; death of 30; Markey, Eugene, battle with 29–30; O'Connell, Peter, shooting at 19–20; O'Rourke, Patrick, killing of 23–24; Waller Defeat, battle of 24–27; "Water War," battle of 21–22
Prior, George 100

Quadro, Dominico 167
Quillen, Johnny 78

Rafferty, Matt see Flynn, Thomas
Raum, Ed 55
Rawlings, Lloyd 27
Raymond, William 120–121
Raymond and Ely Company 49–51, 71–72, 79, 93–94, 120–121
Raymond and Ely Mine **50**, 51
Redfield, Deputy U.S. Marshal 179
Regan, Julia 128, 130
Reid, William 136
Reilly, John 13
Revere, Paul 162, 169
Rice, Henry 72
Rich, Marshall 166–167
Richard, John 38–39
Ridgeley, Charles 18, 83, 88–89, 92
Rieley, Michael 25
Riggs, John L. 173
Rising, Richard 131, 147, 153–154, 155–156, 161
Ritter, John 90
Roberts, Jack Bedford 108–110
Robey, R.H. 38
Robles, Quirino 67
Rodds, Charley "Chicken-thief Charley" 76
Rodriguez, Niconor 77
Rollins, R. 116
Rollins, Volney E. 106
Rosamurgay, William 76
Ross, Richard 42
Roth, George 112, 113–115
Rover, J.W. 133
Ruby Hill, Nevada 51–54, **163**
Rudford, Melissa 79, 80, 81
Russell, William 113
Rutherford, A.H. 121
Rutherford, G.W. 90
Rutherford, George 14–15
Ryan (foot racer) 65
Ryan, Thomas 113

Sacramento, California 5–8, 83, 98
San Francisco, California 5, 11, 14, 17, 24, 27, 49, 58, 64–65, 67, 71, 87, 99, 115, 124, 139, 141
Schoonmaker, Frank 124–125
Schustrich (saloonist) 74
Scott, John 52–54
Sears, James 84
Seawell, William 155, 157
Sedgwick, John 138
Sexton, William 141
Shamp, T.B. 154–155
Sharp, L.N. 133
Shaw, Dave 39
Sheehan, John 14–15
Sheik, William 21–22, 36–37, 63–64, 191n13
Sheridan, James 53
Sherman, Edwin A. 86
Sherman, Thomas 8
Sherwood, Henry 46
Sherwood, John 46–47

Sherwood, O.P. 76, 82
Shibell, Charles 65
Shiftlett, W.D. 25–26
Simpson, J.B. 164, 166–167
Simpson, White Pine County Deputy Sheriff 184
Slingerland, James 111
Sloan, William "Idaho Bill" 117
Smith, Anna 100
Smith, Carrie "Spring Chicken" 100–104
Smith, Fred N. 6–8
Smith, George 166–167
Smith, Jedediah S. 1
Smith (miner) 175
Smith, Sam 178
Smith, T.F. "Fred" 24–25, 27
Smith, Timothy G. 44, 47, 142
Smith, William 144
Smock, George 77
Snell, W.G. 51, 72, 94
Sparks, E. 116
Spencer, Frank 103
Steinbach, A. 90
Steiner, Nick 85
Stewart, Archibald 175, *176*, 177–178
Stewart, Helen 175–178, *186*, 214n44
Stewart, John 164
Stoddard, A. 21
Stone, M.N. 156, 157
Stoner, John 145, 146
Storey, Hank 166–167
Sublette, Milton 1
Sullivan, Cornelius "Con" 124–126, 128–130, 135
Sullivan, James "Yankee" 5
Sullivan, John 164–165
Sullivan, John C. 128–130, 133
Sumner, James 38
Sutter, John 5
Swift, S.T. 55, 112, 113–114
Symons, S. 147
Syphers, Georgia 75

Taft (shooter) 135
Talcott, William 9
Tamkin, Isaac 63
Taylor (card player) 172
Taylor, Dan 111
Terril, Edward 67

"Texas" (old man) 95
Thomas, Charley 66
Thomas, Joe 76
Thompson, Harry 99
Thompson, P.G. 181–182, 184
Thornton, Harry 55
Thornton (killed by Ed Lloyd) 6
Tickner, Henry 118
Toland, Jim 78
Tombstone, Arizona 58, 65–67
Toomey, Joe 164, 166–167
Travis, Wes 73, 75, 77, 126
Treasure City, Nevada 11–13, 35, 47–48
Treese, A.B. 183
Triplett, T.W. 55
Truckee (Paiute Indian Chief) 95
Truckee, California 93, 95–97, 100–103, 104
Turner, Ephraim 80, 182, 183
Twain, Mark 58

Uhler, J. Clem 24
Utah State Prison 116–117, 119, 170, 180

Vance, Sam 18, 84–86, 87–88, 92
Van Hagan, J.B. 73, 76, 79
Vigilantes 85, 86, 95, 97, 98, 100–104, 110, 129, 141, 144–147, 170
Virginia City "Water War" 21–22, 35–37, 63–64
Virginia City Territorial Enterprise 21, 34, 36, 58, 133, 161
Virginia City, Nevada 2, 12, *20*, 21–22, 24, 29–30, 31–32, *33*, 34–37, *41*, 42, 58–65, 87, 95, 100, 128–129, 130–133, 139, *140*, 142, *143*, 144–147, 152–154, 158–159, 187

Wagner, John 52–53, 55
Wales, Jimmy 75
Walker, Wythe 72, 121
Wallace, Robert 105
Waller Defeat 25–28
Ward, Franklin 42
Warren, James "Jimmy Fresh" 159–161
Washington and Creole 49–51, 71–72, 93–94, 121
"Washington and Creole Battle" 49–51, 71–72, 121

Waterhouse, R.M. 88
Watkins, W.F. 85
Weaver, John P. 173
Webster, Jim 149
Wells, Thomas H. 183
Werk, G.W. 25–26
"Wharf runners" 5
Wheeler, Frank 47
Whipley, Jack 100
Whitbeck, J. 116
White, Dr. 56
White, Jack 51, 72, 93–97, 98, 104, 121; Fugate, Andy, killed by 96–97; "Texas," knifed by 95; Washington and Creole, battle of 93–94
White, John 153
Whitford, Andrew 153
Whitman, B.C. 134
Whitney, Al 67–68
Wiedehold, C. 76
Wiggins, Jack 117, 119
Wiggins, Tom 98–99
Williams, Henry 159
Williams, Jack 60
Williams, Jennie 96
Williams, Thomas "Tommy the Headmaker" 76
Williams, Walter 35
Willis, William 112, 113, 115–116, 119, 143, 144
Wilson, Adair 10–11, 17
Winne, Stephen H. 163–164
Winslow, S.L. 52–53
Wise, Joseph 142
Witcher, V.A. 122
Wood, Deputy Sheriff 94
Woodburn, William 155
Woodman, Policeman 139
Woodruff, Henry 73, 74, 125
Woodruff, M. 138
Woods, W.M. 153
Wright, Andy 56
Wright, S.R. 133, 142

Yew, Young 106
Yocum, James 173
Young, A.A. 182

Zerli, Tedora 167
Zimmerman, J.J. 106–107